W9-CXJ-093

Study Guide

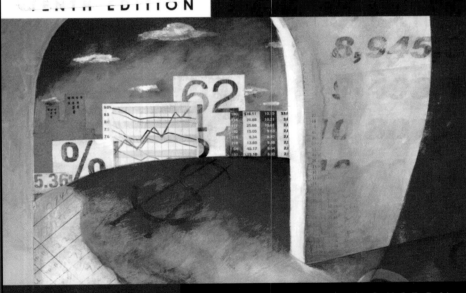

FUNDAMENTALS
OF FINANCIAL
MANAGEMENT

BK08507710

TENTH EDITION

BRIGHAM & HOUSTON

Prepared by

Eugene F. Brigham, Joel F. Houston,
Dana Aberwald Clark

Study Guide

Fundamentals of Financial Management
Tenth Edition

Eugene F. Brigham
University of Florida

Joel F. Houston
University of Florida

Prepared by

Dana Aberwald Clark
University of Florida

THOMSON
™
SOUTH-WESTERN

Australia · Canada · Mexico · Singapore · Spain · United Kingdom · United States

THOMSON
SOUTH-WESTERN

Study Guide for **Fundamentals of Financial Management, 10e**

Eugene F. Brigham, Joel F. Houston, and Dana Aberwald Clark

Editorial Director:
Jack W. Calhoun

Editor-in-Chief:
Michael P. Roche

Executive Editor:
Michael R. Reynolds

Developmental Editor:
Elizabeth R. Thomson

Senior Marketing Manager:
Charlie Stutesman

Senior Production Editor:
Kara ZumBahlen

Manufacturing Coordinator:
Sandee Milewski

Printer:
Edwards Brothers, Ann Arbor, MI

For more information
contact South-Western,
5191 Natorp Boulevard,
Mason, Ohio 45040.
Or you can visit our Internet site at:
http://www.swlearning.com

ISBN: 0-324-17832-8

PREFACE

This *Study Guide* is designed primarily to help you develop a working knowledge of the concepts and principles of financial management. Additionally, it will familiarize you with the types of true/false and multiple-choice test questions that are being used with increasing frequency in introductory finance courses.

The *Study Guide* follows the outline of *Fundamentals of Financial Management: Tenth Edition*. You should read carefully the next section, "How to Use This Study Guide," to familiarize yourself with its specific contents and to gain some insights into how it can be used most effectively.

We would like to thank Lou Gapenski, Susan Whitman, and Sharon Bullivant for their considerable assistance in the preparation of this edition, and Bob LeClair for his helpful ideas in prior editions that we carried over to this one.

We have tried to make the *Study Guide* as clear and error-free as possible. However, some mistakes may have crept in, and there are almost certainly some sections that could be clarified. Any suggestions for improving the *Study Guide* would be greatly appreciated and should be addressed to Joel Houston at the address below. Since instructors almost never read study guides, we address this call for help to students!

Eugene F. Brigham
Joel F. Houston
Dana Aberwald Clark

Houston & Associates
4723 N.W. 53rd Ave., Suite A
Gainesville, FL 32606
email address: fundamentals@joelhouston.com

March 2003

HOW TO USE THIS STUDY GUIDE

Different people will tend to use the *Study Guide* in somewhat different ways. This is natural because both introductory finance courses and individual students' needs vary widely. However, the tips contained in this section should help all students use the *Study Guide* more effectively, regardless of these differences.

Each chapter contains (1) a list of learning objectives, (2) an overview, (3) an outline, (4) definitional self-test questions, (5) conceptual self-test questions, (6) self-test problems, and (7) answers and solutions to the self-test questions and problems. You should begin your study by reading the list of learning objectives and the overview; they will give you an idea of what is contained in the chapter and how this material fits into the overall scheme of things in financial management.

Next, read over the outline to get a better fix on the specific topics covered in the chapter. It is important to realize that the outline does not list every facet of every topic covered in the textbook. The *Study Guide* is intended to highlight and summarize the textbook, not to supplant it. Also, note that web appendix material is clearly marked as such within the outline. Thus, if your instructor does not assign a particular web appendix, you may not want to study that portion of the outline.

The definitional self-test questions are intended to test your knowledge of, and also to reinforce your ability to work with, the terms and concepts introduced in the chapter. If you do not understand the definitions thoroughly, review the outline prior to going on to the conceptual questions and problems.

The conceptual self-test questions focus on the same kinds of ideas that the textbook end-of-chapter questions address, but in the *Study Guide*, the questions are set out in a true/false or multiple-choice format. Thus, for many students these questions can be used to practice for the types of tests that are being used with increasing frequency. However, regardless of the types of tests you must take, working through the conceptual questions will help drive home the key concepts of financial management.

The numeric problems are also written in a multiple-choice format. Generally, the problems are arranged in order of increasing difficulty. Also, note that some of the *Study Guide* problems are convoluted in the sense that information normally available to financial managers is withheld and information normally unknown is given. Such problems are designed to test your knowledge of a subject, and you must work "backwards" to solve them. Furthermore, such problems are included in the *Study Guide* in part because they provide a good test of how well you understand the material and in part because you may well be seeing similar problems on your exams.

Finally, each *Study Guide* chapter provides the answers and solutions to the self-test questions and problems. The rationale behind a question's correct answer is explained where necessary, but the problem solutions are always complete. Note that the problems generally provide "financial calculator" solutions.

Of course, each student must decide how to incorporate the *Study Guide* in his or her overall study program. Many students begin an assignment by reading the *Study Guide's* learning objectives, overview, and outline to get the "big picture." Then, they go on to read the chapter in the textbook. Naturally, the *Study Guide* overview and outline are also used extensively to review for exams. Most students work the textbook questions and problems, using the latter as a self-test and review tool. However, if you are stumped by a text problem, try the *Study Guide* problems first because their detailed solutions can get you over stumbling blocks.

WANT TO DO WELL ON EXAMS? THEN READ THIS!

The goals of a good testing system are (1) to give students direction as to the most important material, (2) to motivate them to study properly, and (3) to determine how much they have learned. In finance, it is easy to construct a combination problem/essay exam that accomplishes these goals, but if essay questions are ruled out by class size, then instructors have a more difficult job. They must then develop complex, unambiguous questions and problems that require students to think through the issues and determine which of several plausible-looking statements is most correct. A good exam will require students to recall how to use a number of equations, graphs, and problem set-ups, to actually set up examples or draw graphs to determine the required answers, and to understand how the results are used in the decision-making process. It is not easy to accomplish these goals in a multiple-choice exam, but it can be done.

Many students in the introductory finance course have never faced this type of an exam, and they are "thrown for a loop" by our questions. Eventually, they catch on to our examination process, and when they do, they think it is both fair and reasonable. Still, learning how to take multiple-choice finance exams can be traumatic and stressful. *The purpose of this section is to try to reduce your stress if you will be faced with multiple-choice exams.* If you will be taking "regular" problem/essay exams, the section will still be useful, but if you will be taking multiple-choice exams, you simply cannot afford to skip it!

How to Take Multiple-Choice Finance Tests

Like it or not, testing is inherently competitive—students compete against one another and also against the instructor. Of course, the instructor wants the students to do well, but he or she also wants to challenge students and to see just how well they understand the material.

You should understand how your instructor makes up his or her exams because this will help you to prepare for them. Obviously, we don't know how your specific instructor will construct exams, but chances are that he or she will do something similar to what we and most other instructors do. So, here are some pointers that will help you as you study finance and prepare for exams.

1. Recognize that finance is inherently quantitative—it deals with numbers and relationships between numbers. It is less intuitive than management or marketing but more intuitive than accounting or statistics. For example, accountants are primarily interested in reporting *historical* data, but in finance we want to know how different actions will affect *future* data. Therefore, as they write out exams, instructors will ask you to do lots of calculations, but to do more than just crank out numerical answers. They will also expect you to know how your answer would tend to change if the data were changed and how the very possibility of such changes might influence actual decisions.

2. You will probably have to answer two types of questions on finance exams: (1) numerical problems and (2) conceptual true/false or multiple-choice questions. You are probably used to taking courses where you can cram just before the exams, memorize some equations and facts, then regurgitate them on the exam and do fine. That won't work in finance—you obviously will need to learn some facts, but you must also learn how to set up and solve relatively complex problems and reason out difficult conceptual multiple-choice questions.

3. You can study for problems in two ways: work all the problems you can find and hope you will get recognizably similar ones on the exam, or, preferably, think about the various types of problems in a generic sense, and try to understand what each type of problem is all about; that is, think about why the particular problem is important, what type of decision it deals with, and why the solution is laid out as it is.

4. The worst way to study homework problems is to just work on each problem until you get the right answer, pat yourself on the back for getting it, and then move on to the next problem. The best way to study problems is to go consciously and systematically through these four steps: (1) Begin by asking yourself what the purpose of the problem is. For example, if the problem deals with a ratio analysis by a banker considering whether or not to make a loan to a company, make note of that fact. (2) Next, ask yourself what formula, table set-up, or what-have-you is necessary to get a solution; in a ratio analysis, you might at this point list the ratios that would be most relevant. (3) Then insert the data to get the required answer. (4) Finally, conclude by asking yourself two sets of questions:

   a. If my instructor were to give us a problem like this on the exam, how might he or she change it to make up a good exam problem? Obviously the numbers could be changed, but could we be required to solve for a different variable? For example, if the problem gave us balance sheet data and then required us to determine the current ratio, could we be given the current ratio plus some balance sheet data and then be required to complete the balance sheet?

   b. If our instructor wants to see if we understand the implications of the answer for decision making, what kind of conceptual question might we be asked? For example, if we calculated a current ratio of 2.3×, how could we tell if that ratio was good, bad, or indifferent, and who might use the current ratio, and for what purposes?

We let our students bring to the exams one 8½" by 11" sheet of paper with as much written on the two sides as they can squeeze on it. We do this partly to reduce their tendency to try to memorize things, but we also want them to think about problems generically, and having them list formulas and prototype examples of each type of problem on their "cheat sheet" helps in this regard.

5. Except for a few definitional questions, most non-numeric (conceptual) exam questions are actually based on problems. When we and most other finance professors make up regular problem/essay exams as opposed to multiple-choice exams, we often ask for the solution to a problem and then ask for an essay explanation of how changes in various factors would affect

the answer. Or, we might just skip the numerical problem part and simply ask you to explain how changes in different input variables would affect some output variable.

For example, we might give you the following partial balance sheet and then ask you to calculate the current ratio:

Inventory	$ 50	Accounts payable	$ 50
Other current assets	45	Short-term bank loans	50
Total current assets	$ 95	Total current liabilities	$100

You would find the current ratio to be 95/100 = 0.95. Then, on an essay exam, we might ask you three additional questions:

a. Would the current ratio be improved (increased) if the company took out a 6-month loan for $100 and used the proceeds to increase inventory?

b. Would your answer in Part a have been the same if the company's original current ratio had been 1.5 rather than 0.95? Explain.

c. What general conclusions can you reach regarding the effects on the current ratio of adding equal dollar amounts to both current assets and current liabilities?

To answer Part a, you would make the necessary changes in the balance sheet, calculate the new current ratio of ($95 + $100)/($100 + $100) = $195/$200 = 0.975, and answer, "Yes, the current ratio would be improved—it would increase from 0.95 to 0.975." To answer Part b, you would increase Other current assets (or Inventory) by $55 to produce a situation where the original current ratio was 1.5, then add $100 to both inventories and bank loans, and get this new current ratio:

$$\text{Current ratio} = (\$150 + \$100)/(\$100 + \$100) = \$250/\$200 = 1.25.$$

Then you would answer Part b as follows: "No. In this case, adding an equal amount to both current assets and current liabilities will cause the current ratio to decrease from 1.5 to 1.25."

To answer Part c, you should first suspect that whether the current ratio increases or decreases depends on whether or not the initial current ratio is above or below 1.0. You might then go back to the original data, add $5 to other current assets to bring the current ratio up to 1.0, and then add $100 to both inventories and bank loans to confirm your hunch. Then you would answer Part c as follows: "If the current ratio is initially below 1.0, then adding equal dollar amounts to current assets and current liabilities will improve the current ratio, while if the initial ratio is greater than 1.0, the current ratio will be reduced. If the initial current ratio is 1.0, then the change will have no effect on the current ratio—it will remain constant at 1.0."

6. The essay questions in Point 5 were derived directly from the problem, and we answered the questions by modifying the data in the problem. Thus, the questions were based on the

problem. *Now note that we could have skipped the problem and gone directly to the conceptual questions.* For example, we could have given you a question like this:

> If a company whose current ratio is 0.95 takes out a 6-month loan from its bank and uses the cash to increase inventory, how would this affect its current ratio?

Now you would probably approach the question by writing out the formula for the current ratio, making up some data where the current ratio is 0.95, then adding some amount to current assets and current liabilities, and finally calculating a new current ratio. Some people can think such questions through abstractly, but most of us find it easier to work out some numbers, get the picture of what's happening, and then reach general conclusions. *Therefore, for most of us it is most efficient to approach conceptual questions that test our knowledge of relationships by first asking what generic problem the question is based on by thinking about the question within the framework of a problem,* in this case the calculation of a current ratio.

7. When we make up multiple-choice exams, we put several false statements plus one true statement into a question and then ask you to identify the correct statement. For example, we might ask you the following question:

If a firm takes out a 6-month loan and uses the proceeds to build inventory, then, other things held constant, its current ratio will

   a.   Increase.
   b.   Decrease.
   c.   Remain constant.
   d.   Fluctuate.
   e.   Increase, decrease, or remain constant, depending on the level of the initial current ratio.

As we saw above, the correct answer is "e," but if we had not just gone through the example, how would you have approached the question? You could try guessing, but a better approach would be to set up a partial balance sheet, put some numbers in, and see what happens to the current ratio. That is the best way for most of us to attack many of the conceptual questions you will face.

8. You should realize that when professors make up conceptual questions, they often start with numerical problems and then frame "word" questions as they look at the details of a problem. For example, we might be looking at a balance sheet and the calculations for the current ratio and then come up with the question posed in Point 7.

9. To take this a step further, many professors write a multiple-choice exam problem and then ask a multiple-choice conceptual question that is related to the problem, *but does not tie the two together* physically on the exam. Thus, you might be asked to calculate some ratios as a problem and then, separately, be asked to answer a conceptual question about ratios that would be easier to answer if you make the connection between the problem and the question.

10. At Florida, we generally give two midterms plus a final exam, and each is a 2-hour exam. We have about 10 multiple-choice conceptual questions first, then about 10 multiple-choice problems. Initially, most students worked straight through the exam, front to back. However, some of the more astute students figured out that if they worked the problems first, they would get some clues that would help with the questions. Now our students generally work the problems first, regardless of their order of appearance on the exams. Note, though, that we and many other instructors include a number of relatively easy questions and problems, along with some difficult ones designed to separate the best students from the rest. Further, the most difficult problems are placed toward the end of the problem set. We warn our students not to spend too much time on any one problem and, if they don't have a clue as to how to handle it, to go on and then come back to it later if they have time.

11. One final comment about studying is appropriate. Some of our less astute students tend to tackle a given problem, not see how to work it, look up the solution or get someone to explain it to them, and then say to themselves, "Oh yes, I see how to work it, and I could work one like it on the exam. Now let's finish the rest of the problems." Too often, this is pure self-deceit: The student really doesn't understand the problem and could not work one like it unless it was virtually identical. Slowing down and going through our checklist will help you to avoid this problem.

CONTENTS OF THE STUDY GUIDE

CHAPTER 1
AN OVERVIEW OF FINANCIAL MANAGEMENT

LEARNING OBJECTIVES

● Explain the career opportunities available within the three interrelated areas of finance.

● Identify some of the forces that will affect financial management in the new millennium.

● Describe the advantages and disadvantages of alternative forms of business organization.

● Briefly explain the responsibilities of the financial staff within an organization.

● State the primary goal in a publicly traded firm, and explain how social responsibility and business ethics fit in with that goal.

● Define an agency relationship, give some examples of potential agency problems, and identify possible solutions.

● Identify major factors that determine the price of a company's stock, including those that managers have control over and those that they do not.

● Discuss whether financial managers should concentrate strictly on cash flow and ignore the impact of their decisions on EPS.

OVERVIEW

This chapter provides an overview of financial management and should give you a better understanding of the following: (1) what career opportunities exist within the three interrelated areas of finance, (2) what forces will affect financial management in the future, (3) how businesses are organized, (4) how finance fits into the structure of a firm's organization, (5) how financial managers relate to their counterparts in other departments, and (6) what the goals of a firm are and how financial managers can contribute to the attainment of these goals.

OUTLINE

Finance consists of three interrelated areas: money and capital markets, investments, and financial management. Career opportunities within each field are varied and numerous, but financial managers must have a knowledge of all three areas.

- Many finance majors go to work for financial institutions, including banks, insurance companies, mutual funds, and investment banking firms.
  - □ For success here, one needs a knowledge of valuation techniques, the factors that cause interest rates to rise and fall, the regulations to which financial institutions are subject, and the various types of financial instruments.

- Finance graduates who go into investments generally work for a brokerage house in sales or as a security analyst; for a bank, a mutual fund, or an insurance company in the management of investment portfolios; for a financial consulting firm, advising individual investors or pension funds on how to invest their funds; for an investment bank whose primary function is to help businesses raise new capital; or as a financial planner whose job is to help individuals develop long-term financial goals and portfolios.

- Financial management, the broadest of the three areas, and the one with the greatest number of job opportunities, is important to all types of businesses. The types of jobs one encounters in this area range from making decisions regarding plant expansions to choosing what types of securities to issue when financing an expansion.

The focus on value maximization continues as we begin the 21st century. However, two other trends are becoming increasingly important: (1) the globalization of business and (2) the increased use of information technology. Both of these trends provide companies with exciting new opportunities to increase profitability and reduce risks. However, these trends are also leading to increased competition and new risks.

- Four factors have led to increased globalization of businesses.
  - □ Transportation and communications improvements have lowered shipping costs and made international trade more feasible.
  - □ Increased political clout of consumers has helped lower trade barriers.
  - □ Due to advanced technology, higher development costs for new products have resulted, necessitating increased unit sales and the need to expand markets.
  - □ Competitive pressures have forced companies to shift manufacturing operations to lower-cost countries.

■ Continued advances in computer and communications technology are revolutionizing the way financial decisions are made. Thus, the new generation of financial managers will need stronger computer and quantitative skills than were required in the past.
   □ Changing technology provides both opportunities and threats.
   □ Improved technology enables businesses to reduce costs and expand markets.
   □ Changing technology can introduce additional competition, which may reduce profitability in existing markets.

The three main forms of business organization are the sole proprietorship, the partnership, and the corporation. About 80 percent of businesses operate as sole proprietorships, but when based on dollar value of sales, 80 percent of all business is conducted by corporations.

■ A *sole proprietorship* is an unincorporated business owned by one individual.
   □ Its advantages are: (a) it is easily and inexpensively formed, (b) it is subject to few government regulations, and (c) it avoids corporate income taxes. (However, all business earnings are taxed as personal income to the owner.)
   □ Its disadvantages are: (a) it is limited in its ability to raise large sums of capital, (b) the proprietor has unlimited personal liability for business debts, and (c) it has a life limited to the life of the individual who created it.

■ A *partnership* exists whenever two or more persons associate to conduct a noncorporate business.
   □ Its major advantage is its low cost and ease of formation.
   □ Its disadvantages are: (a) unlimited liability, (b) limited life, (c) difficulty of transferring ownership, and (d) difficulty of raising large amounts of capital.

■ A *corporation* is a legal entity created by a state, and it is separate and distinct from its owners and managers.
   □ Its advantages are: (a) unlimited life, (b) ownership that is easily transferred through the exchange of stock, and (c) limited liability. Because of these three factors, it is much easier for corporations than for proprietorships or partnerships to raise money in the capital markets.
   □ Its disadvantages are: (a) corporate earnings may be subject to double taxation and (b) setting up a corporation and filing required state and federal reports are more complex and time-consuming than for a sole proprietorship or partnership.
   □ A *charter* must be filed with the state where the firm is incorporated, and *bylaws* that govern the management of the company must be prepared.

■ The value of any business other than a very small one will probably be maximized if it is organized as a corporation for three reasons.

☐ Limited liability reduces the risks borne by investors, and the lower the firm's risk, the higher its value.

☐ A firm's value is dependent on its growth opportunities, which in turn are dependent on the firm's ability to attract capital.

☐ The value of an asset also depends on its liquidity, which means the ease of selling the asset and converting it to cash at a "fair market value."

The financial staff's tasks are to acquire and operate resources so as to maximize the firm's value, which will also contribute to the welfare of consumers and employees. Some specific activities follow.

■ The financial staff *forecasts and plans* to shape the firm's future position.

■ The financial staff *makes major investment and financing decisions*.

■ The financial staff *coordinates and controls* when interacting with other departments so that the firm operates as efficiently as possible.

■ The financial staff *works with the financial markets*.

■ The financial staff is responsible for the firm's overall *risk management* program.

Maximizing the price of the firm's common stock is the most important goal of most corporations.

■ Other objectives, such as personal satisfaction, employee welfare, and the good of the community and of society at large, also have an influence, but for publicly-owned companies, they are less important than stock price maximization.

■ Managers of a firm operating in a competitive market will be forced to undertake actions that are reasonably consistent with shareholder wealth maximization. If they depart from this goal, they run the risk of being removed from their jobs, either by the firm's board of directors or by outside forces.

■ *Social responsibility* is the concept that businesses should be actively concerned with the welfare of society at large. It raises the question of whether businesses should operate strictly in their stockholders' best interests or also be responsible for the welfare of their employees, customers, and the communities in which they operate.

☐ Any voluntary, socially responsible acts that raise costs will be difficult, if not impossible, in industries that are subject to keen competition.

☐ Even highly profitable firms are generally constrained in exercising social responsibility by capital market forces because investors will normally prefer a firm that concentrates on profits over one excessively devoted to social action.

☐ Socially responsible actions that increase costs may have to be put on a mandatory, rather than a voluntary, basis to ensure that the burden falls uniformly on all businesses.

☐ Industry and government must cooperate in establishing the rules of corporate behavior, and the costs as well as the benefits of such actions must be estimated accurately and then taken into account.

■ Most actions that help a firm increase the price of its stock also benefit society at large.

☐ To maximize stock price, a firm must provide a low-cost, high-quality product to consumers. This, in itself, is a benefit to society.

☐ Since financial management plays a crucial role in the operations of successful firms, and since successful firms are absolutely necessary for a healthy, productive economy, it is easy to see why finance is important from a social welfare standpoint.

Business ethics can be thought of as a company's attitude and conduct toward its employees, customers, community, and stockholders. Most firms today have in place strong codes of ethical behavior; however, it is imperative that top management be openly committed to ethical behavior and that they communicate this commitment through their own personal actions as well as company policies. Recent events (Enron and Global Crossing) show that the long-run costs of unethical behavior can often be staggering.

An agency relationship arises whenever one or more individuals (the principals) hire another individual or organization (the agent) to act on their behalf, delegating decision-making authority to that agent. Within the financial management context, the primary agency relationships are those (1) between stockholders and managers and (2) between stockholders (through managers) and creditors (debtholders).

■ A potential *agency problem* arises whenever a manager of a firm owns less than 100 percent of the firm's common stock.

☐ Since the firm's earnings do not go solely to the manager, he or she may not concentrate exclusively on maximizing shareholder wealth.

☐ In most large corporations, potential agency conflicts are important, because large firms' managers generally own only a small percentage of the stock.

■ Specific mechanisms are used to motivate managers to act in shareholders' best interests. These include: (1) managerial compensation, (2) direct intervention by shareholders, (3) the threat of firing, and (4) the threat of takeovers.

☐ A *performance share* is stock that is awarded to executives on the basis of the company's performance.

- ☐ *Executive stock options* are granted to an executive as part of his or her compensation package and allow the executive to purchase stock at some future time at a given price.
- ☐ A *hostile takeover* is the acquisition of a company over the opposition of its management. Hostile takeovers are most likely to occur when a firm's stock is undervalued relative to its potential because of poor management.

■ Another agency problem involves conflicts between stockholders (through managers) and creditors (debtholders).

- ☐ Conflicts arise if (a) management, acting for its stockholders, takes on projects that have greater risk than was anticipated by creditors or (b) the firm increases debt to a level higher than was anticipated. Both of these actions decrease the value of the debt outstanding.
- ☐ To best serve their shareholders in the long run, managers must play fairly with creditors. Managers, as agents of both shareholders and creditors, must act in a manner that is fairly balanced between the interests of the two classes of security holders.

  - Creditors attempt to protect themselves against stockholders by placing restrictive covenants in debt agreements.

  - If creditors perceive that a firm's managers are trying to take advantage of them, they will either refuse to deal with the firm or else will charge a higher-than-normal interest rate to compensate for the risk of possible exploitation.

- ☐ Similarly, because of other constraints and sanctions, management actions that would expropriate wealth from any of the firm's other stakeholders, including its employees, customers, suppliers, and community, will ultimately be to the detriment of its shareholders.
- ☐ In our society, stock price maximization requires fair treatment for all parties whose economic positions are affected by managerial decisions.

What factors determine the price of a company's stock? Three basic principles apply. (1) Any financial asset is valuable only to the extent that the asset generates cash flows. (2) The timing of the cash flows matters. (3) Investors are generally averse to risk, so all else equal, they will pay more for a stock whose cash flows are relatively certain than for one with relatively risky cash flows. Because of these factors, managers can enhance their firm's value (and its stock price) by increasing their firm's expected cash flows, by speeding them up, and by reducing their riskiness.

■ Investment and financing decisions are likely to affect the level, timing, and riskiness of the firm's cash flows, and, therefore, the price of its stock. Managers should make investment and financing decisions designed to maximize the firm's stock price.

■   Although managerial actions affect the value of a firm's stock, external factors also influence stock prices. Some of these external factors are legal constraints, the general level of economic activity, tax laws, interest rates, and conditions in the stock market.

While a growing number of analysts rely on cash flow projections to assess performance, at least as much attention is still paid to accounting measures, especially EPS.

■   Traditional accounting performance measures are appealing because (1) they are easy to use and understand; (2) they are calculated on the basis of standardized accounting practices; and (3) net income is supposed to be reflective of the firm's potential to produce cash flows over time.

■   Generally, there is a high correlation between EPS, cash flow, and stock price, and all generally rise if a firm's sales rise. Nevertheless, stock prices depend not just on today's earnings and cash flows—future cash flows and the riskiness of the future earnings stream also affect stock prices.

■   Even though cash flows ultimately determine stockholder value, financial managers cannot ignore the effects of their decisions on reported EPS, because earnings announcements send messages to investors.

SELF-TEST QUESTIONS

Definitional

1. Finance consists of three interrelated areas: (1) _____ _____ _____ _____, which deals with many of the topics covered in macroeconomics; (2) _____, which focuses on the decisions of individuals and financial institutions as they choose securities for their investment portfolios; and (3) _____ _____ or "business finance."

2. Two increasingly important trends affecting financial management in recent years are the _____ of business and the increased use of _____ _____.

3. Sole proprietorships are easily formed, but often have difficulty raising _____, they subject proprietors to unlimited _____, and they have a limited _____.

4. Partnership profits are taxed as _____ income in proportion to each partner's proportionate ownership.

5. A partnership is dissolved upon the withdrawal or _____ of any one of the partners. In addition, the difficulty in _____ ownership is a major disadvantage of the partnership form of business organization.

6. A(n) _____ is a legal entity created by a state, and it is separate from its owners and managers.

7. The concept of _____ _____ means that a firm's stockholders are not personally liable for the debts of the business.

8. Modern financial theory operates on the assumption that the goal of management is the _____ of shareholder _____. This goal is accomplished if the firm's _____ _____ is maximized.

9. Socially responsible activities that increase a firm's costs will be most difficult in those industries where _____ is most intense.

10. Firms with above-average profit levels will find social actions _____ by capital market factors.

11. _____ _____ can be thought of as a company's attitude and conduct towards its employees, customers, community, and stockholders.

12. A(n) _____ relationship arises whenever one or more individuals (the principals) hire another individual or organization (the agent) to act on their behalf, delegating decision-making authority to that agent.

13. Potential agency problems exist between a firm's shareholders and its _____ and also between shareholders (through managers) and _____.

14. _____ _____ is the concept that businesses should be actively concerned with the welfare of society at large.

15. A(n) _____ _____ is stock that is awarded to executives on the basis of the company's performance.

16. _____ _____ _____ are granted as part of a compensation package and allow managers to purchase stock at some future time at a given price.

17. A(n) _____ _____ is the acquisition of a company over the opposition of its management.

Conceptual

18. The primary objective of the firm is to maximize EPS.

    a. True **b.** False

19. The types of actions that help a firm maximize stock price are generally not directly beneficial to society at large.

    a. True **b.** False

20. There are factors that influence stock price over which managers have virtually no control.

    a. True **b.** False

21. Which of the following factors tend to encourage management to pursue stock price maximization as a goal?

    a. Shareholders link management's compensation to company performance.
    b. Managers' reactions to the threat of firing and hostile takeovers.
    c. Managers do not have goals other than stock price maximization.
    d. Statements a and b are correct.
    e. Statements a, b, and c are all correct.

22. The primary contribution of finance to total social welfare is its

    a. Function as a productive resource.
    b. Contribution to the efficient allocation and use of resources.
    c. Role as an exogenous variable.
    d. Positive impact on the externalities of "other variables."
    e. Contribution to environmental protection.

23. Which of the following represents a significant *disadvantage* to the corporate form of organization?

    a. Difficulty in transferring ownership.
    b. Exposure to taxation of corporate earnings and stockholder dividend income.
    c. Degree of liability to which corporate owners and managers are exposed.
    d. Level of difficulty corporations face in obtaining large amounts of capital in financial markets.
    e. All of the above are disadvantages to the corporate form of organization.

ANSWERS TO SELF-TEST QUESTIONS

1. money and capital markets; investments; financial management
2. globalization; information technology
3. capital; liability; life
4. personal
5. death; transferring
6. corporation
7. limited liability
8. maximization; wealth; stock price

9. competition
10. constrained
11. Business ethics
12. agency
13. managers; creditors (or debtholders)
14. Social responsibility
15. performance share
16. Executive stock options
17. hostile takeover

18. b. An increase in earnings per share will not necessarily increase stock price. For example, if the increase in earnings per share is accompanied by an increase in the riskiness of the firm, stock price might fall. *The primary objective is the maximization of stock price.*

19. b. The actions that maximize stock price generally also benefit society by promoting efficient, low-cost operations; encouraging the development of new technology, products, and jobs; and requiring efficient and courteous service.

20. a. Managers have no control over factors such as (1) external constraints (for example, antitrust laws and environmental regulations), (2) the general level of economic activity, (3) taxes, (4) interest rates, and (5) conditions in the stock market, all of which affect the firm's stock price.

21. d. Specific mechanisms that tend to force managers to act in shareholders' best interests include (1) the proper structuring of managerial compensation, (2) direct intervention by shareholders, (3) the threat of firing, and (4) the threat of takeover.

22. b. Financial management plays a crucial role in the operation of successful firms because of finance's contribution to the efficient allocation and use of resources. Successful firms are absolutely necessary for a healthy, productive economy.

23. b. The double taxation of corporate earnings is a significant disadvantage of the corporate form of organization. The corporations' earnings are taxed, and then any earnings paid out as dividends are taxed again as income to stockholders.

CHAPTER 2
FINANCIAL STATEMENTS, CASH FLOW, AND TAXES

- Briefly explain the history of accounting and financial statements, and how financial statements are used.

- List of types of information in a corporation's annual report.

- Explain what a balance sheet is, the information it provides, and how assets and claims on assets are arranged on a balance sheet.

- Explain what an income statement is and the information it provides.

- Specify the changes reported in a firm's statement of retained earnings.

- Differentiate between net cash flow and accounting profit.

- Identify the purpose of the statement of cash flows, list the factors affecting a firm's cash position that are reflected in this statement, and identify the three categories of activities that are separated out in this statement.

- Discuss how certain modifications to the accounting data are needed and used for corporate decision making and stock valuation purposes. In the process, explain the terms: net operating working capital, total investor-supplied operating capital, NOPAT, free cash flow, and operating cash flow; and explain how each is calculated.

- Define the terms Market Value Added (MVA) and Economic Value Added (EVA), explain how each is calculated, and differentiate between them.

- Explain why financial managers must be concerned with taxation, and list some of the most important elements of the current tax law, such as the differences between the treatment of dividends and interest paid and interest and dividend income received.

OVERVIEW

Financial management requires the consideration of the types of financial statements firms must provide to investors. Thus, this chapter begins with a discussion of the basic financial statements, how they are used, and what kinds of financial information users need. The value of any asset depends on the usable, or after-tax, cash flows the asset is expected to produce, so the chapter also explains the difference between accounting income versus cash flow. Since the traditional financial statements are designed more for use by creditors than for corporate managers and stock analysts, the chapter discusses how to modify accounting data for managerial decisions. In addition, the concepts of Market Value Added (MVA) and Economic Value Added (EVA) are defined and explained. Finally, since it is the after-tax cash flow that is important, the chapter provides an overview of the federal income tax system. A more detailed discussion of the income tax system is contained in Web Appendix 2A.

OUTLINE

Although the economic system has grown enormously since the early days of the barter system, the original reasons for accounting and financial statements still apply. Investors need them to make intelligent decisions, managers need them to see how effectively their enterprises are being run, and taxing authorities need them to assess taxes in a reasonable manner.

A firm's annual report to shareholders presents two important types of information. The first is a verbal statement of the company's recent operating results and its expectations for the coming year. The second is a set of quantitative financial statements that report what actually happened to the firm's financial position, earnings, and dividends over the past few years.

The balance sheet is a statement of the firm's financial position at a specific point in time. It shows the firm's assets and the claims against those assets. Assets, found on the left-hand side of the balance sheet, are typically shown in the order of their liquidity. Claims, found on the right-hand side, are generally listed in the order in which they must be paid.

■ Only cash represents actual money. Noncash assets should produce cash flows eventually, but they do not represent cash in hand.

■ Claims against the assets consist of liabilities and stockholders' equity:

Assets – Liabilities – Preferred stock = Common stockholders' equity (Net worth).

- ☐ *Common stockholders' equity*, or *net worth*, is capital supplied by common stock-holders—common stock, paid-in capital, retained earnings, and occasionally, certain reserves.
  ☐ Preferred stock is a hybrid, or a cross between common stock and debt.

- ■ The common equity section of the balance sheet is divided into two accounts: common stock and retained earnings. The *common stock* account arises from the issuance of stock to raise capital. *Retained earnings* are built up over time as the firm "saves" a part of its earnings rather than paying all earnings out as dividends.

- ■ Different methods, such as FIFO and LIFO, can be used to determine the value of inventory. These methods, in turn, affect the reported cost of goods sold, profits, and EPS.

- ■ Companies often use the most accelerated method permitted under the law to calculate depreciation for tax purposes but use straight-line depreciation, which results in a lower depreciation expense, for stockholder reporting.

- ■ The balance sheet may be thought of as a snapshot of the firm's financial position *at a point in time* (for example, end of year). The balance sheet changes every day as inventory is increased or decreased, as fixed assets are added or retired, as bank loans are increased or decreased, and so on.

The income statement summarizes the firm's revenues and expenses over a period of time (for example, the past year). Earnings per share (EPS) is called "the bottom line," denoting that of all the items on the income statement, EPS is the most important.

- ■ *Depreciation* is an annual noncash charge against income that reflects the estimated dollar cost of the capital equipment used up in the production process. It applies to *tangible assets*, such as plant and equipment, whereas *amortization* applies to *intangible asset*s, such as patents, copyrights, and trademarks. They are often lumped together on the income statement.

- ■ *EBITDA* represents earnings before interest, taxes, depreciation, and amortization.

- ■ For planning and control purposes, management generally forecasts monthly income statements, and it then compares actual results to the budgeted statements.

The statement of retained earnings reports changes in the equity accounts between balance sheet dates.

■ The balance sheet account "retained earnings" represents a claim against assets, not assets per se. Retained earnings as reported on the balance sheet do not represent cash and are not "available" for the payment of dividends or anything else.
  ☐ Retained earnings represent funds that have already been reinvested in the firm's operating assets.

In finance the emphasis is on the cash flow that the company is expected to generate. The firm's net income is important, but cash flows are even more important because dividends must be paid in cash, and cash is also necessary to purchase the assets required to continue operations.

■ A business's net cash flow generally differs from its accounting profit (net income reported on its income statement), because some of the revenues and expenses listed on the income statement were not paid in cash during the year.

Net cash flow = Net income – Noncash revenues + Noncash charges.

  ☐ Typically, depreciation and amortization are by far the largest noncash items, and in many cases the other noncash items roughly net out to zero. For this reason, many analysts assume that

Net cash flows = Net income + Depreciation and amortization.

  ● However, you should remember that this equation will not accurately reflect net cash flow in those instances where there are significant noncash items beyond depreciation and amortization.

The statement of cash flows reports the impact of a firm's operating, investing and financing activities on cash flows over an accounting period.

■ *Net cash flow* represents the amount of cash a business generates for its shareholders in a given year.

■ The company's cash position as reported on the balance sheet is affected by many factors, including cash flow, changes in working capital, fixed assets, and security transactions.

■ The statement separates activities into three categories:
  ☐ *Operating activities*, which includes net income, depreciation, and changes in current assets and current liabilities other than cash and short-term debt.
  ☐ *Investing activities*, which includes investments in or sales of fixed assets.
  ☐ *Financing activities*, which includes cash raised during the year by issuing debt or stock, and dividends paid or cash buy-backs of outstanding stock or bonds.

■ Financial managers generally use this statement, along with the cash budget, when forecasting their companies' cash positions.

The traditional financial statements are designed more for use by creditors and tax collectors than for managers and equity analysts. Certain modifications are used for corporate decision making and stock valuation purposes.

■ To judge managerial performance one needs to compare managers' ability to generate operating income (EBIT) with the operating assets under their control.
  □ *Operating assets* consist of cash, marketable securities, accounts receivable, inventories, and fixed assets necessary to operate the business.
  □ *Nonoperating assets* include cash and marketable securities above the level required for normal operations, investments in subsidiaries, land held for future use, and the like.
  □ Operating assets can be further divided into working capital and fixed assets such as plant and equipment.
  □ Those current assets used in operations are called *operating working capital*, and operating working capital less accounts payable and accrued liabilities is called *net operating working capital (NOWC)*.
    • Net operating working capital is the working capital acquired with investor-supplied funds.
  □ Total investor-supplied operating capital is the sum of net operating working capital and net fixed assets.

■ Net income does not always reflect the true performance of a company's operations or the effectiveness of its managers and employees.
  □ A better measurement for comparing managers' performance is *net operating profit after taxes (NOPAT)*, which is the amount of profit a company would generate if it had no debt and held no nonoperating assets.

$$NOPAT = EBIT(1 - Tax\ rate).$$

■ The value of a company's operations depends on all the future expected free cash flows.
  □ *Free cash flow* is the cash flow actually available for distribution to all investors (stockholders and debtholders) after the company has made all the investments in fixed assets, new products, and working capital necessary to sustain ongoing operations.
    • Free cash flow is defined as after-tax operating profit minus the amount of investment in working capital and fixed assets necessary to sustain the business.

- Free cash flow is calculated as operating cash flow less gross investment in operating capital.
- It also equals NOPAT less net investment in operating capital.

☐ Free cash flow differs from net cash flow in two important ways.

- Free cash flow represents funds available to all investors, whereas net cash flow represents funds available to common stockholders. Consequently, payments to bondholders and preferred stockholders reduce net cash flow, but they are not subtracted out of free cash flow.
- Free cash flow represents the funds available to all investors after subtracting out the investments that are necessary to sustain the firm's ongoing operations. Thus, investments in fixed assets and net working capital reduce free cash flow, but they are not subtracted out of net cash flow.

☐ While analysts often calculate net cash flow to measure the cash generated for shareholders in a given year, free cash flow is often more relevant when estimating the value of a project or firm.

☐ *Operating cash flow* is NOPAT plus any noncash adjustments as shown on the statement of cash flows.

- Operating cash flow = NOPAT + Depreciation and amortization.

■ Negative free cash flow is not always bad. If free cash flow is negative because NOPAT is negative, this is bad, because the company is probably experiencing operating problems.

☐ Exceptions to this might be startup companies; companies that are incurring significant current expenses to launch a new product line; or high-growth companies, which will have large investments in capital that cause low current free cash flow, but that will increase future free cash flow.

Neither traditional accounting data nor the modified data discussed above deal with stock prices. This is a serious omission, since the primary goal of management is to maximize the firm's stock price. In response to these limitations, analysts have come up with adjustments that provide alternative measures of performance. Two of these measures are Market Value Added (MVA) and Economic Value Added (EVA).

■ Shareholders' wealth is maximized by maximizing the difference between the market value of the firm's stock and the amount of equity capital that was supplied by shareholders. This difference is called the *Market Value Added (MVA)*.

$$MVA = \text{Market value of stock} - \text{Equity capital supplied by shareholders}$$
$$= (\text{Shares outstanding})(\text{Stock price}) - \text{Total common equity}.$$

☐ The higher its MVA, the better the job management is doing for the firm's shareholders.

- Whereas MVA measures the effects of managerial actions since the very inception of a company, *Economic Value Added (EVA)* focuses on managerial effectiveness in a given year.

$$\text{EVA} = \text{NOPAT} - \text{After-tax dollar cost of capital used to support operations}$$
$$= \text{EBIT}(1 - T) - \binom{\text{Total investor - supplied}}{\text{operating capital}}\binom{\text{After - tax percentage}}{\text{cost of capital}}.$$

  - ☐ EVA is an estimate of a business's true economic profit for the year.
  - ☐ EVA differs sharply from accounting profit.
    - EVA represents the residual income that remains after the cost of all capital, including equity capital, has been deducted, whereas accounting profit is determined without imposing a charge for equity capital.
  - ☐ When calculating EVA, depreciation is not added back. Although it is not a cash expense, depreciation is a cost, and it is therefore deducted when determining both net income and EVA.
  - ☐ EVA provides a good measure of the extent to which the firm has added to shareholder value.
    - If managers focus on EVA, this will help to ensure that they operate in a manner that is consistent with maximizing shareholder wealth.
  - ☐ EVA can be determined for divisions as well as for the company as a whole, so it provides a useful basis for determining managerial compensation at all levels. MVA must be applied to the entire corporation.

- There is a relationship between MVA and EVA, but it is not a direct one.
  - ☐ If a company has a history of negative EVAs, then its MVA will probably be negative, and vice versa if it has a history of positive EVAs.
    - A company with a history of negative EVAs could have a positive MVA, provided investors expect a turnaround in the future. Stock price, which is the key ingredient in the MVA calculation, depends more on expected future performance than on historical performance.
  - ☐ When EVAs or MVAs are used to evaluate managerial performance as part of an incentive compensation program, EVA is the measure that is typically used.
    - MVA is used primarily to evaluate top corporate officers over periods of five to ten years, or longer.

Corporations must pay a significant portion of their income out as taxes, and individuals are also taxed on their income. A more detailed discussion of the federal income tax system is contained in Web Appendix 2A.

- Corporate income is generally taxed at rates that begin at 15 percent and go up to 35 percent on taxable income of $10 million or more.

☐ The corporate tax rate is *progressive* in the sense that higher rates are imposed on companies with larger incomes.

◼ Individuals are taxed on their taxable income by the federal government at rates that begin at 10 percent and rise to 38.6 percent on incomes of $307,050 or more.
  ☐ Income on investments held in pension accounts are not taxed until the money is withdrawn, presumably after retirement.

◼ Borrowers must pay interest on their debts.
  ☐ For a business, interest payments are regarded as an expense, and they may be deducted when calculating taxable income.
  ☐ Generally, individuals cannot deduct interest payments. However, interest on home loans is deductible within limits.
  ☐ Most interest earned, whether by businesses or individuals, is taxable income, and hence subject to income taxes.
    ● An important exception is that interest on most state and local government debt is exempt from federal taxes. State and local bonds are often called "munis," or municipal bonds, and individuals in high tax brackets generally purchase them.

◼ Corporations pay dividends, and dividends paid are generally not deductible for tax purposes.
  ☐ Our tax system encourages debt financing over equity financing because interest paid is tax deductible while dividends paid are not. Higher interest charges mean lower taxable income, lower taxes, and higher cash flow.
  ☐ Dividends received by an individual are taxed as ordinary income.
    ● There is a double tax on dividend income—the corporation that paid the dividend is first taxed, and then the individual who receives it is taxed again.
    ● A corporation that receives dividend income can exclude some of the dividends from its taxable income. This provision in the Tax Code minimizes the amount of triple taxation that would otherwise occur.

◼ The Tax Code allows firms to carry losses back to offset profits in prior years, and if losses haven't been offset by past profits then carried forward to offset profits in the future, which causes taxes over time to reflect average income over time.

◼ Capital gains are defined as profits from the sale of assets that are not normally bought and sold in the course of business.
  ☐ For these assets, if held for a year or more, then the gain will be taxed at a lower rate than ordinary income.
    ● The long-term capital gains tax rate is generally 20 percent.
    ● This tax treatment has an effect on corporate dividend policy.

■ Congress allows companies to use a different method for calculating depreciation used for tax purposes.

  ☐ Congress authorizes depreciation rates for different types of assets, and those rates generally mean that depreciation charges are higher than what the company uses for stockholder reporting.

  ☐ Congress adjusts depreciation rates periodically as a part of its fiscal policy decisions, recognizing that faster depreciation rates stimulate corporate investment and thus encourage economic growth, but at the cost of lower tax collections in the immediate future.

■ An S corporation enjoys the advantages of the corporate form of organization yet still get the tax advantages of a partnership.

  ☐ Most small business corporations are actually set up as S corporations.

SELF-TEST QUESTIONS

Definitional

1. Of all its communications with shareholders, a firm's _____ report is generally the most important.

2. The income statement reports the results of operations during the past year, the most important item being _____ _____ _____.

3. The _____ _____ lists the firm's assets as well as claims against those assets.

4. Typically, assets are listed in order of their _____, while liabilities are listed in the order in which they must be paid.

5. Assets – Liabilities – Preferred stock = _____ worth, or _____ _____ equity.

6. The two accounts that normally make up the common equity section of the balance sheet are _____ _____ and _____ _____.

7. _____ _____ as reported on the balance sheet represent income earned by the firm in past years that has not been paid out as dividends.

8. Retained earnings are generally reinvested in _____ _____ and are not held in the form of cash.

9. The _____ _____ _____ _____ reports the impact of a firm's operating, investing, and financing activities on cash flows over an accounting period.

10. The three major categories of the Statement of Cash Flows are cash flows associated with _____ activities, _____-_____ _____ activities, and _____ activities.

11. The _____ _____ account arises from the issuance of stock to raise capital.

12. The _____ _____ _____ _____ reports changes in the equity accounts between balance sheet dates.

13. In finance the emphasis is on the _____ _____ that the company is expected to generate.

14. _____ _____ _____ represents the amount of funds that is available to stockholders.

15. The traditional financial statements are designed more for use by _____ and tax collectors than for _____ and equity analysts.

16. _____ _____ consist of cash, marketable securities, accounts receivable, inventories, and fixed assets necessary to operate the business.

17. _____ _____ include cash and marketable securities above the level required for normal operations, investments in subsidiaries, and land held for future use.

18. Those current assets used in operations are called _____ _____ _____.

19. Operating working capital less accounts payable and accrued liabilities is called _____ _____ _____ _____.

20. _____ _____-_____ _____ _____ is the sum of net operating working capital and net fixed assets.

21. A better measurement for comparing managers' performance than net income is _____ _____ _____ _____ _____.

22. _____ _____ _____ is the cash flow actually available for distribution to all investors (stockholders and debtholders) after the company has made all the investments in fixed assets and working capital necessary to sustain ongoing operations.

23. _____ _____ _____ is calculated as net operating profit after taxes plus any noncash adjustments as shown on the statement of cash flows.

24. Shareholder wealth is maximized by maximizing the difference between the market value of the firm's common stock and the amount of equity that was supplied by shareholders. This difference is called _____ _____ _____.

25. _____ _____ _____ focuses on managerial effectiveness in a given year and is an estimate of a business's true economic profit for the year.

26. A(n) _____ tax system is one in which tax rates are higher at higher levels of income.

27. Interest received on _____ bonds is generally not subject to federal income taxes. This feature makes them particularly attractive to investors in _____ tax brackets.

28. In order to qualify as a long-term capital gain or loss, an asset must be held for _____ _____.

29. Another important distinction exists between interest and dividends paid by a corporation. Interest payments are _____ _____, while dividend payments are not.

30. The Tax Code permits a corporation (that meets certain restrictions) to be taxed at the owners' personal tax rates. This type of corporation is called a(n) ___ corporation.

Conceptual

31. The fact that some intercorporate dividends received by a corporation are excluded from taxable income has encouraged debt financing over equity financing.

   a. True   b. False

32. Which of the following statements is most correct?

    a. In order to avoid double taxation and to escape the frequently higher tax rate applied to capital gains, stockholders generally prefer to have corporations pay dividends rather than to retain their earnings and reinvest the money in the business. Thus, earnings should be retained only if the firm needs capital very badly and would have difficulty raising it from external sources.

    b. Under our current tax laws, when investors pay taxes on their dividend income, they are being subjected to a form of double taxation.

    c. The fact that a percentage of the interest received by one corporation, which is paid by another corporation, is excluded from taxable income has encouraged firms to use more debt financing relative to equity financing.

    d. If the tax laws stated that $0.50 out of every $1.00 of interest paid by a corporation was allowed as a tax-deductible expense, this would probably encourage companies to use more debt financing than they presently do, other things held constant.

    e. Statements b and d are correct.

SELF-TEST PROBLEMS

(The following data apply to the next three Self-Test Problems.)

Ryngaert & Sons, Inc. has operating income (EBIT) of $2,250,000. The company's depreciation expense is $450,000, its interest expense is $120,000, and it faces a 40 percent tax rate. Assume the firm has no amortization expense.

1. What is the company's net income?

    a. $1,008,000   **b.** $1,278,000   **c.** $1,475,000   **d.** $1,728,000   **e.** $1,800,000

2. What is its net cash flow?

    a. $1,008,000   **b.** $1,278,000   **c.** $1,475,000   **d.** $1,728,000   **e.** $1,800,000

3. What is its operating cash flow?

    a. $1,008,000   **b.** $1,278,000   **c.** $1,475,000   **d.** $1,728,000   **e.** $1,800,000

(The following data apply to the next two Self-Test Problems.)

GPD Corporation has operating income (EBIT) of $300,000, total assets of $1,500,000, and its capital structure consists of 40 percent debt and 60 percent equity. Total assets were equal to total operating capital. The firm's after-tax cost of capital is 10.5 percent and its tax rate is 40 percent. The firm has 50,000 shares of common stock currently outstanding and the current price of a share of stock is $27.00.

4.   What is the firm's Market Value Added (MVA)?

   a. $22,500   **b.** $87,575   **c.** $187,740   **d.** $450,000   **e.** $575,000

5.   What is the firm's Economic Value Added (EVA)?

   a. $22,500   **b.** $87,575   **c.** $187,740   **d.** $450,000   **e.** $575,000

(The following financial statements apply to the next four Self-Test Problems.)

You have just obtained financial information for the past two years for the Smith Brothers Corporation.

Smith Brothers Corporation
Income Statements for Year Ending December 31
(Millions of Dollars)

	2002	2001
Sales	$360	$300
Operating costs excluding depreciation	306	255
EBITDA	$ 54	$ 45
Depreciation	9	7
EBIT	$ 45	$ 38
Interest	7	6
EBT	$ 38	$ 32
Taxes (40%)	15	13
NI available to common stockholders	$ 23	$ 19
Common dividends	$ 16	$ 10

Smith Brothers Corporation
Balance Sheets as of December 31
(Millions of Dollars)

Assets	2002	2001
Cash	$ 4	$ 3
Accounts receivable	54	45
Inventories	54	60
Total CA	$112	$108
Net plant & equipment	90	75
Total assets	$202	$183

Liabilities and Equity		
Accounts payable	$ 32	$ 28
Notes payable	20	16
Accrued liabilities	22	18
Total CL	$ 74	$ 62
Long-term bonds	45	45
Total debt	$119	$107
Common stock (50,000,000 shares)	15	15
Retained earnings	68	61
Common equity	$ 83	$ 76
Total liabilities and equity	$202	$183

6. What is the net operating profit after taxes (NOPAT) in millions of dollars for 2002?

   a. $18   **b.** $27   **c.** $34   **d.** $40   **e.** $45

7. What is the net operating working capital in millions of dollars in 2002?

   a. $38   **b.** $54   **c.** $58   **d.** $87   **e.** $112

8. What is the total investor-supplied operating capital in millions of dollars for 2002?

   a. $90   **b.** $128   **c.** $144   **d.** $148   **e.** $177

9. What is the free cash flow in millions of dollars for 2002?

   a. $11   **b.** $16   **c.** $20   **d.** $25   **e.** $27

10. In its recent income statement Tyler Toys Inc. reported $72.5 million of net income, and in its year-end balance sheet Tyler reported $1,174 million of retained earnings. The previous year its balance sheet showed $1,131 million of retained earnings. What were the total dividends (in millions of dollars) paid to shareholders during the most recent year?

   a. $10.5   **b.** $17.7   **c.** $24.6   **d.** $29.5   **e.** $33.0

11. Peterson Manufacturing recently reported an EBITDA of $18.75 million and $4.5 million of net income. The company has $5 million of interest expense and the corporate tax rate is 40 percent. What was the company's depreciation and amortization expense in millions of dollars?

   a. $6.25   **b.** $3.75   **c.** $1.50   **d.** $2.25   **e.** $8.50

ANSWERS TO SELF-TEST QUESTIONS

1.	annual	16.	Operating assets
2.	earnings per share	17.	Nonoperating assets
3.	balance sheet	18.	operating working capital
4.	liquidity	19.	net operating working capital
5.	Net; common stockholders'	20.	Total investor-supplied operating capital
6.	common stock, retained earnings		
7.	Retained earnings	21.	net operating profit after taxes
8.	operating assets	22.	Free cash flow
9.	Statement of Cash Flows	23.	Operating cash flow
10.	operating; long-term investing; financing	24.	Market Value Added (MVA)
		25.	Economic Value Added (EVA)
11.	common stock	26.	progressive
12.	Statement of Retained Earnings	27.	municipal; high
13.	cash flow	28.	one year
14.	Net cash flow	29.	tax deductible
15.	creditors; managers	30.	S

31. b. Debt financing is encouraged by the fact that interest payments are tax deductible while dividend payments are not.

32. b. Statement a is incorrect. To avoid double taxation, stockholders would prefer that corporations retain more earnings because long-term capital gains are generally taxed at a maximum rate of 20 percent. Statement c is incorrect. Debt financing has been encouraged by the fact that interest on debt is tax deductible. Statement d is incorrect. Currently, interest on debt is fully tax deductible; allowing 50 percent of interest to be tax deductible would discourage debt financing.

SOLUTIONS TO SELF-TEST PROBLEMS

1. b.
EBIT	$2,250,000
Interest	120,000
EBT	$2,130,000
Taxes (40%)	852,000
Net income	$1,278,000

2. d. Net cash flow = Net income + Depreciation and amortization
    $$= \$1,278,000 + \$450,000$$
    $$= \$1,728,000.$$

3. e. Operating cash flow = EBIT$(1 - T)$ + Depreciation and amortization
    $$= \$2,250,000(0.6) + \$450,000$$
    $$= \$1,800,000.$$

4. d. Market Value Added = (Shares outstanding)(P_0) − Total common equity
    $$= 50,000(\$27.00) - (0.6)(\$1,500,000)$$
    $$= \$1,350,000 - \$900,000$$
    $$= \$450,000.$$

5. a. Economic Value Added = NOPAT − AT dollar cost of capital used to support operations
    $$= \text{EBIT}(1 - T) - (\text{Operating capital})(\text{AT percentage cost})$$
    $$= \$300,000(0.6) - (\$1,500,000)(0.105)$$
    $$= \$180,000 - \$157,500$$
    $$= \$22,500.$$

6. b. NOPAT = EBIT$(1 - T)$
    $$= \$45(0.6)$$
    $$= \$27.$$

7. c. Net operating working capital$_{02}$ = Current assets − Non-interest charging current liabilities
    $$= (\$4 + \$54 + \$54) - (\$32 + \$22)$$
    $$= \$112 - \$54 = \$58.$$

8.   d.   Operating capital$_{02}$ = Net plant and equipment + Net operating working capital
$$= \$90 + \$58$$
$$= \$148.$$

9.   b.   FCF$_{02}$ = NOPAT – Net investment in operating capital
$$= \$27 - (\$148 - \$137)$$
$$= \$16.$$

10.   d.   NI = \$72,500,000; R/E$_{Y/E}$ = \$1,174,000,000; R/E$_{B/Y}$ = \$1,131,000,000; Dividends = ?
R/E$_{B/Y}$ + NI – Div = R/E$_{Y/E}$.

$$\$1,131,000,000 + \$72,500,000 - Div = \$1,174,000,000$$
$$\$1,203,500,000 - Div = \$1,174,000,000$$
$$\$29,500,000 = Div.$$

11.   a.   EBITDA = \$18,750,000; NI = \$4,500,000; Int = \$5,000,000; T = 40%; DA = ?

EBITDA	\$18,750,000	
DA	6,250,000	EBITDA – DA = EBIT; DA = EBITDA – EBIT
EBIT	\$12,500,000	EBIT = EBT + Int = \$7,500,000 + \$5,000,000
Int	5,000,000	(Given)
EBT	\$ 7,500,000	$\dfrac{\$4,500,000}{(1-T)} = \dfrac{\$4,500,000}{0.6}$
Taxes (40%)	3,000,000	
NI	\$ 4,500,000	(Given)

CHAPTER 3
ANALYSIS OF FINANCIAL STATEMENTS

LEARNING OBJECTIVES

- Explain why ratio analysis is usually the first step in the analysis of a company's financial statements.

- List the five groups of ratios, specify which ratios belong in each group, and explain what information each group gives us about the firm's financial position.

- State what trend analysis is, and why it is important.

- Describe how the Du Pont equation is used, and how it may be modified to include the effect of financial leverage.

- Explain "benchmarking" and its purpose.

- List several limitations of ratio analysis.

- Identify some of the problems with ROE that can arise when firms use it as a sole measure of performance.

- Identify some of the qualitative factors that must be considered when evaluating a company's financial performance.

OVERVIEW

Financial analysis is designed to determine the relative strengths and weaknesses of a company. Investors need this information to estimate both future cash flows from the firm and the riskiness of those cash flows. Financial managers need the information provided by analysis both to evaluate the firm's past performance and to map future plans. Financial analysis concentrates on financial statement analysis, which highlights the key aspects of a firm's operations.

Financial statement analysis involves a study of the relationships between income statement and balance sheet accounts, how these relationships change over time (trend analysis), and how a particular firm compares with other firms in its industry (bench-marking). Although financial analysis has limitations, when used with care and judgment, it can provide some very useful insights into a company's operations.

OUTLINE

Financial statements are used to help predict the firm's future earnings and dividends. From an investor's standpoint, predicting the future is what financial statement analysis is all about. From management's standpoint, financial statement analysis is useful both to help anticipate future conditions and, more important, as a starting point for planning actions that will influence the future course of events.

■ Financial ratios are designed to help one evaluate a firm's financial statements.
  ☐ The burden of debt, and the company's ability to repay, can be best evaluated (1) by comparing the company's debt to its assets and (2) by comparing the interest it must pay to the income it has available for payment of interest. Such comparisons are made by *ratio analysis*.

A liquid asset is an asset that can be converted to cash quickly without having to reduce the asset's price very much. Liquidity ratios are used to measure a firm's ability to meet its current obligations as they come due.

■ One of the most commonly used liquidity ratios is the current ratio.
  ☐ The *current ratio* measures the extent to which current liabilities are covered by current assets.
  ☐ It is determined by dividing current assets by current liabilities.
  ☐ It is the most commonly used measure of short-term solvency.

Asset management ratios measure how effectively a firm is managing its assets and whether the level of those assets is properly related to the level of operations as measured by sales.

■ The *inventory turnover ratio* is defined as sales divided by inventories.
  ☐ It is often necessary to use average inventories rather than year-end inventories, especially if a firm's business is highly seasonal, or if there has been a strong upward or downward sales trend during the year.

■ *Days sales outstanding (DSO),* also called the "average collection period" (ACP), is used to appraise accounts receivable, and it is calculated by dividing accounts receivable by average daily sales to find the number of days' sales tied up in receivables.

- ☐ The DSO represents the average length of time that the firm must wait after making a sale before receiving cash.
- ☐ The DSO can also be evaluated by comparison with the terms on which the firm sells its goods.
- ☐ If the trend in DSO over the past few years has been rising, but the credit policy has not been changed, this would be strong evidence that steps should be taken to expedite the collection of accounts receivable.

■ The *fixed assets turnover ratio* is the ratio of sales to net fixed assets.
  - ☐ It measures how effectively the firm uses its plant and equipment.
  - ☐ A potential problem can exist when interpreting the fixed assets turnover ratio of a firm with older, lower-cost fixed assets compared to one with recently acquired, higher-cost fixed assets. Financial analysts recognize that a problem exists and deal with it judgmentally.

■ The *total assets turnover ratio* is calculated by dividing sales by total assets.
  - ☐ It measures the utilization, or turnover, of all the firm's assets.

Debt management ratios measure the extent to which a firm is using debt financing, or financial leverage, and the degree of safety afforded to creditors.

■ Financial leverage has three important implications: (1) By raising funds through debt, stockholders can maintain control of a firm while limiting their investment. (2) Creditors look to the equity, or owner-supplied funds, to provide a margin of safety, so if the stockholders have provided only a small proportion of the total financing, the firm's risks are borne mainly by its creditors. (3) If the firm earns more on investments financed with borrowed funds than it pays in interest, the return on the owners' capital is magnified, or "leveraged."
  - ☐ Firms with relatively high debt ratios have higher expected returns when the economy is normal, but they are exposed to risk of loss when the economy goes into a recession.
  - ☐ Firms with low debt ratios are less risky, but also forgo the opportunity to leverage up their return on equity.
  - ☐ Decisions about the use of debt require firms to balance higher expected returns against increased risk.

■ Analysts use two procedures to examine the firm's debt: (1) They check the balance sheet to determine the extent to which borrowed funds have been used to finance assets, and (2) they review the income statement to see the extent to which fixed charges are covered by operating profits.

- The *debt ratio*, or ratio of total debt to total assets, measures the percentage of funds provided by creditors. Total debt includes both current liabilities and long-term debt.
  - ☐ The lower the ratio, the greater the protection afforded creditors in the event of liquidation.
  - ☐ Stockholders, on the other hand, may want more leverage because it magnifies expected earnings.
  - ☐ A debt ratio that exceeds the industry average raises a red flag and may make it costly for a firm to borrow additional funds without first raising more equity capital.

- The *times-interest-earned (TIE) ratio* is determined by dividing earnings before interest and taxes (EBIT) by the interest charges.
  - ☐ The TIE measures the extent to which operating income can decline before the firm is unable to meet its annual interest costs.
  - ☐ Note that EBIT, rather than net income, is used in the numerator. Because interest is paid with pre-tax dollars, the firm's ability to pay current interest is not affected by taxes.
  - ☐ This ratio has two shortcomings: (1) Interest is not the only fixed financial charge. (2) EBIT does not represent all the cash flow available to service debt, especially if a firm has high depreciation and/or amortization charges.

- To account for the deficiencies of the TIE ratio, bankers and others have developed the *EBITDA coverage ratio*. It is calculated as EBITDA plus lease payments divided by the sum of interest, principal repayments, and lease payments.
  - ☐ The EBITDA coverage ratio is most useful for relatively short-term lenders such as banks, which rarely make loans (except real estate-backed loans) for longer than about five years.
  - ☐ Over a relatively short period, depreciation-generated funds can be used to service debt.
    - • Over a longer time, depreciation-generated funds must be reinvested to maintain the plant and equipment or else the company cannot remain in business.
  - ☐ Banks and other relatively short-term lenders focus on the EDITDA coverage ratio, whereas long-term bondholders focus on the TIE ratio.

Profitability ratios show the combined effects of liquidity, asset management, and debt on operating results.

- The *profit margin on sales* is calculated by dividing net income by sales.
  - ☐ It gives the profit per dollar of sales.

- The *basic earning power (BEP) ratio* is calculated by dividing earnings before interest and taxes (EBIT) by total assets.

> ☐ It shows the raw earning power of the firm's assets, before the influence of taxes and leverage.
> ☐ It is useful for comparing firms with different tax situations and different degrees of financial leverage.

■ The *return on total assets (ROA)* is the ratio of net income to total assets.
> ☐ It measures the return on all the firm's assets after interest and taxes.

■ The *return on common equity (ROE)* measures the rate of return on the stockholders' investment.
> ☐ It is equal to net income divided by common equity. Stockholders invest to get a return on their money, and this ratio tells how well they are doing in an accounting sense.

Market value ratios relate the firm's stock price to its earnings, cash flow, and book value per share, and thus give management an indication of what investors think of the company's past performance and future prospects. If the liquidity, asset management, debt management, and profitability ratios all look good, then the market value ratios will be high, and the stock price will probably be as high as can be expected.

■ The *price/earnings (P/E) ratio*, or price per share divided by earnings per share, shows how much investors are willing to pay per dollar of reported profits.
> ☐ P/E ratios are higher for firms with strong growth prospects, other things held constant, but they are lower for riskier firms.

■ The *price/cash flow ratio* is the ratio of price per share divided by cash flow per share.
> ☐ It shows the dollar amount investors will pay for $1 of cash flow.

■ The *market/book (M/B) ratio*, defined as market price per share divided by book value per share, gives another indication of how investors regard the company.
> ☐ Higher M/B ratios are generally associated with firms with relatively high rates of return on common equity.
> ☐ An M/B ratio greater than 1.0 means that investors are willing to pay more for stocks than their accounting book values.

It is important to analyze trends in ratios as well as their absolute levels. Trend analysis can provide clues as to whether the firm's financial situation is likely to improve or to deteriorate.

The Extended Du Pont Equation shows how return on equity is affected by assets turnover, profit margin, and leverage. This measure was developed by Du Pont managers for evaluating performance and analyzing ways of improving performance.

- The profit margin times the total assets turnover is called the *Du Pont Equation*. This equation gives the rate of return on assets (ROA):

  ROA = Profit margin × Total assets turnover.

- The ROA times the *equity multiplier* (total assets divided by common equity) yields the return on equity (ROE). This equation is referred to as the *Extended Du Pont Equation:*

  ROE = Profit margin × Total assets turnover × Equity multiplier.

- If a company is financed only with common equity, the return on assets (ROA) and the return on equity (ROE) are the same because total assets will equal common equity. This equality holds only if the company uses no debt.

Ratio analysis involves comparisons because a company's ratios are compared with those of other firms in the same industry, that is, to industry average figures. Comparative ratios are available from a number of sources including *ValueLine*, Dun & Bradstreet, Robert Morris Associates, and the U. S. Commerce Department.

- *Benchmarking* is the process of comparing the ratios of a particular company with those of a smaller group of "benchmark" companies, rather than with the entire industry.

- Benchmarking makes it easy for a firm to see exactly where the company stands relative to its competition.

There are some inherent problems and limitations to ratio analysis that necessitate care and judgment. Ratio analysis conducted in a mechanical, unthinking manner is dangerous, but used intelligently and with good judgment, it can provide useful insights into a firm's operations.

- Financial ratios are used by three main groups:
  - ☐ Managers, who employ ratios to help analyze, control, and thus improve their firm's operations.
  - ☐ Credit analysts, such as bank loan officers or bond rating analysts, who analyze ratios to help ascertain a company's ability to pay its debts.
  - ☐ Stock analysts, who are interested in a company's efficiency, risk, and growth prospects.

- Ratios are often not useful for analyzing the operations of large firms that operate in many different industries because comparative ratios are not meaningful.

- The use of industry averages may not provide a very challenging target for high-level performance.

■ Inflation affects depreciation charges, inventory costs, and therefore, the value of both balance sheet items and net income. For this reason, the analysis of a firm over time, or a comparative analysis of firms of different ages, can be misleading.

■ Ratios may be distorted by seasonal factors, or manipulated by management to give the impression of a sound financial condition (*window dressing techniques*).

■ Different operating policies and accounting practices, such as the decision to lease rather than to buy equipment, can distort comparisons.

■ Many ratios can be interpreted in different ways, and whether a particular ratio is good or bad should be based upon a complete financial analysis rather than the level of a single ratio at a single point in time.

Despite its widespread use and the fact that ROE and shareholder wealth are often highly correlated, some problems can arise when firms use ROE as the sole measure of performance.

■ ROE does not consider risk.

■ ROE does not consider the amount of invested capital.

■ A project's return, risk, and size combine to determine its impact on shareholder value.

■ To the extent that ROE focuses only on rate of return and ignores risk and size, increasing ROE may in some cases be inconsistent with increasing shareholder wealth.
  □ Alternative measures of performance have been developed, including Market Value Added (MVA) and Economic Value Added (EVA).

While it is important to understand and interpret financial statements, sound financial analysis involves more than just calculating and interpreting numbers.

■ Good analysts recognize that certain qualitative factors must be considered when evaluating a company. Some of these factors are:
  □ The extent to which the company's revenues are tied to one key customer.
  □ The extent to which the company's revenues are tied to one key product.
  □ The extent to which the company relies on a single supplier.
  □ The percentage of the company's business generated overseas.
  □ Competition.
  □ Future prospects.
  □ Legal and regulatory environment.

SELF-TEST QUESTIONS

Definitional

1. The current ratio is an example of a(n) _____ ratio. It measures a firm's ability to meet its _____ obligations.

2. The days sales outstanding (DSO) ratio is found by dividing average sales per day into accounts _____. The DSO is the length of time that a firm must wait after making a sale before it receives _____.

3. Debt management ratios are used to evaluate a firm's use of financial _____.

4. The debt ratio, which is the ratio of _____ _____ to _____ _____, measures the percentage of funds supplied by creditors.

5. The _____-_____-_____ ratio is calculated by dividing earnings before interest and taxes by the amount of interest charges.

6. The combined effects of liquidity, asset management, and debt on operating results are measured by _____ ratios.

7. Dividing net income by sales gives the _____ _____ on sales.

8. The _____/_____ ratio measures how much investors are willing to pay for each dollar of a firm's reported profits.

9. Firms with higher rates of return on stockholders' equity tend to sell at relatively high ratios of _____ price to _____ value.

10. Individual ratios are of little value in analyzing a company's financial condition. More important are the _____ of a ratio over time and the comparison of the company's ratios to _____ average ratios.

11. The _____ ____ _____ _____ shows how return on equity is affected by total assets turnover, profit margin, and leverage.

12. Return on assets is a function of two variables, the profit _____ and _____ _____ turnover.

13. Analyzing a particular ratio over time for an individual firm is known as _____ analysis.

14. The process of comparing a particular company with a smaller set of companies in the same industry is called _____.

15. Financial ratios are used by three main groups: (1) _____, who employ ratios to help analyze, control, and thus improve their firm's operations; (2) _____ _____, who analyze ratios to help ascertain a company's ability to pay its debts; and (3) _____ _____, who are interested in a company's efficiency, risk, and growth prospects.

16. The _____ _____ _____ ratio measures how effectively the firm uses its plant and equipment.

17. The _____ _____ _____ ratio measures the utilization of all the firm's assets.

18. Analysts use two procedures to examine the firm's debt: (1) They check the _____ _____ to determine the extent to which borrowed funds have been used to finance assets, and, (2) they review the _____ _____ to see the extent to which fixed charges are covered by operating profits.

19. To account for the deficiencies of the TIE ratio, bankers have developed the _____ _____ ratio, which is most useful for relatively short-term lenders.

20. The _____ _____ _____ ratio is useful for comparing firms with different tax situations and different degrees of financial leverage.

21. If a company is financing only with common equity, the firm's return on assets and return on equity will be _____.

22. The _____/_____ _____ ratio shows the dollar amount investors will pay for $1 of cash flow.

Conceptual

23. The equity multiplier can be expressed as 1 − (Debt/Assets).

   a. True   **b.** False

24. A high current ratio is *always* a good indication of a well-managed liquidity position.

   a. True   **b.** False

25. International Appliances Inc. has a current ratio of 0.5. Which of the following actions would improve (increase) this ratio?

    a. Use cash to pay off current liabilities.
    b. Collect some of the current accounts receivable.
    c. Use cash to pay off some long-term debt.
    d. Purchase additional inventory on credit (accounts payable).
    e. Sell some of the existing inventory at cost.

26. Refer to Self-Test Question 25. Assume that International Appliances has a current ratio of 1.2. Now, which of the following actions would improve (increase) this ratio?

    a. Use cash to pay off current liabilities.
    b. Collect some of the current accounts receivable.
    c. Use cash to pay off some long-term debt.
    d. Purchase additional inventory on credit (accounts payable).
    e. Use cash to pay for some fixed assets.

27. Examining the ratios of a particular firm against the same measures for a small group of firms from the same industry, at a point in time, is an example of

    a. Trend analysis.
    b. Benchmarking.
    c. Du Pont analysis.
    d. Simple ratio analysis.
    e. Industry analysis.

28. Which of the following statements is most correct?

    a. Having a high current ratio is always a good indication that a firm is managing its liquidity position well.
    b. A decline in the inventory turnover ratio suggests that the firm's liquidity position is improving.
    c. If a firm's times-interest-earned ratio is relatively high, then this is one indication that the firm should be able to meet its debt obligations.
    d. Since ROA measures the firm's effective utilization of assets (without considering how these assets are financed), two firms with the same EBIT must have the same ROA.
    e. If, through specific managerial actions, a firm has been able to increase its ROA, then, because of the fixed mathematical relationship between ROA and ROE, it must also have increased its ROE.

29. Which of the following statements is most correct?

    a. Suppose two firms with the same amount of assets pay the same interest rate on their debt and earn the same rate of return on their assets and that ROA is positive. However, one firm has a higher debt ratio. Under these conditions, the firm with the higher debt ratio will also have a higher rate of return on common equity.

    b. One of the problems of ratio analysis is that the relationships are subject to manipulation. For example, we know that if we use some cash to pay off some of our current liabilities, the current ratio will always increase, especially if the current ratio is weak initially, for example, below 1.0.

    c. Generally, firms with high profit margins have high asset turnover ratios and firms with low profit margins have low turnover ratios; this result is exactly as predicted by the extended Du Pont equation.

    d. Firms A and B have identical earnings and identical dividend payout ratios. If Firm A's growth rate is higher than Firm B's, then Firm A's P/E ratio must be greater than Firm B's P/E ratio.

    e. Each of the above statements is false.

SELF-TEST PROBLEMS

1. Info Technics Inc. has an equity multiplier of 2.75. The company's assets are financed with some combination of long-term debt and common equity. What is the company's debt ratio?

    a. 25.00%   **b.** 36.36%   **c.** 52.48%   **d.** 63.64%   **e.** 75.00%

2. Refer to Self-Test Problem 1. What is the company's common equity ratio?

    a. 25.00%   **b.** 36.36%   **c.** 52.48%   **d.** 63.64%   **e.** 75.00%

3. Cutler Enterprises has current assets equal to $4.5 million. The company's current ratio is 1.25. What is the firm's level of current liabilities (in millions)?

    a. $0.8   **b.** $1.8   **c.** $2.4   **d.** $2.9   **e.** $3.6

4. Jericho Motors has $4 billion in total assets. The other side of its balance sheet consists of $0.4 billion in current liabilities, $1.2 billion in long-term debt, and $2.4 billion in common equity. The company has 500 million shares of common stock outstanding, and its stock price is $25 per share. What is Jericho's market-to-book ratio?

    a. 2.00   **b.** 4.27   **c.** 5.21   **d.** 3.57   **e.** 1.42

5. Taylor Toys Inc. has $6 billion in assets, and its tax rate is 35 percent. The company's basic earning power (BEP) is 10 percent, and its return on assets (ROA) is 2.5 percent. What is Taylor's times-interest-earned (TIE) ratio?

    a. 1.625   **b.** 2.000   **c.** 2.433   **d.** 2.750   **e.** 3.000

(The following financial statements apply to the next six Self-Test Problems.)

Roberts Manufacturing Balance Sheet
December 31, 2002
(Dollars in Thousands)

Cash	$ 200	Accounts payable	$ 205
Receivables	245	Notes payable	425
Inventory	625	Other current liabilities	115
Total current assets	$1,070	Total current liabilities	$ 745
Net fixed assets	1,200	Long-term debt	420
		Common equity	1,105
Total assets	$2,270	Total liabilities and equity	$2,270

Roberts Manufacturing Income Statement
for Year Ended December 31, 2002
(Dollars in Thousands)

Sales		$2,400
Cost of goods sold:		
Materials	$1,000	
Labor	600	
Heat, light, and power	89	
Indirect labor	65	
Depreciation	80	1,834
Gross profit		$ 566
Selling expenses		175
General and administrative expenses		216
Earnings before interest and taxes (EBIT)		$ 175
Interest expense		35
Earnings before taxes (EBT)		$ 140
Taxes (40%)		56
Net income (NI)		$ 84

6. Calculate the current ratio.

    a. 1.20   **b.** 1.33   **c.** 1.44   **d.** 1.51   **e.** 1.60

7.   Calculate the asset management ratios, that is, the inventory turnover ratio, fixed assets turnover, total assets turnover, and days sales outstanding. Assume a 365-day year.

a. 3.84; 2.00; 1.06; 37.26 days   d. 3.84; 2.00; 1.24; 34.10 days
b. 3.84; 2.00; 1.06; 35.25 days   e. 3.84; 2.20; 1.48; 34.10 days
c. 3.84; 2.00; 1.06; 34.10 days

8.   Calculate the debt and times-interest-earned ratios.

a. 0.39; 3.16   b. 0.39; 5.00   c. 0.51; 3.16   d. 0.51; 5.00   e. 0.73; 3.16

9.   Calculate the profitability ratios, that is, the profit margin on sales, return on total assets, return on common equity, and basic earning power of assets.

a. 3.50%; 4.25%; 7.60%; 8.00%   d. 3.70%; 3.50%; 8.00%; 8.00%
b. 3.50%; 3.70%; 7.60%; 7.71%   e. 4.25%; 3.70%; 7.60%; 8.00%
c. 3.70%; 3.50%; 7.60%; 7.71%

10.   Calculate the market value ratios, that is, the price/earnings ratio, the price/cash flow ratio, and the market/book value ratio. Roberts had an average of 10,000 shares outstanding during 2002, and the stock price on December 31, 2002, was $40.00.

a. 4.21; 2.00; 0.36   d. 4.76; 2.44; 1.54
b. 3.20; 1.75; 1.54   e. 4.76; 2.44; 0.36
c. 3.20; 2.44; 0.36

11.   Use the Extended Du Pont Equation to determine Roberts' return on equity.

a. 6.90%   b. 7.24%   c. 7.47%   d. 7.60%   e. 8.41%

12.   Lewis Inc. has sales of $2 million per year, all of which are credit sales. Its days sales outstanding is 42 days. What is its average accounts receivable balance? Assume a 365-day year.

a. $230,137   b. $266,667   c. $333,333   d. $350,000   e. $366,750

13.   Southeast Jewelers Inc. sells only on credit. Its days sales outstanding is 73 days, and its average accounts receivable balance is $500,000. What are its sales for the year? Assume a 365-day year.

a. $1,500,000   b. $2,500,000   c. $2,000,000   d. $2,750,000   e. $3,000,000

14. A firm has total interest charges of $20,000 per year, sales of $2 million, a tax rate of 40 percent, and a profit margin of 6 percent. What is the firm's times-interest-earned ratio?

   a. 10   **b.** 11   **c.** 12   **d.** 13   **e.** 14

15. Refer to Self-Test Problem 14. What is the firm's TIE, if its profit margin decreases to 3 percent and its interest charges double to $40,000 per year?

   a. 3.0   **b.** 2.5   **c.** 3.5   **d.** 4.2   **e.** 3.7

16. Wilson Watercrafts Company has $12 billion in total assets. The company's basic earning power (BEP) is 15 percent, and its times-interest-earned ratio is 4.0. Wilson's depreciation and amortization expense totals $1.28 billion. It has $0.8 billion in lease payments and $0.4 billion must go towards principal payments on outstanding loans and long-term debt. What is Wilson's EBITDA coverage ratio?

   a. 1.00   **b.** 1.33   **c.** 1.50   **d.** 2.10   **e.** 2.35

17. A fire has destroyed many of the financial records at Anderson Associates. You are assigned to piece together information to prepare a financial report. You have found that the firm's return on equity is 12 percent and its debt ratio is 0.40. What is its return on assets?

   a. 4.90%   **b.** 5.35%   **c.** 6.60%   **d.** 7.20%   **e.** 8.40%

18. Refer to Self-Test Problem 17. What is the firm's debt ratio if its ROE is 15 percent and its ROA is 10 percent?

   a. 67%   **b.** 50%   **c.** 25%   **d.** 33%   **e.** 45%

19. Rowe and Company has a debt ratio of 0.50, a total assets turnover of 0.25, and a profit margin of 10 percent. The president is unhappy with the current return on equity, and he thinks it could be doubled. This could be accomplished (1) by increasing the profit margin to 14 percent and (2) by increasing debt utilization. Total assets turnover will not change. What new debt ratio, along with the 14 percent profit margin, is required to double the return on equity?

   a. 0.55   **b.** 0.60   **c.** 0.65   **d.** 0.70   **e.** 0.75

20. Altman Corporation has $1,000,000 of debt outstanding, and it pays an interest rate of 12 percent annually. Altman's annual sales are $4 million, its federal-plus-state tax rate is 40 percent, and its net profit margin on sales is 10 percent. If the company does not maintain a TIE ratio of at least 5 times, its bank will refuse to renew the loan, and bankruptcy will result. What is Altman's TIE ratio?

a. 9.33   b. 4.44   c. 2.50   d. 4.00   e. 6.56

21. Refer to Self-Test Problem 20. What is the maximum amount Altman's EBIT could decrease and its bank still renew its loan?

a. $186,667   b. $45,432   c. $66,767   d. $47,898   e. $143,925

22. Pinkerton Packaging's ROE last year was 2.5 percent, but its management has developed a new operating plan designed to improve things. The new plan calls for a total debt ratio of 50 percent, which will result in interest charges of $240 per year. Management projects an EBIT of $800 on sales of $8,000, and it expects to have a total assets turnover ratio of 1.6. Under these conditions, the federal-plus-state tax rate will be 40 percent. If the changes are made, what return on equity will Pinkerton earn?

a. 2.50%   b. 13.44%   c. 13.00%   d. 14.02%   e. 14.57%

(The following financial statement applies to the next three Self-Test Problems.)

Baker Corporation Balance Sheet
December 31, 2002

Cash and marketable securities	$ 50	Accounts payable	$ 250
Accounts receivable	200	Accrued liabilities	250
Inventory	250	Notes payable	500
Total current assets	$ 500	Total current liabilities	$1,000
Net fixed assets	1,500	Long-term debt	250
		Common stock	400
		Retained earnings	350
Total assets	$2,000	Total liabilities and equity	$2,000

23. What is Baker Corporation's current ratio as of December 31, 2002?

a. 0.35   b. 0.65   c. 0.50   d. 0.25   e. 0.75

24. If Baker uses $50 of cash to pay off $50 of its accounts payable, what is its new current ratio after this action?

a. 0.47   b. 0.44   c. 0.54   d. 0.33   e. 0.62

25. If Baker uses its $50 cash balance to pay off $50 of its long-term debt, what will be its new current ratio?

a. 0.35   **b.** 0.50   **c.** 0.55   **d.** 0.60   **e.** 0.45

(The following financial statements apply to the next Self-Test Problem.)

Whitney Inc. Balance Sheet
December 31, 2002

Total current liabilities		$100
Long-term debt		250
Common stockholders' equity		400
Total assets	$750	Total liabilities and equity	$750

Whitney Inc. Income Statement
for Year Ended December 31, 2002

Sales		$1,000
Cost of goods sold (excluding depreciation)	$550	
Other operating expenses	100	
Depreciation	50	
Total operating costs		700
Earnings before interest and taxes (EBIT)		$ 300
Interest expense		25
Earnings before taxes (EBT)		$ 275
Taxes (40%)		110
Net income		$ 165

26. What are Whitney Inc.'s basic earning power and ROA ratios?

a. 30%; 22%   **b.** 40%; 30%   **c.** 50%; 22%   **d.** 40%; 22%   **e.** 40%; 40%

(The following financial statements apply to the next Self-Test Problem.)

Cotner Enterprises Balance Sheet
December 31, 2002

Total current liabilities		$ 300
Long-term debt		500
Common stockholders' equity		450
Total assets	$1,250	Total liabilities and equity	$1,250

**Cotner Enterprises Income Statement
for Year Ended December 31, 2002**

Sales		$1,700
Cost of goods sold (excluding depreciation)	$1,190	
Other operating expenses	135	
Depreciation	75	
Total operating costs		1,400
Earnings before interest and taxes (EBIT)		$ 300
Interest expense		54
Earnings before taxes (EBT)		$ 246
Taxes (35%)		86
Net income		$ 160

27. What are Cotner Enterprise's basic earning power and ROA ratios?

    a. 20%; 12.8%   **d.** 17.5%; 12.8%
    b. 24%; 12.8%   **e.** 24%; 10.5%
    c. 24%; 15.8%

28. Dauten Enterprises is just being formed. It will need $2 million of assets, and it expects to have an EBIT of $400,000. Dauten will own no securities, so all of its income will be operating income. If it chooses to, Dauten can finance up to 50 percent of its assets with debt that will have a 9 percent interest rate. Dauten has no other liabilities. Assuming a 40 percent federal-plus-state tax rate on all taxable income, what is the difference between the expected ROE if Dauten finances with 50 percent debt versus the expected ROE if it finances entirely with common stock?

    a. 7.2%   **b.** 6.6%   **c.** 6.0%   **d.** 5.8%   **e.** 9.0%

29. Helen's Fashion Designs recently reported net income of $3,500,000. The company has 700,000 shares of common stock, and it currently trades at $25 a share. The company continues to expand and anticipates that one year from now its net income will be $4,500,000. Over the next year the company also anticipates issuing an additional 100,000 shares of stock, so that one year from now the company will have 800,000 shares of common stock. Assuming the company's price/earnings ratio remains at its current level, what will be the company's stock price one year from now?

    a. $25.25   **b.** $27.50   **c.** $28.125   **d.** $31.00   **e.** $33.00

30. Henderson Chemical Company has $5 million in sales. Its ROE is 10 percent and its total assets turnover is 2.5×. The company is 60 percent equity financed. What is the company's net income?

    a. $95,750   **b.** $105,300   **c.** $110,250   **d.** $120,000   **e.** $145,000

31. Bradberry Bolts Inc. recently reported the following information:

Net income	$750,000
ROA	6%
Interest expense	$210,000

The company's tax rate is 35 percent. What is the company's basic earning power (BEP)?

    a. 7.25%   **b.** 8.33%   **c.** 9.45%   **d.** 10.00%   **e.** 10.91%

ANSWERS TO SELF-TEST QUESTIONS

1.	liquidity; current		13.	trend
2.	receivable; cash		14.	benchmarking
3.	leverage		15.	managers; credit analysts; stock analysts
4.	total debt; total assets			
5.	times-interest-earned		16.	fixed assets turnover
6.	profitability		17.	total assets turnover
7.	profit margin		18.	balance sheet; income statement
8.	price/earnings		19.	EBITDA coverage
9.	market; book		20.	basic earning power
10.	trend; industry		21.	equal
11.	Extended Du Pont Equation		22.	price/cash flow
12.	margin; total assets			

23.   b. 1 – (Debt/Assets) = Equity/Assets. The equity multiplier is equal to Assets/Equity.

24.   b. Excess cash resulting from poor management could produce a high current ratio. Similarly, if accounts receivable are not collected promptly, this could also lead to a high current ratio. In addition, excess inventory which might include obsolete inventory could also lead to a high current ratio.

25.   d. This question is best analyzed using numbers. For example, assume current assets equal $50 and current liabilities equal $100; thus, the current ratio equals 0.5. For answer a, assume $5 in cash is used to pay off $5 in current liabilities. The new current ratio would be $45/$95 = 0.47. For answer d, assume a $10 purchase of inventory is made on credit (accounts payable). The new current ratio would be $60/$110 = 0.55, which is an increase over the old current ratio of 0.5

26.   a.   Again, this question is best analyzed using numbers. For example, assume current assets equal $120 and current liabilities equal $100; thus, the current ratio equals 1.2. For answer a, assume $5 in cash is used to pay off $5 in current liabilities. The new current ratio would be $115/$95 = 1.21, which is an increase over the old current ratio of 1.2. For answer d, assume a $10 purchase of inventory is made on credit (accounts payable). The new current ratio would be $130/$110 = 1.18, which is a decrease over the old current ratio of 1.2.

27.   b.   The correct answer is benchmarking. A trend analysis compares the firm's ratios over time, while a Du Pont analysis shows how return on equity is affected by assets turnover, profit margin, and leverage.

28.   c.   Excess cash resulting from poor management could produce a high current ratio; thus statement a is false. A decline in the inventory turnover ratio suggests that either sales have decreased or inventory has increased, which suggests that the firm's liquidity position is *not* improving; thus statement b is false. ROA = Net income/Total assets, and EBIT does not equal net income. Two firms with the same EBIT could have different financing and different tax rates resulting in different net incomes. Also, two firms with the same EBIT do not necessarily have the same total assets; thus, statement d is false. ROE = ROA × Assets/Equity. If ROA increases because total assets decrease, then the equity multiplier decreases, and depending on which effect is greater, ROE may or may not increase; thus, statement e is false. Statement c is correct; the TIE ratio is used to measure whether the firm can meet its debt obligation, and a high TIE ratio would indicate this is so.

29.   a.   Ratio analysis is subject to manipulation; however, if the current ratio is less than 1.0 and we use cash to pay off some current liabilities, the current ratio will decrease, *not* increase; thus statement b is false. Statement c is just the reverse of what actually occurs. Firms with high profit margins have low turnover ratios and vice versa. Statement d is false; it does not necessarily follow that if a firm's growth rate is higher that its stock price will be higher. Statement a is correct. From the information given in statement a, one can determine that the two firms' net incomes are equal; thus, the firm with the higher debt ratio (lower equity ratio) will indeed have a higher ROE.

SOLUTIONS TO SELF-TEST PROBLEMS

1.   d. $2.75 = A/E$

          $E/A = 1/2.75$

          $E/A = 36.36\%.$

          $D/A = 1 - E/A$

               $= 1 - 36.36\%$

               $= 63.64\%.$

2.   b.   From Self-Test Problem #1 above, $E/A = 36.36\%.$

3.   e. $CA = \$4.5$ million; $CA/CL = 1.25.$

          $\$4.5/CL = 1.25$

        $1.25(CL) = \$4.5$

             $CL = \$3.6$ million.

4.   c. $TA = \$4,000,000,000$; $CL = \$400,000,000$; $LT\ debt = \$1,200,000,000$; $CE = \$2,400,000,000$; Shares outstanding $= 500,000,000$; $P_0 = \$25$; $M/B = ?$

$$\text{Book value} = \frac{\$2,400,000,000}{500,000,000} = \$4.80.$$

$$M/B = \frac{\$25.00}{\$4.80} = 5.2083 \approx 5.21.$$

5.   a. $TA = \$6,000,000,000$; $T = 35\%$; $EBIT/TA = 10\%$; $ROA = 2.5\%$; $TIE = ?$

$$\frac{EBIT}{\$6,000,000,000} = 0.10$$

                       $EBIT = \$600,000,000.$

$$\frac{NI}{\$6,000,000,000} = 0.025$$

                      $NI = \$150,000,000.$

Now use the income statement format to determine interest so you can calculate the firm's TIE ratio.

EBIT	$600,000,000	See above.
INT	369,230,769	
EBT	$230,769,231	EBT = $150,000,000/0.65
Taxes (35%)	80,769,231	
NI	$150,000,000	See above.

$$\boxed{\begin{aligned} INT &= EBIT - EBT \\ &= \$600,000,000 - \$230,769,231 \end{aligned}}$$

$$TIE = EBIT/INT$$
$$= \$600,000,000/\$369,230,769$$
$$= 1.625.$$

6. c. $\text{Current ratio} = \dfrac{\text{Current assets}}{\text{Current liabilities}} = \dfrac{\$1,070}{\$745} = 1.44\times.$

7. a. $\text{Inventory turnover} = \dfrac{\text{Sales}}{\text{Inventory}} = \dfrac{\$2,400}{\$625} = 3.84\times.$

$\text{Fixed assets turnover} = \dfrac{\text{Sales}}{\text{Net fixed assets}} = \dfrac{\$2,400}{\$1,200} = 2.00\times.$

$\text{Total assets turnover} = \dfrac{\text{Sales}}{\text{Total assets}} = \dfrac{\$2,400}{\$2,270} = 1.06\times.$

$\text{DSO} = \dfrac{\text{Accounts receivable}}{\text{Sales}/365} = \dfrac{\$245}{\$2,400/365} = 37.26\,\text{days}.$

8. d. Debt ratio = Total debt/Total assets = $1,165/$2,270 = 0.51 = 51%.

TIE ratio = EBIT/Interest = $175/$35 = 5.00×.

9. b. $\text{Profit margin} = \dfrac{\text{Net income}}{\text{Sales}} = \dfrac{\$84}{\$2,400} = 0.0350 = 3.50\%.$

$\text{ROA} = \dfrac{\text{Net income}}{\text{Total assets}} = \dfrac{\$84}{\$2,270} = 0.0370 = 3.70\%.$

$$\text{ROE} = \frac{\text{Net income}}{\text{Common equity}} = \frac{\$84}{\$1,105} = 0.0760 = 7.60\%.$$

$$\text{BEP} = \frac{\text{EBIT}}{\text{Total assets}} = \frac{\$175}{\$2,270} = 0.0771 = 7.71\%.$$

10. e. $\text{EPS} = \dfrac{\text{Net income}}{\text{Number of shares outstanding}} = \dfrac{\$84,000}{10,000} = \$8.40.$

$$\text{P/E ratio} = \frac{\text{Price}}{\text{EPS}} = \frac{\$40.00}{\$8.40} = 4.76\times.$$

$$\text{Cash flow/share} = \frac{\text{Net income} + \text{Depreciation}}{\text{Number of shares outstanding}} = \frac{\$84,000 + \$80,000}{10,000} = \$16.40.$$

$$\text{Price/cash flow} = \frac{\$40.00}{\$16.40} = 2.44\times.$$

$$\text{Market/Book value} = \frac{\text{Market price}}{\text{Book value}} = \frac{\$40(10,000)}{\$1,105,000} = 0.36\times.$$

11. d. ROE $= \text{Profit margin} \times \text{Total assets turnover} \times \text{Equity multiplier}$

$$= \frac{\$84}{\$2,400} \times \frac{\$2,400}{\$2,270} \times \frac{\$2,270}{\$1,105} = 0.035 \times 1.057 \times 2.054$$

$$= 0.0760 = 7.60\%.$$

12. a. $\text{DSO} = \dfrac{\text{Accounts receivable}}{\text{Sales}/365}$

$$42 \text{ days} = \frac{\text{AR}}{\$2,000,000 / 365}$$

$$\text{AR} = \$230,137.$$

13. b. $\quad\quad\text{DSO} = \text{Accounts receivable}/(\text{Sales}/365)$

$$73 \text{ days} = \$500,000/(\text{Sales}/365)$$

$$73(\text{Sales}/365) = \$500,000$$

$$\text{Sales} = \$2,500,000.$$

14. b. Net income = $2,000,000(0.06) = $120,000.

Earnings before taxes = $120,000/(1 − 0.4) = $200,000.

EBIT = $200,000 + $20,000 = $220,000.

TIE = EBIT/Interest = $220,000/$20,000 = 11×.

15. c. Net income = $2,000,000(0.03) = $60,000.

Earnings before taxes = $60,000/(1 − 0.4) = $100,000.

EBIT = $100,000 + $40,000 = $140,000.

TIE = EBIT/Interest = $140,000/$40,000 = 3.5×.

16. e. TA = $12,000,000,000; EBIT/TA = 15%; TIE = 4; DA = $1,280,000,000; Lease payments = $800,000,000; Principal payments = $400,000,000; EBITDA coverage = ?

$$EBIT/\$12,000,000,000 = 0.15$$
$$EBIT = \$1,800,000,000.$$

$$4 = EBIT/INT$$
$$4 = \$1,800,000,000/INT$$
$$INT = \$450,000,000.$$

$$EBITDA = EBIT + DA$$
$$= \$1,800,000,000 + \$1,280,000,000$$
$$= \$3,080,000,000.$$

$$EBITDA \text{ coverage ratio} = \frac{EBITDA + \text{Lease payments}}{INT + \text{Princ. pmts} + \text{Lease pmts}}$$
$$= \frac{\$3,080,000,000 + \$800,000,000}{\$450,000,000 + \$400,000,000 + \$800,000,000}$$
$$= \frac{\$3,880,000,000}{\$1,650,000,000} = 2.3515 \approx 2.35.$$

17. d. If Total debt/Total assets = 0.40, then Total equity/Total assets = 0.60, and the equity multiplier (Assets/Equity) = 1/0.60 = 1.667.

$$\frac{NI}{E} = \frac{NI}{A} \times \frac{A}{E}$$

ROE = ROA × EM

12% = ROA × 1.667

ROA = 7.20%.

18. d. ROE = ROA × Equity multiplier

15% = 10% × TA/Equity

1.5 = TA/Equity.

Equity/TA = 1/1.5 = 0.67.

Debt/TA = 1 − Equity/TA = 1 − 0.67 = 0.33 = 33%.

19. c. If Total debt/Total assets = 0.50, then Total equity/Total assets = 0.50 and the equity multiplier (Assets/Equity) = 1/0.50 = 2.0.

ROE = PM × Total assets turnover × EM.

Before: ROE = 10% × 0.25 × 2.00 = 5.00%.

After: 10.00% = 14% × 0.25 × EM; thus EM = 2.8571.

$$\text{Equity multiplier} = \frac{\text{Assets}}{\text{Equity}}$$

$$2.8571 = \frac{1}{\text{Equity/ Assets}}$$

$$0.35 = \text{Equity/Assets.}$$

Debt/TA = 1 − Equity/TA = 100% − 35% = 65%.

20. e. TIE = EBIT/Interest, so find EBIT and Interest.

Interest = $1,000,000(0.12) = $120,000.

Net income = $4,000,000(0.10) = $400,000.

Pre-tax income = $400,000/(1 − T) = $400,000/0.6 = $666,667.

EBIT = $666,667 + $120,000 = $786,667.

TIE = $786,667/$120,000 = 6.56×.

21.   a.   TIE = EBIT/INT

$$5 = \text{EBIT}/\$120,000$$

EBIT = $600,000.

From Self-Test Problem #20, EBIT = $786,667, so EBIT could decrease by $786,667 − $600,000 = $186,667.

22.   b.   ROE = Profit margin × Total assets turnover × Equity multiplier

            = NI/Sales × Sales/TA × TA/Equity.

Now we need to determine the inputs for the equation from the data that were given. On the left we set up an income statement, and we put numbers in it on the right:

Sales (given)	$8,000
Cost	NA
EBIT (given)	$ 800
Interest (given)	240
EBT	$ 560
Taxes (40%)	224
Net income	$ 336

Now we can use some ratios to get some more data:

Total assets turnover = S/TA = 1.6× (given).

D/A = 50%, so E/A = 50%, and therefore TA/E = 1/(E/A) = 1/0.5 = 2.00×.

Now we can complete the Extended Du Pont Equation to determine ROE:

ROE = $336/$8,000 × 1.6 × 2.0 = 13.44%.

23.   c.   Baker Corporation's current ratio equals Current assets/Current liabilities = $500/$1,000 = 0.50×.

24.   a.   Baker Corporation's new current ratio equals ($500 − $50)/($1,000 − $50) = $450/$950 = 0.47×.

25.   e.   Only the current assets balance is affected by this action. Baker's new current ratio = ($500 − $50)/$1,000 = $450/$1,000 = 0.45×.

26. d. Whitney's BEP ratio equals EBIT/Total assets = $300/$750 = 40%.

Whitney's ROA equals Net income/Total assets = $165/$750 = 22%.

27. b. Cotner's BEP ratio equals EBIT/Total assets = $300/$1,250 = 24%.

Cotner's ROA equals Net income/Total assets = $160/$1,250 = 12.8%.

28. b. Known data: Total assets = $2,000,000; EBIT = $400,000; k_d = 9%, T = 40%.

D/A = 0.5 = 50%, so Equity = 0.5($2,000,000) = $1,000,000.

	D/A = 0%	D/A = 50%
EBIT	$400,000	$400,000
Interest	0	90,000*
Taxable income	$400,000	$310,000
Taxes (40%)	160,000	124,000
Net income (NI)	$240,000	$186,000

*If D/A = 50%, then half of assets are financed by debt, so Debt = 0.5($2,000,000) = $1,000,000. At a 9 percent interest rate, INT = 0.09($1,000,000) = $90,000.

For D/A = 0%, ROE = NI/Equity = $240,000/$2,000,000 = 12%. For D/A = 50%, ROE = $186,000/$1,000,000 = 18.6%. Difference = 18.6% – 12.0% = 6.6%.

29. c. The current EPS is $3,500,000/700,000 shares or $5.00. The current P/E ratio is then $25/$5 = 5.00×. The new number of shares outstanding will be 800,000. Thus, the new EPS = $4,500,000/800,000 = $5.625. If the shares are selling for 5 times EPS, then they must be selling for $5.625(5) = $28.125.

30. d. Step 1: Calculate total assets from information given.
Sales = $5 million.

$$2.5× = Sales/TA$$
$$2.5× = \frac{\$5,000,000}{Assets}$$
Assets = $2,000,000.

Step 2: Calculate net income.
There is 40% debt and 60% equity, so Equity = $2,000,000 × 0.6 = $1,200,000.

$$ROE = NI/S \times S/TA \times TA/E$$
$$0.10 = NI/\$5,000,000 \times 2.5 \times \$2,000,000/\$1,200,000$$
$$0.10 = \frac{4.1667(NI)}{\$5,000,000}$$
$$\$500,000 = 4.1667(NI)$$
$$\$120,000 = NI.$$

31.   e. Given ROA = 6% and net income of $750,000, then total assets must be $12,500,000.

$$ROA = \frac{NI}{TA}$$
$$6\% = \frac{\$750,000}{TA}$$
$$TA = \$12,500,000.$$

To calculate BEP, we still need EBIT. To calculate EBIT construct a partial income statement:

EBIT	$1,363,846	($210,000 + $1,153,846)
Interest	210,000	(Given)
EBT	$1,153,846	$750,000/0.65
Taxes (35%)	403,846	
NI	$ 750,000	

$$BEP = \frac{EBIT}{TA}$$
$$= \frac{\$1,363,846}{\$12,500,000}$$
$$= 0.1091 = 10.91\%.$$

CHAPTER 4
THE FINANCIAL ENVIRONMENT:
MARKETS, INSTITUTIONS, AND INTEREST RATES

LEARNING OBJECTIVES

- List some of the many different types of financial markets, and identify several recent trends taking place in the financial markets.

- Identify some of the most important money and capital market instruments, and list the characteristics of each.

- Describe three ways in which the transfer of capital takes place.

- Compare and contrast major financial institutions.

- Distinguish between the two basic types of stock markets.

- Explain how capital is allocated in a supply/demand framework, and list the fundamental factors that affect the cost of money.

- Write out two equations for the nominal, or quoted, interest rate, and briefly discuss each component.

- Define what is meant by the term structure of interest rates, and graph a yield curve for a given set of data.

- Explain the two key factors that determine the shape of the yield curve.

- Discuss country risk.

- List four additional factors that influence the level of interest rates and the slope of the yield curve.

- Briefly explain how interest rate levels affect business decisions.

OVERVIEW

It is critical that financial managers understand the environment and markets within which they operate. In this chapter, we examine the markets in which capital is raised, securities are traded, and stock prices are established. We examine the institutions that operate in these markets and through which securities transactions are conducted. In the process, we shall see how money costs are determined, and we shall explore the principal factors that determine both the general level of interest rates in the economy and the interest rate on a particular debt security.

OUTLINE

Financial markets bring together people and organizations wanting to borrow money with those having surplus funds.

■ There are many different financial markets in a developed economy, each dealing with a different type of instrument, serving a different set of customers, or operating in a different part of the country.

■ The major types of financial markets include the following:
- □ *Physical asset markets* (also called "tangible" or "real" asset markets) are the markets for such products as wheat, autos, real estate, computers, and machinery.
- □ *Financial asset markets* deal with stocks, bonds, notes, mortgages, and other claims on real assets.
- □ *Spot markets* are markets in which assets are bought or sold for "on-the-spot" delivery.
- □ *Futures markets* are markets in which participants agree today to buy or sell an asset at some future date.
- □ *Money markets* are the markets for short-term, highly liquid debt securities, those securities that mature in less than one year.
- □ *Capital markets* are the markets for long-term debt and corporate stocks.
- □ *Primary markets* are the markets in which corporations sell newly issued securities to raise capital.
- □ *Secondary markets* are the markets in which existing, already outstanding securities are traded among investors.
- □ The *initial public offering (IPO) market* is a subset of the primary market. Here firms "go public" by offering shares to the public for the first time.
- □ *Private markets* are the markets where transactions are worked out directly between two parties.

- ☐ *Public markets* are the markets where standardized contracts are traded on organized exchanges.

■ A healthy economy is dependent on efficient transfers of funds from people who are net savers to firms and individuals who need capital.

■ Financial markets have experienced tremendous change during the last two decades.
  - ☐ Technological advances in computers and telecommunications, along with the globalization of banking and commerce, have led to deregulation, and this has increased competition throughout the world.
  - ☐ The result is a much more efficient, internationally linked market, but one that is far more complex than existed a few years ago.
    - • With globalization has come the need for greater cooperation among regulators at the international level.

■ Another important trend in recent years has been the increased use of derivatives.
  - ☐ A *derivative* is any financial asset whose value is derived from the value of some other "underlying" asset.
  - ☐ The market for derivatives has grown faster than any other market in recent years, providing corporations with additional opportunities but also exposing them to new risks.
  - ☐ Derivatives can be used either to reduce risks or as speculative investments, which increase risk.
  - ☐ In theory, derivatives should allow companies to manage risk better, but it is not clear whether recent innovations have "increased or decreased the inherent stability of the financial system."

Transfers of capital between savers and borrowers take place in three different ways.

■ *Direct transfers* of money and securities occur when a business sells its stocks or bonds directly to savers, without going through any type of financial institution.

■ Transfers through an *investment banking house* occur when a brokerage firm, such as Merrill Lynch, serves as a middleman and facilitates the issuance of securities.
  - ☐ These middlemen help corporations design securities that will be attractive to investors, buy these securities from the corporations, and then resell them to savers in the primary markets.

■ Transfers through a *financial intermediary* occur when a bank or mutual fund obtains funds from savers, issues its own securities in exchange, and then uses these funds to purchase other securities.

- ☐ The existence of intermediaries greatly increases the efficiency of money and capital markets.
- ☐ Intermediaries literally create new forms of capital.
- ☐ Some major classes of intermediaries include commercial banks, savings and loan (S&L) associations, mutual savings banks, credit unions, pension funds, life insurance companies, and mutual funds.
  - A mutual fund that invests in short-term, low-risk securities and allows investors to write checks against their accounts is known as a *money market fund*.
- ☐ The result of ongoing regulatory changes has been a blurring of the distinctions between the different types of financial institutions. As a result, in the United States the trend has been toward huge *financial service corporations*, which own any number of financial intermediaries with national and even global operations.

The stock market is one of the most important markets to financial managers because it is here that the price of each stock, and hence the value of all publicly-owned firms, is established. There are two basic types of stock markets.

- ■ The *physical location exchanges*, typified by the New York Stock Exchange (NYSE) and the American Stock Exchange (AMEX), are tangible, physical entities.

- ■ The *electronic dealer-based markets* include the Nasdaq stock market, the less formal over-the-counter market, and the recently developed electronic communications networks (ECNs). They include all facilities that are needed to conduct security transactions not conducted on the physical location exchanges. This has traditionally been referred to as the *over-the-counter market (OTC)*.
  - ☐ Brokers and dealers who participate in the over-the-counter market are members of a self-regulating body known as the *National Association of Securities Dealers (NASD)*, which licenses brokers and oversees trading practices.
  - ☐ Over the past decade the competition between the NYSE and Nasdaq has become increasingly fierce.
  - ☐ In an effort to become more competitive with the NYSE and with international markets, the Nasdaq and the AMEX merged in 1998 to form the Nasdaq-Amex Market Group, which might best be referred to as an *organized investment network*. This investment network is often referred to as Nasdaq, but stocks continue to be traded and reported separately on the two markets.
  - ☐ Since most of the largest companies trade on the NYSE, the market capitalization of NYSE-traded stocks is much higher than for stocks traded on Nasdaq. However, reported volume (number of shares traded) is often larger on Nasdaq, and more companies are listed on Nasdaq.

Capital in a free economy is allocated through the price system. The interest rate is the price paid to borrow debt capital. With equity capital, investors expect to receive dividends and capital gains, whose sum is the cost of equity money.

■   There are four fundamental factors that affect the supply of, and demand for, investment capital, hence the cost of money.
- ☐ *Production opportunities,* the returns available within an economy from investments in productive (cash-generating) assets.
- ☐ Consumers' *time preferences for consumption* of current versus future consumption.
- ☐ *Risk,* the chance that an investment will provide a low or negative return.
- ☐ *Inflation,* the tendency of prices to increase over time.

■   The higher the perceived risk, the higher the required rate of return, and the higher the expected rate of inflation, the higher the required return.

Capital is allocated among borrowers by interest rates: Firms with the most profitable investment opportunities are willing and able to pay the most for capital, so they tend to attract it away from inefficient firms or from those whose products are not in demand.

■   Supply and demand interact to determine interest rates in capital markets.
- ☐ If the demand for funds declines, as it typically does during business recessions, the market-clearing, or equilibrium, interest rate declines.
- ☐ If the Federal Reserve tightens credit, lowering the supply of funds, interest rates rise and the level of borrowing in the economy declines.

■   Capital markets are interdependent.
- ☐ Investors are willing to accept higher risk in exchange for a risk premium.

■   There are many capital markets in the U.S.
- ☐ U.S. firms also invest and raise capital throughout the world, and foreigners both borrow and lend in the U.S.

■   There is a price for each type of capital, and these prices change over time as shifts occur in supply and demand conditions.
- ☐ Short-term interest rates are especially prone to rise during booms, as the demand for capital increases and inflationary pressures push rates up.
- ☐ Conditions are reversed during recessions due to a drop in interest rates, as demand for credit is reduced and the inflation rate falls. The Federal Reserve often lowers rates during recessions to help stimulate the economy.

- ☐ The gap between the current interest rate and the current inflation rate is defined as the "current real rate of interest." It is called the "real rate" because it shows how much investors really earned after taking out the effects of inflation.
- ☐ Tendencies in interest rate fluctuations do not hold exactly. The level of interest rates varies with changes in the current rate of inflation and changes in expectations about future inflation.

The quoted (or nominal) interest rate on a debt security, k, is composed of a real risk-free rate of interest, k*, plus several premiums that reflect inflation, the riskiness of the security, and the security's marketability (or liquidity):

$$\text{Quoted interest rate} = k* + IP + DRP + LP + MRP.$$
$$k = k_{RF} + DRP + LP + MRP.$$

- ■ The *real risk-free rate of interest (k*)* is the interest rate that would exist on a riskless security if no inflation were expected, and it may be thought of as the rate of interest on short-term U.S. Treasury securities in an inflation-free world.
  - ☐ The real risk-free rate is not static—it changes over time depending on economic conditions, especially (1) on the rate of return corporations and other borrowers expect to earn on productive assets and (2) on people's time preferences for current versus future consumption.

- ■ The *quoted,* or *nominal, risk-free rate of interest (k_{RF})* on a security such as a U.S. Treasury bill is the real risk-free rate plus a premium for expected inflation: $k_{RF} = k* + IP$.
  - ☐ An indexed U.S. Treasury security is free of most risks. These securities are free of default, maturity, and liquidity risks, and also of risk due to changes in the general level of interest rates.
  - ☐ The term risk-free rate without a modifier generally means the nominal rate.
  - ☐ In general, we use the T-bill rate to approximate the short-term risk-free rate, and the T-bond rate to approximate the long-term risk-free rate.

- ■ The *inflation premium (IP),* which is the average inflation rate *expected* over the life of the security, compensates investors for the expected loss of purchasing power.
  - ☐ It is important to note that the inflation rate built into interest rates is the inflation rate expected in the future, not the rate experienced in the past.
  - ☐ Expectations for future inflation are closely, but not perfectly, correlated with rates experienced in the recent past.

- ■ The *default risk premium (DRP)* compensates investors for the risk that a borrower will default and hence not pay the interest or principal on a loan.
  - ☐ DRP is zero for U.S. Treasury securities, but it rises as the riskiness of issuers increases.

- ☐ The greater the default risk, the higher the interest rate.
- ☐ For corporate bonds, the higher the bond's rating, the lower its default risk, and, consequently, the lower its interest rate.
- ☐ The difference between the quoted interest rate on a T-bond and that on a corporate bond with similar maturity, liquidity, and other features is the default risk premium.

- ■ A security that can be converted to cash on short notice at a "reasonable" price is said to be *liquid*. A *liquidity,* or *marketability, premium (LP)* is also added to the real rate for securities that are not liquid.

- ■ Long-term securities are more price sensitive to interest rate changes than are short-term securities, so all long-term bonds have an element of risk called *interest rate risk.* Therefore, a *maturity risk premium (MRP)* is added to longer-term securities to compensate investors for interest rate risk.
  - ☐ The MRP is higher the longer the years to maturity.
  - ☐ This premium, like the others, is difficult to measure, but it varies somewhat over time, rising when interest rates are more volatile and uncertain, then falling when interest rates are more stable.
  - ☐ Although long-term bonds are heavily exposed to interest rate risk, short-term bills are heavily exposed to *reinvestment rate risk.* This is the risk that a decline in interest rates will lead to lower income when bonds mature and funds are reinvested.
    - ● Although "investing short" preserves one's principal, the interest income provided by short-term T-bills is less stable than the interest income on long-term bonds.

The term structure of interest rates is the relationship between bond yields and maturities.

- ■ When plotted, this relationship produces a *yield curve.*

- ■ Yield curves have different shapes depending on expected inflation rates and perceptions about the relative riskiness of securities with different maturities.
  - ☐ The *"normal" yield curve* is upward sloping because investors charge higher rates on longer-term bonds, even when inflation is expected to remain constant.
  - ☐ An *inverted,* or *"abnormal" yield curve* is downward sloping, and signifies that investors expect inflation to decrease.
  - ☐ A *"humped" yield curve* occurs when interest rates on medium-term maturities are higher than rates on both short- and long-term maturities.

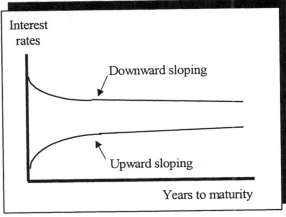

The shape of the yield curve depends on two key factors: (1) expectations about future inflation, and (2) perceptions about the relative riskiness of securities with different maturities.

- The *expectations theory*, sometimes referred to as the pure expectations theory, assumes that investors establish bond prices and interest rates strictly on the basis of expectations for interest rates.
  - ☐ The expectations theory holds that long-term interest rates are a weighted average of current and expected future short-term interest rates.
  - ☐ If the interest rate is expected to decline, the curve will be downward sloping, and if the interest rate is expected to increase, the curve will be upward sloping.
  - ☐ According to the pure expectations theory, the maturity risk premium is equal to zero because investors are indifferent with respect to maturity in the sense that they do not view long-term bonds as being riskier than short-term bonds.

In addition to inflation and liquidity, investors should consider other risk factors before investing overseas.

- *Country risk* is the risk that arises from investing or doing business in a particular country.
  - ☐ This risk depends on the country's economic, political, and social environment.
  - ☐ Examples of country risk include the risk associated with changes in tax rates, regulations, currency conversion, and exchange rates. It also includes the risk that property will be expropriated without adequate compensation, as well as new host country stipulations about local production, sourcing or hiring practices, and damage or destruction of facilities due to internal strife.

- Investors should keep in mind when investing overseas, more often than not, the security will be denominated in a currency other than the dollar.
  - ☐ This means the value of the investment will depend on what happens to exchange rates, and this is known as *exchange rate risk.*
  - ☐ The effective rate of return on a foreign investment will depend on both the performance of the foreign security and on what happens to exchange rates over the life of the investment.

There are other factors that influence both the general level of interest rates and the shape of the yield curve. The four most important factors are (1) Federal Reserve policy; (2) the federal budget deficit or surplus; (3) international factors, including the foreign trade balance and interest rates in other countries; and (4) the level of business activity.

- Expansionary monetary policy (growth in monetary supply) by the Federal Reserve initially lowers the interest rate but inflationary pressures could cause a rise in the interest rate in the long term. Contractionary monetary policy has the opposite effect.
  - □ During periods when the Fed is actively intervening in the markets, the yield curve may be temporarily distorted.
  - □ Short-term rates will be temporarily "too low" if the Fed is easing credit, and "too high" if it is tightening credit.

- Federal budget deficits drive interest rates up due to increased demand for loanable funds, while surpluses drive rates down due to increased supply of loanable funds.

- Foreign trade deficits (when imports are greater than exports) push interest rates up because deficits must be financed from abroad and rates must be high enough relative to world interest rates to attract foreign investors.

- In relation to the business cycle, there is a general tendency for interest rates to decline during a recession.

Interest rate movements have a significant impact on business decisions.

- Wrong decisions, such as using short-term debt to finance long-term projects just before interest rates rise, can be very costly.

- It is extremely difficult, if not impossible, to predict future interest rate levels. Interest rates will fluctuate—they always have, and they always will.

- Sound financial policy calls for using a mix of long- and short-term debt and equity, to position the firm so that it can survive in almost any interest rate environment.
  - □ The optimal financial policy depends in an important way on the nature of the firm's assets—the easier it is to sell off assets to generate cash, the more feasible it is to use large amounts of short-term debt. This makes it more feasible for a firm to finance its current assets than its fixed assets with short-term debt.

- Changes in interest rates also have implications for savers. A saver's choice of maturity would have a major effect on investment performance, hence future income.

SELF-TEST QUESTIONS

Definitional

1.   Markets for short-term debt securities are called _____ markets, while markets for long-term debt and equity are called _____ markets.

2.   Firms raise capital by selling newly issued securities in the _____ markets, while existing, already outstanding securities are traded in the _____ markets.

3.   An institution that issues its own securities in exchange for funds and then uses these funds to purchase other securities is called a financial _____.

4.   A(n) _____ _____ firm facilitates the transfer of capital between savers and borrowers by acting as a middleman.

5.   The two basic types of stock markets are the _____ _____ exchanges, such as the NYSE, and the _____-_____ or _____-_____-_____ market.

6.   The risk that a borrower will not pay the interest or principal on a loan is _____ risk.

7.   _____ ____ _____ securities have zero default risk.

8.   A(n) _____ premium is added to the real risk-free rate to protect investors against loss of purchasing power.

9.   The nominal rate of interest is determined by adding a(n) _____ premium plus a(n) _____ risk premium plus a(n) _____ premium plus a(n) _____ risk premium to the real risk-free rate of return.

10. The relationship between bond yields and maturities is called the _____ _____ of interest rates, while the resulting plotted curve is the _____ curve.

11. The "normal" yield curve has a(n) _____ slope.

12. The _____ theory holds that long-term interest rates are a weighted average of current and expected future short-term interest rates.

13. Because interest rates fluctuate, a sound financial policy calls for using a mix of _____- and _____-_____ debt and _____.

14. _____ _____ bring together people and organizations wanting to borrow money with those having surplus funds.

15. _____ _____ of money and securities occur when a business sells its stock or bonds directly to savers, without going through any type of financial institution.

16. A(n) _____ is any financial asset whose value is derived from the value of some other "underlying" asset.

17. The result of the ongoing regulatory changes has been a blurring of the distinctions between the different types of financial institutions. As a result, in the U.S. the trend has been toward huge _____ _____ corporations, which own any number of financial intermediaries with national and even global operations.

18. The _____ market is one of the most important markets to financial managers because it is here that the value of all publicly-owned firms is established.

19. The _____ _____ is the price paid to borrow debt capital.

20. A(n) _____ _____ premium is added to longer-term securities to compensate investors for interest rate risk.

21. _____ risk is the risk that arises from investing or doing business in a particular country.

22. The value of an investment made overseas will depend on what happens to exchange rates, and this is known as _____ _____ risk.

23. The _____ _____ _____ market is the market in which firms "go public" by offering shares to the public for the first time.

24. In an effort to become more competitive with the NYSE and with international markets, the Nasdaq and the AMEX merged to form the Nasdaq-Amex Market Group, which might best be referred to as a(n) _____ _____ _____.

25. There are four fundamental factors that affect the supply of, and demand for, investment capital: _____ _____, _____ _____ for consumption, _____, and _____.

26. A security that can be converted to cash on short notice at a "reasonable" price is said to be _____.

27. Long-term securities are more price sensitive to interest rate changes than are short-term securities, so all long-term bonds have an element of risk called _____ _____ _____.

28. Short-term bills are heavily exposed to _____ _____ risk.

29. _____ _____ are markets in which transactions are worked out directly between two parties.

30. _____ _____ are markets in which standardized contracts are traded on organized exchanges.

31. _____ _____ are the markets in which assets are bought or sold for "on-the-spot" delivery.

32. _____ _____ are the markets in which participants agree today to buy or sell an asset at some future date.

Conceptual

33. If management is sure that the economy is at the peak of a boom and is about to enter a recession, a firm that needs to borrow money should probably use short-term rather than long-term debt.

    a. True   **b.** False

34. Long-term interest rates reflect expectations about future inflation. Inflation has varied greatly from year to year over the last 10 years, and, as a result, long-term rates have fluctuated more than short-term rates.

    a. True   **b.** False

35. Suppose the Fed takes actions that lower expectations for inflation this year by 1 percentage point, but these same actions raise expectations for inflation in Years 2 and thereafter by 2 percentage points. Other things held constant, the yield curve becomes steeper.

    a. True   **b.** False

36. Assume interest rates on 30-year government and corporate bonds were as follows: T-bond = 7.72%; AAA = 8.72%; A = 9.64%; BBB = 10.18%. The differences in rates among these issues are caused primarily by:

    a. Tax effects.   **d.** Inflation differences.
    b. Default risk differences.   **e.** Both statements b and d.
    c. Maturity risk differences.

37. Which of the following statements is most correct?

    a. Suppose financial institutions, such as savings and loans, were required by law to make long-term, fixed interest rate mortgages, but, at the same time, they were largely restricted, in terms of their capital sources, to taking deposits that could be withdrawn on demand. Under these conditions, these financial institutions should prefer a "normal" yield curve to an inverted curve.

    b. You are considering establishing a new firm, the University Assistance Company (UAC). UAC would obtain funds in the short-term money market and write long-term mortgage loans to students so that they might buy condominiums rather than rent. A downward sloping yield curve, if it persisted over time, would be best for UAC.

    c. The yield curve is upward sloping, or normal, if short-term rates are higher than long-term rates.

    d. All of the above statements are correct.

    e. Only statements a and b are correct.

38. Which of the following statements is most correct?

    a. One of the major benefits of well-developed stock markets is that they increase liquidity, which makes it easier for firms to raise capital.

    b. In the United States, we have a number of specialized financial institutions, but, according to the text, the trend is toward larger, more diversified institutions that offer broad arrays of financial services.

    c. If the expected rate of inflation rose by 2 percentage points, from 5 to 7 percent, then the *real* risk-free rate (k^*) would also rise by 2 percentage points.

    d. Statements a, b, and c are all true.

    e. Only statements a and b are true.

SELF-TEST PROBLEMS

1. The real risk-free rate of interest is 2 percent. Inflation is expected to be 3 percent the next 2 years and 5 percent during the next 3 years after that. Assume that the maturity risk premium is zero. What is the yield on 3-year Treasury securities?

    a. 5.2%   **b.** 5.7%   **c.** 6.0%   **d.** 6.2%   **e.** 6.5%

2. Refer to Self-Test Problem 1. What is the yield on 5-year Treasury securities?

    a. 5.2%   **b.** 5.7%   **c.** 6.0%   **d.** 6.2%   **e.** 6.5%

3. A Treasury bond that matures in 20 years has a yield of 8 percent. A 20-year corporate bond has a yield of 11 percent. Assume that the liquidity premium on the corporate bond is 1.0 percent. What is the default risk premium on the corporate bond?

   a. 0.50%   **b.** 1.00%   **c.** 1.50%   **d.** 1.75%   **e.** 2.00%

4. You have determined the following data for a given bond: Real risk-free rate (k^*) = 3%; inflation premium = 8%; default risk premium = 2%; liquidity premium = 2%; and maturity risk premium = 1%. What is the nominal risk-free rate, k_{RF}?

   a. 10%   **b.** 11%   **c.** 12%   **d.** 13%   **e.** 14%

5. Refer to Self-Test Problem 4. What is the interest rate on long-term Treasury securities, or T-bonds, of the relevant maturity?

   a. 10%   **b.** 11%   **c.** 12%   **d.** 13%   **e.** 14%

6. Assume that a 3-year Treasury note has no maturity risk or liquidity risk and that the real risk-free rate of interest falls to 2 percent. A 3-year T-note carries a yield to maturity of 12 percent. If the expected inflation rate is 12 percent for the coming year and 10 percent the year after, what is the implied expected inflation rate for the third year?

   a. 8%   **b.** 9%   **c.** 10%   **d.** 11%   **e.** 12%

7. Assume that the real risk-free rate is 2 percent, that the expected inflation rate during Year 2 is 3 percent, and that 2-year T-bonds yield 5.5 percent. If the maturity risk premium is zero, what is the inflation rate during Year 1?

   a. 3.0%   **b.** 5.0%   **c.** 3.5%   **d.** 4.0%   **e.** 2.5%

8. Refer to Self-Test Problem 7. Given the same information, what is the rate of return on 1-year T-bonds?

   a. 5.5%   **b.** 6.0%   **c.** 5.0%   **d.** 6.5%   **e.** 4.5%

9. Assume that the real risk-free rate, k^*, is 4 percent and that inflation is expected to be 7 percent in Year 1, 4 percent in Year 2, and 3 percent thereafter. Assume also that all Treasury bonds are highly liquid and free of default risk. If 2-year and 5-year Treasury bonds both yield 11 percent, what is the difference in the maturity risk premiums (MRPs) on the two bonds; that is, what is $MRP_5 - MRP_2$?

   a. 0.5%   **b.** 1.0%   **c.** 2.25%   **d.** 1.5%   **e.** 1.25%

10. Due to the recession, the rate of inflation expected for the coming year is only 3.5 percent. However, the rate of inflation in Year 2 and thereafter is expected to be constant at some level above 3.5 percent. Assume that the real risk-free rate is k* = 2% for all maturities and that the expectations theory fully explains the yield curve, so there are no maturity risk premiums. If 3-year Treasury bonds yield 3 percentage points (0.03) more than 1-year Treasury bonds, what rate of inflation is expected after Year 1?

   a. 4%   **b.** 5%   **c.** 7%   **d.** 6%   **e.** 8%

11. You read in *The Wall Street Journal* that 30-day T-bills are currently yielding 5 percent. Your brother-in-law, a broker at Fast Track Securities, has given you the following estimates of current interest rate premiums:

- Inflation premium = 2.85%.
- Liquidity premium = 0.5%.
- Maturity risk premium = 1.5%.
- Default risk premium = 2.0%.

On the basis of these data, what is the real risk-free rate of return?

   a. 1.85%   **b.** 2.00%   **c.** 2.15%   **d.** 2.25%   **e.** 2.50%

12. The 5-year bonds of Englewood Enterprises are yielding 8.10 percent per year. Treasury bonds with the same maturity are yielding 5.65 percent per year. The real risk-free rate (k*) has not changed in recent years and is 2.5 percent. The average inflation premium is 2.75 percent and the maturity risk premium takes the form: MRP = 0.1%(t − 1), where t = number of years to maturity. If the liquidity premium is 1.2 percent, what is the default risk premium on Englewood's corporate bonds?

   a. 0.50%   **b.** 0.85%   **c.** 1.00%   **d.** 1.25%   **e.** 1.60%

13. An investor in Treasury securities expects inflation to be 2.25 percent in Year 1, 2.75 percent in Year 2, and 3.30 percent each year thereafter. Assume that the real risk-free rate is 2.40 percent, and that this rate will remain constant over time. Three-year Treasury securities yield 5.60 percent, while 5-year Treasury securities yield 6.20 percent. What is the difference in the maturity risk premiums (MRPs) on the two securities, that is, what is $MRP_5 - MRP_3$?

   a. 0.39%   **b.** 0.55%   **c.** 0.75%   **d.** 0.90%   **e.** 1.20%

ANSWERS TO SELF-TEST QUESTIONS

1.	money; capital	**17.**	financial service
2.	primary; secondary	**18.**	stock
3.	intermediary	**19.**	interest rate
4.	investment banking	**20.**	maturity risk
5.	physical location; dealer-based; over-the-counter (OTC)	**21.**	Country
		22.	exchange rate
6.	default	**23.**	initial public offering
7.	U.S. Treasury	**24.**	organized investment network
8.	inflation	**25.**	production opportunities; time preferences; risk; inflation
9.	inflation; default; liquidity; maturity		
10.	term structure; yield	**26.**	liquid
11.	upward	**27.**	interest rate risk
12.	expectations	**28.**	reinvestment rate
13.	short-; long-term; equity	**29.**	Private markets
14.	Financial markets	**30.**	Public markets
15.	Direct transfers	**31.**	Spot markets
16.	derivative	**32.**	Futures markets

33. a. The firm should borrow short-term until interest rates drop due to the recession, then go long-term. Predicting interest rates is extremely difficult, for managers can rarely be sure about what is going to happen to the economy.

34. b. Fluctuations in long-term rates are smaller because the long-term inflation premium is an average of inflation expectations over many years, and hence the IP on long-term bonds is quite stable relative to the IP on short-term bonds. Also, short-term rates fluctuate as a result of Federal Reserve policy (the Fed intervenes in the short-term rather than the long-term market).

35. a. The yield curve becomes steeper. Although interest rates in Year 1 decrease by 1 percent, interest rates in the following years increase by 2 percent, making the yield curve steeper.

36. b. $k = k^* + IP + DRP + LP + MRP$. Since each of these bonds has a 30-year maturity, the MRP and IP would all be equal. Thus, the differences in the interest rates among these issues are the default risk and liquidity premiums.

37. a. Statement b is incorrect. If a downward-sloping yield curve existed, long-term interest rates would be lower than short-term rates. This would be very serious for UAC: UAC receives as income the interest it charges on its long-term mortgage loans, but it has to pay out interest for obtaining funds in the short-term money market. Therefore, UAC would be receiving low interest income, but it would be paying out even higher interest. Statement c is incorrect. An upward-sloping yield curve would indicate higher interest rates for long-term securities than for short-term securities.

38.   e.   Statement c is incorrect because the nominal rate ($k_{RF} = k^* + IP$) would increase (not the real risk-free rate, k^*) if inflation increased by 2 percentage points.

SOLUTIONS TO SELF-TEST PROBLEMS

1.   b. $k^* = 2\%$; $I_1 = 3\%$; $I_2 = 3\%$; $I_3 = 5\%$; $I_4 = 5\%$; $I_5 = 5\%$; MRP = 0; $k_{T3} = ?$
Since these are Treasury securities, DRP = LP = 0.

$k_{T3} = k^* + IP_3$.

$IP_3 = (3\% + 3\% + 5\%)/3 = 3.67\%$.

$k_{T3} = 2\% + 3.67\% = 5.67\% \approx 5.7\%$.

2.   d. $k^* = 2\%$, $I_1 = 3\%$; $I_2 = 3\%$; $I_3 = 5\%$; $I_4 = 5\%$; $I_5 = 5\%$; MRP = 0; $k_{T5} = ?$
Since these are Treasury securities, DRP = LP = 0.

$k_{T5} = k^* + IP_5$.

$IP_5 = (3\% + 3\% + 5\% + 5\% + 5\%)/5 = 4.2\%$.

$k_{T5} = 2\% + 4.2\% = 6.2\%$.

3.   e. $k_{T20} = 8\%$; $k_{C20} = 11\%$; LP = 1.0%; DRP = ?

$k = k^* + IP + DRP + LP + MRP$.

$k_{T20} = 8\% = k^* + IP + MRP$; DRP = LP = 0.

$k_{C20} = 11\% = k^* + IP + DRP + 1.0\% + MRP$.

Because both bonds are 20-year bonds the inflation premium and maturity risk premium on both bonds are equal. The only differences between them are the liquidity and default risk premiums.

$k_{C20} = 11\% = k^* + IP + MRP + 1.0\% + DRP$. But we know from above that $k^* + IP + MRP = 8\%$; therefore,

$11\% = 8\% + 1.0\% + DRP$
$ 2\% = DRP$.

4. b. $k_{RF} = k^* + IP = 3\% + 8\% = 11\%$.

5. c. There is virtually no risk of default on a U.S. Treasury security, and they trade in active markets, which provide liquidity, so

$k = k^* + IP + DRP + LP + MRP$
$ = 3\% + 8\% + 0\% + 0\% + 1\%$
$ = 12\%$.

6. a. $k_{T3} = k^* + IP_3 + DRP_3 + LP_3 + MRP_3$
$12\% = 2\% + IP_3 + 0\% + 0\% + 0\%$
$ IP_3 = 10\%$.

Thus, the average expected inflation rate over the next three years (IP) is 10 percent. Given that the average expected inflation rate over the next three years is 10%, we can find the implied expected inflation rate for the third year by solving the equation that sets the two known plus the one unknown expected inflation rates equal to 10%:

$$\frac{12\% + 10\% + I_3}{3} = 10\%$$

$$I_3 = 8\%.$$

7. d.

Year	k^*	Inflation	Average Inflation	k_t
1	2%	?	$I_1/1 = ?$	?
2	2%	3	$(I_1 + 3\%)/2$	5.5%

$2\% + (I_1 + 3\%)/2 = 5.5\%$
$ (I_1 + 3\%)/2 = 3.5\%$
$ I_1 + 3\% = 7\%$
$ I_1 = 4\%$.

8. b. $I_1 = IP = 4\%$. $k_{T1} = k^* + IP = 2\% + 4\% = 6\%$.

9.   d.   First, note that we will use the equation $k_t = 4\% + IP_t + MRP_t$. We have the data needed to find the IPs:

$IP_5 = (7\% + 4\% + 3\% + 3\% + 3\%)/5 = 20\%/5 = 4\%$.
$IP_2 = (7\% + 4\%)/2 = 5.5\%$.

Now we can substitute into the equation:

$k_{T2} = 4\% + 5.5\% + MRP_2 = 11\%$.
$k_{T5} = 4\% + 4\% + MRP_5 = 11\%$.

Now we can solve for the MRPs, and find the difference:

$MRP_5 = 11\% - 8\% = 3\%$.
$MRP_2 = 11\% - 9.5\% = 1.5\%$.
Difference $= 3\% - 1.5\% = 1.5\%$.

10.   e.   Basic relevant equations:

$k_t = k^* + IP_t + DRP_t + MRP_t + LP_t$. But $DRP_t = MRP_t = LP_t = 0$, so
$k_t = k^* + IP_t$.

$$IP_t = \frac{\text{Average}}{\text{inflation}} = \frac{I_1 + I_2 + \ldots}{N}.$$

We know that $I_1 = IP_1 = 3.5\%$ and $k^* = 2\%$. Therefore,

$k_{T1} = 2\% + 3.5\% = 5.5\%$.
$k_{T3} = k_{T1} + 3\% = 5.5\% + 3\% = 8.5\%$.

But $k_{T3} = k^* + IP_3 = 2\% + IP_3 = 8.5\%$, so
$IP_3 = 8.5\% - 2\% = 6.5\%$.

We also know that $I_t = $ Constant after $t = 1$.

$(3.5\% + 2I)/3 = 6.5\%$
$3.5\% + 2(I) = 19.5\%$
$2(I) = 16\%$
$I = 8\%$.

We can set up this table:

Year	k*	I_t	Avg. I = IP_t	k = k* + IP_t
1	2%	3.5%	3.5%/1 = 3.5%	5.5%
2	2%	I	(3.5% + I)/2 = IP_2	
3	2%	I	(3.5 + I + I)/3 = IP_3	8.5%, so IP_3 = 8.5% − 2% = 6.5%

11.   c. T-bill rate = k* + IP

$$5\% = k^* + 2.85\%$$
$$k^* = 2.15\%.$$

12.   d. We're given all the components to determine the yield on the Englewood bonds except the default risk premium (DRP) and MRP. Calculate the MRP as 0.1%(5 − 1) = 0.4%. Now, we can solve for the DRP as follows:

8.1% = 2.5% + 2.75% + 0.4% + 1.2% + DRP, or DRP = 1.25%.

13.   a. First, calculate the inflation premiums for the next three and five years, respectively. They are IP_3 = (2.25% + 2.75% + 3.3%)/3 = 2.77% and IP_5 = (2.25% + 2.75% + 3.3% + 3.3% + 3.3%)/5 = 2.98%. The real risk-free rate is given as 2.40%. Since the default and liquidity premiums are zero on Treasury bonds, we can now solve for the default risk premium. Thus, 5.60% = 2.40% + 2.77% + MRP_3, or MRP_3 = 0.43%. Similarly, 6.20% = 2.40% + 2.98% + MRP_5, or MRP_5 = 0.82%. Thus, $MRP_5 - MRP_3$ = 0.82% − 0.43% = 0.39%.

CHAPTER 5
RISK AND RATES OF RETURN

LEARNING OBJECTIVES

- Define dollar return and rate of return.

- Define risk and calculate the expected rate of return, standard deviation, and coefficient of variation for a probability distribution.

- Specify how risk aversion influences required rates of return.

- Graph diversifiable risk and market risk; explain which of these is relevant to a well-diversified investor.

- State the basic proposition of the Capital Asset Pricing Model (CAPM) and explain how and why a portfolio's risk may be reduced.

- Explain the significance of a stock's beta coefficient, and use the Security Market Line to calculate a stock's required rate of return.

- List changes in the market or within a firm that would cause the required rate of return on the firm's stock to change.

- Identify concerns about beta and the CAPM.

- Explain how stock price volatility is more likely to imply risk than earnings volatility.

OVERVIEW

Risk is an important concept in financial analysis, especially in terms of how it affects security prices and rates of return. Investment risk is associated with the probability of low or negative future returns.

The riskiness of an asset can be con-sidered in two ways: (1) on a stand-alone basis, where the asset's cash flows are analyzed all by themselves, or (2) in a portfolio context, where the cash flows from a number of assets are combined, and then the consolidated cash flows are analyzed.

In a portfolio context, an asset's risk can be divided into two components: (1) a diversifiable risk component, which can be diversified away and hence is of little concern to diversified investors, and (2) a market risk component, which reflects the risk of a general stock market decline and cannot be eliminated by diversification, and therefore, is of concern to investors. Only market risk is relevant; diversifiable risk is irrelevant because it can be eliminated.

An attempt has been made to quantify market risk with a measure called beta. Beta is a measurement of how a particular firm's stock returns move relative to overall movements of stock market returns. The Capital Asset Pricing Model (CAPM), using the concept of beta and investors' aversion to risk, specifies the relationship between market risk and the required rate of return. This relationship can be visualized graphically with the Security Market Line (SML). The slope of the SML can change, or the line can shift upward or downward, in response to changes in risk or required rates of return.

OUTLINE

With most investments, an individual or business spends money today with the expectation of earning even more money in the future. The concept of return provides investors with a convenient way of expressing the financial performance of an investment.

■ One way of expressing an investment return is in *dollar terms*.

$$\text{Dollar return} = \text{Amount received} - \text{Amount invested}.$$

☐ Expressing returns in dollars is easy, but two problems arise.
- To make a meaningful judgment about the adequacy of the return, you need to know the scale (size) of the investment.
- You also need to know the timing of the return.

■ The solution to the scale and timing problems of dollar returns is to express investment results as *rates of return*, or *percentage returns*.

$$\text{Rate of return} = \frac{\text{Amount received} - \text{Amount invested}}{\text{Amount invested}}.$$

☐ The rate of return calculation "standardizes" the return by considering the return per unit of investment.
☐ Expressing rates of return on an annual basis solves the timing problem.
☐ Rate of return is the most common measure of investment performance.

Risk refers to the chance that some unfavorable event will occur. Investment risk is related to the probability of actually earning a low or negative return; thus, the greater the chance of low or negative returns, the riskier the investment.

■ An asset's risk can be analyzed in two ways: (1) on a *stand-alone basis,* where the asset is considered in isolation, and (2) on a *portfolio basis,* where the asset is held as one of a number of assets in a portfolio.

■ No investment will be undertaken unless the expected rate of return is high enough to compensate the investor for the perceived risk of the investment.

■ The *probability distribution* for an event is the listing of all the possible outcomes for the event, with mathematical probabilities assigned to each.
   □ An event's *probability* is defined as the chance that the event will occur.
   □ The sum of the probabilities for a particular event must equal 1.0.

■ *The expected rate of return* $(\hat{k})$ is the sum of the products of each possible outcome times its associated probability—it is a weighted average of the various possible outcomes, with the weights being their probabilities of occurrence:

$$\text{Expected rate of return} = \hat{k} = \sum_{i=1}^{n} P_i k_i .$$

   □ Where the number of possible outcomes is virtually unlimited, *continuous probability distributions* are used in determining the expected rate of return of the event.
   □ The tighter, or more peaked, a distribution, the more likely it is that the actual outcome will be close to the expected value, and, consequently, the less likely it is that the actual return will end up far below the expected return. Thus, the tighter the probability distribution, the lower the risk assigned to a stock.

■ One measure for determining the tightness of a distribution is the *standard deviation,* σ.

$$\text{Standard deviation} = \sigma = \sqrt{\sum_{i=1}^{n} (k_i - \hat{k})^2 P_i} .$$

   □ The standard deviation is a probability-weighted average deviation from the expected value, and it provides an idea of how far above or below the expected value the actual value is likely to be.
   • The smaller the standard deviation, the tighter the probability distribution, and, accordingly, the lower the riskiness of the stock.

- If a probability distribution is normal, the actual return will be within ±1 standard deviation of the expected return 68.26 percent of the time.
  □ The *variance, σ^2,* is the square of the standard deviation.

■ Another useful measure of risk is the *coefficient of variation (CV),* which is the standard deviation divided by the expected return.

  □ It shows the risk per unit of return and provides a more meaningful basis for comparison when the expected returns on two alternatives are not the same:

$$\text{Coefficient of variation (CV)} = \frac{\sigma}{\hat{k}}.$$

  □ Because the coefficient of variation captures the effects of both risk and return, it is a better measure than the standard deviation for evaluating risk in situations in which investments have substantially different expected returns.

■ Most investors are *risk averse.* This means that for two alternatives with the same expected rate of return, investors will choose the one with the lower risk. The average investor is risk averse with regard to his or her serious money.

  □ Risk-averse investors require higher rates of return as an inducement to buy riskier securities.
  □ The higher a security's risk, the lower its price and the higher its required return.

■ *Risk premium, RP,* is the difference between the expected rate of return on a given risky asset and that on a less risky asset. It represents the additional compensation investors require for assuming additional risk.

  □ In a market dominated by risk-averse investors, riskier securities must have higher expected returns, as estimated by the marginal investor, than less risky securities. If this situation does not exist, buying and selling in the market will force it to occur.

An asset held as part of a portfolio is less risky than the same asset held in isolation. This is important, because most financial assets are not held in isolation; rather, they are held as parts of portfolios. From the investor's standpoint, what is important is the return on his or her portfolio, and the portfolio's risk—not the fact that a particular stock goes up or down. Thus, the risk and return of an individual security should be analyzed in terms of how it affects the risk and return of the portfolio in which it is held.

■ The expected return on a portfolio, $\hat{k}_p$ is the weighted average of the expected returns on the individual assets in the portfolio, with the weights being the fraction of the total portfolio invested in each asset:

$$\hat{k}_p = \sum_{i=1}^{n} w_i \hat{k}_i .$$

■ The *realized rate of return, $\bar{k}$,* is the return that was actually earned during some past period, and usually is different from the expected return, $\hat{k}$.

■ The riskiness of a portfolio, σ_p, is generally *not* a weighted average of the standard deviations of the individual assets in the portfolio; the portfolio's risk will be smaller than the weighted average of the assets' σ's. The riskiness of a portfolio depends not only on the standard deviations of the individual stocks, but also on the *correlation between the stocks*.
   □ The *correlation coefficient, r,* measures the tendency of two variables to move together. With stocks, these variables are the individual stock returns.
   □ Diversification does nothing to reduce risk if the portfolio consists of *perfectly positively correlated* stocks.
   □ As a rule, the riskiness of a portfolio will decline as the number of stocks in the portfolio increases.
   □ However, in the typical case, where the correlation among the individual stocks is positive, but less than +1.0, some, but not all, risk can be eliminated.
   □ In the real world, it is impossible to form completely riskless stock portfolios. Diversification can reduce risk, but cannot eliminate it.

■ A portfolio consisting of all stocks is called the *market portfolio*. While very large portfolios end up with a substantial amount of risk, it is not as much risk as if all the money were invested in only one stock.
   □ Almost half of the riskiness inherent in an average individual stock can be eliminated if the stock is held in a reasonably well diversified portfolio, which is one containing 40 or more stocks. Some risk always remains, however, so it is virtually impossible to diversify away the effects of broad stock market movements that affect almost all stocks.
   □ *Diversifiable risk* is that part of the risk of a stock that can be eliminated by proper diversification. It is caused by random events that are unique to a particular firm.
   □ *Market risk* is that part of the risk that cannot be eliminated, and it stems from factors that systematically affect most firms, such as war, inflation, recessions, and high interest rates.

- Market risk can be measured by the degree to which a given stock tends to move up or down with the market.
- Market risk is the *relevant* risk, which reflects a security's contribution to the portfolio's risk.

☐ The *Capital Asset Pricing Model* is an important tool for analyzing the relationship between risk and rates of return.

- The model is based on the proposition that a stock's required rate of return is equal to the risk-free rate of return plus a risk premium, where risk reflects diversification.
- The model's primary conclusion is: The relevant riskiness of an individual stock is its contribution to the riskiness of a well-diversified portfolio.

The tendency of a stock to move with the market is reflected in its beta coefficient, b, which is a measure of the stock's volatility relative to that of an average stock.

■ An average-risk stock is defined as one that tends to move up and down in step with the general market. By definition it has a beta of 1.0.

■ A stock that is twice as volatile as the market will have a beta of 2.0, while a stock that is half as volatile as the market will have a beta coefficient of 0.5.

■ The beta coefficient of a portfolio of securities is the weighted average of the individual securities' betas:

$$b_p = \sum_{i=1}^{n} w_i b_i.$$

■ Since a stock's beta coefficient determines how the stock affects the riskiness of a diversified portfolio, beta is the most relevant measure of any stock's risk.

The Capital Asset Pricing Model (CAPM) employs the concept of beta, which measures risk as the relationship between a particular stock's movements and the movements of the overall stock market. The CAPM uses a stock's beta, in conjunction with the average investor's degree of risk aversion, to calculate the return that investors require, k_s, on that particular stock.

■ The *Security Market Line (SML)* shows the relationship between risk as measured by beta and the required rate of return for individual securities. The SML equation can be used to find the required rate of return on Stock i:

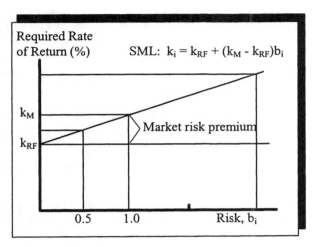

$$\text{SML: } k_i = k_{RF} + (k_M - k_{RF})b_i.$$

☐ Here k_{RF} is the interest rate on risk-free securities, b_i is the ith stock's beta, and k_M is the return on the market or, alternatively, on an average stock.

☐ The term $k_M - k_{RF}$ is the *market risk premium, RP_M*. This is a measure of the additional return over the risk-free rate needed to compensate investors for assuming an average amount of risk.

 • The size of this premium depends on the perceived risk of the stock market and investors' degree of risk aversion.

☐ In the CAPM, the market risk premium, $k_M - k_{RF}$, is multiplied by the stock's beta coefficient to determine the additional premium over the risk-free rate that is required to compensate investors for the risk inherent in a particular stock.

 • This premium may be larger or smaller than the premium required on an average stock, depending on the riskiness of that stock in relation to the overall market as measured by the stock's beta.

☐ The risk premium calculated by $(k_M - k_{RF})b_i$ is added to the risk-free rate, k_{RF} (the rate on Treasury securities), to determine the total rate of return required by investors on a particular stock, k_s.

☐ Both the Security Market Line and a company's position on it change over time due to changes in interest rates, investors' aversion to risk, and individual companies' betas.

■ The risk-free (also known as the nominal, or quoted) rate of interest consists of two elements: (1) a real inflation-free rate of return, k*, and (2) an inflation premium, IP, equal to the anticipated inflation rate.

☐ The real risk-free rate on long-term Treasury bonds has historically ranged from 2 to 4 percent.

☐ As the expected inflation rate increases, a higher premium must be added to the real risk-free rate of return to compensate for the loss of purchasing power.

■ As risk aversion increases, so do the risk premium and the slope of the SML. The greater the average investor's aversion to risk, then (1) the steeper the slope of the line, (2) the greater the risk premium for all stocks, and (3) the higher the required rate of return on all stocks.

■ Many factors can affect a company's beta. When such changes occur, the required rate of return also changes.
  ☐ A firm can influence its market risk, hence its beta, through changes in the composition of its assets and also through its use of debt.
  ☐ A company's beta can also change as a result of external factors such as increased competition in its industry, the expiration of basic patents, and the like.

For a management whose primary goal is stock price maximization, the overriding consideration is the riskiness of the firm's stock, and the relevant risk of any physical asset must be measured in terms of its effect on the stock's risk as seen by investors.

A number of recent studies have raised concerns about the validity of the CAPM.

■ A recent study by Fama and French found no historical relationship between stocks' returns and their market betas.
  ☐ They found two variables that are consistently related to stock returns: (1) a firm's size and (2) its market/book ratio.
  ☐ After adjusting for other factors, they found that smaller firms have provided relatively high returns, and that returns are higher on stocks with low market/book ratios. By contrast, they found no relationship between a stock's beta and its return.

■ As an alternative to the traditional CAPM, researchers and practitioners have begun to look to more general multi-beta models that encompass the CAPM and address its shortcomings.
  ☐ In the multi-beta model, market risk is measured relative to a set of risk factors that determine the behavior of asset returns, whereas the CAPM gauges risk only relative to the market return.
  ☐ The risk factors in the multi-beta model are all nondiversifiable sources of risk.
    • Empirical research has discovered several systematic empirical risk factors, including the bond default premium, the bond term structure premium, and inflation.

Earnings volatility does not necessarily imply investment risk. The causes of the volatility need to be considered before reaching any conclusions as to whether earnings volatility indicates risk. However, stock price volatility does signify risk (except for stocks that are negatively correlated with the market, which are few and far between).

Web Appendix 5A contains a discussion of calculating beta coefficients. The discussion concentrates on graphic and least squares regression techniques.

SELF-TEST QUESTIONS

Definitional

1. Investment risk is associated with the _____ of low or negative returns; the greater the chance of loss, the riskier the investment.

2. A listing of all possible _____, with a probability assigned to each, is known as a probability _____.

3. Weighting each possible outcome of a distribution by its _____ of occurrence and summing the results give the expected _____ of the distribution.

4. One measure of the tightness of a probability distribution is the _____ _____, a probability-weighted average deviation from the expected value.

5. Investors who prefer outcomes with a high degree of certainty to those that are less certain are described as being _____ _____.

6. Owning a portfolio of securities enables investors to benefit from _____.

7. Diversification of a portfolio can result in lower _____ for the same level of return.

8. Diversification of a portfolio is achieved by selecting securities that are not perfectly _____ correlated with each other.

9. That part of a stock's risk that can be eliminated is known as _____ risk, while the portion that cannot be eliminated is called _____ risk.

10. The _____ coefficient measures a stock's volatility relative to that of an average stock.

11. A stock that is twice as volatile as the market would have a beta coefficient of _____, while a stock with a beta of 0.5 would be only _____ as volatile as the market.

12. The beta coefficient of a portfolio is the _____ _____ of the betas of the individual stocks.

13. The minimum expected return that will induce investors to buy a particular security is the _____ rate of return.

14. The security used to measure the _____-_____ rate is a U.S. Treasury security.

15. The risk premium for a particular stock may be calculated by multiplying the market risk premium times the stock's _____ _____.

16. A stock's required rate of return is equal to the _____-_____ rate plus the stock's _____ _____.

17. The risk-free rate on a short-term Treasury security is made up of two parts: the _____ _____-_____ rate of return plus a(n) _____ premium.

18. Changes in investors' risk aversion alter the _____ of the Security Market Line.

Conceptual

19. The Y-axis intercept of the Security Market Line (SML) indicates the required rate of return on an individual stock with a beta of 1.0.

   a. True   **b.** False

20. If a stock has a beta of zero, it will be riskless when held in isolation.

   a. True   **b.** False

21. A group of 200 stocks each has a beta of 1.0. We can be certain that each of the stocks was positively correlated with the market.

   a. True   **b.** False

22. Refer to Self-Test Question 21. If we combined these same 200 stocks into a portfolio, market risk would be reduced below the average market risk of the stocks in the portfolio.

   a. True   **b.** False

23. Refer to Self-Test Question 22. The standard deviation of the portfolio of these 200 stocks would be lower than the standard deviations of the individual stocks.

   a. True   **b.** False

24. Suppose k_{RF} = 7% and k_M = 12%. If investors became more risk averse, k_M would be likely to decrease.

   a. True   **b.** False

25. Refer to Self-Test Question 24. The required rate of return for a stock with b = 0.5 would increase more than for a stock with b = 2.0.

   a. True   b. False

26. Refer to Self-Test Questions 24 and 25. If the expected inflation rate increased, the required rate of return on a b = 2.0 stock would rise by more than that of a b = 0.5 stock.

   a. True   b. False

27. Which is the best measure of risk for an asset held in a well-diversified portfolio?

   a. Variance   d. Semi-variance
   b. Standard deviation   e. Expected value
   c. Beta

28. In a portfolio of three different stocks, which of the following could *not* be true?

   a. The riskiness of the portfolio is less than the riskiness of each stock held in isolation.
   b. The riskiness of the portfolio is greater than the riskiness of one or two of the stocks.
   c. The beta of the portfolio is less than the beta of each of the individual stocks.
   d. The beta of the portfolio is greater than the beta of one or two of the individual stocks.
   e. The beta of the portfolio is equal to the beta of one of the individual stocks.

29. If investors expected inflation to increase in the future, and they also became more risk averse, what could be said about the change in the Security Market Line (SML)?

   a. The SML would shift up and the slope would increase.
   b. The SML would shift up and the slope would decrease.
   c. The SML would shift down and the slope would increase.
   d. The SML would shift down and the slope would decrease.
   e. The SML would remain unchanged.

30. Which of the following statements is most correct?

    a. The SML relates required returns to firms' market risk. The slope and intercept of this line *cannot* be controlled by the financial manager.

    b. The slope of the SML is determined by the value of beta.

    c. If you plotted the returns of a given stock against those of the market, and if you found that the slope of the regression line was negative, then the CAPM would indicate that the required rate of return on the stock should be less than the risk-free rate for a well-diversified investor, assuming that the observed relationship is expected to continue on into the future.

    d. If investors become less risk averse, the slope of the Security Market Line will increase.

    e. Statements a and c are both true.

31. Which of the following statements is most correct?

    a. Normally, the Security Market Line has an upward slope. However, at one of those unusual times when the yield curve on bonds is downward sloping, the SML will also have a downward slope.

    b. The market risk premium, as it is used in the CAPM theory, is equal to the required rate of return on an average stock minus the required rate of return on an average company's bonds.

    c. If the marginal investor's aversion to risk decreases, then the slope of the yield curve would, other things held constant, tend to increase. If expectations for inflation also increased at the same time risk aversion was decreasing—say the expected inflation rate rose from 5 percent to 8 percent—the net effect could possibly result in a parallel upward shift in the SML.

    d. According to the text, it is theoretically possible to combine two stocks, each of which would be quite risky if held as your only asset, and to form a 2-stock portfolio that is riskless. However, the stocks would have to have a correlation coefficient of expected future returns of -1.0, and it is hard to find such stocks in the real world.

    e. Each of the above statements is false.

32. Which of the following statements is most correct?

   a. The expected future rate of return, $\hat{k}$, is always *above* the past realized rate of return, $\bar{k}$, except for highly risk-averse investors.

   b. The expected future rate of return, $\hat{k}$, is always *below* the past realized rate of return, $\bar{k}$, except for highly risk-averse investors.

   c. The expected future rate of return, $\hat{k}$, is always *below* the required rate of return, k, except for highly risk-averse investors.

   d. There is no logical reason to think that any relationship exists between the expected future rate of return, $\hat{k}$, on a security and the security's required rate of return, k.

   e. Each of the above statements is false.

33. Which of the following statements is most correct?

   a. Someone who is highly risk averse should invest in stocks with high betas (above +1.0), other things held constant.

   b. The returns on a stock might be highly uncertain in the sense that they could actually turn out to be much higher or much lower than the expected rate of return (that is, the stock has a high standard deviation of returns), yet the stock might still be regarded by most investors as being less risky than some other stock whose returns are less variable.

   c. The standard deviation is a better measure of risk when comparing securities than the coefficient of variation. This is true because the standard deviation "standardizes" risk by dividing each security's variance by its expected rate of return.

   d. Market risk can be reduced by holding a large portfolio of stocks, and if a portfolio consists of all traded stocks, market risk will be completely eliminated.

   e. The market risk in a portfolio declines as more stocks are added to the portfolio, and the risk decline is linear, that is, each additional stock reduces the portfolio's risk by the same amount.

SELF-TEST PROBLEMS

1. Stock A has the following probability distribution of expected returns:

Probability	Rate of Return
0.1	-15%
0.2	0
0.4	5
0.2	10
0.1	25

What is Stock A's expected rate of return and standard deviation?

   a. 8.0%; 9.5%   **b.** 8.0%; 6.5%   **c.** 5.0%; 3.5%   **d.** 5.0%; 6.5%   **e.** 5.0%; 9.5%

2. If $k_{RF} = 5\%$, $k_M = 11\%$, and $b = 1.3$ for Stock X, what is k_X, the required rate of return for Stock X?

    a. 18.7%   **b.** 16.7%   **c.** 14.8%   **d.** 12.8%   **e.** 11.9%

3. Refer to Self-Test Problem 2. What would k_X be if investors expected the inflation rate to increase by 2 percentage points?

    a. 18.7%   **b.** 16.7%   **c.** 14.8%   **d.** 12.8%   **e.** 11.9%

4. Refer to Self-Test Problem 2. What would k_X be if an increase in investors' risk aversion caused the market risk premium to increase by 3 percentage points? k_{RF} remains at 5 percent.

    a. 18.7%   **b.** 16.7%   **c.** 14.8%   **d.** 12.8%   **e.** 11.9%

5. Refer to Self-Test Problem 2. What would k_X be if investors expected the inflation rate to increase by 2 percentage points *and* their risk aversion increased by 3 percentage points?

    a. 18.7%   **b.** 16.7%   **c.** 14.8%   **d.** 12.8%   **e.** 11.9%

6. A stock has a required return of 12 percent. The risk-free rate is 6 percent and the market risk premium is 5 percent. What is the stock's beta?

    a. 0.80   **b.** 0.95   **c.** 1.20   **d.** 1.50   **e.** 1.75

7. Refer to Self-Test Problem 6. If the market risk premium increases to 8 percent, what will happen to the stock's required rate of return? Assume the risk-free rate and the stock's beta remain unchanged.

    a. 11.75%   **b.** 12.80%   **c.** 13.10%   **d.** 14.25%   **e.** 15.60%

8. Jan Middleton owns a 3-stock portfolio with a total investment value equal to $300,000.

Stock	Investment	Beta
A	$100,000	0.5
B	100,000	1.0
C	100,000	1.5
Total	$300,000	

    What is the weighted average beta of Jan's 3-stock portfolio?

    a. 0.9   **b.** 1.3   **c.** 1.0   **d.** 0.4   **e.** 1.2

9. The Apple Investment Fund has a total investment of $450 million in five stocks.

Stock	Investment (Millions)	Beta
1	$130	0.4
2	110	1.5
3	70	3.0
4	90	2.0
5	50	1.0
Total	$450	

What is the fund's overall, or weighted average, beta?

a. 1.14   b. 1.22   c. 1.35   d. 1.46   e. 1.53

10. Refer to Self-Test Problem 9. If the risk-free rate is 12 percent and the market risk premium is 6 percent, what is the required rate of return on the Apple Fund?

a. 20.76%   b. 19.92%   c. 18.81%   d. 17.62%   e. 15.77%

11. Stock A has a beta of 1.2, Stock B has a beta of 0.6, the expected rate of return on an average stock is 12 percent, and the risk-free rate of return is 7 percent. By how much does the required return on the riskier stock exceed the required return on the less risky stock?

a. 4.00%   b. 3.25%   c. 3.00%   d. 2.50%   e. 3.75%

(The following data apply to the next three Self-Test Problems.)

Stock A has an expected return of 8 percent, a beta coefficient of 0.72, and a standard deviation of expected returns of 28 percent. Stock B has an expected return of 10 percent, a beta coefficient of 0.96, and a standard deviation of expected returns of 20 percent. The risk-free rate is 5.5 percent and the market risk premium is 4 percent.

12. What are the coefficients of variation for Stocks A and B?

a. 3.5; 2.2   b. 3.2; 2.0   c. 3.5; 2.0   d. 3.2; 2.2   e. 3.5; 1.8

13. What are the required rates of return for Stocks A and B?

a. 7.75%; 9.34%   d. 7.75%; 10.25%
b. 8.38%; 9.34%   e. 6.50%; 9.34%
c. 8.38%; 10.25%

14. What is the required return of a portfolio that has $60,000 invested in Stock A and $40,000 invested in Stock B?

   a. 9.00%   **b.** 8.25%   **c.** 8.55%   **d.** 9.22%   **e.** 8.76%

15. You are managing a portfolio of 10 stocks that are held in equal dollar amounts. The current beta of the portfolio is 1.8, and the beta of Stock A is 2.0. If Stock A is sold and the proceeds are used to purchase a replacement stock, what does the beta of the replacement stock have to be to lower the portfolio beta to 1.7?

   a. 1.4   **b.** 1.3   **c.** 1.2   **d.** 1.1   **e.** 1.0

16. Consider the following information for the Alachua Retirement Fund, with a total investment of $4 million.

Stock	Investment	Beta
A	$ 400,000	1.2
B	600,000	-0.4
C	1,000,000	1.5
D	2,000,000	0.8
Total	$4,000,000	

   The market required rate of return is 12 percent, and the risk-free rate is 6 percent. What is its required rate of return?

   a. 9.98%   **b.** 10.45%   **c.** 11.01%   **d.** 11.50%   **e.** 12.56%

17. You are given the following distribution of returns:

Probability	Return
0.4	$30
0.5	25
0.1	-20

   What is the coefficient of variation of the expected dollar returns?

   a. 206.2500   **b.** 0.6383   **c.** 14.3614   **d.** 0.7500   **e.** 1.2500

18. If the risk-free rate is 8 percent, the expected return on the market is 13 percent, and the expected return on Security J is 15 percent, then what is the beta of Security J?

   a. 1.40   **b.** 0.90   **c.** 1.20   **d.** 1.50   **e.** 0.75

19. Consider the following information for three stocks, Stock X, Stock Y, and Stock Z. The returns on each of the three stocks are positively correlated, but they are not perfectly correlated. (That is, all of the correlation coefficients are between 0 and 1.)

Stock	Expected Return	Standard Deviation	Beta
Stock X	7.6%	15%	0.60
Stock Y	10.2%	15	1.25
Stock Z	12.0%	15	1.70

Portfolio P has half of its funds invested in Stock X and half invested in Stock Y. Portfolio Q has one third of its funds invested in each of these three stocks. The risk-free rate is 5.2 percent, and the market is in equilibrium. (That is, required returns equal expected returns.) What is the market risk premium $(k_M - k_{RF})$?

a. 5.25%   b. 3.30%   c. 6.00%   d. 4.00%   e. 4.75%

20. Hammond Industries (HI) has a beta of 1.75, while Longwood-Ocala Enterprises' (LOE) beta is 0.45. The risk-free rate is 5.5 percent, and the required rate of return on an average stock is 11.75 percent. Now the expected rate of inflation built into k_{RF} falls by 1.25 percentage points, the real risk-free rate remains constant, the required return on the market falls to 10.3 percent, and the betas remain constant. When all of these changes are made, what will be the difference in the required returns on HI's and LOE's stocks?

a. 7.865%   b. 6.355%   c. 5.765%   d. 7.333%   e. 5.250%

21. You have been managing a $3 million portfolio. The portfolio has a beta of 1.10 and a required rate of return of 10 percent. The current risk-free rate is 5.6 percent. Assume that you receive another $600,000. If you invest the money in a stock that has a beta of 0.60, what will be the required return on your $3.6 million portfolio?

a. 9.20%   b. 9.67%   c. 8.75%   d. 9.95%   e. 10.20%

Web Appendix 5A

A-1. Given the information below, calculate the betas for Stocks A and B. (Hint: Think rise over run.)

Year	Stock A	Stock B	Market
1	-5%	10%	-10%
2	10	20	10
3	25	30	30

a. 1.0; 0.5   b. 0.75; 0.5   c. 0.75; 1.0   d. 0.5; 0.5   e. 0.75; 0.25

(The following data apply to the next two Self-Test Problems.)

You are given the following information:

Year	Stock N	Market
1	-5%	10%
2	-8	15
3	7	-10

The risk-free rate is equal to 7 percent and the market required return is equal to 10 percent.

A-2. What is Stock N's beta coefficient?

   a. 1.00   **b.** -0.50   **c.** 0.60   **d.** -0.75   **e.** -0.60

A-3. What is Stock N's required rate of return?

   a. 6.40%   **b.** 5.20%   **c.** 8.80%   **d.** 5.90%   **e.** 7.00%

A-4. Stock Y and the Market had the following rates of return during the last 4 years. What is Stock Y's beta? (Hint: You will need a financial calculator to calculate the beta coefficient.)

Year	Y	Market
1999	10.0%	10.0%
2000	16.0	13.5
2001	-7.5	-4.0
2002	0.0	5.5

   a. 1.25   **b.** 0.75   **c.** 1.00   **d.** 1.34   **e.** 1.57

A-5. Stock Y, Stock Z, and the Market had the following rates of return during the last 4 years:

Year	Y	Z	Market
1999	10.0%	10.0%	10.0%
2000	16.0	11.5	13.5
2001	-7.5	1.0	-4.0
2002	0.0	6.0	5.5

The expected future return on the market is 15 percent, the real risk-free rate is 3.75 percent, and the expected inflation rate is a constant 5 percent. If the market risk premium rises by 3 percentage points, what will be the change in the required rate of return of the riskier stock?

   a. 4.01%   **b.** 3.67%   **c.** 4.88%   **d.** 3.23%   **e.** 4.66%

ANSWERS TO SELF-TEST QUESTIONS

1. probability
2. outcomes; distribution
3. probability; return
4. standard deviation
5. risk averse
6. diversification
7. risk
8. positively
9. diversifiable; market

10. beta
11. 2.0; half
12. weighted average
13. required
14. risk-free
15. beta coefficient
16. risk-free; risk premium
17. real risk-free; inflation
18. slope

19.   b.   The Y-axis intercept of the SML is k_{RF}, which is the required rate of return of a security with a beta of zero.

20.   b.   A zero beta stock could be made riskless if it were combined with enough other zero beta stocks, but it would still have company-specific risk and be risky when held in isolation.

21.   a.   By definition, if a stock has a beta of 1.0 it moves exactly with the market. In other words, if the market moves up by 7 percent, the stock will also move up by 7 percent, while if the market falls by 7 percent, the stock will fall by 7 percent.

22.   b.   Market risk is measured by the beta coefficient. The portfolio beta is a weighted average of the betas of the stocks, so b_p would also be 1.0. Thus, the market risk for the portfolio would be the same as the market risk of the stocks in the portfolio.

23.   a.   Note that with a 200-stock portfolio, the actual returns would all be on or close to the regression line. However, when the portfolio (and the market) returns are quite high, some individual stocks would have higher returns than the portfolio, and some would have much lower returns. Thus, the range of returns, and the standard deviation, would be higher for the individual stocks.

24.   b. RP_M, which is equal to $k_M - k_{RF}$, would rise, leading to an increase in k_M.

25.   b.   The required rate of return for a stock with b = 0.5 would increase less than the return of a stock with b = 2.0.

26.   b.   If the expected inflation rate increased, the SML would shift parallel due to an increase in k_{RF}. Thus, the effect on the required rates of return for both the b = 0.5 and b = 2.0 stocks would be the same.

27.   c.   The best measure of risk is the beta coefficient, which is a measure of the extent to which the returns on a given stock move with the stock market.

28.   c.   The beta of the portfolio is a weighted average of the individual securities' betas, so it could not be less than the betas of all of the stocks.

29.   a.   The increase in inflation would cause the SML to shift up, and more risk-averse investors would cause the slope to increase.

30.   e.   Statement b is false because the slope of the SML is $k_M - k_{RF}$. Statement d is false because as investors become less risk averse the slope of the SML decreases. Statement a is correct because the financial manager has no control over k_M or k_{RF}. ($k_M - k_{RF}$ = slope and k_{RF} = intercept of the SML.) Statement c is correct because the slope of the regression line is beta and beta would be negative; thus, the required return would be less than the risk-free rate.

31.   d.   Statement a is false. The yield curve determines the value of k_{RF}; however, SML = $k_{RF} + (k_M - k_{RF})b$. The average return on the market will always be greater than the risk-free rate; thus, the SML will always be upward sloping. Statement b is false because RP_M is equal to $k_M - k_{RF}$. k_{RF} is equal to the risk-free rate, not the rate on an average company's bonds. Statement c is false. A decrease in an investor's aversion to risk would indicate a downward sloping yield curve. A decrease in risk aversion and an increase in inflation would cause the SML slope to decrease and to shift upward simultaneously.

32.   e.   All the statements are false. For equilibrium to exist, the expected return must equal the required return.

33.   b.   Statement b is correct because the stock with the higher standard deviation might not be highly correlated with most other stocks, hence have a relatively low beta, and thus not be very risky if held in a well-diversified portfolio. The other statements are simply false.

SOLUTIONS TO SELF-TEST PROBLEMS

1.   e. $\hat{k}_A = 0.1(-15\%) + 0.2(0\%) + 0.4(5\%) + 0.2(10\%) + 0.1(25\%) = 5.0\%$.

Variance $= 0.1(-0.15 - 0.05)^2 + 0.2(0.0 - 0.05)^2 + 0.4(0.05 - 0.05)^2$
$+ 0.2(0.10 - 0.05)^2 + 0.1(0.25 - 0.05)^2$
$= 0.009$.

Standard deviation $= \sqrt{0.009} = 0.0949 = 9.5\%$.

2. d. $k_X = k_{RF} + (k_M - k_{RF})b_X = 5\% + (11\% - 5\%)1.3 = 12.8\%$.

3. c. $k_X = k_{RF} + (k_M - k_{RF})b_X = 7\% + (13\% - 7\%)1.3 = 14.8\%$.

    A change in the inflation premium does *not* change the market risk premium $(k_M - k_{RF})$ since both k_M and k_{RF} are affected.

4. b. $k_X = k_{RF} + (k_M - k_{RF})b_X = 5\% + (14\% - 5\%)1.3 = 16.7\%$.

5. a. $k_X = k_{RF} + (k_M - k_{RF})b_X = 7\% + (16\% - 7\%)1.3 = 18.7\%$.

6. c. $k = 12\%$; $k_{RF} = 6\%$; $RP_M = 5\%$; $b = ?$

    $$
    \begin{aligned}
    k &= k_{RF} + (k_M - k_{RF})b \\
    12\% &= 6\% + (5\%)b \\
    6\% &= 5\%b \\
    b &= 1.20.
    \end{aligned}
    $$

7. e. $k_{RF} = 6\%$; $RP_M = 8\%$; $b = 1.2$; $k = ?$

    $$
    \begin{aligned}
    k &= k_{RF} + (k_M - k_{RF})b \\
    k &= 6\% + (8\%)(1.2) \\
    k &= 15.60\%.
    \end{aligned}
    $$

8. c. The calculation of the portfolio's beta is as follows:

    $$b_p = (1/3)(0.5) + (1/3)(1.0) + (1/3)(1.5) = 1.0.$$

9. d. $b_p = \displaystyle\sum_{i=1}^{5} w_i b_i$

    $$= \frac{\$130}{\$450}(0.4) + \frac{\$110}{\$450}(1.5) + \frac{\$70}{\$450}(3.0) + \frac{\$90}{\$450}(2.0) + \frac{\$50}{\$450}(1.0) = 1.46.$$

10. a. $k_p = k_{RF} + (k_M - k_{RF})b_p = 12\% + (6\%)1.46 = 20.76\%$.

11.   c.   We know $b_A = 1.20$, $b_B = 0.60$; $k_M = 12\%$, and $k_{RF} = 7\%$.

$k_i = k_{RF} + (k_M - k_{RF})b_i = 7\% + (12\% - 7\%)b_i$.

$k_A = 7\% + 5\%(1.20) = 13.0\%$.

$k_B = 7\% + 5\%(0.60) = 10.0\%$.

$k_A - k_B = 13\% - 10\% = 3\%$.

12.   c. $CV_A = 28\%/8\% = 3.50$.

$CV_B = 20\%/10\% = 2.00$.

13.   b. $k_A = k_{RF} + (k_M - k_{RF})b_A$
$k_A = 5.5\% + (4\%)(0.72)$
$k_A = 8.38\%$.

$k_B = k_{RF} + (k_M - k_{RF})b_B$
$k_B = 5.5\% + (4\%)(0.96)$
$k_B = 9.34\%$.

14.   e. $b_p = 0.6(0.72) + 0.4(0.96)$
$b_p = 0.432 + 0.384$
$b_p = 0.816$.

$k_p = k_{RF} + (k_M - k_{RF})b_p$
$k_p = 5.5\% + (4\%)(0.816)$
$k_p = 8.764\% \approx 8.76\%$.

15.   e.   First find the beta of the remaining 9 stocks:

$1.8 = 0.9(b_R) + 0.1(b_A)$
$1.8 = 0.9(b_R) + 0.1(2.0)$
$1.8 = 0.9(b_R) + 0.2$
$1.6 = 0.9(b_R)$
$b_R = 1.7778$.

Now find the beta of the new stock that produces $b_p = 1.7$.

$1.7 = 0.9(1.7778) + 0.1(b_N)$
$1.7 = 1.6 + 0.1(b_N)$
$0.1 = 0.1(b_N)$
$b_N = 1.0$.

16. c. Determine the weight each stock represents in the portfolio:

Stock	Investment	w_i	Beta	$w_i \times$ Beta
A	400,000	0.10	1.2	0.1200
B	600,000	0.15	-0.4	-0.0600
C	1,000,000	0.25	1.5	0.3750
D	2,000,000	0.50	0.8	0.4000
				$b_p = \underline{0.8350}$ = Portfolio beta

Write out the SML equation, and substitute known values including the portfolio beta. Solve for the required portfolio return.

$k_p = k_{RF} + (k_M - k_{RF})b_p$
$\quad = 6\% + (12\% - 6\%)0.8350$
$\quad = 6\% + 5.01\% = 11.01\%$.

17. b. Use the given probability distribution of returns to calculate the expected value, variance, standard deviation, and coefficient of variation.

P_i		k_i		$P_i k_i$	k_i	$\hat{k}$		$(k_i - \hat{k})$	$(k_i - \hat{k})^2$	$P(k_i - \hat{k})^2$
0.4	×	$30	=	$12.0	$30 −	$22.5	=	$ 7.5	$ 56.25	$ 22.500
0.5	×	25	=	12.5	25 −	22.5	=	2.5	6.25	3.125
0.1	×	-20	=	-2.0	-20 −	22.5	=	-42.5	1,806.25	180.625
		$\hat{k}$	=	$22.5				σ^2 = Variance = $206.250		

The standard deviation (σ) of $\hat{k}$ is $\sqrt{\$206.25} = \$14.3614$.

Use the standard deviation and the expected return to calculate the coefficient of variation: $\$14.3614/\$22.5 = 0.6383$.

18.   a.   Use the SML equation, substitute in the known values, and solve for beta.

$k_{RF} = 8\%$; $k_M = 13\%$; $\hat{k}_J = 15\%$.

$$\hat{k}_J = k_J = k_{RF} + (k_M - k_{RF})b_J$$
$$15\% = 8\% + (13\% - 8\%)b_J$$
$$7\% = (5\%)b_J$$
$$b_J = 1.4.$$

19.   d.   Using Stock X (or any stock):
$$7.6\% = k_{RF} + (k_M - k_{RF})b_X$$
$$7.6\% = 5.2\% + (k_M - k_{RF})0.6$$
$$(k_M - k_{RF}) = 4\%.$$

20.   a. $b_{HI} = 1.75$; $b_{LOE} = 0.45$.   No changes occur.

$k_{RF} = 5.5\%$.   Decreases by 1.25% to 4.25%.

$k_M = 11.75\%$.   Falls to 10.3%.

Now SML: $k_i = k_{RF} + (k_M - k_{RF})b_i$.

$k_{HI} = 4.25\% + (10.3\% - 4.25\%)1.75 = 4.25\% + 6.05\%(1.75) = 14.8375\%$
$k_{LOE} = 4.25\% + (10.3\% - 4.25\%)0.45 = 4.25\% + 6.05\%(0.45) = \underline{\ 6.9725\%}$
Difference $\underline{7.8650\%}$

21.   b.   Step 1:   Determine the market risk premium from the CAPM:
$$0.10 = 0.056 + (k_M - k_{RF})1.10$$
$$(k_M - k_{RF}) = 0.04.$$

Step 2:   Calculate the beta of the new portfolio:
The beta of the new portfolio is
($600,000/$3,600,000)(0.60) + ($3,000,000/$3,600,000)(1.10) = 1.01667.

Step 3:   Calculate the required return on the new portfolio:
The required return on the new portfolio is
5.6% + (4%)(1.01667) = 9.67%.

Web Appendix 5A

A-1. b. Stock A: $b_A = \dfrac{\text{Rise}}{\text{Run}} = \dfrac{10-(-5)}{10-(-10)} = \dfrac{15}{20} = 0.75.$

Stock B: $b_B = \dfrac{\text{Rise}}{\text{Run}} = \dfrac{20-10}{10-(-10)} = \dfrac{10}{20} = 0.50.$

This problem can also be worked using most financial calculators with statistical functions.

A-2. e. $b_N = \text{Rise/Run} = [-8 - (-5)]/(15 - 10) = -3/5 = -0.60.$

Again, this problem can also be worked using most financial calculators with statistical functions.

A-3. b. $k_N = 7\% + (10\% - 7\%)(-0.60) = 7\% + (-1.80\%) = 5.20\%.$

A-4. d. Use the regression feature of the calculator. Enter data for the Market and Stock Y, and then find $\text{Beta}_Y = 1.3374$ rounded to 1.34.

A-5. a. We know $k_M = 15\%$; $k^* = 3.75\%$; $IP = 5\%$.
Original $RP_M = k_M - k_{RF} = 15\% - (3.75\% + 5\%) = 6.25\%.$

RP_M increases by 3% to 9.25%.

Find the change in $k = \Delta k$ for the riskier stock.

First, find the betas for the two stocks. Enter data in the regression register, then find $b_Y = 1.3374$ and $b_Z = 0.6161.$

Y is the riskier stock. Originally, its required return was $k_Y = 8.75\% + 6.25\%(1.3374)$ = 17.11%. When RP_M increases by 3 percent, $k_Y = 8.75\% + (6.25\% + 3\%)(1.3374) =$ 21.12%. Difference = 21.12% – 17.11% = 4.01%.

CHAPTER 6
TIME VALUE OF MONEY

LEARNING OBJECTIVES

- Convert time value of money (TVM) problems from words to time lines.

- Explain the relationship between compounding and discounting, between future and present value.

- Calculate the future value of some beginning amount, and find the present value of a single payment to be received in the future.

- Solve for time or interest rate, given the other three variables in the TVM equation.

- Find the future value of a series of equal, periodic payments (an annuity) as well as the present value of such an annuity.

- Explain the difference between an ordinary annuity and an annuity due, and calculate the difference in their values.

- Calculate the value of a perpetuity.

- Demonstrate how to find the present and future values of an uneven series of cash flows.

- Distinguish among the following interest rates: Nominal (or Quoted) rate, Periodic rate, and Effective (or Equivalent) Annual Rate; and properly choose between securities with different compounding periods.

- Solve time value of money problems with fractional time periods.

- Construct loan amortization schedules for both fully-amortized and partially-amortized loans.

OVERVIEW

A dollar in the hand today is worth more than a dollar to be received in the future because, if you had it now, you could invest that dollar and earn interest. Of all the techniques used in finance, none is more important than the concept of time value of money, also called discounted cash flow (DCF) analysis. It is essential for financial managers to have a clear understanding of the time value of money and its impact on stock prices.

Future value and present value techniques can be applied to a single cash flow (lump sum), ordinary annuities, annuities due, and uneven cash flow streams. Future and present values can be calculated using a regular calculator, a calculator with financial functions, or a computer spreadsheet program. The principles of time value analysis have many applications, ranging from setting up schedules for paying off loans to decisions about whether to acquire new equipment.

OUTLINE

The time line is one of the most important tools in time value of money calculations. Time lines help visualize what is happening in a particular problem. Cash flows are placed directly below the tick marks, and interest rates are shown directly above the time line; unknown cash flows are indicated by question marks. Thus, to find the future value of $100 after 5 years at 5 percent interest, the following time line can be set up:

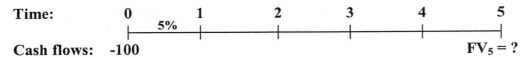

Finding the future value (FV), or compounding, is the process of going from today's values (or present values) to future amounts (or future values). The future value is calculated as

$$FV_n = PV(1 + i)^n,$$

where PV = present value, or beginning amount; i = interest rate per year; and n = number of periods involved in the analysis. This equation can be solved in one of three ways: numerically, with a financial calculator, or with a computer spreadsheet program. For calculations, assume the following data that were presented in the time line above: present value (PV) = $100, interest rate (i) = 5%, and number of years (n) = 5.

■   To solve numerically, use a regular calculator to find 1 + i = 1.05 raised to the fifth power, which equals 1.2763. Multiply this figure by PV = $100 to get the final answer of $FV_5 = \$127.63$.

■ With a financial calculator, the future value can be found by using the time value of money input keys, where N = number of periods, I = interest rate per period, PV = present value, PMT = payment, and FV = future value. By entering N = 5, I = 5, PV = -100, and PMT = 0, and then pressing the FV key, the answer 127.63 is displayed.
  ☐ Some financial calculators require that all cash flows be designated as either inflows or outflows, thus an outflow must be entered as a negative number (for example, PV = -100 instead of PV = 100).
  ☐ Some calculators require you to press a "Compute" key before pressing the FV key.

■ Spreadsheet programs are ideally suited for solving many financial problems, including time value of money problems. With very little effort, the spreadsheet itself becomes a time line.

■ A graph of the compounding process shows how any sum grows over time at various interest rates. The greater the interest rate, the faster the growth rate.
  ☐ Time value concepts can be applied to anything that is growing—sales, population, earnings per share, or your future salary.

Finding present values is called discounting, and it is simply the reverse of compounding. In general, the present value of a cash flow due n years in the future is the amount which, if it were on hand today, would grow to equal the future amount. By solving for PV in the future value equation, the present value, or discounting, equation can be developed and written as follows:

$$PV = \frac{FV_n}{(1+i)^n} = FV_n \left(\frac{1}{1+i}\right)^n.$$

■ To solve for the present value of $127.63 discounted back 5 years at a 5% *opportunity cost rate*, the rate of return that could be earned on an alternative investment of similar risk, one can utilize any of the three solution methods:
  ☐ Numerical solution: Divide $127.63 by 1.05 five times to get PV = $100.
  ☐ Financial calculator solution: Enter N = 5, I = 5, PMT = 0, and FV = 127.63, and then press the PV key to get PV = -100.
  ☐ With *Excel*, you can use the built-in spreadsheet PV function to solve for PV = 100.

■ A graph of the *discounting process* shows how the present value of any sum to be received in the future diminishes as the years to receipt increases. At relatively high interest rates, funds due in the future are worth very little today, and even at a relatively low discount rate, the present value of a sum due in the very distant future is quite small.

There are four variables in the time value of money compounding and discounting equations: PV, FV, i, and n. If three of the four variables are known, you can find the value of the fourth.

■ If we are given PV, FV, and n, we can determine i by substituting the known values into either the present value or future value equations, and then solving for i. Thus, if you can buy a security at a price of $78.35 that will pay you $100 after 5 years, what is the interest rate earned on the investment?

   ☐ Numerical solution: Use a trial and error process to reach the 5% value for i. This is a tedious and inefficient process.

   ☐ Financial calculator solution: Enter N = 5, PV = -78.35, PMT = 0, and FV = 100, then press the I key, and I = 5 is displayed.

   ☐ Computer spreadsheet program: Most spreadsheets have a built-in function to find the interest rate.

■ Likewise, if we are given PV, FV, and i, we can determine n by substituting the known values into either the present value or future value equations, and then solving for n. Thus, if you can buy a security with a 5 percent interest rate at a price of $78.35 today, how long will it take for your investment to return $100?

   ☐ Numerical solution: Use a trial and error process to reach the value of 5 for n. This is a tedious and inefficient process.

   ☐ Financial calculator solution: Enter I = 5, PV = -78.35, PMT = 0, and FV = 100, then press the N key, and N = 5 is displayed.

   ☐ Computer spreadsheet program: In *Excel* you can use either the goal-seeking or solver functions on the Tools menu to solve the TVM equation for n.

An annuity is a series of equal payments made at fixed intervals for a specified number of periods. If the payments occur at the end of each period, as they typically do, the annuity is an ordinary (or deferred) annuity. If the payments occur at the beginning of each period, it is called an annuity due.

■ The *future value of an annuity, FVA$_n$*, is the total amount one would have at the end of the annuity period if each payment were invested at a given interest rate and held to the end of the annuity period.

   ☐ Defining FVA$_n$ as the compound sum of an ordinary annuity of n years, and PMT as the periodic payment, we can write

$$FVA_n = PMT \sum_{t=1}^{n} (1+i)^{n-t} .$$

☐ With a financial calculator, the future value of an ordinary annuity can be found as follows: Enter N = 3, I = 5, PV = 0, and PMT = -100. Then press the FV key, and 315.25 is displayed.

☐ Most spreadsheets have a built-in function to find the future value of an annuity. The function allows you to specify the annuity "type," that is, whether the annuity is an ordinary annuity or an annuity due.

☐ For an annuity due, each payment is compounded for one additional period, so the future value of the entire annuity is equal to the future value of an ordinary annuity compounded for one additional period.

☐ Most financial calculators have a switch, or key, marked "DUE" or "BEG" that permits you to switch from end-of-period payments (an ordinary annuity) to beginning-of-period payments (an annuity due). Switch your calculator to "BEG" mode, and calculate as you would for an ordinary annuity. Do not forget to switch your calculator back to "END" mode when you are finished.

■ The *present value of an annuity* is the single (lump sum) payment today that would be equivalent to the annuity payments spread over the annuity period. It is the amount today that would permit withdrawals of an equal amount (PMT) at the end (or beginning for an annuity due) of each period for n periods.

☐ Defining PVA_n as the present value of an ordinary annuity of n years and PMT as the periodic payment, we can write

$$PVA_n = PMT \sum_{t=1}^{n} \left(\frac{1}{1+i} \right)^t .$$

☐ Using a financial calculator, enter N = 3, I = 5, PMT = -100, and FV = 0, and then press the PV key, for an answer of $272.32.

☐ Most spreadsheets have a built-in function to find the present value of an annuity. The function allows you to specify the annuity "type," that is, whether the annuity is an ordinary annuity or an annuity due.

☐ For an annuity due, each payment is discounted for one less period, so the present value of the entire annuity is equal to the present value of an ordinary annuity multiplied by (1 + i).

☐ Using a financial calculator, switch to the "BEG" mode, and then enter N = 3, I = 5, PMT = -100, and FV = 0, and then press PV to get the answer, $285.94. Again, do not forget to switch your calculator back to "END" mode when you are finished.

An annuity that goes on indefinitely is called a perpetuity. The payments of a perpetuity constitute an infinite series.

■　　The present value of a perpetuity is:

$$PV \text{ (Perpetuity)} = \text{Payment/Interest rate} = PMT/i.$$

■　　For example, if the interest rate were 12 percent, a perpetuity of $1,000 a year would have a present value of $1,000/0.12 = $8,333.33.

■　　The value of a perpetuity changes dramatically when interest rates change.

Many financial decisions require the analysis of uneven, or nonconstant, cash flows rather than a stream of fixed payments such as an annuity.

■　　The present value of an uneven stream of income is the sum of the PVs of the individual cash flow components. Similarly, the future value of an uneven stream of income is the sum of the FVs of the individual cash flow components. *PMT (payment)* is the term designated for equal cash flows coming at regular intervals, while *CF (cash flow)* is the term designated for uneven cash flows.

　　☐ With a financial calculator, enter each cash flow (beginning with the $t = 0$ cash flow) into the cash flow register, CF_j, enter the appropriate interest rate, and then press the NPV key to obtain the PV of the cash flow stream.

　　☐ Some calculators have a net future value (NFV) key that allows you to obtain the FV of an uneven cash flow stream, or *terminal value*.

　　　　● Even if your calculator doesn't have the NFV feature, you can use the cash flow stream's net present value to find its net future value:

$$NFV = NPV(1 + i)^n.$$

　　☐ Spreadsheets are especially useful for solving problems with uneven cash flows. Just as with a financial calculator, you must enter the cash flows in the spreadsheet. To find the PV of an uneven cash flow stream, you can use *Excel's* NPV function.

■　　If one knows the relevant cash flows, the effective interest rate can be calculated efficiently with a financial calculator. Enter each cash flow (beginning with the $t = 0$ cash flow) into the cash flow register, CF_j, and then press the IRR key to obtain the interest rate of an uneven cash flow stream.

　　☐ *Excel* has an IRR function that can be used to obtain the interest rate of an uneven cash flow stream.

Semiannual, quarterly, and other compounding periods more frequent than an annual basis are often used in financial transactions. Compounding on a nonannual basis requires an adjustment to both the compounding and discounting procedures discussed previously.

■ The *effective annual rate* (*EAR* or *EFF%*) is the rate that would have produced the final compounded value under annual compounding. The effective annual percentage rate is given by the following formula:

$$\text{Effective annual rate (EAR)} = \text{EFF\%} = (1 + i_{Nom}/m)^m - 1.0,$$

where i_{Nom} is the *nominal, or quoted, interest rate* and m is the number of compounding periods per year. The EAR is useful in comparing securities with different compounding periods.

■ For example, to find the effective annual rate if the nominal rate is 6 percent and semiannual compounding is used, we have:

$$\text{EAR} = (1 + 0.06/2)^2 - 1.0 = 6.09\%.$$

■ For annual compounding use the formula to find the future value of a single payment (lump sum):

$$FV_n = PV(1 + i)^n.$$

☐ When compounding occurs more frequently than once a year, use this formula:

$$FV_n = PV(1 + i_{Nom}/m)^{mn}.$$

Here m is the number of times per year compounding occurs, and n is the number of years.

■ The *annual percentage rate (APR)* is the periodic rate times the number of periods per year.

■ The amount to which $1,000 will grow after 5 years if quarterly compounding is applied to a nominal 8 percent interest rate is found as follows:

$$FV_n = \$1,000(1 + 0.08/4)^{(4)(5)} = \$1,000(1.02)^{20} = \$1,485.95.$$

☐ Financial calculator solution: Enter N = 20, I = 2, PV = -1000, and PMT = 0, and then press the FV key to find FV = $1,485.95.
☐ Spreadsheet program solution: The spreadsheet developed to find the future value of a lump sum under quarterly compounding would look like the one for annual compounding, with two changes: The interest rate would be quartered, and the time line would show four times as many periods.

■ The present value of a 5-year future investment equal to $1,485.95, with an 8 percent nominal interest rate, compounded quarterly, is found as follows:

$$\$1,485.95 = PV(1 + 0.08/4)^{(4)(5)}$$
$$PV = \frac{\$1,485.95}{(1.02)^{20}} = \$1,000.$$

- ☐ Financial calculator solution: Enter N = 20, I = 2, PMT = 0, and FV = 1485.95, and then press the PV key to find PV = -$1,000.00.
- ☐ Spreadsheet program solution: The spreadsheet developed to find the present value of a lump sum under quarterly compounding would look like the one for annual compounding, with two changes: The interest rate would be quartered, and the time line would show four times as many periods.

The nominal rate is the rate that is quoted by borrowers and lenders. Nominal rates can only be compared with one another if the instruments being compared use the same number of compounding periods per year. Note also that the nominal rate is never shown on a time line, or used as an input in a financial calculator, unless compounding occurs only once a year. In general, nonannual compounding can be handled one of two ways:

- ■ State everything on a periodic rather than on an annual basis. Thus, n = 6 periods rather than n = 3 years and i = 3% instead of i = 6% with semiannual compounding.

- ■ Find the effective annual rate (EAR) with the equation below and then use the EAR as the rate over the given number of years.

$$EAR = \left(1 + \frac{i_{Nom}}{m}\right)^m - 1.0.$$

Fractional time periods are used when payments occur within periods, instead of at either the beginning or the end of periods. Solving these problems requires using the fraction of the time period for n, number of periods, and then solving numerically, with a financial calculator, or with a computer spreadsheet program. (Some older calculators will produce incorrect answers because of their internal "solution" programs.)

An important application of compound interest involves amortized loans, which are paid off in equal installments over time.

- ■ With a financial calculator, enter N (number of years), I (interest rate), PV (amount borrowed), and FV = 0, and then press the PMT key to find the periodic payment.

- ■ Each payment consists partly of interest and partly of the repayment of principal. This breakdown is often developed in a *loan amortization schedule*.

☐ The interest component is largest in the first period, and it declines over the life of the loan.

☐ The repayment of principal is smallest in the first period, and it increases thereafter.

■ Financial calculators are programmed to calculate amortization tables.

■ Spreadsheets are ideal for developing amortization tables.

■ Many loans are set up on a *partial amortization basis*, with a *balloon payment* coming due at some date before the loan has been fully amortized.

☐ The set up is similar to a regular amortization schedule except that the final payment includes a balloon payment because the loan was only partially amortized.

Web Appendix 6B discusses the formulas necessary for continuous compounding and discounting. The equation for continuous compounding is $FV_n = PV(e^{in})$ where e is the approximate value 2.7183; the equation for continuous discounting is $PV = FV_n(e^{-in})$.

SELF-TEST QUESTIONS

Definitional

1. The beginning value of an account or investment in a project is known as its _____ _____.

2. The difference between a savings account's present value and its future value at the end of the period is due to _____ earned during the period.

3. The process of finding present values is often referred to as _____ and is the reverse of the _____ process.

4. A series of payments of a constant amount for a specified number of periods is a(n) _____. If the payments occur at the end of each period it is a(n) _____ annuity, while if the payments occur at the beginning of each period it is an annuity _____.

5. The present value of an uneven stream of future payments is the _____ of the PVs of the individual payments.

6. Since different types of investments use different compounding periods, it is important to distinguish between the quoted, or _____, rate and the _____ annual interest rate.

7. The _____ _____ is one of the most important tools in time value of money calculations; it helps visualize what is happening.

8. An annuity that goes on indefinitely is called a(n) _____.

9. _____ loans are those that are paid off in equal installments over time.

10. The breakdown of each payment as partly interest and partly principal is developed in a(n) _____ _____ _____.

11. The _____ _____ _____ is the rate of return that could be earned on an alternative investment of similar risk.

12. _____ is the term designated for equal cash flows coming at regular intervals, while ____ is the term designated for uneven cash flows.

13. The _____ _____ _____ is that rate that would have produced the final compounded value under annual compounding.

14. The _____ _____ _____ is the periodic rate times the number of periods per year.

15. Many loans are set up on a partial amortization basis, with a(n) _____ _____ coming due at some date before the loan has been fully amortized.

Conceptual

16. If a bank uses quarterly compounding for savings accounts, the nominal rate will be greater than the effective annual rate (EAR).

    a. True   **b.** False

17. If money has time value (that is, i > 0), the future value of some amount of money will always be more than the amount invested. The present value of some amount to be received in the future is always less than the amount to be received.

    a. True   **b.** False

18.   You have determined the profitability of a planned project by finding the present value of all the cash flows from that project. Which of the following would cause the project to look less appealing, that is, have a lower present value?

a.   The discount rate decreases.
b.   The cash flows are extended over a longer period of time.
c.   The discount rate increases.
d.   Statements b and c are correct.
e.   Statements a and b are correct.

19.   As the discount rate increases without limit, the present value of a future cash inflow

a.   Gets larger without limit.
b.   Stays unchanged.
c.   Approaches zero.
d.   Gets smaller without limit; that is, approaches minus infinity.
e.   Goes to e^{in}.

20.   Which of the following statements is most correct?

a.   Except in situations where compounding occurs annually, the periodic interest rate exceeds the nominal interest rate.
b.   The effective annual rate always exceeds the nominal rate, no matter how few or many compounding periods occur each year.
c.   If compounding occurs more frequently than once a year, and if payments are made at times other than at the end of compounding periods, it is impossible to determine present or future values, even with a financial calculator. The reason is that under these conditions, the basic assumptions of discounted cash flow analysis are not met.
d.   Assume that compounding occurs quarterly, that the nominal interest rate is 8 percent, and that you need to find the present value of $1,000 due 6 months from today. You could get the correct answer by discounting the $1,000 at 2 percent for 2 periods.
e.   All of the above statements are false.

SELF-TEST PROBLEMS

(Note: In working these problems, you may get an answer that differs from ours by a few cents due to rounding differences. This should not concern you; just pick the closest answer.)

1.   Assume that you purchase a 6-year, 8 percent savings certificate for $1,000. If interest is compounded annually, what will be the value of the certificate when it matures?

a. $630.17   b. $1,469.33   c. $1,677.10   d. $1,586.87   e. $1,766.33

2. Refer to Self-Test Problem 1. A savings certificate similar to the one in the previous problem is available with the exception that interest is compounded semiannually. What is the difference between the ending value of the savings certificate compounded semiannually and the one compounded annually?

    a. The semiannual is worth $14.16 more than the annual.
    b. The semiannual is worth $14.16 less than the annual.
    c. The semiannual is worth $21.54 more than the annual.
    d. The semiannual is worth $21.54 less than the annual.
    e. The semiannual is worth the same as the annual.

3. A friend promises to pay you $600 two years from now if you loan him $500 today. What annual interest rate is your friend offering?

    a. 7.5%   b. 8.5%   c. 9.5%   d. 10.5%   e. 11.5%

4. At an inflation rate of 9 percent, the purchasing power of $1 would be cut in half in just over 8 years (some calculators round to 9 years). How long, to the nearest year, would it take for the purchasing power of $1 to be cut in half if the inflation rate were only 4 percent?

    a. 12 years   b. 15 years   c. 18 years   d. 20 years   e. 23 years

5. Jane Smith has $20,000 in a brokerage account, and she plans to contribute an additional $7,500 to the account at the end of every year. The brokerage account has an expected annual return of 8 percent. If Jane's goal is to accumulate $375,000 in the account, how many years will it take for Jane to reach her goal?

    a. 5.20   b. 10.00   c. 12.50   d. 16.33   e. 18.40

6. You are offered an investment opportunity with the "guarantee" that your investment will double in 5 years. Assuming annual compounding, what annual rate of return would this investment provide?

    a. 40.00%   b. 100.00%   c. 14.87%   d. 20.00%   e. 18.74%

7. You decide to begin saving towards the purchase of a new car in 5 years. If you put $1,000 at the end of each of the next 5 years in a savings account paying 6 percent compounded annually, how much will you accumulate after 5 years?

    a. $6,691.13   b. $5,637.09   c. $1,338.23   d. $5,975.32   e. $5,731.94

8.   Refer to Self-Test Problem 7. What would be the ending amount if the payments were made at the beginning of each year?

   a. $6,691.13   **b.** $5,637.09   **c.** $1,338.23   **d.** $5,975.32   **e.** $5,731.94

9.   Refer to Self-Test Problem 7. What would be the ending amount if $500 payments were made at the end of each 6-month period for 5 years and the account paid 6 percent compounded semiannually?

   a. $6,691.13   **b.** $5,637.09   **c.** $1,338.23   **d.** $5,975.32   **e.** $5,731.94

10. Calculate the present value of $1,000 to be received at the end of 8 years. Assume an interest rate of 7 percent.

   a. $582.01   **b.** $1,718.19   **c.** $531.82   **d.** $5,971.30   **e.** $649.37

11. How much would you be willing to pay today for an investment that would return $800 each year at the end of each of the next 6 years? Assume a discount rate of 5 percent.

   a. $5,441.53   **b.** $4,800.00   **c.** $3,369.89   **d.** $4,060.55   **e.** $4,632.37

12. You have applied for a mortgage of $60,000 to finance the purchase of a new home. The bank will require you to make annual payments of $7,047.55 at the end of each of the next 20 years. Determine the interest rate in effect on this mortgage.

   a. 8.0%   **b.** 9.8%   **c.** 10.0%   **d.** 51.0%   **e.** 11.2%

13. If you would like to accumulate $7,500 over the next 5 years, how much must you deposit each six months, starting six months from now, given a 6 percent interest rate and semiannual compounding?

   a. $1,330.47   **b.** $879.23   **c.** $654.23   **d.** $569.00   **e.** $732.67

14. A company is offering bonds that pay $100 per year indefinitely. If you require a 12 percent return on these bonds—that is, the discount rate is 12 percent—what is the value of each bond?

   a. $1,000.00   **b.** $962.00   **c.** $904.67   **d.** $866.67   **e.** $833.33

15. What is the present value (t = 0) of the following cash flows if the discount rate is 12 percent?

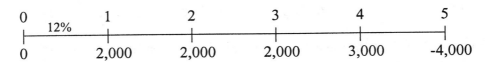

a. $4,782.43 b. $4,440.51 c. $4,221.79 d. $4,041.23 e. $3,997.98

16. What is the effective annual rate (EAR) of 12 percent compounded monthly?

a. 12.00% b. 12.55% c. 12.68% d. 12.75% e. 13.00%

17. Martha Mills, manager of Plaza Gold Emporium, wants to sell on credit, giving customers 4 months in which to pay. However, Martha will have to borrow from her bank to carry the accounts receivable. The bank will charge a nominal 18 percent, but with monthly compounding. Martha wants to quote a nominal rate to her customers (all of whom are expected to pay on time at the end of 4 months) *that will exactly cover her financing costs*. What nominal annual rate should she quote to her credit customers?

a. 15.44% b. 19.56% c. 17.11% d. 18.41% e. 16.88%

18. Self-Test Problem 12 refers to a 20-year mortgage of $60,000. This is an amortized loan. How much principal will be repaid in the second year?

a. $1,152.30 b. $1,725.70 c. $5,895.25 d. $7,047.55 e. $1,047.55

19. You have $1,000 invested in an account that pays 16 percent compounded annually. A commission agent (called a "finder") can locate for you an equally safe deposit that will pay 16 percent, compounded quarterly, for 2 years. What is the maximum amount you should be willing to pay him now as a fee for locating the new account?

a. $10.92 b. $13.78 c. $16.14 d. $16.78 e. $21.13

20. The present value (t = 0) of the following cash flow stream is $11,958.20 when discounted at 12 percent annually. What is the value of the missing t = 2 cash flow?

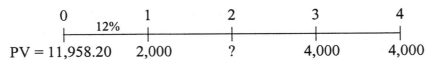

a. $4,000.00 b. $4,500.00 c. $5,000.33 d. $5,500.50 e. $6,000.16

21. Today is your birthday, and you decide to start saving for your college education. You will begin college on your 18th birthday and will need $4,000 per year at the *end* of each of the following 4 years. You will make a deposit 1 year from today in an account paying 12 percent annually and continue to make an identical deposit each year up to and including the year you begin college. If a deposit amount of $2,542.05 will allow you to reach your goal, what birthday are you celebrating today?

    a. 13   **b.** 14   **c.** 15   **d.** 16   **e.** 17

22. Assume that your aunt sold her house on December 31 and that she took a mortgage in the amount of $50,000 as part of the payment. The mortgage has a stated (or nominal) interest rate of 8 percent, but it calls for payments every 6 months, beginning on June 30, and the mortgage is to be amortized over 20 years. Now, one year later, your aunt must file Schedule B of her tax return with the IRS informing them of the interest that was included in the two payments made during the year. (This interest will be income to your aunt and a deduction to the buyer of the house.) What is the total amount of interest that was paid during the first year?

    a. $1,978.95   **b.** $526.17   **c.** $3,978.95   **d.** $2,000.00   **e.** $750.02

23. Assume that you inherited some money. A friend of yours is working as an unpaid intern at a local brokerage firm, and her boss is selling some securities that call for five payments, $75 at the end of each of the next 4 years, plus a payment of $1,075 at the end of Year 5. Your friend says she can get you some of these securities at a cost of $960 each. Your money is now invested in a bank that pays an 8 percent nominal (quoted) interest rate, but with quarterly compounding. You regard the securities as being just as safe, and as liquid, as your bank deposit, so your required effective annual rate of return on the securities is the same as that on your bank deposit. You must calculate the value of the securities to decide whether they are a good investment. What is their present value to you?

    a. $957.75   **b.** $888.66   **c.** $923.44   **d.** $1,015.25   **e.** $970.51

24. Your company is planning to borrow $500,000 on a 5-year, 7 percent, annual payment, fully amortized term loan. What fraction of the payment made at the end of the second year will represent repayment of principal?

    a. 76.29%   **b.** 42.82%   **c.** 50.28%   **d.** 49.72%   **e.** 60.27%

25. Your firm can borrow from its bank for one month. The loan will have to be "rolled over" at the end of the month, but you are sure the rollover will be allowed. The nominal interest rate is 14 percent, but interest will have to be paid at the end of each month, so the bank interest rate is 14 percent, monthly compounding. Alternatively, your firm can borrow from an insurance company at a nominal rate that would involve quarterly compounding. What nominal quarterly rate would be equivalent to the rate charged by the bank?

   a. 12.44%   **b.** 14.16%   **c.** 13.55%   **d.** 13.12%   **e.** 12.88%

26. Assume that you have $15,000 in a bank account that pays 5 percent annual interest. You plan to go back to school for a combination MBA/law degree 5 years from today. It will take you an additional 5 years to complete your graduate studies. You figure you will need a fixed income of $25,000 in today's dollars; that is, you will need $25,000 of today's dollars during your first year and each subsequent year. (*Thus, your real income will decline while you are in school.*) You will withdraw funds for your annual expenses at the beginning of each year. Inflation is expected to occur at the rate of 3 percent per year. How much must you save during each of the next 5 years in order to achieve your goal? The first increment of savings will be deposited one year from today.

   a. $20,241.66   **b.** $19,224.55   **c.** $18,792.11   **d.** $19,559.42   **e.** $20,378.82

27. You plan to buy a new HDTV. The dealer offers to sell the set to you on credit. You will have 3 months in which to pay, but the dealer says you will be charged a 15 percent interest rate; that is, the nominal rate is 15 percent, quarterly compounding. As an alternative to buying on credit, you can borrow the funds from your bank, but the bank will make you pay interest each month. At what nominal bank interest rate should you be indifferent between the two types of credit?

   a. 13.7643%   **b.** 14.2107%   **c.** 14.8163%   **d.** 15.5397%   **e.** 15.3984%

28. Assume that your father is now 40 years old, that he plans to retire in 20 years, and that he expects to live for 25 years after he retires, that is, until he is 85. He wants a fixed retirement income that has the same purchasing power at the time he retires as $75,000 has today. (He realizes that the real value of his retirement income will decline year-by-year after he retires.) His retirement income will begin the day he retires, 20 years from today, and he will then get 24 additional annual payments. Inflation is expected to be 4 percent per year from today forward; he currently has $200,000 saved up; and he expects to earn a return on his savings of 7 percent per year, annual compounding. To the nearest dollar, how much must he save during each of the next 20 years (with deposits being made at the end of each year) to meet his retirement goal?

   a. $31,105.90   **b.** $35,709.25   **c.** $54,332.88   **d.** $41,987.33   **e.** $62,191.25

29. A rookie quarterback is in the process of negotiating his first contract. The team's general manager has offered him three possible contracts. Each of the contracts lasts for four years. All of the money is guaranteed and is paid at the end of each year. The payment terms of the contracts are listed below:

Year	Contract 1	Contract 2	Contract 3
1	$1.5 million	$1.0 million	$3.5 million
2	1.5 million	1.5 million	0.5 million
3	1.5 million	2.0 million	0.5 million
4	1.5 million	2.5 million	0.5 million

The quarterback discounts all cash flows at 12 percent. Which of the three contracts offers the most value?

   a. Contract 1; its present value is $4.56 million.
   b. Contract 2; its present value is $5.10 million.
   c. Contract 3; its present value is $4.20 million.
   d. Either Contract 2 or Contract 3; each provides a present value of $5.10 million.
   e. Either Contract 1 or Contract 2; each provides a present value of $5.10 million.

(The following data apply to the next four Self-Test Problems.)

The Wade family is interested in buying a home. The family is applying for a $200,000 30-year mortgage. Under the terms of the mortgage, they will receive $200,000 today to help purchase their home. The loan will be fully amortized over the next 30 years. Current mortgage rates are 7.5 percent. Interest is compounded monthly and all payments are due at the end of the month.

30. What is the monthly mortgage payment?

   a. $989.66   b. $1,047.50   c. $1,111.25   d. $1,398.43   e. $1,563.97

31. What portion of the mortgage payments during the first year will go toward interest?

   a. 89%   b. 100%   c. 75%   d. 65%   e. 95%

32. What will be the remaining balance on the mortgage after five years?

   a. $73,141   b. $166,752   c. $189,235   d. $195,750   e. $190,433

33. How much could the Wades borrow today if they were willing to have an $1,800 monthly mortgage payment? (Assume that the interest rate and the length of the loan remain the same.)

    a. $225,557   **b.** $257,432   **c.** $210,333   **d.** $244,125   **e.** $253,456

(The following data apply to the next three Self-Test Problems.)

Janet and Denise have both been given $15,000 by their grandparents today on their 21st birthdays. They want to save for their future and have aspirations of one day being millionaires. Each woman plans to make annual contributions on her birthday, beginning next year. Janet and Denise have each opened investment accounts at the 1st National Bank and 2nd National Bank, respectively, and they expect to earn nominal returns of 6% and 7%, respectively. Janet has already decided to deposit $7,500 each year into her investment account, while Denise is unsure of the amount she will deposit annually.

34. How many years will it take Janet before she reaches her investment goal of $1 million?

    a. 20.33   **b.** 25.50   **c.** 30.00   **d.** 32.45   **e.** 35.76

35. If Denise decides to make the same annual contributions as Janet, how much sooner (in years) would she reach the investment goal?

    a. 2.50   **b.** 3.18   **c.** 3.75   **d.** 4.00   **e.** 4.25

36. Suppose Denise was interested in reaching the investment goal at the same time as Janet. What is the minimum monthly contribution she could make in order to reach $1 million at the same time as Janet?

    a. $5,683.44   **b.** $4,250.00   **c.** $6,195.76   **d.** $5,333.33   **e.** $4,888.97

(The following data apply to the next three Self-Test Problems.)

John has just won the state lottery and has three award options to choose from. He can elect to receive a lump sum payment today of $46 million, 10 annual end-of-year payments of $7 million, or 30 annual end-of-year payments of $4 million.

37. If he expects to earn a 7% annual return on his investments, which option should he choose?

    a. Lump sum   **b.** 10 payments   **c.** 30 payments

38. If he expects to earn an 8% annual return on his investments, which option should he choose?

   a. Lump sum   **b.** 10 payments   **c.** 30 payments

39. If he expects to earn a 9% annual return on his investments, which option should he choose?

   a. Lump sum   **b.** 10 payments   **c.** 30 payments

(The following data apply to the next two Self-Test Problems.)

Henry has saved $5,000 and intends to use his savings as a down payment on a new car. After careful examination of his income and expenses, Henry has concluded that the most he can afford to spend every month on his car payment is $425. The car loan that Henry uses to buy the car will have an APR of 10%.

40. What is the price of the most expensive car that Henry can afford if he finances his new car for 48 months?

   a. $16,756.97   **b.** $17,500.00   **c.** $19,125.25   **d.** $21,756.97   **e.** $22,450.50

41. What is the price of the most expensive car that Henry can afford if he finances his new car for 60 months?

   a. $18,333.33   **b.** $20,002.78   **c.** $21,756.97   **d.** $23,750.00   **e.** $25,002.78

Web Appendix 6B

B-1. If you receive $30,000 today and can invest it at a 4 percent annual rate compounded continuously, then what will its future value be in 10 years?

   a. $31,224.32   **b.** $38,327.77   **c.** $40,765.66   **d.** $44,754.74   **e.** $42,121.00

B-2. What is the present value of $125,000 due in 15 years, if the appropriate continuous discount rate is 6 percent?

   a. $44,754.74   **b.** $50,821.21   **c.** $38,327.77   **d.** $42,121.00   **e.** $40,765.66

ANSWERS TO SELF-TEST QUESTIONS

1. present value
2. interest
3. discounting; compounding
4. annuity; ordinary; due
5. sum
6. nominal; effective
7. time line
8. perpetuity

9. Amortized
10. loan amortization schedule
11. opportunity cost rate
12. PMT; CF
13. effective annual rate
14. annual percentage rate
15. balloon payment

16. b. The EAR is always greater than or equal to the nominal rate.

17. a. Both these statements are correct.

18. d. The slower the cash flows come in and the higher the interest rate, the smaller the present value.

19. c. As the discount rate increases, the present value of a future sum decreases and eventually approaches zero.

20. d. Statement a is false because the periodic interest rate is equal to the nominal rate divided by the number of compounding periods, so it will be equal to or smaller than the nominal rate. Statement b is false because the EAR will equal the nominal rate if there is one compounding period per year (annual compounding). Statement c is false because we can determine present or future values under the stated conditions. Statement d is correct; using a financial calculator, enter N = 2, I = 2, PMT = 0, and FV = 1000 to find PV = -961.1688.

SOLUTIONS TO SELF-TEST PROBLEMS

1. d.

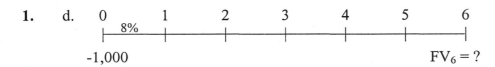

With a financial calculator, input N = 6, I = 8, PV = -1000, PMT = 0, and solve for FV = $1,586.87.

2. a.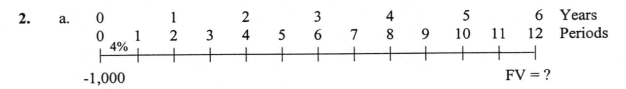

    With a financial calculator, input N = 12, I = 4, PV = -1000, and PMT = 0, and then solve for FV = $1,601.03. The difference, $1,601.03 – $1,586.87 = $14.16.

3. c.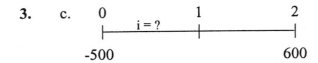

    With a financial calculator, input N = 2, PV = -500, PMT = 0, FV = 600, and solve for I = 9.54% ≈ 9.5%.

4. c. 0   N = ?
           4%
        ├──────────────┤
        1.00   0.50

    With a financial calculator, input I = 4, PV = -1.00, PMT = 0, and FV = 0.50. Solve for N = 17.67 ≈ 18 years.

5. e. Using your financial calculator, enter the following data: I = 8; PV = -20000; PMT = -7500; FV = 375000; N = ? Solve for N = 18.4. It will take 18.4 years for Jane to accumulate $375,000.

6. c. 0   1   2   3   4   5
           i = ?
        ├──┼──────┼──────┼──────┼──────┤
        -1   2

    Assume any value for the present value and double it:

    With a financial calculator, input N = 5, PV = -1, PMT = 0, FV = 2, and solve for I = 14.87%.

7. **b.**

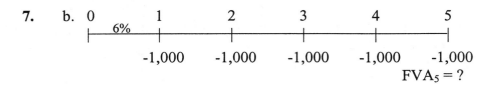

With a financial calculator, input N = 5, I = 6, PV = 0, PMT = -1000, and solve for FV = $5,637.09.

8. **d.**

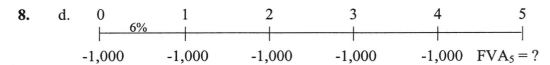

With a financial calculator, switch to "BEG" mode, then input N = 5, I = 6, PV = 0, PMT = -1000, and solve for FV = $5,975.32. Be sure to switch back to "END" mode.

9. **e.**

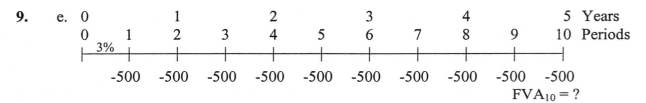

With a financial calculator, input N = 10, I = 3, PV = 0, PMT = -500, and solve for FV = $5,731.94.

10. **a.**

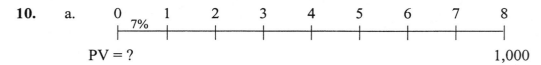

With a financial calculator, input N = 8, I = 7, PMT = 0, FV = 1000, and solve for PV = -$582.01.

(Note: Annual compounding is assumed if not otherwise specified.)

11. **d.**

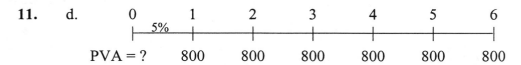

With a financial calculator, input N = 6, I = 5, PMT = 800, FV = 0, and solve for PV = -$4,060.55.

12. **c.**

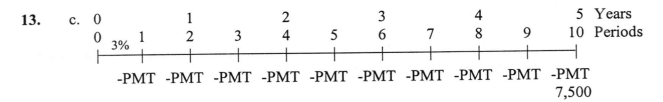

With a financial calculator, input N = 20, PV = 60000, PMT = -7047.55, FV = 0, and solve for I = 10.00%.

13. **c.**

-PMT -PMT -PMT -PMT -PMT -PMT -PMT -PMT -PMT -PMT
7,500

With a financial calculator, input N = 10, I = 3, PV = 0, FV = 7500, and solve for PMT = -$654.23.

14. **e.** PV = PMT/i = $100/0.12 = $833.33.

15. **b.** With a financial calculator, using the cash flow register, CF_j, input 0; 2000; 2000; 2000; 3000; and -4000. Enter I = 12 and solve for NPV = $4,440.51.

16. **c.**
$$EAR = (1 + i_{Nom}/m)^m - 1.0$$
$$= (1 + 0.12/12)^{12} - 1.0$$
$$= (1.01)^{12} - 1.0$$
$$= 1.1268 - 1.0$$
$$= 0.1268 = 12.68\%.$$

With a financial calculator, enter P/YR = 12 and NOM% = 12, and then solve for EFF% = 12.68%. Don't forget to return P/YR = 1 after solving this problem.

17. **d.** Here we want to have the same effective annual rate on the credit extended as on the bank loan that will be used to finance the credit extension.

First, we must find the EAR = EFF% on the bank loan. With a financial calculator, enter P/YR = 12, NOM% = 18, and press EFF% to get EAR = 19.56%.

Because 4 months of credit is being given there are 3 credit periods in a year, so enter P/YR = 3, EFF% = EAR = 19.56, and press NOM% to find the nominal rate of

18.41%. Therefore, if Martha charges an 18.41% nominal rate and gives credit for 4 months, she will cover the cost of her bank loan.

Alternative solution: First, we need to find the effective annual rate charged by the bank:

$$EAR = (1 + i_{Nom}/m)^m - 1$$
$$= (1 + 0.18/12)^{12} - 1$$
$$= (1.0150)^{12} - 1 = 19.56\%.$$

Now, we can find the nominal rate Martha must quote her customers so that her financing costs are exactly covered:

$$19.56\% = (1 + i_{Nom}/3)^3 - 1$$
$$1.1956 = (1 + i_{Nom}/3)^3$$
$$1.0614 = 1 + i_{Nom}/3$$
$$0.0614 = i_{Nom}/3$$
$$i_{Nom} = 18.41\%.$$

18. a.

Year	Payment	Interest	Repayment on Principal	Remaining Principal Balance
1	$7,047.55	$6,000.00	$1,047.55	$58,952.45
2	7,047.55	5,895.25	1,152.30	57,800.15

19. d. Currently:

Find the future value of your current account:
With a financial calculator, input N = 2, I = 16, PV = -1000, PMT = 0, and solve for FV = $1,345.60.

Find the future value of the new account:
With a financial calculator, input N = 8, I = 4, PV = -1000, PMT = 0, and solve for FV = $1,368.57.

Thus, the new account will be worth $1,368.57 – $1,345.60 = $22.97 more after 2 years.

Determine how much you're willing to pay the agent:
With a financial calculator, input N = 8, I = 4, PMT = 0, FV = 22.97, and solve for PV = -$16.78.

Therefore, the most you should be willing to pay the agent for locating the new account is $16.78.

20. e. With a financial calculator, input cash flows into the cash flow register, using -11,958.20 as the cash flow for time 0 (CF_0), and using 0 as the value for the unknown cash flow, input I = 12, and then press the NPV key to solve for the present value of the unknown cash flow, $4,783.29. This value should be compounded by $(1.12)^2$, so that $4,783.29(1.2544) = $6,000.16.

21. b. First, how much must you accumulate on your 18th birthday?

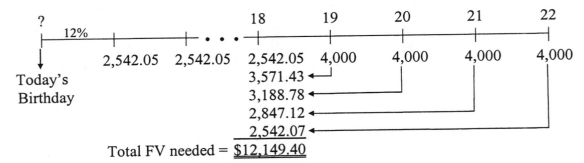

Total FV needed = $12,149.40

Using a financial calculator (with the calculator set for an ordinary annuity), enter N = 4, I = 12, PMT = 4000, FV = 0, and solve for PV = -$12,149.40. This is the amount (or lump sum) that must be present in your bank account on your 18th birthday in order for you to be able to withdraw $4,000 at the end of each year for the next 4 years.

Now, how many payments of $2,542.05 must you make to accumulate $12,149.40?

Using a financial calculator, enter I = 12, PV = 0, PMT = -2542.05, FV = 12149.40, and solve for N = 4. Therefore, if you make payments at 18, 17, 16, and 15, you are now 14.

22. c. This can be done with a calculator by specifying an interest rate of 4 percent per period for 40 periods.

N = 20 × 2 = 40.
I = 8/2 = 4.
PV = -50000.
FV = 0.
PMT = $2,526.17.

Set up an amortization table:

Period	Beginning Balance	Payment	Interest	Payment of Principal	Ending Balance
1	$50,000.00	$2,526.17	$2,000.00	$526.17	$49,473.83
2	49,473.83	2,526.17	1,978.95		
			$3,978.95		

You can really just work the problem with a financial calculator using the amortization function. Find the interest in each 6-month period, sum them, and you have the answer. Even simpler, with some calculators such as the HP-17BII, just input 2 for periods and press INT to get the interest during the first year, $3,978.95.

23. e.

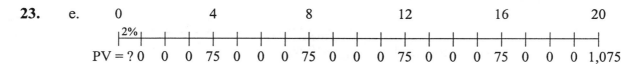

Input the cash flows in the cash flow register, input I = 2, and solve for NPV = $970.51.

24. a. Input N = 5, I = 7, PV = -500000, and FV = 0 to solve for PMT = $121,945.35.

Year	Beginning Balance	Payment	Interest	Payment of Principal	Ending Balance
1	$500,000.00	$121,945.35	$35,000.00	$86,945.35	$413,054.65
2	413,054.65	121,945.35	28,913.83	93,031.52	320,023.13

The fraction that is principal is $93,031.52/$121,945.35 = 76.29%.

25. b. Start with a time line to picture the situation:

Bank: 14% nominal; EAR = 14.93%.

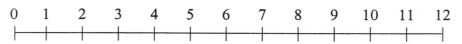

Insurance company: EAR = 14.93%; Nominal = 14.16%.

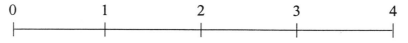

Here we must find the EAR on the bank loan and then find the quarterly nominal rate for that EAR. The bank loan rate is a nominal 14 percent with monthly compounding.

Using the interest conversion feature of the calculator, or the EAR formula, we must find the EAR on the bank loan. Enter P/YR = 12 and NOM% = 14, and then press the EFF% key to find EAR bank loan = 14.93%.

Now, we can find the nominal rate with quarterly compounding that also has an EAR of 14.93 percent. Enter P/YR = 4 and EFF% = 14.93, and then press the NOM% key to get 14.16%. If the insurance company quotes a nominal rate of 14.16%, with quarterly compounding, then the bank and insurance company loans would be equivalent in the sense that they both have the same effective annual rate, 14.93%.

Alternative solution:

$$EAR = (1 + i_{Nom}/12)^{12} - 1$$
$$= (1 + 0.14/12)^{12} - 1$$
$$= 14.93\%.$$

$$14.93\% = (1 + i_{Nom}/4)^4 - 1$$
$$1.1493 = (1 + i_{Nom}/4)^4$$
$$1.0354 = 1 + i_{Nom}/4$$
$$0.0354 = i_{Nom}/4$$
$$i_{Nom} = 14.16\%.$$

26. e. Inflation = 3%.

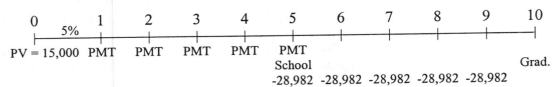

Fixed income = $25,000(1.03)^5$ = \$28,981.85.

1. Find the FV of \$25,000 compounded for 5 years at 3 percent; that FV, \$28,981.85, is the amount you will need each year while you are in school. (Note: Your real income will decline.)

2. You must have enough in 5 years to make the \$28,981.85 payments to yourself. These payments will begin as soon as you start school, so we are dealing with a 5-year, 5 percent interest rate *annuity due*. Set the calculator to "BEG" mode, because we are dealing with an annuity due, and then enter N = 5, I = 5, PMT = -28981.85, and FV = 0. Then press the PV key to find the PV, \$131,750.06. This is the amount you must have in your account 5 years from today. (Do not forget to switch the calculator back to "END" mode.)

3. You now have $15,000. It will grow at 5 percent to $19,144.22 after 5 years. Enter N = 5, I = 5, PV = -15000, and PMT = 0, to solve for FV = $19,144.22. You can subtract this amount to determine the FV of the amount you must save: $131,750.06 – $19,144.22 = $112,605.84.

4. Therefore, you must accumulate an additional $112,605.84 by saving PMT per year for 5 years, with the first PMT being deposited at the end of this year and earning a 5 percent interest rate. Now we have an ordinary annuity, so be sure you returned your calculator to "END" mode. Enter N = 5, I = 5, PV = 0, FV = 112605.84, and then press PMT to find the required payments, -$20,378.82.

27. c. Find the EAR on the TV dealer's credit. Use the interest conversion feature of your calculator. First, though, note that if you are charged a 15 percent nominal rate, you will have to pay interest of 15%/4 = 3.75% after 3 months. The dealer then has the use of the interest, so he can earn 3.75 percent on it for the next three months, and so forth. Thus, we are dealing with quarterly compounding. The nominal rate is 15 percent, quarterly compounding.

Enter NOM% = 15, P/YR = 4, and then press EFF% to get EAR = 15.8650%.

You should be indifferent between the dealer credit and the bank loan if the bank loan has an EAR of 15.8650 percent. The bank is using monthly compounding, or 12 periods per year. To find the nominal rate at which you should be indifferent, enter P/YR = 12, EFF% = 15.8650, and then press NOM% to get NOM% = 14.8163%.

Conclusion: A loan that has a 14.8163 percent nominal rate with monthly compounding is equivalent to a 15 percent nominal rate loan with quarterly compounding. Both have an EAR of 15.8650 percent.

Alternative Solution

$$
\begin{aligned}
EAR &= (1 + i_{Nom}/4)^4 - 1 \\
&= (1 + 0.15/4)^4 - 1 \\
&= (1.0375)^4 - 1 \\
&= 15.8650\%.
\end{aligned}
$$

$$
\begin{aligned}
15.8650\% &= (1 + i_{Nom}/12)^{12} - 1 \\
1.15865 &= (1 + i_{Nom}/12)^{12} \\
1.012347 &= 1 + i_{Nom}/12 \\
i_{Nom} &= 14.8163\%.
\end{aligned}
$$

28. a. Information given:

1. Will save for 20 years, then receive payments for 25 years.

2. Wants payments of $75,000 per year in today's dollars for first payment only. Real income will decline. Inflation will be 4 percent. Therefore, to find the inflated fixed payments, we have this time line:

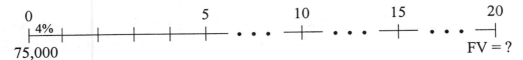

Enter N = 20, I = 4, PV = -75000, PMT = 0, and press FV to get FV = $164,334.24.

3. He now has $200,000 in an account that pays 7 percent, annual compounding. We need to find the FV of $200,000 after 20 years. Enter N = 20, I = 7, PV = -200000, PMT = 0, and press FV to get FV = $773,936.89.

4. He wants to withdraw, or have payments of, $164,334.24 per year for 25 years, with the first payment made at the beginning of the first retirement year. So, we have a 25-year annuity due with PMT = $164,334.24, at an interest rate of 7 percent. (The interest rate is 7 percent annually, so no adjustment is required.) Set the calculator to "BEG" mode, then enter N = 25, I = 7, PMT = -164334.24, FV = 0, and press PV to get PV = $2,049,138.53. This amount must be on hand to make the 25 payments.

5. Since the original $200,000, which grows to $773,936.89, will be available, he must save enough to accumulate $2,049,138.53 – $773,936.89 = $1,275,201.64.

6. The $1,275,201.64 is the FV of a 20-year ordinary annuity. The payments will be deposited in the bank and earn 7 percent interest. Therefore, set the calculator to "END" mode and enter N = 20, I = 7, PV = 0, FV = 1275201.64, and press PMT to find PMT = $31,105.90.

29. b. Contract 1: Using your financial calculator, enter the following data: $CF_0 = 0$; CF_{1-4} = 1500000; I = 12; NPV = ? Solve for NPV = $4,556,024.02

Contract 2: Using your financial calculator, enter the following data: $CF_0 = 0$; $CF_1 =$ 1000000; $CF_2 = 1500000$; $CF_3 = 2000000$; $CF_4 = 2500000$; I = 12; NPV = ? Solve for NPV = $5,101,003.65.

Contract 3:   Using your financial calculator, enter the following data: $CF_0 = 0$; $CF_1 =$ 3500000; $CF_2 = 500000$; $CF_3 = 500000$; $CF_4 = 500000$; $I = 12$; $NPV = ?$ Solve for NPV = \$4,197,246.10.

Contract 2 gives the quarterback the highest present value; therefore, he should accept Contract 2.

30.   d.   Using your financial calculator, input the following data: $N = 30 \times 12 = 360$; $I = 7.5/12 = 0.6250$; $PV = -200000$; $FV = 0$; $PMT = ?$ Solve for PMT = \$1,398.43.

31.   a.   After finding the monthly mortgage payment, use the amortization feature of your calculator to find interest and principal repayments during the year and the remaining mortgage balance as follows: 1 INPUT 12 ■ AMORT

= \$14,937.47 (Interest)
= \$1,843.69 (Principal)
= \$198,156.31 (Balance)

Total mortgage payments made during the first year equals $12 \times \$1,398.43 = \$16,781.16$.

Portion of first year mortgage payments that go towards interest equals \$14,937.47/\$16,781.16 = 89.01 ≈ 89%.

32.   c.   After finding the monthly mortgage payment, use the amortization feature of your calculator to find interest and principal payments during the first five years and the remaining mortgage balance as follows: 1 INPUT 60 ■ AMORT

= \$73,140.61 (Interest)
= \$10,765.19 (Principal)
= \$189,234.81 (Balance)

The remaining mortgage balance after 5 years will be \$189,234.81 ≈ \$189,235.

33.   b.   Using your financial calculator, input the following data: $N = 30 \times 12 = 360$; $I = 7.5/12 = 0.6250$; $PMT = 1800$; $FV = 0$; $PV = ?$ Solve for PV = \$257,431.73 ≈ \$257,432.

If the Wades are willing to have a \$1,800 monthly mortgage payment, they can borrow \$257,432 today.

34.   e.   Using the information given in the problem, you can solve for the number of years required to reach \$1 million.

I = 6; PV = 15000; PMT = 7500; FV = -1000000; and then solve for N = 35.76.

Therefore, it will take Janet 35.76 years to reach her investment goal.

35.   b.   Again, you can solve for the number of years required to reach $1 million.

I = 7; PV = 15000; PMT = 7500; FV = -1000000; and then solve for N = 32.58.

It will take Denise 32.58 years to reach her investment goal. The difference in time is 35.76 – 32.58 = 3.18 years.

36.   a.   Using the 35.76 year target, you can solve for the required payment.

N = 35.76; I = 7; PV = 15000; FV = -1000000; then solve for PMT = $5,683.44.

If Denise wishes to reach the investment goal at the same time as Janet, she can contribute as little as $5,683.44 every year.

37.   c.   If John expects a 7% annual return on his investments:

1 payment	10 payments	30 payments
	N = 10	N = 30
	I = 7	I = 7
	PMT = 7000000	PMT = 4000000
	FV = 0	FV = 0
PV = 46,000,000	PV = 49,165,071	PV = 49,636,165

John should accept the 30-year payment option as it carries the highest present value ($49,636,165).

38.   b.   If John expects an 8% annual return on his investments:

1 payment	10 payments	30 payments
	N = 10	N = 30
	I = 8	I = 8
	PMT = 7000000	PMT = 4000000
	FV = 0	FV = 0
PV = 46,000,000	PV = 46,970,570	PV = 45,031,133

John should accept the 10-year payment option as it carries the highest present value ($46,970,570).

39.   a.   If John expects a 9% annual return on his investments:

1 payment	10 payments	30 payments
	N = 10	N = 30
	I = 9	I = 9
	PMT = 7000000	PMT = 4000000
	FV = 0	FV = 0
PV = 46,000,000	PV = 44,923,604	PV = 41,094,616

John should accept the lump-sum payment option as it carries the highest present value ($46,000,000).

40.   d.   Using the information given in the problem, you can solve for the maximum attainable car price.

Financed for 48 months
N = 48
I = 0.8333 (10/12 = 0.8333)
PMT = 425
FV = 0

PV = $16,756.97

You must add the value of the down payment to the present value of the car payments. If financed for 48 months, Henry can afford a car valued up to $21,756.97 ($16,756.97 + $5,000).

41.   e.   Using the information given in the problem, you can solve for the maximum attainable car price.

Financed for 60 months
N = 60
I = 0.8333
PMT = 425
FV = 0

PV = $20,002.78

If financing for 60 months, Henry can afford a car valued up to $25,002.78 ($20,002.78 + $5,000).

Web Appendix 6B

B-1.   d. $FV_n = PV\ e^{in}$

$$FV_{10} = \$30,000\ e^{0.04(10)}$$
$$= \$30,000\ e^{0.4}$$
$$= \$44,754.74.$$

B-2.   b. $PV = FV_n\ e^{-in}$

$$= \$125,000\ e^{-0.90}$$
$$= \$50,821.21.$$

CHAPTER 7
BONDS AND THEIR VALUATION

LEARNING OBJECTIVES

- List the four main classifications of bonds and differentiate among them.

- Identify the key characteristics common to all bonds.

- Calculate the value of a bond with annual or semiannual interest payments.

- Explain why the market value of an outstanding fixed-rate bond will fall when interest rates rise on new bonds of equal risk, or vice versa.

- Calculate the current yield, the yield to maturity, and/or the yield to call on a bond.

- Differentiate between interest rate risk, reinvestment rate risk, and default risk.

- List major types of corporate bonds and distinguish among them.

- Explain the importance of bond ratings and list some of the criteria used to rate bonds.

- Differentiate among the following terms: Insolvent, liquidation, and reorganization.

- Read and understand the information provided on the bond market page of your newspaper.

OVERVIEW

This chapter presents a discussion of the key characteristics of bonds, and then uses time value of money concepts to determine bond values. Bonds are one of the most important types of securities to investors and a major source of financing for corporations and governments.

The value of any financial asset is the present value of the cash flows expected from that asset. Therefore, once the cash flows have been estimated and a discount rate determined, the value of the financial asset can be calculated.

A bond is valued as the present value of the stream of interest payments (an annuity) plus the present value of the par value that is received by the investor on the bond's maturity date. Depending on the relationship between the current interest rate and the bond's coupon rate, a bond can sell at its par value, at a discount, or at a premium. The total rate of return on a bond is comprised of two components: an interest yield and a capital gains yield.

The bond valuation concepts developed earlier in the chapter are used to illustrate interest rate and reinvestment rate risk. In addition, default risk, various types of corporate bonds, bond ratings, and bond markets are discussed.

OUTLINE

A bond is a long-term contract under which a borrower agrees to make payments of interest and principal, on specific dates, to the holders of the bond. There are four main types of bonds: Treasury, corporate, municipal, and foreign. Each type differs with respect to expected return and degree of risk.

- *Treasury bonds*, sometimes referred to as government bonds, are issued by the Federal government and are not exposed to default risk.
  - ☐ Treasury bond prices decline when interest rates rise, so they are not free of all risk.

- *Corporate bonds* are issued by corporations and are exposed to default risk.
  - ☐ Different corporate bonds have different levels of default risk, depending on the issuing company's characteristics and on the terms of the specific bond.

- *Municipal bonds* are issued by state and local governments.
  - ☐ The interest earned on most municipal bonds is exempt from federal taxes and also from state taxes if the holder is a resident of the issuing state.
  - ☐ Consequently, municipal bonds carry interest rates that are considerably lower than those on corporate bonds with the same default risk.

- *Foreign bonds* are issued by foreign governments or foreign corporations.
  - ☐ These bonds are not only exposed to default risk, but are also exposed to an additional risk if the bonds are denominated in a currency other than that of the investor's home currency.

Differences in contractual provisions, and in the underlying strength of the companies backing the bonds, lead to major differences in bonds' risks, prices, and expected returns. It is important to understand both the key characteristics, which are common to all bonds, and how differences in these characteristics affect the values and risks of individual bonds.

■ The *par value* is the stated face value of a bond, usually $1,000.
  ☐ This is the amount of money that the firm borrows and promises to repay on the maturity date.

■ The *coupon payment* is the dollar amount that is paid each period to a bondholder by the issuer for use of the $1,000 loan. This payment is a fixed amount, established at the time the bond is issued. The *coupon interest rate* is obtained by dividing the coupon payment by the par value of the bond.
  ☐ *Floating rate bonds* are bonds with a coupon payment that varies over time.
    ● Floating rate debt is popular with investors because the market value of the debt is stabilized.
    ● It is advantageous to corporations because firms can issue long-term debt without committing themselves to paying a historically high interest rate for the entire life of the loan.
  ☐ *Zero coupon bonds* pay no coupons at all, but are offered at a substantial discount below their par values.
    ● They provide capital appreciation rather than interest income.
    ● Web Appendix 7A discusses zero coupon bonds and their valuation in more detail.
  ☐ In general, any bond originally offered at a price significantly below its par value is called an *original issue discount bond (OID)*.

■ The *maturity date* is the date on which the par value must be repaid. Most bonds have original maturities of from 10 to 40 years, but any maturity is legally permissible.
  ☐ *Original maturity* is the number of years to maturity at the time a bond is issued.

■ A *call provision* gives the issuing corporation the right to call the bonds for redemption under specified terms prior to the normal maturity date.
  ☐ The call provision generally states that if the bonds are called, the company must pay the bondholders an amount greater than the par value, a *call premium*.
    ● The call premium is often set equal to one year's interest if the bonds are called during the first year, and the premium declines at a constant rate of INT/N each year thereafter, where INT = annual interest and N = original maturity in years.
  ☐ A *deferred call* occurs when bonds are not callable until several years after they are issued. These bonds are said to have *call protection*.
  ☐ The call privilege is valuable to the firm but potentially detrimental to the investor, especially if the bonds were issued in a period when interest rates were cyclically high. Accordingly, the interest rate on a new issue of callable bonds will exceed that on a new issue of noncallable bonds.

☐ The process of using the proceeds of a new lower-interest-rate bond issue to retire a higher-interest-rate issue and reduce the firm's interest expense is called a *refunding operation.*

■ A *sinking fund provision* facilitates the orderly retirement of a bond issue. This can be achieved in one of two ways, and the firm will choose the least-cost method:
  ☐ The company can call in for redemption (at par value) a certain percentage of bonds each year. If interest rates have fallen, a firm will call the bonds.
  ☐ The company may buy the required amount of bonds on the open market. If interest rates have risen, causing bond prices to fall, it will buy bonds in the open market at a discount.
    ● Bonds that have a sinking fund are regarded as being safer than those without such a provision, so at the time they are issued sinking fund bonds have lower coupon rates than otherwise similar bonds without sinking funds.
    ● A sinking fund call typically requires no call premium, but only a small percentage of the issue is normally callable in any one year.

■ *Convertible bonds* are securities that are exchangeable into shares of common stock, at a fixed price, at the option of the bondholder.
  ☐ Convertibles have a lower coupon rate than nonconvertible debt, but they offer investors a chance for capital gains in exchange for the lower coupon rate.

■ Bonds issued with *warrants* are similar to convertibles. Warrants are options that permit the holder to buy stock for a stated price, thereby providing a capital gain if the stock price rises.
  ☐ Bonds that are issued with warrants carry lower coupon rates than straight bonds.

■ *Putable bonds* contain provisions that allow the bonds' investors to sell the bonds back to the company prior to maturity at a prearranged price.

■ *Income bonds* pay interest only if the interest is earned.
  ☐ These securities cannot bankrupt a company, but from an investor's standpoint they are riskier than "regular" bonds.

■ The interest rate of an *indexed,* or *purchasing power, bond* is based on an inflation index such as the consumer price index (CPI), so the interest paid rises automatically when the inflation rate rises, thus protecting the bondholders against inflation.

The value of any financial asset is simply the present value of the cash flows the asset is expected to produce. The cash flows from a specific bond depend on its contractual features.

■ A bond represents an annuity plus a lump sum, and its value is found as the present value of this payment stream:

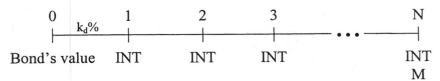

$$\text{Bond value} = V_B = \sum_{t=1}^{N} \frac{\text{INT}}{(1+k_d)^t} + \frac{M}{(1+k_d)^N}.$$

☐ Here INT = dollars of interest paid each year, M = par, or maturity, value, which is typically $1,000, k_d = market interest rate on the bond, and N = number of years until the bond matures.

■ For example, consider a 15-year, $1,000 bond paying $100 annually, when the appropriate interest rate, k_d, is 10 percent. Using a financial calculator, enter N = 15, k_d = I = 10, PMT = 100, and FV = 1000, and then press the PV key for an answer of $1,000. The NPV function of a spreadsheet program can also be used to find the answer.

■ A *new issue* is the term applied to a bond that has just been issued.
☐ At the time of issue, the coupon payment is generally set at a level that will force the market price of the bond to equal its par value.
☐ Once the bond has been on the market for a while, it is classified as an *outstanding bond*, or a *seasoned issue*.

■ Bond prices and interest rates are inversely related; that is, they tend to move in the opposite direction from one another. Interest rates do change over time, but for a fixed-rate bond the coupon rate remains fixed after the bond has been issued.
☐ A fixed-rate bond will sell at par when its coupon interest rate is equal to the going rate of interest, k_d.
☐ A *discount bond* is a bond that sells below its par value, when the going rate of interest rises above the coupon rate.
☐ A *premium bond* is a bond that sells above its par value, when the going rate of interest falls below the coupon rate.
☐ The percentage rate of return on a bond consists of an interest yield, or current yield, plus a capital gains yield.
☐ The market value of a bond will always approach its par value as its maturity date approaches, provided the firm does not go bankrupt.

Unlike the coupon interest rate, which is fixed, a bond's yield varies from day to day depending on current market conditions. The expected interest rate on a bond, also called its "yield," can be calculated in a variety of different ways.

■ The rate of return earned on a bond if it is held until maturity is known as the *yield to maturity (YTM)*.

  ☐ The yield to maturity is generally the same as the market rate of interest, k_d.

  ☐ The YTM for a bond that sells at par consists entirely of an interest yield, but if the bond sells at a price other than its par value, the YTM consists of the interest yield plus a positive or negative capital gains yield.

  ☐ The yield to maturity can also be viewed as the bond's promised rate of return.

  ☐ The yield to maturity equals the expected rate of return only if the probability of default is zero and the bond cannot be called.

  ☐ An investor who purchases a bond and holds it until it matures will receive the YTM that existed on the purchase date, but the bond's calculated YTM will change frequently between the purchase date and the maturity date.

■ If current interest rates are well below an outstanding bond's coupon rate, then a *callable bond* is likely to be called, and investors should estimate the expected rate of return on the bond as the *yield to call (YTC)* rather than as the yield to maturity. To calculate the YTC, solve this equation for k_d:

$$\text{Price of bond} = \sum_{t=1}^{N} \frac{\text{INT}}{(1+k_d)^t} + \frac{\text{Call price}}{(1+k_d)^N}.$$

  ☐ Here N is the number of years until the company can call the bond; call price is the price the company must pay in order to call the bond (which is often set equal to the par value plus one year's interest); and k_d is the YTC.

■ The *current yield* is the annual interest payment divided by the bond's current price.

  ☐ The current yield provides information regarding the amount of cash income that a bond will generate in a given year.

  ☐ The current yield does not take account of capital gains or losses that will be realized if the bond is held until maturity (or call), so it does not provide an accurate measure of the bond's total expected return.

    ● Since zeros pay no annual income, they always have a current yield of zero. This indicates that the bond will not provide any cash interest income, but since the bond will appreciate in value over time, its total rate of return clearly exceeds zero.

The bond valuation model must be adjusted when interest is paid semiannually:

$$V_B = \sum_{t=1}^{2N} \frac{\text{INT}/2}{(1+k_d/2)^t} + \frac{M}{(1+k_d/2)^{2N}}.$$

■ The value with semiannual interest payments is larger than the value when interest is paid annually. This higher value occurs because interest payments are received somewhat faster under semiannual compounding.

Interest rates fluctuate over time, and an increase in interest rates leads to a decline in the value of outstanding bonds.

■ People or firms who invest in bonds are exposed to risk from changing interest rates, or *interest rate risk.*
  ☐ For bonds with similar coupons, the longer the maturity of the bond, the greater the exposure to interest rate risk.

■ The shorter the maturity of the bond, the greater the risk of a decrease in interest rates. The risk of a decline in income due to a drop in interest rates is called *reinvestment rate risk.*
  ☐ Reinvestment rate risk is obviously high on callable bonds. It is also high on short maturity bonds, because the shorter the maturity of a bond, the fewer the years when the relatively high old interest rate will be earned, and the sooner the funds will have to be reinvested at the new low rate.

■ Interest rate risk relates to the value of the bonds in a portfolio, while reinvestment rate risk relates to the income the portfolio produces. No fixed-rate bond can be considered totally riskless.

■ A bond's risk depends critically on how long the investor plans to hold the bond. This is often referred to as the *investment horizon.*
  ☐ Even a small change in interest rates can have a large effect on the prices of long-term securities.
  ☐ Investors with shorter investment horizons view long-term bonds as risky investments.
  ☐ Short-term bonds tend to be riskier than long-term bonds for investors who have longer investment horizons.
  ☐ One simple way to minimize interest rate and reinvestment rate risk is to buy a zero-coupon Treasury security with a maturity that equals your investment horizon.
    ● Investors in zeros have to pay taxes each year on their amortized gain in value, even though the bonds don't produce any cash until the bond matures or is sold.
    ● Purchasing a zero coupon bond with a maturity equal to your investment horizon enables you to lock in a nominal cash flow, but the value of that cash flow will still depend on what happens to inflation during your investment horizon.
  ☐ A positive maturity risk premium would suggest that a majority of bond investors have short-term investment horizons.

Another important risk associated with bonds is default risk. If the issuer defaults, investors receive less than the promised return on the bond. Default risk is influenced by both the financial strength of the issuer and the terms of the bond contract, especially whether collateral has been pledged to secure the bond.

■ The greater the default risk, the higher the bond's yield to maturity. Default risk on Treasury securities is zero, but default risk can be substantial for corporate and municipal bonds.

☐ If a bond's default risk changes, this will affect the bond's price.

■ Corporations can influence the default risk of their bonds by changing the type of bonds they issue.

☐ Under a *mortgage bond*, the corporation pledges certain assets as security for the bond.

● All mortgage bonds are written subject to an *indenture*, which is a legal document that spells out in detail the rights of both the bondholders and the corporation.

● These indentures are generally "open ended," meaning that new bonds can be issued from time to time under the same indenture.

☐ A *debenture* is an unsecured bond, and as such, it provides no lien against specific property as security for the obligation.

● Debenture holders are general creditors whose claims are protected by property not otherwise pledged.

● In practice, the use of debentures depends both on the nature of the firm's assets and on its general credit strength.

☐ *Subordinated debentures* have claims on assets, in the event of bankruptcy, only after senior debt as named in the subordinated debt's indenture has been paid.

● Subordinated debentures may be subordinated to designated notes payable or to all other debt.

● How subordination works, and how it strengthens the position of senior debtholders, is explained in detail in Web Appendix 7B.

■ Bond issues are normally assigned quality ratings by rating agencies. The three major rating agencies are Moody's Investors Service (Moody's), Standard & Poor's Corporation (S&P), and Fitch's Investor Service. These ratings reflect the probability that a bond will go into default.

☐ Aaa (Moody's) and AAA (S&P) are the highest ratings. The triple- and double-A bonds are extremely safe. Single-A and triple-B bonds are also strong enough to be called *investment grade bonds* and they are the lowest-rated bonds that many banks and other institutional investors are permitted by law to hold.

☐ Double-B and lower bonds are speculative, or *junk bonds*, which have a significant probability of going into default.

☐ Bond rating assignments are based on both qualitative and quantitative factors including the firm's financial ratios, mortgage, subordination and guarantee provisions, regulation, antitrust and environmental factors, product and pension liabilities, labor concerns, as well as accounting policies.

- Companies with lower debt ratios, higher free cash flow to debt, higher returns on invested capital, higher EBITDA coverage ratios, and higher times-interest-earned (TIE) ratios typically have higher bond ratings.

☐ Bond ratings are important both to firms and to investors.

☐ Because a bond's rating is an indicator of its default risk, the rating has a direct, measurable influence on the bond's interest rate and the firm's cost of debt.

☐ Most bonds are purchased by institutional investors rather than individuals, and many institutions are restricted to investment grade securities, securities with ratings of Baa/BBB or above.

☐ Changes in a firm's bond rating affect both its ability to borrow long-term capital and the cost of that capital.

☐ Rating agencies review outstanding bonds on a periodic basis, occasionally upgrading or downgrading a bond as the issuer's circumstances change.

- If a company issues more bonds, this will trigger a review by the rating agencies.

- On balance, bond ratings generally do a good job of measuring the average credit risk of bonds, and bond rating agencies do their best to change ratings whenever they perceive a change in credit quality. However, bond ratings do not immediately adjust to changes in credit quality, and in some cases there can be a considerable lag between a change in credit quality and a change in bond rating.

■ In the event of *bankruptcy*, debtholders have a prior claim over the claims of both common and preferred stockholders to a firm's income and assets.

☐ When a business becomes *insolvent*, it does not have enough cash to meet scheduled interest and principal payments. Thus, it must decide whether to dissolve the firm through *liquidation* or to permit it to reorganize and thus stay alive. These issues are discussed in Chapters 7 and 11 of the federal bankruptcy statutes.

☐ In a *reorganization*, a plan may call for restructuring of the firm's debt, in which case the interest rate may be reduced, the term to maturity lengthened, or some of the debt may be exchanged for equity.

- The point of the restructuring is to reduce the financial charges to a level that the firm's cash flows can support.

☐ Liquidation occurs if the company is deemed to be too far gone to be saved. Upon liquidation, assets are sold and the cash is distributed as specified in Chapter 7 of the Bankruptcy Act, beginning with highest priority to secured creditors and ending with lowest priority to common stockholders (assuming anything is left).

☐ Web Appendix 7B discusses bankruptcy and reorganization in more detail.

Bonds are traded primarily in the over-the-counter market.

■   Most bonds are owned by and traded among the large financial institutions, and it is relatively easy for the over-the-counter bond dealers to arrange the transfer of large blocks of bonds among the relatively few holders of the bonds.

■   Information on bond trades in the over-the-counter market is not published, but a representative group of bonds is listed and traded on the bond division of the NYSE.

SELF-TEST QUESTIONS

Definitional

1.   A(n) _____ is a long-term contract under which a borrower agrees to make payments of interest and principal on specific dates.

2.   _____ bonds are issued by state and local governments, and the _____ earned on these bonds is exempt from federal taxes.

3.   The stated face value of a bond is referred to as its _____ value and is usually set at $_____.

4.   The "coupon interest rate" on a bond is determined by dividing the _____ _____ by the _____ _____ of the bond.

5.   The date on which the par value of a bond is repaid to each bondholder is known as the _____ _____.

6.   A(n) _____ _____ bond is one whose interest rate fluctuates with shifts in the general level of interest rates.

7.   A(n) _____ _____ bond is one that pays no annual interest but is sold at a discount below par, thus providing compensation to investors in the form of capital appreciation.

8.   The legal document setting forth the terms and conditions of a bond issue is known as the _____.

9.   In meeting its sinking fund requirements, a firm may _____ the bonds or purchase them on the _____ _____.

10. Except when the call is for sinking fund purposes, when a bond issue is called, the firm must pay a(n) _____ _____, or an amount in excess of the _____ value of the bond.

11. A bond with annual coupon payments represents an annuity of INT dollars per year for N years, plus a lump sum of M dollars at the end of N years, and its value, V_B, is the _____ _____ of this payment stream.

12. At the time a bond is issued, the coupon interest rate is generally set at a level that will cause the _____ _____ and the _____ _____ of the bond to be approximately equal.

13. Market interest rates and bond prices move in _____ directions from one another.

14. The rate of return earned by purchasing a bond and holding it until maturity is known as the bond's _____ ____ _____.

15. To adjust the bond valuation formula for semiannual coupon payments, the _____ _____ and _____ _____ must be divided by 2, and the number of _____ must be multiplied by 2.

16. A bond secured by real estate is known as a(n) _____ bond.

17. _____ bonds are issued by the Federal government and are not exposed to default risk.

18. _____ bonds pay interest only if the interest is earned.

19. The interest rate of a(n) _____, or _____ _____, bond is based on an inflation index, so the interest paid rises automatically when the inflation rate rises, thus protecting the bondholders against inflation.

20. Any bond originally offered at a price significantly below its par value is called a(n) _____ _____ _____ bond.

21. Once a bond has been on the market for a while, it is classified as an outstanding bond, or a(n) _____ _____.

22. The _____ _____ is the annual interest payment divided by the bond's current price.

23. _____ _____ is the number of years to maturity at the time a bond is issued.

24. A(n) _____ _____ _____ facilitates the orderly retirement of a bond issue.

25. The process of using the proceeds of a new lower-interest-rate bond issue to retire a higher-interest-rate issue and reduce the firm's interest expense is called a(n) _____ _____.

26. A(n) _____ _____ gives the issuing corporation the right to call bonds for redemption under specified terms prior to the normal maturity date.

27. A(n) _____ _____ is a bond that has just been issued.

28. A(n) _____ bond sells above its par value, when the going rate of interest falls below the coupon rate.

29. If current interest rates are well below an outstanding bond's coupon rate, then a callable bond is likely to be called, and investors should estimate the expected rate of return on the bond as the _____ ____ _____.

30. A(n) _____ is an unsecured bond, and as such, it provides no lien against specific property as security for the obligation.

31. A(n) _____ _____ occurs when bonds are not callable until several years after they are issued. These bonds are said to have _____ _____.

32. _____ _____ are securities that are exchangeable into shares of common stock, at a fixed price, at the option of the bondholder.

33. _____ _____ contain provisions that allow the bonds' investors to sell the bonds back to the company prior to maturity at a prearranged price.

34. For bonds with similar coupons, the longer the maturity of the bond, the greater the exposure to _____ _____ _____.

35. The risk of a decline in income due to a drop in interest rates is called _____ _____ _____.

36. A bond's risk depends critically on how long the investor plans to hold the bond. This is often referred to as the _____ _____.

37. In practice, the use of debentures depends both on the nature of the firm's _____ and on its general _____ strength.

38. Single-A and triple-B bonds are strong enough to be called _____ _____ bonds, and they are the lowest-rated bonds that many banks and other institutional investors are permitted by law to hold.

39. In the event of _____, debtholders have a prior claim over the claims of both common and preferred stockholders to a firm's income and assets.

40. When a business becomes _____, it does not have enough cash to meet scheduled interest and principal payments.

Conceptual

41. Changes in economic conditions cause interest rates and bond prices to vary over time.

    a. True   b. False

42. If the appropriate rate of interest on a bond is greater than its coupon rate, the market value of that bond will be above par value.

    a. True   b. False

43. A 20-year, annual coupon bond with one year left to maturity has the same interest rate risk as a 10-year, annual coupon bond with one year left to maturity. Both bonds are of equal risk, have the same coupon rate, and the prices of the two bonds are equal.

    a. True   b. False

44. There is a direct relationship between bond ratings and the required rate of return on bonds; that is, the higher the rating, the higher is the required rate of return.

    a. True   b. False

45. The "penalty" for having a low bond rating is less severe when the Security Market Line is relatively steep than when it is not so steep.

    a. True   b. False

46. Which of the following statements is *false*? In all of the statements, assume that "other things are held constant."

    a. Price sensitivity—that is, the change in price due to a given change in the required rate of return—increases as a bond's maturity increases.

    b. For a given bond of any maturity, a given percentage point increase in the going interest rate (k_d) causes a *larger* dollar capital loss than the capital gain stemming from an identical decrease in the interest rate.

    c. For any given maturity, a given percentage point increase in the interest rate causes a *smaller* dollar capital loss than the capital gain stemming from an identical decrease in the interest rate.

    d. From a borrower's point of view, interest paid on bonds is tax deductible.

    e. A 20-year zero-coupon bond has less reinvestment rate risk than a 20-year coupon bond.

47. Which of the following statements is most correct?

    a. Ignoring interest accrued between payment dates, if the required rate of return on a bond is less than its coupon interest rate, and k_d remains below the coupon rate until maturity, then the market value of that bond will be below its par value until the bond matures, at which time its market value will equal its par value.

    b. Assuming equal coupon rates, a 20-year original maturity bond with one year left to maturity has more interest rate risk than a 10-year original maturity bond with one year left to maturity.

    c. Regardless of the size of the coupon payment, the price of a bond moves in the same direction as interest rates; for example, if interest rates rise, bond prices also rise.

    d. For bonds, price sensitivity to a given change in interest rates generally increases as years remaining to maturity increases.

    e. Because short-term interest rates are much more volatile than long-term rates, you would, in the real world, be subject to more interest rate risk if you purchased a 30-*day* bond than if you bought a 30-*year* bond.

48. Which of the following statements is most correct?

    a. Bonds C and Z both have a $1,000 par value and 10 years to maturity. They have the same default risk, and they both have an effective annual rate (EAR) of 8 percent. If Bond C has a 15 percent annual coupon and Bond Z a zero coupon (paying just $1,000 at maturity), then Bond Z will be exposed to more *interest rate risk*, which is defined as the *percentage* loss of value in response to a given increase in the going interest rate.

    b. If the words "interest rate risk" were replaced by the words "reinvestment rate risk" in Statement a, then the statement would be true.

    c. The interest rate paid by the state of Florida on its debt would be lower, other things held constant, if interest on the debt were not exempt from federal income taxes.

    d. Given the conditions in Statement a, we can be sure that Bond Z would have the higher price.

    e. Statements a, b, c, and d are false.

49. If a company's bonds are selling at a *discount*, then:

    a. The YTM is the return investors probably expect to earn.

    b. The YTC is probably the expected return.

    c. Either a or b could be correct, depending on the yield curve.

    d. The current yield will exceed the expected rate of return.

    e. The after-tax cost of debt to the company will have to be less than the coupon rate on the bonds.

SELF-TEST PROBLEMS

1. Delta Corporation has a bond issue outstanding with an annual coupon rate of 7 percent and 4 years remaining until maturity. The par value of the bond is $1,000. Determine the current value of the bond if present market conditions justify a 14 percent required rate of return. The bond pays interest annually.

    a. $1,126.42   **b.** $1,000.00   **c.** $796.04   **d.** $791.00   **e.** $536.38

2. Refer to Self-Test Problem 1. Suppose the bond had a semiannual coupon. Now what would be its current value?

    a. $1,126.42   **b.** $1,000.00   **c.** $796.04   **d.** $791.00   **e.** $536.38

3. Refer to Self-Test Problem 1. Assume an annual coupon but 20 years remaining to maturity. What is the current value under these conditions?

    a. $1,126.42   **b.** $1,000.00   **c.** $796.04   **d.** $791.00   **e.** $536.38

4. Refer to Self-Test Problem 3. What is the bond's current yield?

   a. 12.20%   **b.** 13.05%   **c.** 13.75%   **d.** 14.00%   **e.** 14.50%

5. A bond that matures in 6 years sells for $950. The bond has a face value of $1,000 and a 5.5 percent annual coupon. What is the bond's current yield?

   a. 5.50%   **b.** 6.00%   **c.** 5.79%   **d.** 6.25%   **e.** 6.50%

6. Refer to Self-Test Problem 5. What is the bond's yield to maturity?

   a. 5.50%   **b.** 5.79%   **c.** 6.33%   **d.** 6.53%   **e.** 7.00%

7. Refer to Self-Test Problems 5 and 6. Assume that the yield to maturity remains constant for the next two years. What will be the price of the bond two years from today?

   a. $964.61   **b.** $975.25   **c.** $988.89   **d.** $1,000.00   **e.** $1,250.00

8. Acme Products has a bond issue outstanding with 8 years remaining to maturity, a coupon rate of 10 percent with interest paid annually, and a par value of $1,000. If the current market price of the bond issue is $814.45, what is the yield to maturity, k_d?

   a. 12%   **b.** 13%   **c.** 14%   **d.** 15%   **e.** 16%

9. A bond that matures in 8 years has a 10 percent coupon rate, semiannual payments, a face value of $1,000, and an 8.5 percent current yield. What is the bond's nominal yield to maturity (YTM)?

   a. 6.9%   **b.** 7.1%   **c.** 7.7%   **d.** 8.5%   **e.** 10.0%

10. You have just been offered a bond for $863.73. The coupon rate is 8 percent, payable annually, and interest rates on new issues with the same degree of risk are 10 percent. You want to know how many more interest payments you will receive, but the party selling the bond cannot remember. If the par value is $1,000, how many interest payments remain?

    a. 10   **b.** 11   **c.** 12   **d.** 13   **e.** 14

11. Bird Corporation's 12 percent coupon rate, semiannual payment, $1,000 par value bonds that mature in 20 years are callable at a price of $1,100 five years from now. The bonds sell at a price of $1,300, and the yield curve is flat. Assuming that interest rates in the economy are expected to remain at their current level, what is the best estimate of Bird's *nominal interest rate* on the new bonds?

    a. 8.46%   **b.** 6.16%   **c.** 9.28%   **d.** 6.58%   **e.** 8.76%

12. The Graf Company needs to finance some new R&D programs, so it will sell new bonds for this purpose. Graf's currently outstanding bonds have a $1,000 par value, a 10 percent coupon rate, and pay interest semiannually. The outstanding bonds have 25 years remaining to maturity, are callable after 5 years at a price of $1,090, and currently sell at a price of $700. The yield curve is expected to remain flat. On the basis of these data, what is the best estimate of Graf's *nominal interest rate* on the new bonds it plans to sell?

   a. 21.10%   b. 14.48%   c. 15.67%   d. 16.25%   e. 18.29%

13. Suppose Hadden Inc. is negotiating with an insurance company to sell a bond issue. Each bond has a par value of $1,000, it would pay 10 percent per year in quarterly payments of $25 per quarter for 10 years, and then it would pay 12 percent per year ($30 per quarter) for the next 10 years (Years 11-20). The $1,000 principal would be returned at the end of 20 years. The insurance company's alternative investment is in a 20-year mortgage that has a nominal rate of 14 percent and provides monthly payments. If the mortgage and the bond issue are equally risky, how much should the insurance company be willing to pay Hadden for each bond?

   a. $750.78   b. $781.50   c. $804.65   d. $710.49   e. $840.97

14. You have just purchased a 15-year, $1,000 par value bond. The coupon rate on this bond is 7.5 percent and interest is paid semiannually. If you require an "effective" annual interest rate of 6.09 percent then how much should you have paid for this bond?

   a. $995.00   b. $1,056.50   c. $1,210.25   d. $1,100.00   e. $1,147.00

(The following data apply to the next three Self-Test Problems.)

Hooper Printing, Inc. has a bond issue outstanding with 14 years left to maturity. The bond issue has a 7 percent annual coupon rate and a par value of $1,000, but due to changes in interest rates, each bond's value has fallen to $749.04. The capital gains yield earned by investors over the last year was -25.10 percent.

15. What is the expected current yield for the next year on this bond issue?

   a. 8.24%   b. 9.35%   c. 10.00%   d. 10.50%   e. 8.75%

16. What is the yield to maturity on this bond issue?

   a. 8.24%   b. 9.35%   c. 10.00%   d. 10.50%   e. 8.75%

17. What is the expected capital gains yield for the next year on this bond issue?

   a. -1.00%   b. 0.50%   c. 1.15%   d. 1.75%   e. 2.00%

Web Appendix 7A

A-1. J.C. Nickel is planning a zero coupon bond issue. The bond has a par value of $1,000, matures in 10 years, and will be sold at an 80 percent discount, or for $200. The firm's marginal federal-plus-state tax rate is 40 percent. What is the annual after-tax cost of debt to Nickel on this issue?

    a. 10.48%   **b.** 10.00%   **c.** 11.62%   **d.** 14.79%   **e.** 17.46%

A-2. Assume that the city of Miami sold an issue of $1,000 maturity value, tax-exempt (muni), zero coupon bonds 10 years ago. The bonds had a 30-year maturity when they were issued, and the interest rate built into the issue was a nominal 12 percent, but with semiannual compounding. The bonds are now callable at a premium of 12 percent over the accrued value. What effective annual rate of return would an investor who bought the bonds when they were issued and who still owns them earn if they are called today?

    a. 13.33%   **b.** 12.00%   **c.** 12.37%   **d.** 11.76%   **e.** 13.64%

Web Appendix 7B

B-1. The Stanton Marble Company has the following balance sheet:

Current assets	$15,120	Accounts payable	$ 3,240
		Notes payable (to bank)	1,620
		Accrued taxes	540
		Accrued wages	540
		Total current liabilities	$ 5,940
Fixed assets	8,100	First mortgage bonds	2,700
		Second mortgage bonds	2,700
		Total mortgage bonds	$ 5,400
		Subordinated debentures	3,240
		Total debt	$14,580
		Preferred stock	1,080
		Common stock	7,560
Total assets	$23,220	Total liabilities and equity	$23,220

The debentures are subordinated only to the notes payable. Suppose Stanton Marble goes bankrupt and is liquidated with $5,400 being received from the sale of the fixed assets, which were pledged as security for the first and second mortgage bonds, and $8,640 received from the sale of current assets. The trustee's costs total $1,440. How much will the holders of subordinated debentures receive?

    a. $2,052   **b.** $2,448   **c.** $3,240   **d.** $2,709   **e.** $3,056

ANSWERS TO SELF-TEST QUESTIONS

1. bond
2. Municipal; interest
3. par; 1,000
4. coupon payment; par value
5. maturity date
6. floating rate
7. zero coupon
8. indenture
9. call; open market
10. call premium; par
11. present value
12. market price; par value
13. opposite
14. yield to maturity
15. coupon payment; interest rate; years
16. mortgage
17. Treasury
18. Income
19. indexed; purchasing power
20. original issue discount

21. seasoned issue
22. current yield
23. Original maturity
24. sinking fund provision
25. refunding operation
26. call provision
27. new issue
28. premium
29. yield to call
30. debenture
31. deferred call; call protection
32. Convertible bonds
33. Putable bonds
34. interest rate risk
35. reinvestment rate risk
36. investment horizon
37. assets; credit
38. investment grade
39. bankruptcy
40. insolvent

41. a. For example, if inflation increases, the interest rate (or required return) will increase, resulting in a decline in bond price.

42. b. It will sell at a discount.

43. a. Both bonds are valued as 1-year bonds regardless of their original issue dates, and since they are of equal risk and have the same coupon rate, their prices must be equal.

44. b. The relationship is inverse. The higher the rating, the lower is the default risk and hence the lower is the required rate of return. Aaa/AAA is the highest rating, and as we go down the alphabet, the ratings are lower.

45. b. A steeper SML implies a higher risk premium on risky securities and thus a greater "penalty" on lower-rated bonds.

46. b. Statements a, d, and e are true. To determine which of the remaining statements is false, it is best to use an example. Assume you have a 10-year, 10 percent annual coupon bond that sold at par. If interest rates increase to 13 percent, the value of the bond decreases to $837.21, while if interest rates decrease to 7 percent, the value of the bond

increases to $1,210.71. Thus, the capital gain is greater than the capital loss and statement b is false.

47. d. Statement a is false because the bond would have a premium and thus sell above par value. Statement b is false because both bonds would have the same interest rate risk because they both have one year left to maturity. Statement c is false because the price of a bond moves in the opposite direction as interest rates. Statement e is false because the 30-year bond would have more interest rate risk than the 30-day bond. Statement d is correct. As years to maturity increase for a bond, the number of discount periods used in finding the current bond value also increases. Therefore, bonds with longer maturities will have more price sensitivity to a given change in interest rates.

48. a. Statement a is correct. Bond C has a high coupon (hence its name), so bondholders get cash flows right away. Bond Z has a zero coupon, so its holders will get no cash flows until the bond matures. Since all of the cash flows on Z come at the end, a given increase in the interest rate will cause this bond's value to fall sharply relative to the decline in value of the coupon bond.

You could also use the data in the problem to find the value of the two bonds at two different interest rates, and then calculate the percentage change. For example, at $k_d = 15\%$, $V_C = \$1,000$ and $V_Z = \$247.18$. At $k_d = 20\%$, $V_C = \$790.38$ and $V_Z = \$161.51$. Therefore, Bond Z declines in value by 34.66 percent, while Bond C declines by only 20.96 percent. Note that Bond Z is exposed to *less* reinvestment rate risk than Bond C.

49. a. When bonds sell at a discount, the going interest rate (k_d) is above the coupon rate. If a company called the old discount bonds and replaced them with new bonds, the new coupon would be above the old coupon. This would increase a firm's interest cost; hence, the company would not call the discount bonds. Therefore, the YTM would be the expected rate of return. The shape of the yield curve would have no effect in the situation described in this question, but if the bonds had been selling at a premium, making the YTC the relevant yield, then the yield curve in a sense would have an effect. The YTC would be below the cost if the company were to sell new long-term bonds, if the yield curve were steeply upward sloping. Statement d is false because the expected rate of return would include a current yield component and a capital gains component (because the bond's price will rise from its current discounted price to par as maturity approaches). Therefore, the current yield will *not* exceed the expected rate of return. The after-tax cost of debt is the expected rate adjusted for taxes, $k_d(1 - T)$. Because the bonds are selling at a discount, the coupon rate could be quite low, even zero, so we know that statement e is false. Therefore, statement a is correct.

SOLUTIONS TO SELF-TEST PROBLEMS

1.　c.　Calculator solution: Input N = 4, I = 14, PMT = 70, FV = 1000, and solve for PV = $796.04.

2.　d.　Calculator solution: Input N = 8, I = 7, PMT = 35, FV = 1000, and solve for PV = $791.00.

3.　e.　Calculator solution: Input N = 20, I = 14, PMT = 70, FV = 1000, and solve for PV = $536.38.

4.　b.　From Self-Test Problem 3 we know that the current price of the bond is $536.38.

$$\text{Therefore, the current yield} = \frac{\text{Annual Interest}}{\text{Current Price}}$$
$$= \frac{\$70}{\$536.38}$$
$$= 13.05\%.$$

5.　c.　$V_B = \$950$; $M = \$1,000$; $INT = 0.055 \times \$1,000 = \$55$.

Current yield = Annual interest/Current price of bond
$$= \$55.00/\$950.00$$
$$= 5.79\%.$$

6.　d.　$N = 6$; $PV = -950$; $PMT = 55$; $FV = 1000$; $YTM = ?$

Solve for I = YTM = 6.5339% ≈ 6.53%.

7.　a.　$N = 4$; $I = 6.5339$; $PMT = 55$; $FV = 1000$; $PV = ?$

Solve for $V_B = PV = \$964.61$.

8.　c.　Calculator solution: Input N = 8, PV = -814.45, PMT = 100, FV = 1000, and solve for I = k_d = 14.00%.

9.   b. $N = 8 \times 2 = 16$; $PMT = 0.10/2 \times \$1,000 = 50$; $FV = 1000$; $PV = ?$; $YTM = ?$

Solve for PV using the 8.5% current yield:
Current yield = Annual interest payment/Current bond price

$$8.5\% = \$100/V_B$$
$$V_B = \$100/0.085$$
$$V_B = \$1,176.47.$$

Now, solve for YTM:
$N = 16$; $PV = -1176.47$; $PMT = 50$; $FV = 1000$; $YTM = ?$
Solve for $YTM = k_d/2 \times 2 = 3.5368\% \times 2 = 7.0736\% \approx 7.1\%$.

Remember, when calculating the YTM realize that the interest rate first obtained is a periodic rate. To arrive at the correct answer, the periodic interest rate must be put on an annual basis.

10.   c.   Using a financial calculator, input $I = 10$, $PV = -863.73$, $PMT = 80$, $FV = 1000$, and solve for $N = 12$.

11.   d.   The bond is selling at a large premium, which means that its coupon rate is much higher than the going rate of interest. Therefore, the bond is likely to be called—it is more likely to be called than to remain outstanding until it matures. Thus, it will probably provide a return equal to the YTC rather than the YTM. So, there is no point in calculating the YTM; just calculate the YTC. Enter these values: $N = 10$, $PV = -1300$, $PMT = 60$, and $FV = 1100$. The periodic rate is 3.29 percent, so the nominal YTC is $2(3.29\%) = 6.58\%$. This would be close to the going rate, and it is about what Bird would have to pay on new bonds.

12.   b.   Investors would expect to earn either the YTM or the YTC, and the expected return on the old bonds is the cost Graf would have to pay in order to sell new bonds.

YTM: Enter $N = 2(25) = 50$; $PV = -700$; $PMT = 100/2 = 50$; and $FV = 1000$. Press I to get $I = k_d/2 = 7.24\%$. Multiply $7.24\%(2) = 14.48\%$ to get the YTM.

YTC: Enter $N = 2(5) = 10$, $PV = -700$, $PMT = 50$, $FV = 1090$, and then press I to get $I=10.55\%$. Multiply by 2 to get $YTC = 21.10\%$.

Would investors expect the company to call the bonds? Graf currently pays 10 percent on its debt (the coupon rate). New debt would cost at least 14.48 percent. Because $k_d > 10\%$ coupon rate, it would be stupid for the company to call the bonds, so investors would not expect a call. Therefore, they would expect to earn 14.48 percent on the bonds. This is k_d, so 14.48 percent is the rate Graf would probably have to pay on new bonds.

13.   a.   Time line:

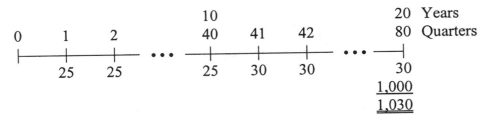

1. You could enter the time line values into the cash flow register, but one element is missing: the interest rate. Once we have the interest rate, we could press the NPV key to get the value of the bond.

2. We need a *periodic* interest rate, and it needs to be a quarterly rate, found as the annual nominal rate divided by 4: $k_{PER} = k_{Nom}/4$. So, we need to find k_{Nom} so that we can find k_{PER}.

3. The insurance company will insist on earning at least the same effective annual rate on the bond issue as it can earn on the mortgage. The mortgage pays 14 percent monthly, which is equivalent to an EAR = 14.93%. Using a financial calculator, enter NOM% = 14, P/YR = 12, and press EFF% to obtain 14.93%. So, the bond issue will have to have a k_{Nom}, with quarterly payments, which translates into an EAR of 14.93 percent.

4. EAR = 14.93% is equivalent to a quarterly nominal rate of 14.16 percent; that is, a nominal rate of 14.16 percent with quarterly compounding is equivalent to an EAR of 14.93 percent. You can find this by entering EFF% = 14.93, P/YR = 4, and pressing the NOM% key to get NOM% = 14.16%. If this nominal rate is set on the bond issue, the insurance company will earn the same effective rate as it can get on the mortgage.

5. The periodic rate for a 14.16 percent nominal rate, with quarterly compounding, is 14.16%/4 = 3.54%. This 3.54% is the rate to use in the time line calculations.

With an HP-10BII calculator, enter the following data:
$CF_0 = 0$, $CF_j = 25$; $N_j = 40$; $CF_j = 30$; $N_j = 39$; $CF_j = 1030$; I = 3.54.
Solve for NPV = $750.78 = Value of each bond.

With an HP-17BII calculator, enter the following data:
Flow(0) = 0 Input; Flow(1) = 25 Input; # Times = 40 Input; Flow(2) = 30 Input; # Times = 39 Input; Flow(3) = 1030 Input; # Times = 1 Input; Exit; Calc; I = 3.54.
Solve for NPV = $750.78 = Value of each bond.

If each bond is priced at $750.78, the insurance company will earn the same effective rate of return on the bond issue as on the mortgage.

14. e. Before you can solve for the price, we must find the appropriate semiannual rate at which to evaluate this bond.

$$
\begin{aligned}
\text{EAR} &= (1 + \text{NOM}/2)^2 - 1 \\
0.0609 &= (1 + \text{NOM}/2)^2 - 1 \\
1.0609 &= (1 + \text{NOM}/2)^2 \\
1.03 &= 1 + \text{NOM}/2 \\
0.03 &= \text{NOM}/2 \\
\text{NOM} &= 0.06.
\end{aligned}
$$

Semiannual interest rate = 0.06/2 = 0.03 = 3%.

Solving for price:
N = 30, I = 3, PMT = 37.50, FV = 1000
PV = -$1,147.00. V_B = $1,147.00.

15. b. The current yield is defined as the annual coupon payment divided by the current price.

CY = $70/$749.04 = 9.35%.

16. d. Solving for YTM:
N = 14, PV = -749.04, PMT = 70, FV = 1000
I = YTM = 10.50%.

17. c. Expected capital gains yield can be found as the difference between YTM and the current yield.

CGY = YTM – CY = 10.50% – 9.35% = 1.15%.

Alternatively, you can solve for the capital gains yield by first finding the expected price next year.

N = 13, I = 10.5, PMT = 70, FV = 1000
PV = -$757.69. V_B = $757.69.

Hence, the capital gains yield is the percent price appreciation over the next year.

CGY = $(P_1 - P_0)/P_0$ = ($757.69 – $749.04)/$749.04 = 1.16%.

Web Appendix 7A

A-1. a. Maturity = N = 10; Issue price = PV = 200; PMT = 0; Maturity value = FV = 1000; Corporate tax rate = 40%.

Enter into a financial calculator: N = 10, PV = 200, PMT = 0, and FV = -1000, and then solve for k_d = I = 17.46%. However, this is a before-tax cost of debt. $k_d(1 - T)$ = 17.46%(1 − 0.4) = 10.48%.

Alternatively, set the analysis up on a time line:

	0	1	2	3	4	5	6	7	8	9	10
Year-end accrued value[1]	200	234.92	275.94	324.12	380.71	447.18	525.25	616.96	724.69	851.22	-1,000.00
Interest deduction[2]		34.92	41.02	48.18	56.59	66.47	78.07	91.71	107.73	126.53	148.78
Tax savings (40%)[3]		13.97	16.41	19.27	22.64	26.59	31.23	36.68	43.09	50.61	59.51
Cash flow[4]	200	13.97	16.41	19.27	22.64	26.59	31.23	36.68	43.09	50.61	-940.49

Enter cash flows in CF register and solve for IRR.
After-tax cost of debt: 10.48%.

Notes:
[1]Year-end accrued value = Issue price $\times (1 + k_d)^n$.
[2]Interest in Year n = Accrued value$_n$ − Accrued value$_{n-1}$.
[3]Tax savings = (Interest deduction)(T).
[4]Cash flow in Year 10 = Tax savings − Maturity value.

A-2. e.

Periodic rate = 6.6024%.
EAR = $(1.066024)^2 - 1$ = 0.1364 = 13.64%.

The solution to this problem requires three steps:

1. Solve for the PV of the original issue. Using a financial calculator, enter N = 60, I = 6, PMT = 0, and FV = 1000, and then solve for PV = $30.3143.

2. Determine the accrued value at the end of 20 periods, and multiply by the call premium.

$$\$30.3143 \times (1.06)^{20} \times 1.12 = \$108.8889.$$

3. Solve for the EAR to an investor if the bonds are called today. Using a financial calculator, enter $N = 20$, $PV = -30.3143$, $PMT = 0$, and $FV = 108.8889$, and then solve for $k_d/2 = I = 6.6024\%$.

$$EAR = (1.066024)^2 - 1 = 0.1364 = 13.64\%.$$

Web Appendix 7B

B-1. a.

Claimant	Claim Amount (1)	Pro Rata Distribution (2)	Distribution after Subordinate Adjustment (3)	Percent of Claim (4)
Accounts payable	$ 3,240	$ 2,448	$ 2,448	75.56%
Notes payable	1,620	1,224	1,620	100.00
Accrued taxes	540	540	540	100.00
Accrued wages	540	540	540	100.00
1st mortgage bonds	2,700	2,700	2,700	100.00
2nd mortgage bonds	2,700	2,700	2,700	100.00
Subordinated debentures	3,240	2,448	2,052	63.33
Preferred stock	1,080	0	0	0.00
Common stock	7,560	0	0	0.00
Trustee	1,440	1,440	1,440	100.00
Total	$24,660	$14,040	$14,040	56.93%

Explanation of the columns:

(1) Values are taken from the balance sheet.

(2) Since the firm's total debt is $16,020 ($14,580 + $1,440) and only $14,040 ($5,400 + $8,640) is received from the sale of assets, the preferred and common stockholders are wiped out. These stockholders receive nothing.

The $5,400 from the sale of fixed assets is immediately allocated to the mortgage bonds. The holders of the first mortgage bonds are paid off first, so they receive $2,700. The remaining $2,700 from the sale of fixed assets is allocated to the second mortgage bonds, so these bondholders are also paid.

By law, trustee expenses have first claim on the remaining available funds, wages have second priority, and taxes have third priority. Thus, these claims are paid in full.

We now have $6,120 remaining and claims of $8,100, so the general creditors will receive 75.56 cents on the dollar:

$$\frac{\text{Funds available}}{\text{Unsatisfied debt}} = \frac{\$14,040 - \$5,400 - \$1,080 - \$1,440}{\$3,240 + \$1,620 + \$3,240} = 0.7556.$$

General creditors are now initially allocated 75.56 percent of their original claims.

(3) This column reflects a transfer of funds from the subordinated debentures to the notes payable to the bank. Since subordinated debentures are subordinate to bank debt, notes payable to the bank must be paid in full before the debentures receive anything. The notes are paid in full by transferring the difference between their book value and initial allocation ($1,620 − $1,224 = $396) from subordinated debentures to notes payable. This reduces the allocation to subordinated debentures and increases the allocation to notes payable by $396.

LEARNING OBJECTIVES

- Identify some of the more important rights that come with stock ownership and define the following terms: proxy, proxy fight, takeover, and preemptive right.

- Briefly explain why classified stock might be used by a corporation and what founders' shares are.

- Differentiate between closely held and publicly owned corporations and list the three distinct types of stock market transactions.

- Determine the value of a share of common stock when: (1) dividends are expected to grow at some constant rate, (2) dividends are expected to remain constant, and (3) dividends are expected to grow at some supernormal, or nonconstant, growth rate.

- Calculate the expected rate of return on a constant growth stock.

- Apply the total company (corporate value) model to value a firm in situations when the firm does not pay dividends or is privately held.

- Explain why a stock's intrinsic value might differ between the total company model and the dividend growth model.

- Explain the following terms: equilibrium, marginal investor, and Efficient Markets Hypothesis (EMH); distinguish among the three levels of market efficiency; briefly explain the implications of the EMH on financial decisions; and discuss the results of empirical studies on market efficiency and the implication of behavioral finance on those results.

- Read and understand the stock market page given in the daily newspaper.

- Explain the reasons for investing in international stocks and identify the "bets" an investor is making when he does invest overseas.

- Define preferred stock, determine the value of a share of preferred stock, or given its value, calculate its expected return.

OVERVIEW

Common stock constitutes the ownership position in a firm. As owners, common stockholders have certain rights and privileges, including the right to control the firm through election of directors and the right to the firm's residual earnings.

Firms generally begin their corporate life as closely held companies, with all the common stock held by the founding managers. Then, as the company grows, it is often necessary to sell stock to the general public (that is, to go public) to raise more funds. Eventually, the firm may choose to list its stock on one of the physical location exchanges.

A common stock is valued as the present value of its expected future dividend stream.

The total company model is a valuation model used as an alternative to the dividend growth model to determine the value of a firm, especially one that does not pay dividends or is privately held. The total rate of return on a stock is comprised of a dividend yield plus a capital gains yield. If a stock is in equilibrium, its total expected return must equal the average investor's required rate of return.

Preferred stock is a hybrid—it is similar to bonds in some respects and to common stock in others. The value of a share of preferred stock that is expected to pay a constant dividend forever is found as the dividend divided by the required rate of return.

OUTLINE

The corporation's common stockholders are the owners of the corporation, and as such, they have certain rights and privileges.

■ Common stockholders have control of the firm through their election of the firm's directors, who in turn elect officers who manage the business.

□ In a large, publicly owned firm, the managers typically have some stock, but their personal holdings are generally insufficient to give them voting control.

□ Managements of most publicly owned firms can be removed by the stockholders if the management team is not effective.

□ Stockholders who are unable to attend annual meetings may still vote for directors by means of a *proxy*. Proxies can be solicited by any party seeking to control the firm.

□ If earnings are poor and stockholders are dissatisfied, an outside group may solicit the proxies in an effort to overthrow management and take control of the business. This is known as a *proxy fight*.

□ A *takeover* is an action whereby a person or group succeeds in ousting a firm's management and taking control of the company.

□ A *poison pill* makes a possible acquisition unattractive and wards off hostile takeover attempts.

■ The *preemptive right* gives current shareholders the right to purchase any new shares issued in proportion to their current holdings. The preemptive right may or may not be required by state law.

    ☐ The purpose of the preemptive right is twofold:

        ● It enables current stockholders to maintain their proportionate share of ownership and control of the business, which prevents management from seizing control of the corporation and frustrating the will of current stockholders.

        ● It also prevents the sale of shares at low prices to new stockholders, which would dilute the value of the previously issued shares.

Special classes of common stock are sometimes created by a firm to meet special needs and circumstances. If two classes of stock were desired, one would normally be called "Class A" and the other "Class B." Common stock that is given a special designation is called classified stock.

■ Class A might be entitled to receive dividends before dividends can be paid on Class B stock.

■ Class B might have the exclusive right to vote.

    ☐ Note that Class A and Class B have no standard meanings.

■ *Founders' shares* are stock owned by the firm's founders that have sole voting rights but restricted dividends for a specified number of years.

Some companies are so small that their common stocks are not actively traded; they are owned by only a few people, usually the companies' managers. These companies are closely held corporations. In contrast, the stocks of most larger companies are owned by a large number of investors, most of whom are not active in management. These companies are publicly owned corporations. Larger, publicly owned companies generally apply for listing on physical location exchanges, and they and their stocks are said to be listed.

■ Stock market transactions may be separated into three distinct categories.

    ☐ The *secondary market* deals with trading in previously issued, or outstanding, shares of established, publicly owned companies. The company receives no new money when sales are made in the secondary market.

    ☐ The *primary market* handles additional shares sold by established, publicly owned companies. Companies can raise additional capital by selling in this market.

    ☐ The primary market also handles new public offerings of shares in firms that were formerly closely held. Capital for the firm can be raised by *going public*, and this market is called the *initial public offering (IPO) market*.

        ● Initial offerings are generally *oversubscribed*, which means that the demand for shares at the offering price exceeds the number of shares issued.

- Small investors can buy the stock in the after-market, but evidence suggests that if you do not get in on the ground floor, the average IPO underperforms the overall market over the longer run.
- Lawmakers and regulators have recently begun to take a much closer look at the IPO market. They are concerned about Wall Street's practice of allocating hot IPOs to the personal accounts of officers and directors of companies. The review of this practice may ultimately lead to additional regulations in this market.
- It is important to recognize that firms can go public without raising any additional capital.

Common stocks are valued by finding the present value of the expected future cash flow stream.

■ People typically buy common stock expecting to earn *dividends* plus a *capital gain* when they sell their shares at the end of some holding period. The capital gain may or may not be realized, but most people expect a gain or else they would not buy stocks.

■ The expected dividend yield on a stock during the coming year is equal to the expected dividend, D_1, divided by the current stock price, P_0.

■ $(\hat{P}_1 - P_0)/P_0$ is the expected capital gains yield.

■ The expected dividend yield plus the expected capital gains yield equals the expected total return.

■ The value of the stock today is calculated as the present value of an infinite stream of dividends. For any investor, cash flows consist of dividends plus the expected future sales price of the stock. This sales price, however, depends on dividends expected by future investors:

$$\text{Value of stock} = \hat{P}_0 = \text{PV of expected future dividends}$$

$$= \frac{D_1}{(1+k_s)^1} + \frac{D_2}{(1+k_s)^2} + \cdots + \frac{D_\infty}{(1+k_s)^\infty}$$

$$= \sum_{t=1}^{\infty} \frac{D_t}{(1+k_s)^t}.$$

☐ Here k_s is the discount rate used to find the present value of the dividends.

■ Dividends can be rising, falling, fluctuating randomly, or can even be zero for several years. The generalized equation above can be used to value the stock.

☐ With a computer spreadsheet this equation can easily be used to find a stock's intrinsic value for any dividend pattern. The hard part is getting an accurate forecast of the future dividends.

■ For many companies, earnings and dividends are expected to grow at some normal, or constant, rate. Dividends in any future Year t may be forecasted as $D_t = D_0(1 + g)^t$, where D_0 is the last dividend paid and g is the expected growth rate.

☐ For a company that last paid a $2.00 dividend and has an expected 6 percent constant growth rate, the estimated dividend one year from now would be $D_1 = \$2.00(1.06) = \$2.12$; D_2 would be $\$2.00(1.06)^2 = \$2.25$, and the estimated dividend 4 years hence would be $D_t = D_0(1 + g)^t = \$2.00(1.06)^4 = \$2.525$. Using this method of estimating future dividends, the expected stock price today, $\hat{P}_0$, is determined as follows:

$$\hat{P}_0 = \frac{D_0(1+g)}{k_s - g} = \frac{D_1}{k_s - g}.$$

■ This equation for valuing a constant growth stock is often called the *constant growth model*, or the *Gordon Model,* after Myron J. Gordon, who developed it.

☐ A necessary condition of this equation is that $k_s > g$. If the equation is used in situations when k_s is not greater than g, the results will be both wrong and meaningless.

☐ Growth in dividends occurs primarily as a result of growth in earnings per share.

• Earnings growth results from a number of factors, including inflation, the amount of earnings the company retains and reinvests, and the rate of return the company earns on its equity (ROE).

☐ The constant growth model is often appropriate for mature companies with a stable history of growth.

• Expected growth rates vary somewhat among companies, but future dividend growth for most mature firms is generally expected to continue at about the same rate as nominal gross domestic product (real GDP plus inflation).

■ The constant growth model is sufficiently general to handle the case of a *zero growth stock*, where the dividend is expected to remain constant over time. If g = 0, then the stock can be valued as $P_0 = D/k_s$.

☐ This is the same equation as that used for a perpetuity.

■ For all stocks, the total expected return consists of an expected dividend yield plus an expected capital gains yield. For a constant growth stock, the formula for the total expected return can be written as:

$$\hat{k}_s = \frac{D_1}{P_0} + g.$$

☐ For a constant growth stock, the following conditions must hold:
- The dividend is expected to grow forever at a constant rate, g.
- The stock price is expected to grow at this same rate.
- The expected dividend yield is a constant.
- The expected capital gains yield is also a constant, and it is equal to g.
- The expected total rate of return, $\hat{k}_s$, is equal to the expected dividend yield plus the expected growth rate.

■ Firms typically go through periods of nonconstant growth, after which time their growth rate settles to a rate close to that of the economy as a whole. The value of such a firm is equal to the present value of its expected future dividends. To find the value of such a stock, we proceed in three steps:
☐ Find the present value of the dividends during the period of nonconstant growth.
☐ Find the price of the stock at the end of the nonconstant growth period, at which point it has become a constant growth stock, and discount this price back to the present.
☐ Add these two components to find the intrinsic value of the stock, $\hat{P}_0$.
- *Supernormal (nonconstant) growth* firms are firms that are in that part of their life cycle in which they grow much faster than the economy as a whole.
- The *terminal, or horizon, date* is the date when the growth rate becomes constant. At this date it is no longer necessary to forecast the individual dividends.
- The *horizon, or terminal, value* is the value at the horizon date of all dividends expected thereafter.

The total company, or corporate value, model is a valuation model used as an alternative to the dividend growth model to determine the value of a firm, especially one that does not pay dividends or is privately held. This model discounts a firm's free cash flows at the WACC to determine its value.

■ The value of a firm's stock is directly linked to a firm's total value.

■ The steps to the corporate value model approach are as follows:
☐ Find the firm's total value, which is the present value of its future FCFs.
☐ Subtract out the market value of the debt and preferred stock from the firm's total value.
☐ Divide the total value of the common equity by the number of shares outstanding to obtain an estimate of the value per share.
- This estimate should, in theory, be identical to the share value found using the discounted dividend model.

■ The total company model generally requires more data than the discounted dividend model, these data are often more reliable, particularly for companies that do not pay dividends and where future dividends are especially difficult to predict.

■ The market value of any company can be expressed as follows:

$$V_{Company} = \text{PV of expected future free cash flows}$$

$$= \frac{FCF_1}{(1 + WACC)^1} + \frac{FCF_2}{(1 + WACC)^2} + \cdots + \frac{FCF_\infty}{(1 + WACC)^\infty}.$$

☐ Free cash flow represents the cash generated in a given year minus the cash needed to finance the capital expenditures and operating working capital needed to support future growth.

$$FCF = NOPAT - \text{Net new investment in operating capital.}$$

● Free cash flow is the cash generated before making any payments to common or preferred stockholders, or to bondholders, so it is the cash flow that is available to all investors.

☐ The FCF should be discounted at the company's weighted average cost of debt, preferred stock, and common stock, or the WACC.

■ To find the firm's total value, proceed as follows:
☐ Assume the firm will experience nonconstant growth for N years, after which it will grow at some constant rate.
☐ Calculate the expected FCF for each of the N nonconstant growth years, and find the PV of these cash flows.
☐ After Year N growth will be constant. Use the constant growth formula to find the firm's value at Year N. This terminal value is the sum of the PVs of the FCFs for N + 1 and all subsequent years, discounted back to Year N. The Year N value must be discounted back to the present to find its PV at Year 0.
☐ Sum all the PVs, those of the annual free cash flows during the nonconstant period plus the PV of the terminal value, to find the firm's value.

■ Estimates of intrinsic value will often deviate considerably from the actual stock price.
☐ Deviations occur because the forecaster's assumptions are different from those of the marginal investor in the marketplace.

■ Much can be learned from the corporate value model, so analysts today use it for all types of valuations.
☐ The process of projecting future financial statements can reveal quite a bit about the company's operations and financing needs.
☐ This type of analysis can provide insights into actions that might be taken to increase the company's value.

The relationship between a stock's required and expected rates of return determines the equilibrium price level where buying and selling pressures will just offset each other.

■ The *marginal investor* is a representative investor whose actions reflect the beliefs of those people who are currently trading a stock.
  □ It is the marginal investor who determines a stock's price.

■ If the expected rate of return is less than the required rate, investors will desire to sell the stock; there will also be a tendency for the price to decline.

■ When the expected rate of return is greater than the required rate, investors will try to purchase shares of the stock; this will drive the price upward.

■ Only at the *equilibrium* price, where the expected and required rates are equal, will the stock be stable.

■ Equilibrium will generally exist for a given stock because security prices, especially those of large companies, adjust rapidly to disequilibrium situations.
  □ Stock prices certainly change, but this simply reflects changing conditions and expectations.

■ Changes in the equilibrium price can be brought about (1) by a change in risk aversion, (2) by a change in the risk-free rate, (3) by a change in the stock's beta coefficient, or (4) by a change in the stock's expected growth rate.

■ The *Efficient Markets Hypothesis (EMH)* holds that stocks are always in equilibrium and that it is impossible for an investor to consistently "beat the market."
  □ The *weak form* of the EMH states that all information contained in past price movements is fully reflected in current market prices.
  □ The *semistrong form* of the EMH states that current market prices reflect all *publicly available* information.
    • If this is true, no abnormal returns can be gained by analyzing stocks.
    • Another implication of semistrong-form efficiency is that whenever information is released to the public, stock prices will respond only if the information is different from what had been expected.
  □ The *strong form* of the EMH states that current market prices reflect all pertinent information, whether publicly available or privately held (inside information).
    • If this form holds, even insiders would find it impossible to earn abnormal returns in the stock market.

■ Up until 10 years ago, most of the empirical tests on the EMH suggested that, in its weak and semistrong forms, the EMH was valid. However, the strong-form EMH does not hold, so abnormal profits can be made by those who possess inside information.
  □ More recently, empirical support for the EMH has diminished.

- Skeptics point to the stock market bubble and suggest that at the height of the boom, the prices of many companies exceeded their intrinsic values.
- Skeptics suggest that investors are not simply machines that rationally process all available information. A variety of psychological and irrational factors come into play.
- *Behavioral finance* incorporates elements of cognitive psychology to finance in an effort to better understand how individuals and entire markets respond to different circumstances.

■ The logic behind the EMH is compelling, and most researchers believe that markets are generally efficient in the long run.
   ☐ It is generally safe to assume that $\hat{k} = k$, that $\hat{P}_0 = P_0$, and that stocks plot on the SML.

Anyone who has ever invested in the stock market knows that there can be, and generally are, large differences between expected and realized prices and returns.

■ Investors always expect positive returns from stock investments or else they would not buy them. However, in some years negative returns are actually earned.

■ Even in bad years, some individual stocks do well, and the "name of the game" in security analysis is to pick the winners.
   ☐ Financial managers are trying to take those actions that will help put their companies in the winners' column, but they don't always succeed.

■ When investing overseas, you are making two bets: (1) that foreign stocks will increase in their local markets and (2) that the currencies in which you will be paid will rise relative to the dollar.
   ☐ Although U.S. stocks have generally outperformed foreign stocks in recent years, this by no means suggests that investors should ignore foreign stocks.
      - Foreign investments still improve diversification, and it is inevitable that there will be years when foreign stocks outperform domestic stocks.

Preferred stock is a hybrid—it is similar to bonds in some respects and to common stock in others.

■ Preferred dividends are similar to interest payments on bonds in that they are fixed in amount and generally must be paid before common stock dividends can be paid.

■ If the preferred dividend is not earned, the directors can omit (or "pass") it without throwing the company into bankruptcy.
   ☐ Although preferred stock has a fixed payment like bonds, a failure to make this payment will not lead to bankruptcy.

■ Most preferred stocks entitle their owners to regular fixed dividend payments. If the payments last forever, the issue is a *perpetuity* whose value, V_p, is found as follows:

$$V_p = \frac{D_p}{k_p}.$$

☐ Here D_p is the dividend to be received in each year and k_p is the required rate of return on the preferred stock.

SELF-TEST QUESTIONS

Definitional

1. One of the fundamental rights of common stockholders is to elect a firm's _____, who in turn elect officers who manage the business.

2. If a stockholder cannot vote in person, participation in the annual meeting is still possible through a(n) _____.

3. The preemptive right protects stockholders against loss of _____ of the corporation as well as _____ of market value from the sale of new shares below market value.

4. Firms may find it desirable to separate the common stock into different _____. Generally, this classification is designed to differentiate stock in terms of the right to receive _____ and the right to _____.

5. A(n) _____ _____ corporation is one whose stock is held by a small group, normally its management.

6. The trading of previously issued shares of a corporation takes place in the _____ market, while new issues are offered in the _____ market.

7. _____ _____ refers to the sale of shares of a closely held business to the general public.

8. Securities traded on the physical location exchanges are known as _____ securities.

9. Like other financial assets, the value of common stock is the _____ value of a future stream of income.

10. The income stream expected from a common stock consists of a(n) _____ yield and a(n) _____ _____ yield.

11. If the future growth rate of dividends is expected to be _____, the rate of return is simply the _____ yield.

12. Investors always expect a(n) _____ return on stock investments, but in some years _____ returns may actually be earned.

13. Preferred stock is referred to as a hybrid because it is similar to _____ in some respects and to _____ _____ in others.

14. If earnings are poor and stockholders are dissatisfied, an outside group may solicit the votes of stockholders, unable to attend the annual meeting, in an effort to overthrow management and take control of the business. This is known as a(n) _____ _____.

15. A(n) _____ is an action whereby a person or group succeeds in ousting a firm's management and gaining control of the company.

16. A(n) _____ _____ makes a possible acquisition unattractive and wards off hostile takeover attempts.

17. The market in which capital is raised for firms that were formerly closely held companies is often termed the _____ _____ _____ market.

18. _____ is the term used when the demand for shares at the offering price exceeds the number of shares issued.

19. A zero growth stock can be thought of as a(n) _____.

20. If the expected rate of return on a stock is less than its required rate of return, investors will desire to _____ the stock; there will also be a tendency for the stock's price to _____.

21. Only at the _____ price, where the expected and required rates of return are equal, will the stock's price be stable.

22. The _____ _____ _____ holds that stocks are always in equilibrium and that it is impossible for an investor to consistently "beat the market."

23. The _____ form of the EMH states that all information contained in past price movements is fully reflected in current market prices.

24. When investing overseas, you are making two bets: (1) that foreign stock prices will _____ in their local markets and (2) that the currencies in which you will be paid will _____ relative to the dollar.

25.   The _____ _____ gives the current shareholders the right to purchase any new shares issued in proportion to their current holdings.

26.   Common stock that is given a special designation is called _____ stock.

27.   The _____ _____ is a representative investor whose actions reflect the beliefs of those people who are currently trading a stock and determines a stock's price.

28.   Growth in dividends occurs primarily as a result of growth in _____ _____ _____.

29.   _____ _____ firms are those that are in that part of their life cycle in which they grow much faster than the economy as a whole.

30.   The _____ _____ is the date when the growth rate becomes constant.

31.   The _____ _____ model is a valuation model used as an alternative to the dividend growth model to determine a firm's value, especially one that does not pay dividends or is privately held.

32.   _____ _____ _____ is the cash generated before making any payments to common and preferred stockholders, and bondholders, so it is available to all investors.

33.   The _____ _____ is the value at the horizon date of all dividends expected thereafter.

34.   _____ _____ are stock owned by the firm's founders that have sole voting rights but restricted dividends for a specified number of years.

35.   The constant growth model is often appropriate for _____ companies with a(n) _____ history of growth.

36.   Stocks of most larger companies are owned by a large number of investors, most of whom are not active in management. These companies are _____ _____ corporations.

37.   The equation for valuing a constant growth stock is often called the constant growth model, or the _____ _____, after the individual who developed it.

38.   The corporate value model discounts a firm's _____ _____ _____ at the _____ to determine the firm's value.

39.   When the expected rate of return is greater than the required rate, investors will _____ shares of the stock; this will drive the stock price _____.

40. _____ _____ incorporates elements of cognitive psychology to finance in an effort to better understand how individuals and entire markets respond to different circumstances.

Conceptual

41. According to the valuation model developed in this chapter, the value that an investor assigns to a share of stock is independent of the length of time the investor plans to hold the stock.

    a. True   **b.** False

42. Which of the following assumptions would cause the constant growth stock valuation model to be invalid? The constant growth model is given below:

$$\hat{P}_0 = \frac{D_0(1+g)}{k_s - g}.$$

    a. The growth rate is negative.
    b. The growth rate is zero.
    c. The growth rate is less than the required rate of return.
    d. The required rate of return is above 30 percent.
    e. None of the above assumptions would invalidate the model.

43. Assume that a company's dividends are expected to grow at a rate of 25 percent per year for 5 years and then to slow down and to grow at a constant rate of 5 percent thereafter. The required (and expected) total return, k_s, is expected to remain constant at 12 percent. Which of the following statements is most correct?

    a. The dividend yield will be higher in the early years and then will decline as the annual capital gains yield gets larger and larger, other things held constant.
    b. Right now, it would be easier (require fewer calculations) to find the dividend yield expected in Year 7 than the dividend yield expected in Year 3.
    c. The stock price will grow each year at the same rate as the dividends.
    d. The stock price will grow at a different rate each year during the first 5 years, but its average growth rate over this period will be the same as the average growth rate in dividends; that is, the average stock price growth rate will be (25 + 5)/2.
    e. Statements a, b, c, and d are false.

44. Which of the following statements is most correct?

    a. According to the text, the constant growth stock valuation model is especially useful in situations where g is greater than 15 percent and k_s is 10 percent or less.

    b. According to the text, the constant growth model can be used as one part of the process of finding the value of a stock that is expected to experience a very rapid rate of growth for a few years and then to grow at a constant ("normal") rate.

    c. According to the text, the constant growth model cannot be used unless g is greater than zero.

    d. According to the text, the constant growth model cannot be used unless the constant g is greater than k.

    e. Statements a, b, c, and d are true.

45. When stockholders assign their right to vote to another party, this is called

    a. A privilege.
    b. A preemptive right.
    c. An ex right.
    d. A proxy.
    e. A takeover.

SELF-TEST PROBLEMS

1. Stability Inc. has maintained a dividend rate of $4 per share for many years. The same rate is expected to be paid in future years. If investors require a 12 percent rate of return on similar investments, determine the present value of the company's stock.

    a. $15.00   **b.** $30.00   **c.** $33.33   **d.** $35.00   **e.** $40.00

2. Your sister-in-law, a stockbroker at Invest Inc., is trying to sell you a stock with a current market price of $25. The stock's last dividend (D_0) was $2.00, and earnings and dividends are expected to increase at a constant growth rate of 10 percent. Your required return on this stock is 20 percent. From a strict valuation standpoint, you should:

    a. Buy the stock; it is fairly valued.
    b. Buy the stock; it is undervalued by $3.00.
    c. Buy the stock; it is undervalued by $2.00.
    d. Not buy the stock; it is overvalued by $2.00.
    e. Not buy the stock; it is overvalued by $3.00.

3. Lucas Laboratories' last dividend was $1.50. Its current equilibrium stock price is $15.75, and its expected growth rate is a constant 5 percent. If the stockholders' required rate of return is 15 percent, what is the expected dividend yield and expected capital gains yield for the coming year?

    a. 0%; 15%   **b.** 5%; 10%   **c.** 10%; 5%   **d.** 15%; 0%   **e.** 15%; 15%

4. The Canning Company has been hard hit by increased competition. Analysts predict that earnings (and dividends) will decline at a rate of 5 percent annually into the foreseeable future. If Canning's last dividend (D_0) was $2.00, and investors' required rate of return is 15 percent, what will be Canning's stock price *in 3 years*?

    a. $8.15   **b.** $9.50   **c.** $10.00   **d.** $10.42   **e.** $10.96

    (The following data apply to the next three Self-Test Problems.)

    The Club Auto Parts Company has just recently been organized. It is expected to experience no growth for the next 2 years as it identifies its market and acquires its inventory. However, Club will grow at an annual rate of 5 percent in the third year and, beginning with the fourth year, should attain a 10 percent growth rate that it will sustain thereafter. The first dividend (D_1) to be paid at the end of the first year is expected to be $0.50 per share. Investors require a 15 percent rate of return on Club's stock.

5. What is the current equilibrium stock price?

    a. $5.00   **b.** $8.75   **c.** $9.56   **d.** $12.43   **e.** $15.00

6. What will Club's stock price be at the end of the first year ($\hat{P}_1$)?

    a. $5.00   **b.** $8.75   **c.** $9.57   **d.** $12.43   **e.** $15.00

7. What dividend yield and capital gains yield should an investor in Club expect for the first year?

    a. 7.5%; 7.5%   **b.** 4.7%; 10.3%   **c.** 5.7%; 9.3%   **d.** 10.5%; 4.5%   **e.** 11.5%; 3.5%

8. Johnson Corporation's stock is currently selling at $45.83 per share. The last dividend paid (D_0) was $2.50. Johnson is a constant growth firm. If investors require a return of 16 percent on Johnson's stock, what do they think Johnson's growth rate will be?

    a. 6%   **b.** 7%   **c.** 8%   **d.** 9%   **e.** 10%

9. Assume that the average firm in your company's industry is expected to grow at a constant rate of 7 percent and its dividend yield is 8 percent. Your company is about as risky as the average firm in the industry, but it has just successfully completed some R&D work that leads you to expect that its earnings and dividends will grow at a rate of 40 percent $[D_1 = D_0(1 + g) = D_0(1.40)]$ this year and 20 percent the following year, after which growth should match the 7 percent industry average rate. The last dividend paid (D_0) was $1. What is the current value per share of your firm's stock?

    a. $22.47 **b.** $24.15 **c.** $21.00 **d.** $19.48 **e.** $22.00

10. Assume that as investment manager of Maine Electric Company's pension plan (which is exempt from income taxes), you must choose between Exxon Mobil bonds and GM preferred stock. The bonds have a $1,000 par value; they mature in 20 years; they pay $35 each 6 months; they are callable at Exxon Mobil's option at a price of $1,150 after 5 years (ten 6-month periods); and they sell at a price of $815.98 per bond. The preferred stock is a perpetuity; it pays a dividend of $1.50 each quarter, and it sells for $75 per share. Assume interest rates do not change. What is the most likely *effective annual rate of return (EAR)* on the *higher* yielding security?

    a. 9.20% **b.** 8.24% **c.** 9.00% **d.** 8.00% **e.** 8.50%

11. Chadmark Corporation is expanding rapidly, and it currently needs to retain all of its earnings, hence it does not pay any dividends. However, investors expect Chadmark to begin paying dividends, with the first dividend of $0.75 coming 2 years from today. The dividend should grow rapidly, at a rate of 40 percent per year, during Years 3 and 4. After Year 4, the company should grow at a constant rate of 10 percent per year. If the required return on the stock is 16 percent, what is the value of the stock today?

    a. $16.93 **b.** $17.54 **c.** $15.78 **d.** $18.87 **e.** $16.05

12. Some investors expect Endicott Industries to have an irregular dividend pattern for several years, and then to grow at a constant rate. Suppose Endicott has $D_0 = $2.00; no growth is expected for 2 years; then the expected growth rate is 8 percent for 2 years; and finally the growth rate is expected to be constant at 15 percent thereafter. If the required return is 20 percent, what will be the value of the stock?

    a. $28.53 **b.** $25.14 **c.** $31.31 **d.** $21.24 **e.** $23.84

13. Today is December 31, 2002. The following information applies to Harrison Corporation:

- After-tax operating income [EBIT(1 – T)] for 2003 is expected to be $950 million.
- The company's depreciation expense for 2003 is expected to be $190 million.
- The company's capital expenditures for 2003 are expected to be $380 million.
- No change is expected in the company's net operating working capital.
- The company's free cash flow is expected to grow at a constant rate of 4 percent per year.
- The company's cost of equity is 13 percent.
- The company's WACC is 9 percent.
- The market value of the company's debt is $5.2 billion.
- The company has 250 million shares of stock outstanding.

Using the free cash flow approach, what should the company's stock price be today?

a. $35.00   b. $40.00   c. $37.50   d. $43.50   e. $52.50

14. Hidden Technologies Inc. (HTI) is expected to generate $75 million in free cash flow next year, and it is expected to grow at a constant rate of 6 percent per year. The firm has no debt or preferred stock and has a WACC of 9 percent. If HTI has 50 million shares of stock outstanding, what is the value of the company's stock per share?

a. $40.00   b. $43.33   c. $45.75   d. $50.00   e. $55.25

(The following data apply to the next two Self-Test Problems.)

Hanebury Manufacturing Company (HMC) has preferred stock outstanding with a par value of $50. The stock pays a quarterly dividend of $1.25 and has a current price of $71.43.

15. What is the nominal rate of return on the preferred stock?

a. 9.25%   b. 8.75%   c. 10.50%   d. 8.33%   e. 7.00%

16. What is the effective rate of return on the preferred stock?

a. 8.67%   b. 7.19%   c. 9.55%   d. 8.24%   e. 10.68%

17. Helen's Pottery Co.'s stock recently paid a $1.50 dividend ($D_0 = \$1.50$). This dividend is expected to grow by 15% for the next 3 years, and then grow forever at a constant rate, g. The current stock price is $40.92. If $k_s = 10\%$, at what constant rate is the stock expected to grow following Year 3?

a. 5.00%   b. 4.25%   c. 3.33%   d. 6.50%   e. 5.67%

18.   A stock is expected to pay a dividend of $2.25 at the end of the year (D_1 = $2.25). The dividend is expected to grow at a constant rate of 4 percent a year. The stock has a required return of 11 percent. What is the expected price of the stock five years from today?

    a. $32.14   **b.** $36.67   **c.** $39.11   **d.** $40.25   **e.** $42.00

ANSWERS TO SELF-TEST QUESTIONS

1.	directors		**21.**	equilibrium
2.	proxy		**22.**	Efficient Markets Hypothesis
3.	control; dilution		**23.**	weak
4.	classes; dividends; vote		**24.**	increase; increase
5.	closely held		**25.**	preemptive right
6.	secondary; primary		**26.**	classified
7.	Going public		**27.**	marginal investor
8.	listed		**28.**	earnings per share
9.	present		**29.**	Supernormal (Nonconstant) growth
10.	dividend; capital gains		**30.**	terminal (horizon) date
11.	zero; dividend		**31.**	total company (corporate value)
12.	positive; negative		**32.**	Free cash flow
13.	debt; common stock		**33.**	horizon (terminal) value
14.	proxy fight		**34.**	Founders' shares
15.	takeover		**35.**	mature; stable
16.	poison pill		**36.**	publicly owned
17.	initial public offering		**37.**	Gordon Model
18.	Oversubscribed		**38.**	free cash flows; WACC
19.	perpetuity		**39.**	purchase; upward
20.	sell; decline		**40.**	Behavioral finance

41.   a.   The model considers all future dividends. This produces a current value that is appropriate for all investors independent of their expected holding period.

42.   e.   The model would be invalid, however, if the growth rate *exceeded* the required rate of return.

43.   b.   Statement b is correct. We know that after Year 5, the stock will have a constant growth rate, and the capital gains yield will be equal to that growth rate. We also know that the total return is expected to be constant. Therefore, we could find the expected dividend yield in Year 7 simply by subtracting the growth rate from the total return: yield = 12% − 5% = 7% in Year 7.

The other statements are all false. This could be confirmed by thinking about how the dividend growth rate starts high, ends up at the constant growth rate, and must lie between these two rates and be declining between Years 1 and 5. The average growth rate in dividends during Years 1 through 5 will be $(25 + 5)/2 = 15\%$, which is above $k_s = 12\%$, so statements c and d must be false.

44.   b.   Statement b is correct. In the case of a nonconstant growth stock that is expected to grow at a constant rate after Year N, we would find the value of D_{N+1} and use it in the constant growth model to find P_N. The other statements are all false. Note that the constant growth model can be used for $g = 0$, $g < 0$, and $g < k$.

45.   d.   Recently, there has been a spate of proxy fights, whereby a dissident group of stockholders solicits proxies in competition with the firm's management. If the dissident group gets a majority of the proxies, then it can gain control of the board of directors and oust existing management.

SOLUTIONS TO SELF-TEST PROBLEMS

1.   c.   This is a zero-growth stock, or perpetuity: $\hat{P}_0 = D/k_s = \$4.00/0.12 = \$33.33$.

2.   e. $\hat{P}_0 = \dfrac{D_0(1+g)}{k_s - g} = \dfrac{\$2.00(1.10)}{0.20 - 0.10} = \$22.00$.

Since the stock is currently selling for $25.00, the stock is not in equilibrium and is overvalued by $3.00.

3.   c. $\dfrac{\text{Dividend}}{\text{yield}} = \dfrac{D_1}{P_0} = \dfrac{D_0(1+g)}{P_0} = \dfrac{\$1.50(1.05)}{\$15.75} = 0.10 = 10\%$.

$\dfrac{\text{Capital}}{\text{gains yield}} = \dfrac{\hat{P}_1 - P_0}{P_0} = \dfrac{P_0(1+g) - P_0}{P_0} = \dfrac{\$16.5375 - \$15.75}{\$15.75} = g = 5\%$.

4.   a. $\hat{P}_0 = \dfrac{D_0(1+g)}{k_s - g} = \dfrac{\$2.00(0.95)}{0.15 - (-0.05)} = \dfrac{\$1.90}{0.20} = \$9.50$.

$\hat{P}_3 = \hat{P}_0(1+g)^3 = \$9.50(0.95)^3 = \$9.50(0.8574) = \$8.15$.

The Gordon model can also be used:

$$\hat{P}_3 = \frac{D_4}{k_s - g} = \frac{D_0(1+g)^4}{0.15 - (-0.05)} = \frac{\$2.00(0.95)^4}{0.20} = \frac{\$2.00(0.8145)}{0.20} = \$8.15.$$

5. b. To calculate the current value of a nonconstant growth stock, follow these steps:

1. Determine the expected stream of dividends during the nonconstant growth period. Also, calculate the expected dividend at the end of the first year of constant growth that will be used later to calculate the stock price.

   $D_1 = \$0.50.$
   $D_2 = D_1(1 + g) = \$0.50(1 + 0.0) = \$0.50.$
   $D_3 = D_2(1 + g) = \$0.50(1.05) = \$0.525.$
   $D_4 = D_3(1 + g) = \$0.525(1.10) = \$0.5775.$

2. Discount the expected dividends during the nonconstant growth period at the investor's required rate of return to find their present value.

3. Calculate the expected stock price at the end of the final year of nonconstant growth. This occurs at the end of Year 3. Use the Gordon model for this calculation.

   $$\hat{P}_3 = \frac{D_4}{k_s - g} = \frac{\$0.5775}{0.15 - 0.10} = \$11.55.$$

   Then discount this stock price back 3 periods at the investor's required rate of return to find its present value.

   $PV = \$11.55\,[1/(1.15)^3] = \$11.55(0.6575) = \$7.59.$

4. Add the present value of the stock price expected at the end of Year 3 plus the dividends expected in Years 1, 2, and 3 to find the present value of the stock, P_0.

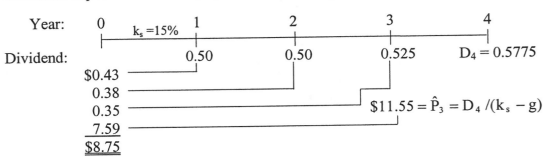

Alternatively, input 0, 0.5, 0.5, 12.075 (0.525 + 11.55) into the cash flow register, input I = 15, and then solve for NPV = $8.75.

6. c. To calculate the expected stock price at the end of Year 1, $\hat{P}_1$, follow the same procedure you did to find the value of the nonconstant growth stock in Self-Test Problem 5. However, discount values to Year 1 instead of Year 0. Also, remember that the dividend in Year 1, D_1, is not included in the valuation because it has already been paid and therefore adds nothing to the wealth of the investor buying the stock at the end of Year 1.

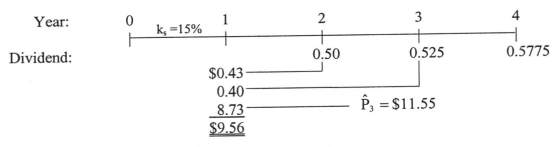

Alternatively, input 0, 0.5, 12.075 (0.525 + 11.55) into the cash flow register, input I = 15, and then solve for NPV = $9.5652 ≈ $9.57.

7. c. $$\text{Dividend yield} = \frac{D_1}{P_0} = \frac{\$0.50}{\$8.75} = 5.7\%.$$

$$\text{Capital gains yield} = \frac{\hat{P}_1 - P_0}{P_0} = \frac{\$9.5652 - \$8.75}{\$8.75} = 9.3\%.$$

The Total yield = Dividend yield + Capital gains yield = 5.7% + 9.3% = 15%. The total yield must equal the required rate of return. Also, the capital gains yield is not equal to the growth rate during the nonconstant growth phase of a nonconstant growth stock. Finally, the dividend and capital gains yields are not constant until the constant growth state is reached.

8. e.

$$P_0 = \frac{D_0(1+g)}{k_s - g}$$

$$\$45.83 = \frac{\$2.50(1+g)}{0.16 - g}$$

$$\$7.33 - \$45.83g = \$2.50 + \$2.50g$$
$$\$48.33g = \$4.83$$
$$g = 0.0999 \approx 10\%.$$

9. d. $D_0 = \$1.00$; $k_s = 8\% + 7\% = 15\%$; $g_1 = 40\%$; $g_2 = 20\%$; $g_n = 7\%$, $P_0 = ?$

Year:	0		1		2		3
		$k_s = 15\%$					
Dividend:		$g = 40\%$	1.40	$g = 20\%$	1.68	$g = 7\%$	1.7976
		$\times 1/1.15$			22.47*		
	\$1.22	$\times 1/(1.15)^2$			24.15		
	18.26						
	\$19.48						

$$*\hat{P}_2 = \frac{\$1.7976}{0.15 - 0.07} = \$22.47.$$

Alternatively, input 0, 1.40, 24.15 (1.68 + 22.47) into the cash flow register, input I = 15, and then solve for NPV = \$19.48.

10. a. Exxon Mobil bonds: Price = \$815.98, Maturity = 20 years, PMT = \$35 per 6 months, and they are callable at \$1,150 after 10 periods (5 years).

Will the bond's YTM or YTC be applicable? The bond is selling at a discount, so $k_d >$ Coupon interest rate. Therefore, the bond is not likely to be called, so calculate the YTM.

Input N = 2 × 20 = 40, PV = -815.98, PMT = 35, FV = 1000, and solve for I = $k_d/2$ = 4.5%. EAR = $(1.045)^2 - 1 = 9.2\%$.

Preferred: $D_p = \$1.50$ per quarter and $P_p = \$75$.
$k_p = \$1.50/\$75 = 2\% =$ periodic rate. EAR = $(1.02)^4 - 1 = 8.24\%$.

Thus, the Exxon Mobil bonds provide the higher effective annual rate of return at 9.2%.

11.   **a.**   To calculate Chadmark's current stock price, follow the following steps: (1) Determine the expected stream of dividends during the nonconstant growth period. You will need to calculate the expected dividend at the end of Year 5, which is the first year of constant growth. This dividend will be used in the next step to calculate the stock price. (2) Calculate the expected stock price at the end of the final year of nonconstant growth. This occurs at the end of Year 4. Use the Gordon model for this calculation. (3) Add the value obtained in Step 2 to the dividend expected in Year 4. (4) Put the values obtained in the prior steps on a time line and discount them at the required rate of return to find the present value of Chadmark's stock. These steps are shown below.

$D_0 = \$0$; $D_1 = \$0$; $D_2 = \$0.75$; $D_3 = \$0.75(1.4) = \$1.05$; $D_4 = \$0.75(1.4)^2 = \$1.47$; $D_5 = \$0.75(1.4)^2(1.10) = \$1.617$.

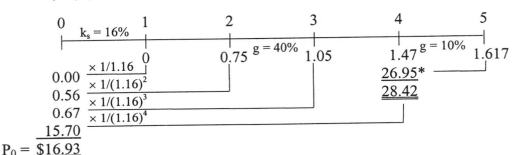

$*\hat{P}_4 = \$1.617/(0.16 - 0.10) = \$26.95$.

$CF_0 = 0$; $CF_1 = 0$; $CF_2 = 0.75$; $CF_3 = 1.05$; $CF_4 = 28.42$.

Alternatively, using a financial calculator you could input the cash flows as shown above into the cash flow register, input $I = 16$, and press NPV to obtain the stock's value today of $16.93.

12.   **c.**   First, set up the time line as follows. Note that D_5 is used to find $\hat{P}_4$, which is treated as part of the cash flow at $t = 4$:

0		1		2		3		4		5
$k_s = 20\%$										

$g = 0\%$ 2.00   2.00 $g = 8\%$ 2.16   2.333 $g = 15\%$ 2.6827

1.667 × 1/1.20
1.389 × 1/(1.20)²   53.654*
1.250 × 1/(1.20)³   55.987
27.000 × 1/(1.20)⁴

$P_0 = \underline{\$31.306}$

$*\hat{P}_4 = \$2.6827/(0.20 - 0.15) = \$53.654$.

Enter the time line values into the cash flow register, with I = 20, to find NPV = $31.31. Be sure to enter $CF_0 = 0$. Note that $\hat{P}_4$ is the PV, at t = 4, of dividends from t = 5 to infinity; that is, the PV of the dividends after the stock is expected to become a constant growth stock.

13. b. $FCF_1 = EBIT(1 - T) + Depreciation - \dfrac{Capital}{expenditures} - \Delta \left(\begin{array}{c} Net\ operating \\ working\ capital \end{array} \right)$

$= \$950,000,000 + \$190,000,000 - \$380,000,000 - \$0$

$= \$760,000,000.$

$$Firm\ value = \frac{FCF_1}{WACC - g}$$

$$= \frac{\$760,000,000}{0.09 - 0.04}$$

$$= \frac{\$760,000,000}{0.05}$$

$$= \$15,200,000,000.$$

This is the total firm value. Now find the market value of its equity.

$$MV_{Total} = MV_{Equity} + MV_{Debt}$$
$$\$15,200,000,000 = MV_{Equity} + \$5,200,000,000$$
$$MV_{Equity} = \$10,000,000,000.$$

This is the market value of all the equity. Divide by the number of shares to find the price per share. $\$10,000,000,000/250,000,000 = \$40.00$.

14. d. The firm's free cash flow is expected to grow at a constant rate, hence we can apply a constant growth formula to determine the total value of the firm.

Firm value = $FCF_1/(WACC - g)$
Firm value = $\$75,000,000/(0.09 - 0.06)$
Firm value = $\$2,500,000,000.$

To find the value of an equity claim upon the company (share of stock), we must subtract out the market value of debt and preferred stock. This firm happens to be entirely equity funded, and this step is unnecessary. Hence, to find the value of a share of stock, we divide equity value (or in this case, firm value) by the number of shares outstanding.

Equity value per share = Equity value/Shares outstanding
Equity value per share = $2,500,000,000/50,000,000
Equity value per share = $50.

Each share of common stock is worth $50, according to the corporate valuation model.

15.   e.   The preferred stock pays $5 annually in dividends. Therefore, its nominal rate of return would be:

Nominal rate of return = $5/$71.43 = 7%.

Or alternatively, you could determine the security's periodic return and multiply by 4.

Periodic rate of return = $1.25/$71.43 = 1.75%.
Nominal rate of return = 1.75% × 4 = 7%.

16.   b. $EAR = (1 + NOM/4)^4 - 1$
$EAR = (1 + 0.07/4)^4 - 1$
$EAR = (1.0175)^4 - 1$
$EAR = 1.0719 - 1$
$EAR = 0.0719 = 7.19\%.$

17.   a.   The value of any asset is the present value of all future cash flows expected to be generated from the asset. Hence, if we can find the present value of the dividends during the period preceding long-run constant growth and subtract that total from the current stock price, the remaining value would be the present value of the cash flows to be received during the period of long-run constant growth.

$D_1 = \$1.50 \times (1.15)^1 = \$1.7250$ $PV(D_1) = \$1.7250/(1.10)^1$ $= \$1.5682$
$D_2 = \$1.50 \times (1.15)^2 = \$1.98375$ $PV(D_2) = \$1.98375/(1.10)^2$ $= \$1.6395$
$D_3 = \$1.50 \times (1.15)^3 = \$2.2813125$ $PV(D_3) = \$2.2813125/(1.10)^3$ $= \$1.7140$

$\Sigma\ PV(D_1\ to\ D_3)$ $= \$4.9217$

Therefore, the PV of the remaining dividends is: $40.9200 − $4.9217 = $35.9983. Compounding this value forward to Year 3, we find that the value of all dividends received during constant growth is $47.9137. [$35.9983(1.10)^3 = $47.9137.] Applying the constant growth formula, we can solve for the constant growth rate:

$$\hat{P}_3 = D_3(1 + g)/(k_s - g)$$
$$\$47.9137 = \$2.2813125(1 + g)/(0.10 - g)$$
$$\$4.7914 - \$47.9137g = \$2.2813125 + \$2.2813125g$$
$$\$2.5101 = \$50.1950g$$
$$5.00\% = g.$$

18.   c.   First, solve for the current price.

$P_0 = D_1/(k_s - g)$
$P_0 = \$2.25/(0.11 - 0.04)$
$P_0 = \$32.1429 \approx \$32.14.$

If the stock is in a constant growth state, the constant dividend growth rate is also the capital gains yield for the stock and the stock price growth rate. Hence, to find the price of the stock five years from today:

$\hat{P}_5 = P_0(1 + g)^5$

$\hat{P}_5 = \$32.1429(1.04)^5$

$\hat{P}_5 = \$39.1067 \approx \$39.11.$

LEARNING OBJECTIVES

- Explain what is meant by a firm's weighted average cost of capital.

- Define and calculate the component costs of debt and preferred stock.

- Explain why retained earnings are not free and use three approaches to estimate the component cost of retained earnings.

- Briefly explain why the cost of new common equity is higher than the cost of retained earnings, calculate the cost of new common equity, and calculate the retained earnings breakpoint—which is the point where new common equity would have to be issued.

- Briefly explain the two alternative approaches that can be used to account for flotation costs.

- Calculate the firm's composite, or weighted average, cost of capital.

- Identify some of the factors that affect the overall, composite cost of capital.

- Briefly explain how firms should evaluate projects with different risks, and the problems encountered when divisions within the same firm all use the firm's composite WACC when considering capital budgeting projects.

- List and briefly explain the three separate and distinct types of risk that can be identified, and explain the procedure many firms use when developing subjective risk-adjusted costs of capital.

- List some problem areas in estimating the cost of capital.

OVERVIEW

When companies issue stocks or bonds, they are raising capital that can be invested in various projects. Capital is a necessary factor of production, and like any other factor, it has a cost. This cost is equal to the marginal investor's required return on the security in question.

Recall that the firm's primary financial objective is to maximize shareholder value. Companies can increase shareholder value by investing in projects that earn more than the cost of capital. For this reason, the cost of capital is sometimes referred to as a hurdle rate: For a project to be accepted, it must earn more than its hurdle rate.

Although its most important use is in capital budgeting, the cost of capital is also used for at least three other purposes: (1) It is a key input required for determining a firm's or division's Economic Value Added (EVA); (2) managers estimate and use the cost of capital when deciding if they should lease or purchase assets; and, (3) the cost of capital has also been important over time in the regulation of electric, gas, and telephone companies.

The same factors that affect required rates of return on securities by investors also determine a firm's cost of capital, so investors and corporate treasurers often use exactly the same models.

OUTLINE

Determining the firm's cost of capital, or the proper discount rate for use in calculating the present value of the cash inflows for the firm's projects, is an important element of the capital budgeting process. The cost of capital used in capital budgeting should be calculated as a weighted average, or composite, of the various types of funds a firm generally uses, regardless of the specific financing used to fund a particular project.

- ■ *Capital components* are items on the right-hand side of the balance sheet such as debt, preferred stock, and common equity. Any increase in total assets must be financed by an increase in one or more of these capital components.
  - ☐ Each element of capital has a component cost that can be identified as follows:
    - k_d = interest rate on the firm's new debt, before taxes.
    - $k_d(1 - T)$ = after-tax cost of new debt where T is the firm's marginal tax rate.
    - k_p = component cost of preferred stock.
    - k_s = cost of retained earnings; it is equal to the required rate of return investors require on a firm's common stock.
    - WACC = the weighted average cost of capital.

The after-tax cost of debt, $k_d(1 - T)$, is the interest rate on new debt, k_d, less the tax savings that result because interest is tax deductible. The value of the firm's stock depends on

after-tax cash flows. So, we are concerned with after-tax cash flows, and since cash flows and rates of return should be placed on a comparable basis, the interest rate should be adjusted downward to take account of the preferential tax treatment of debt.

■ If a firm has a tax rate of 40 percent and can borrow at a rate of 10 percent, then its after-tax cost of debt is $k_d = 10\%(1 - 0.40) = 10\%(0.60) = 6.0\%$.

■ In effect, the government pays part of the cost of debt because interest is tax deductible.

■ k_d is the interest rate on new debt, the marginal cost of debt, not that on already outstanding debt.
  □ The primary concern with the cost of capital is to use it for capital budgeting decisions. The rate at which the firm has borrowed in the past is irrelevant.

The component cost of preferred stock, k_p, is the preferred dividend, D_p, divided by the current price of the preferred stock, P_p: $k_p = D_p/P_p$.

■ No tax adjustments are made when calculating k_p because preferred dividends, unlike interest expense on debt, are not deductible, and hence there are no tax savings.
  □ Some companies have tried to come up with ways to issue securities that are similar to preferred stock but that are structured in ways that enable them to deduct the payments made on these securities.

■ If a firm's preferred stock pays a $10 dividend per share and sells for $97.50 per share, the firm's cost of preferred stock, k_p, is calculated as: $k_p = \$10.00/\$97.50 = 10.3\%$.

The cost of retained earnings, k_s, is the rate of return stockholders require on the company's common stock.

■ New common equity is raised in two ways: (1) By retaining some of the firm's current earnings and (2) by issuing new common stock.
  □ A corporation's management might be tempted to think that retained earnings are "free" because they represent money that is "left over" after paying dividends, but this capital still has a cost.
  □ The reason we must assign a cost of capital to retained earnings involves the *opportunity cost principle*. The firm's after-tax earnings belong to its stockholders. Stockholders could have received the earnings as dividends and invested this money in other stocks, in bonds, in real estate, or in anything else.
  □ The firm should earn on its retained earnings at least as much as the stockholders themselves could earn on alternative investments of comparable risk.
  □ People experienced in estimating equity capital costs recognize that both careful analysis and sound judgment are required.

■ There are three approaches used to estimate k_s:

☐ The Capital Asset Pricing Model (CAPM) works as follows:

- Estimate the risk-free rate, k_{RF}, usually based on U.S. Treasury securities.
- Estimate the stock's beta coefficient, b_i, as an index of risk.
- Estimate the expected rate of return on the market, or on an "average" stock, k_M.
- Substitute the preceding values into the CAPM equation, $k_s = k_{RF} + (k_M - k_{RF})b_i$, to estimate the required rate of return on the stock in question.
- Thus, if $k_{RF} = 8\%$, $k_M = 13\%$, and b_i is 0.7, then $k_s = 8\% + (13\% - 8\%)0.7 = 11.5\%$.

☐ The *bond-yield-plus-risk-premium approach* is a subjective, ad hoc procedure to estimate a firm's cost of common equity. It estimates k_s by adding a risk premium of three to five percentage points to the firm's own bond yield. Thus, $k_s =$ Bond yield + Risk premium.

- It is logical to think that firms with risky, low-rated, and consequently high-interest-rate debt will also have risky, high-cost equity. This approach utilizes this logic.
- If the firm uses a risk premium of 4 percentage points, and its bond rate is 12 percent, then $k_s = 12\% + 4\% = 16\%$.
- Because the risk premium is a judgmental estimate, this method is not likely to produce a precise cost of equity; however, it does get us "into the right ballpark."

☐ The required rate of return, k_s, may also be estimated by the *discounted cash flow (DCF) approach*. This approach is also called the *dividend-yield-plus-growth rate approach*, as it combines the expected dividend yield, D_1/P_0, with the expected future growth rate, g, of earnings and dividends, or

$$k_s = \hat{k}_s = \frac{D_1}{P_0} + \text{Expected g.}$$

- The DCF approach assumes that stocks are normally in equilibrium and that growth is expected to be at a constant rate. If growth is not constant, then a nonconstant growth model must be used.
- The expected growth rate may be based on projections of past growth rates, if they have been relatively stable, or on expected future growth rates as estimated in some other manner.
- Security analysts regularly make earnings and dividend growth forecasts, looking at such factors as projected sales, profit margins, and competitive factors.
- Another method for estimating g involves first forecasting the firm's average future dividend payout ratio and its complement, the retention rate, and then multiplying the retention rate by the company's expected future rate of return on equity (ROE):

$$g = (\text{Retention rate})(\text{ROE}) = (1.0 - \text{Payout rate})(\text{ROE}).$$

- Intuitively, firms that are more profitable and retain a larger portion of their earnings for reinvestment in the firm will tend to have higher growth rates than firms that are less profitable and pay out a higher percentage of their earnings as dividends.
- If the firm's next expected dividend is $1.24, its expected growth rate is 8 percent per year, and its stock is selling for $23 per share, then

$$k_s = \hat{k}_s = \frac{\$1.24}{\$23} + 8.0\%$$
$$= 5.4\% + 8.0\%$$
$$= 13.4\%.$$

- ☐ If the firm cannot earn about 13.4 percent on reinvested equity capital, then it should pay its earnings to stockholders and let them invest directly in other assets that do provide this return. Thus, k_s is an opportunity cost.
- ☐ It is recommended that all three approaches be used in estimating the required rate of return on common stock. When the methods produce widely different results, judgment must be used in selecting the best estimate.

Companies generally hire an investment banker to assist them when they issue common stock, preferred stock, or bonds. In return for a fee, the investment banker helps the company structure the terms, sets a price for the issue, and then sells the issue to investors. The banker's fees are often referred to as flotation costs, and the total cost of capital should include not only the required return paid to investors but also the flotation fees paid to the investment banker for marketing the issue.

- ■ *Flotation costs* should be included in a complete analysis of the cost of capital. Two alternative approaches can be used to account for flotation costs.
  - ☐ The first approach simply adds the estimated dollar amount of flotation costs for each project to the project's up-front cost. Because of the now-higher investment cost, the project's expected rate of return and NPV are decreased.
  - ☐ The second approach involves adjusting the cost of capital rather than increasing the project's cost. If the firm plans to continue to use the capital in the future, as is generally true for equity, then this second approach is better. When calculating the cost of common equity, the DCF approach can be adapted to account for flotation costs. For a constant growth stock, the *cost of new common stock, k_e,* can be expressed as follows:

$$k_e = \frac{D_1}{P_0(1-F)} + g.$$

- Here F is the percentage flotation cost required to sell new stock, so $P_0(1-F)$ is the net price per share received by the company.

- If the firm has a flotation cost of 10 percent, its cost of new outside equity is computed as follows:

$$k_e = \frac{\$1.24}{\$23(1 - 0.10)} + 8.0\% = 14\%.$$

- If the firm can earn 14 percent on investments financed by new common stock, then earnings, dividends, and the growth rate will be maintained, and the price per share will not fall. If it earns more than 14 percent, the price will rise; while if it earns less, the price will fall.

■ Because of flotation costs, dollars raised by selling new stock must "work harder" than dollars raised by retained earnings. Moreover, since no flotation costs are involved, retained earnings have a lower cost than new stock. Therefore, firms should utilize retained earnings to the extent possible to avoid the cost of issuing new common stock.

☐ The *retained earnings breakpoint* represents the total amount of financing that can be raised before the firm is forced to sell new common stock, and is calculated as:

Retained earnings breakpoint = Addition to retained earnings/Equity fraction.

- It is important to recognize that this breakpoint is only suggestive—it is not written in stone. Rather than issuing new common stock, the company could use more debt (hence, less equity), or it could increase its additional retained earnings by reducing its dividend payout ratio. Both actions would increase the retained earnings breakpoint.
- Firms that have a large number of good investment opportunities generally maximize their retained earnings by paying out a smaller percentage of income as dividends than firms with fewer good investment opportunities.

■ Flotation cost adjustments can also be made for preferred stock and debt.

☐ For preferred stock, the flotation-adjusted cost is the preferred dividend, D_p, divided by the net issuing price, P_n, the price the firm receives on preferred after deducting flotation costs.

☐ If debt is issued to the public and flotation costs are incurred, the after-tax cost is found by calculating the after-tax yield to maturity, where the issue price is the bond's par value less the flotation expense.

Each firm has an optimal capital structure, defined as that mix of debt, preferred, and common equity that causes its stock price to be maximized.

■ A value-maximizing firm will establish a *target (optimal) capital structure* and then raise new capital in a manner designed to keep the actual capital structure on target over time.

■ The target proportions of debt, preferred stock, and common equity, along with the component costs of capital, are used to calculate the firm's *weighted average cost of capital (WACC)*.

■ The weighted average cost of capital calculation is shown below for a firm that finances 45 percent with debt, 2 percent with preferred stock, and 53 percent with common equity and that has the following after-tax component costs:

Component	Weight	×	After-tax Cost	=	Weighted Cost
Debt	0.45	×	6.0%	=	2.700%
Preferred	0.02	×	10.3	=	0.206
Common	0.53	×	13.4	=	7.102
			WACC	=	10.008% ≈ 10.0%

■ In more general terms, and in equation format,

$$WACC = w_d k_d (1 - T) + w_p k_p + w_c k_s.$$

■ Theoretically, the weights used should be based on the market values of the different securities, but if a firm's book value weights are reasonably close to its market value weights, book value weights can be used as a proxy for market value weights.

■ Note that total debt includes both long-term debt and bank debt (notes payable). Investor-supplied capital does not include other current liabilities such as accounts payable and accrued liabilities. Therefore, these other items are not included as part of the firm's capital structure.

The cost of capital is affected by a variety of factors. The two most important factors that are beyond the firm's direct control are the level of interest rates and tax rates.

■ If interest rates in the economy rise, the cost of debt capital increases because firms will have to pay bondholders a higher interest rate. Higher interest rates also increase the cost of common and preferred equity capital.

■ Tax rates are used in the calculation of the cost of debt, which is one of the components of WACC.
   □ There are other less apparent ways in which tax policy can affect the cost of capital. Lowering the capital gains tax rate relative to the rate on ordinary income would make stocks more attractive, which would reduce the cost of equity relative to that of debt. This would lead to a change in a firm's optimal capital structure.

■ A firm can affect its cost of capital through its capital structure policy, its dividend policy, and its investment (capital budgeting) policy.

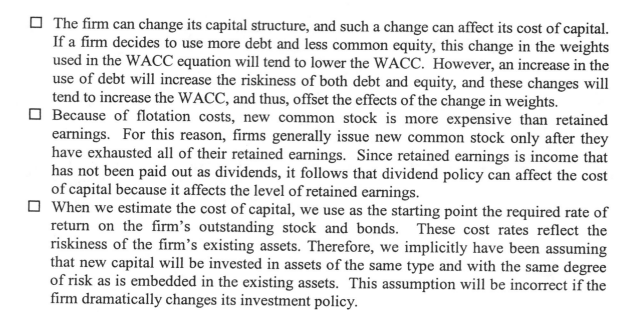

☐ The firm can change its capital structure, and such a change can affect its cost of capital. If a firm decides to use more debt and less common equity, this change in the weights used in the WACC equation will tend to lower the WACC. However, an increase in the use of debt will increase the riskiness of both debt and equity, and these changes will tend to increase the WACC, and thus, offset the effects of the change in weights.

☐ Because of flotation costs, new common stock is more expensive than retained earnings. For this reason, firms generally issue new common stock only after they have exhausted all of their retained earnings. Since retained earnings is income that has not been paid out as dividends, it follows that dividend policy can affect the cost of capital because it affects the level of retained earnings.

☐ When we estimate the cost of capital, we use as the starting point the required rate of return on the firm's outstanding stock and bonds. These cost rates reflect the riskiness of the firm's existing assets. Therefore, we implicitly have been assuming that new capital will be invested in assets of the same type and with the same degree of risk as is embedded in the existing assets. This assumption will be incorrect if the firm dramatically changes its investment policy.

The cost of capital is a key element in the capital budgeting process. A project should be accepted only if its estimated return exceeds its cost of capital. For this reason, the cost of capital is sometimes referred to as the "hurdle rate," because project returns must jump the "hurdle" to be accepted.

■ Investors require higher returns for riskier investments. Consequently, a company that is raising capital to take on risky projects will have a higher cost of capital than a company that is investing in safer projects.

■ Ideally, the hurdle rate for each project should reflect the risk of the project itself, not necessarily the risks associated with the firm's average project as reflected in the firm's composite WACC.

■ Applying a specific hurdle rate to each project insures that every project is evaluated properly.

■ In general, failing to adjust for differences in risk would lead a firm to accept too many risky projects and reject too many safe ones. Over time, the firm will become more risky, its WACC will increase, and its shareholder value will suffer.

It is often difficult to estimate project risk. Three separate and distinct types of risk can be identified in capital budgeting: (1) stand-alone risk, (2) corporate, or within-firm, risk, and (3) market, or beta, risk.

■ *Stand-alone risk* is the risk an asset would have if it were a firm's only asset.
   □ It is measured by the variability of the project's expected returns.

■ *Corporate,* or *within-firm, risk* is the project's risk to the corporation, giving consideration to the fact that the project represents only one of the firm's portfolio of assets.
   □ It is measured by a project's impact on uncertainty about the firm's future earnings.

■ *Market,* or *beta, risk* is the riskiness of the project as seen by a well-diversified stockholder who recognizes that the project is only one of the firm's assets and that the firm's stock is but one small part of the investor's total portfolio.
   □ It is measured by the project's effect on the firm's beta coefficient.

■ Taking on a project with a high degree of either stand-alone or corporate risk will not necessarily affect the firm's beta. However, if the project has highly uncertain returns, and if those returns are highly correlated with returns on the firm's other assets and with most other assets in the economy, the project will have a high degree of all types of risk.

■ Of the three risk measures, market risk is theoretically the most relevant measure because of its effect on stock prices. However, market risk is the most difficult to estimate.
   □ Most decision makers consider all three risk measures in a judgmental manner and then classify projects into subjective risk categories.
   □ *Risk-adjusted costs of capital* are developed for each risk category using the composite WACC as a starting point.
      • While this approach is better than not making any risk adjustments, these adjustments are subjective and somewhat arbitrary.

■ Risk adjustments are necessarily subjective and somewhat arbitrary. Unfortunately, there is no completely satisfactory way to specify exactly how much higher or lower we should go in setting risk-adjusted costs of capital.

A number of difficult issues relating to the cost of capital are listed below. These topics are covered in advanced finance courses.

■ Depreciation-generated funds are the largest single source of capital for many firms. The cost of depreciation-generated funds is approximately equal to the weighted average cost of capital that comes from retained earnings and low-cost debt.

■ As a general rule, the same principles of cost of capital estimation apply to both privately held and publicly owned firms, but the problems of obtaining input data are somewhat difficult for each.

■ One cannot overemphasize the practical difficulties encountered when one actually attempts to estimate the cost of equity.

■ It is difficult to assign proper risk-adjusted discount rates to capital budgeting projects of differing degrees of riskiness.

■ Establishing the target capital structure is a major task in itself.

Web Appendix 9A

As an alternative to the subjective approach, some firms use the CAPM to directly estimate the cost of capital for specific projects or divisions.

■ The Security Market Line (SML) equation expresses the risk/return relationship as follows:

$$k_s = k_{RF} + (k_M - k_{RF})b_i.$$

☐ For example, if a firm has a beta of 1.1, $k_M = 12\%$, and $k_{RF} = 8\%$, then its required rate of return would be $k_s = 8\% + (12\% - 8\%)1.1 = 12.4\%$. Stockholders would be willing to let the firm invest their money if the firm could earn 12.4 percent on their equity capital.

■ The acceptance of a particular capital budgeting project may cause a firm's overall beta to rise or fall, causing a change in the firm's cost of equity.
☐ The impact of any one project on a firm's beta will depend upon the size of the project relative to the firm's existing "portfolio" of projects.
☐ The beta of a portfolio of assets is equal to the weighted average of the betas of the individual assets.
☐ Holding other factors constant, an increase in a firm's beta coefficient will clearly result in a higher required return, k_s, and hence a decrease in price. To maintain a given price, there must be an increase in the expected rate of growth, dividends, or both. These factors, in turn, will result in an increase in the expected return. Therefore, an increase in the firm's beta coefficient will cause the stock price to decline unless the increased beta is offset by a higher expected rate of return.

■ If the beta coefficient for each project can be determined, then a *project cost of capital,* k_p, for each individual project could be found as follows:

$$k_p = k_{RF} + (k_M - k_{RF})b_p.$$

☐ High-beta, or high-risk, projects will have a relatively high cost of equity capital, while low-beta projects will have a correspondingly low cost of capital.

■ If the expected rate of return on a given capital project lies above the SML, the expected rate of return on the project is more than enough to compensate for its risk, and the project should be accepted. Conversely, if the project's rate of return lies below the SML, it should be rejected.

Web Appendix 9B

The estimation of project betas is even more difficult than that for stocks. However, two approaches have been developed for this purpose: the pure play method and the accounting beta method.

■ In the *pure play method*, the company tries to find several single-product companies in the same line of business as the project being evaluated, and it then averages those companies' betas to determine the cost of capital for its own project.
   ☐ The pure play approach can only be used for major assets such as whole divisions, and even then it's frequently difficult to implement because it is often impossible to find pure play proxy firms.

■ In the *accounting beta method*, a project's (or perhaps a division's) return on assets (ROA) is regressed against the average ROA for a large sample of firms, such as those included in the S&P 400. The resulting accounting beta is then used as a proxy for the market beta.
   ☐ Accounting betas for a totally new project can be calculated only after the project has been accepted, placed in operation, and begun to generate output and accounting results—too late for the capital budgeting decision.

SELF-TEST QUESTIONS

Definitional

1. The firm should calculate its cost of capital as a(n) _____ _____ of the after-tax costs of the various types of funds it uses.

2. Capital components are items on the right-hand side of the balance sheet such as the following: (1) _____, (2) _____ _____, and (3) _____ _____.

3. The cost of equity capital is defined as the _____ ____ _____ stockholders require on the firm's common stock.

4. There are _____ approaches that can be used to determine the cost of common equity.

5.   Assigning a cost to retained earnings is based on the _____ _____ principle.

6.   The cost of new outside equity capital is higher than the cost of internal equity (retained earnings) due to _____ _____.

7.   Using the Capital Asset Pricing Model (CAPM), the required rate of return on common equity is found as a function of the _____-_____ _____, the firm's _____ _____, and the required rate of return on an average _____.

8.   The cost of common equity may also be found by adding a(n) _____ _____ to the interest rate on the firm's own _____ yield.

9.   The required rate of return on common equity may also be estimated as the expected _____ _____ on the common stock plus the expected future _____ _____ of the dividends.

10.   The proportions of _____, _____ _____, and _____ _____ in the target capital structure should be used to calculate the _____ _____ cost of capital.

11.   The component cost of preferred stock is calculated as the _____ _____ divided by the preferred stock's _____ _____.

12.   One method for estimating g is by multiplying the _____ _____ by the company's expected future rate of return on equity (ROE).

13.   The capital structure that minimizes a firm's weighted average cost of capital also _____ its stock price.

14.   The two most important factors that affect the cost of capital and that are beyond the firm's direct control are the level of _____ rates and _____ rates.

15.   A firm can affect its cost of capital through its _____ _____ policy, its _____ policy, and its _____ policy.

16.   Two approaches can be used to account for flotation costs: (1) Add the estimated dollar amount of flotation costs for each project to the project's ____-_____ _____ and (2) _____ the cost of capital.

17.   Firms that are more profitable and retain a larger portion of their earnings for reinvestment in the firm will tend to have _____ growth rates than firms who are less profitable and pay out a greater portion of their earnings as _____.

18. Flotation cost adjustments can also be made for _____ stock and _____, as well as for common stock.

19. The cost of capital is sometimes referred to as the _____ rate because projects must jump over it to be accepted.

20. Ideally, the hurdle rate for each project should reflect the _____ of the project itself, not necessarily those associated with the firm's _____ project as reflected in the firm's composite WACC.

21. In general, failing to adjust for differences in risk would lead a firm to accept too many risky projects and reject too many safe ones. Over time, it will become _____ risky, its WACC will _____, and its shareholder value will suffer.

22. Three separate and distinct types of risk can be identified in capital budgeting: _____- _____ risk, _____ risk, and _____ risk.

23. Of the three risk measures, _____ risk is theoretically the most relevant measure because of its effect on stock prices.

24. If the expected rate of return on a given capital project lies _____ the SML, the expected rate of return on the project is more than enough to compensate for its risk and the project should be accepted.

25. _____-_____ risk is the risk an asset would have if it were a firm's only asset.

26. The cost of depreciation-generated funds is approximately equal to the weighted average cost of capital in the interval in which capital comes from _____ _____ and low-cost _____.

27. Projects are classified into subjective risk categories and then _____-_____ _____ ____ _____ are developed for each category using the composite WACC as a starting point.

28. In effect, the government pays part of the cost of debt because interest is _____ _____.

29. New common equity is raised in two ways: (1) by _____ some of the firm's current earnings and (2) by _____ new common stock.

30. The _____ _____ _____ represents the total amount of financing that can be raised before the firm is forced to sell new common stock.

31. A value-maximizing firm will establish a(n) _____ _____ _____ and then raise new capital in a manner designed to keep the actual capital structure on target over time.

32. The impact of any one project on a firm's beta will depend upon the _____ of the project relative to the firm's existing "portfolio" of projects.

33. The primary concern with the cost of capital is to use it for capital budgeting decisions. Consequently, the rate at which the firm has borrowed in the past is _____.

34. Other current liabilities such as _____ _____ and _____ _____ should not be included as part of the firm's capital structure.

35. It is important to recognize that the retained earnings breakpoint is not written in stone. Rather than issuing new common stock, the company could use more _____, or it could increase its additional retained earnings by reducing its _____ _____ _____.

Conceptual

36. Funds acquired by the firm through preferred stock have a cost to the firm equal to the preferred dividend divided by the net issuing price, P_n, the price the firm receives on preferred after deducting flotation costs.

    a. True   **b.** False

37. Which of the following statements could be true concerning the costs of debt and equity?

    a. The cost of debt for Firm A is greater than the cost of equity for Firm A.
    b. The cost of debt for Firm A is greater than the cost of equity for Firm B.
    c. The cost of retained earnings for Firm A is less than its cost of new outside equity.
    d. The cost of retained earnings for Firm A is less than its cost of debt.
    e. Both statements b and c could be true.

38. Which of the following statements is most correct?

    a. If Congress raised the corporate tax rate, this would lower the effective cost of debt but probably would also reduce the amount of retained earnings available to corporations, so the effect on the marginal cost of capital is uncertain.

    b. For corporate investors, 70 percent of the dividends received on both common and preferred stocks is exempt from taxes. However, neither preferred nor common dividends may be deducted by the issuing company. Therefore, the dividend exclusion has no effect on a company's cost of capital, so its WACC would probably not change at all if the dividend exclusion rule were rescinded by Congress.

    c. The calculation for a firm's WACC includes an adjustment to the cost of debt for taxes, since interest is deductible, and includes the cost of all current liabilities.

    d. Each of the above statements is true.

    e. Each of the above statements is false.

SELF-TEST PROBLEMS

1. Roland Corporation's next expected dividend (D_1) is $2.50. The firm has maintained a constant payout ratio of 50 percent during the past 7 years. Seven years ago its EPS was $1.50. The firm's beta coefficient is 1.2. The required return on an average stock in the market is 13 percent, and the risk-free rate is 7 percent. Roland's A-rated bonds are yielding 10 percent, and its current stock price is $30. Which of the following values is the most reasonable estimate of Roland's cost of common stock, k_s?

    a. 10%   **b.** 12%   **c.** 14%   **d.** 20%   **e.** 26%

2. The director of capital budgeting for See-Saw Inc., manufacturers of playground equipment, is considering a plan to expand production facilities in order to meet an increase in demand. He estimates that this expansion will produce a rate of return of 11 percent. The firm's target capital structure calls for a debt/equity ratio of 0.8. See-Saw currently has a bond issue outstanding that will mature in 25 years and has a 7 percent annual coupon rate. The bonds are currently selling for $804. The firm has maintained a constant growth rate of 6 percent. See-Saw's next expected dividend is $2 ($D_1$) and its current stock price is $40. Its tax rate is 40 percent. Should it undertake the expansion? (Assume that there is no preferred stock outstanding and that any new debt will have a 25-year maturity.)

    a. No; the expected return is 2.5 percentage points lower than the cost of capital.

    b. No; the expected return is 1.0 percentage point lower than the cost of capital.

    c. Yes; the expected return is 0.5 percentage point higher than the cost of capital.

    d. Yes; the expected return is 1.0 percentage point higher than the cost of capital.

    e. Yes; the expected return is 2.5 percentage points higher than the cost of capital.

3. The management of Florida Phosphate Industries (FPI) is planning next year's capital budget. The company's earnings and dividends are growing at a constant rate of 5 percent. The last dividend, D_0, was $0.90; and the current equilibrium stock price is $7.73. FPI can raise new debt at a 14 percent before-tax cost. FPI is at its optimal capital structure, which is 40 percent debt and 60 percent equity, and the firm's marginal tax rate is 40 percent. FPI has the following independent, indivisible, and equally risky investment opportunities:

Project	Cost	Rate of Return
A	$15,000	17%
B	15,000	16
C	12,000	15
D	20,000	13

What is FPI's optimal capital budget?

a. $62,000   b. $42,000   c. $30,000   d. $15,000   e. $0

4. Gator Products Company (GPC) is at its optimal capital structure of 70 percent common equity and 30 percent debt. GPC's WACC is 14 percent. GPC has a marginal tax rate of 40 percent. Next year's dividend is expected to be $2.00 per share, and GPC has a constant growth in earnings and dividends of 6 percent. The after-tax cost of common stock used in the WACC is based on new outside equity with a flotation cost of 10 percent, while the before-tax cost of debt is 12 percent. What is GPC's current equilibrium stock price?

a. $12.73   b. $17.23   c. $20.37   d. $23.70   e. $37.20

(The following data apply to the next four Self-Test Problems.)

Sun Products Company (SPC) uses only debt and equity. It can borrow unlimited amounts at an interest rate of 12 percent so long as it finances at its target capital structure, which calls for 45 percent debt and 55 percent common equity. Its last dividend was $2.40, its expected constant growth rate is 5 percent, and its stock sells for $24. SPC's tax rate is 40 percent. Four projects are available: Project A has a cost of $240 million and a rate of return of 13 percent, Project B has a cost of $125 million and a rate of return of 12 percent, Project C has a cost of $200 million and a rate of return of 11 percent, and Project D has a cost of $150 million and a rate of return of 10 percent. All of the company's potential projects are independent and equally risky.

5. What is SPC's cost of common stock?

a. 15.50%   b. 13.40%   c. 7.20%   d. 12.50%   e. 16.00%

6. What is SPC's weighted average cost of capital? In other words, what WACC cost rate should it use to evaluate capital budgeting projects (these four projects plus any others that might arise during the year, provided the WACC remains as it is currently)?

    a. 12.05%   **b.** 13.40%   **c.** 11.77%   **d.** 12.50%   **e.** 10.61%

7. What is SPC's optimal capital budget (in millions)?

    a. $240   **b.** $325   **c.** $365   **d.** $565   **e.** $715

8. Assume now that all four projects are independent; however, Project A has been judged a very risky project, while Projects C and D have been judged low-risk projects. Project B remains an average-risk project. If SPC adjusts its WACC by 2 percentage points up or down to account for risk, what is its optimal capital budget (in millions) now?

    a. $365   **b.** $390   **c.** $440   **d.** $475   **e.** $715

9. Hodor Manufacturing Co.'s (HMC) common stock currently sells for $50.00 per share. Assume the stock is in a state of constant growth, has an expected dividend yield of 4.5%, and an expected capital gains yield of 6.5%. The current dividend payout ratio is 30% and the firm's return on equity is 9.3%. The firm requires external funds for a new project and anticipates issuing additional shares of common stock at its current price of $50.00. However, the process of issuing this new equity is expected to result in a flotation expense equivalent to 10% of the price of the stock. If the firm goes ahead with its equity issue, what will be the firm's cost for this new common stock?

    a. 10.75%   **b.** 11.50%   **c.** 9.65%   **d.** 12.00%   **e.** 13.25%

    (The following data apply to the next two Self-Test Problems.)

    Helena's Candies Co. (HCC) has a target capital structure of 55% equity and 45% debt to fund its $5 billion in operating assets. Furthermore, HCC has a weighted average cost of capital (WACC) of 12.0%. Its before-tax cost of debt is 9%; and its tax rate is 40%. The company's retained earnings are adequate to fund the common equity portion of the capital budget. The firm's expected dividend next year (D_1) is $4 and the current stock price is $40.

10. What is the company's expected growth rate?

    a. 4.50%   **b.** 5.25%   **c.** 5.75%   **d.** 6.30%   **e.** 7.40%

11. If the firm's net income is expected to be $500 million, what portion of its net income is the firm expected to pay out as dividends?

  a. 33.33%   **b.** 40.00%   **c.** 59.30%   **d.** 50.00%   **e.** 45.00%

12. Sunrise Canoes Inc. has determined that its optimal capital structure consists of 55% equity and 45% debt. Sunrise must raise additional capital to fund its upcoming expansion. The firm has $0.5 million in retained earnings that has a cost of 11%. Its investment bankers have informed the company that it can issue an additional $3 million of new common stock at a cost of 14%. Furthermore, the firm can raise up to $1.5 million of debt at 10% and an additional $2 million at 12%. The firm has estimated that the proposed expansion will require an investment of $2.6 million. What is the weighted average cost of capital for the funds Sunrise will be raising?

  a. 10.40%   **b.** 10.75%   **c.** 11.20%   **d.** 10.00%   **e.** 11.50%

ANSWERS TO SELF-TEST QUESTIONS

1.	weighted average		**18.**	preferred; debt
2.	debt; preferred stock; common equity		**19.**	hurdle
3.	rate of return		**20.**	risk; average
4.	three		**21.**	more; increase
5.	opportunity cost		**22.**	stand-alone; corporate (within-firm); market (beta)
6.	flotation costs			
7.	risk-free rate (k_{RF}); beta coefficient (b); stock (k_M)		**23.**	market
			24.	above
8.	risk premium; bond		**25.**	Stand-alone
9.	dividend yield; growth rate		**26.**	retained earnings; debt
10.	debt; preferred stock; common equity; weighted average		**27.**	risk-adjusted costs of capital
			28.	tax deductible
11.	preferred dividends; current price		**29.**	retaining; issuing
12.	retention rate		**30.**	retained earnings breakpoint
13.	maximizes		**31.**	target (optimal) capital structure
14.	interest; tax		**32.**	size
15.	capital structure; dividend; investment		**33.**	irrelevant
16.	up-front cost; adjust		**34.**	accounts payable; accrued liabilities
17.	higher; dividends		**35.**	debt; dividend payout ratio

36. a. This statement is true.

37. e. If Firm A has more business risk than Firm B, Firm A's cost of debt could be greater than Firm B's cost of equity. Also, the cost of retained earnings is less than the cost of new outside equity due to flotation costs.

38. a. Statement a is correct. If Congress were to raise the tax rate, this would lower the cost of debt; however, a bigger chunk of the firm's earnings would go to Uncle Sam. The effect on the WACC would depend on which had the greater effect on the WACC. Statement b is false. Preferred stock generally has a lower before-tax cost than debt due to the dividend exclusion; however, if the dividend exclusion were omitted, preferred stock would have an increased before-tax cost. Statement c is false because the debt considered in the calculation of WACC includes only long-term debt and bank debt (notes payable).

SOLUTIONS TO SELF-TEST PROBLEMS

1. c. Use all three methods to estimate k_s.

CAPM: $k_s = k_{RF} + (k_M - k_{RF})b = 7\% + (13\% - 7\%)1.2 = 14.2\%$.

Risk Premium: k_s = Bond yield + Risk premium = $10\% + 4\% = 14\%$.

DCF: $k_s = D_1/P_0 + g$ = $2.50/$30 + g$, where g can be estimated as follows using a financial calculator:
Enter N = 7, PV = -0.75, PMT = 0, FV = 2.50, and solve for I = g = 18.77% $\approx$ 18.8%.

Therefore, $k_s = 0.083 + 0.188 = 27.1\%$.

Roland Corporation has apparently been experiencing supernormal growth during the past 7 years, and it is not reasonable to assume that this growth will continue. The first two methods yield a k_s of about 14 percent, which appears reasonable.

2. e. Cost of equity = k_s = $2/$40 + 0.06 = 0.11 = 11\%$.

Cost of debt = k_d = Yield to maturity on outstanding bonds based on current market price.

Using a financial calculator: Input N = 25, PV = -804, PMT = 70, FV = 1000, and solve for I = k_d = 9%.

In determining the capital structure weights, note that Debt/Equity = 0.8 or, for example, 4/5. Therefore, Debt/Assets is

$$\frac{D}{A} = \frac{Debt}{Debt + Equity} = \frac{4}{4+5} = \frac{4}{9},$$

and Equity/Assets = 5/9. Hence, the weighted average cost of capital is calculated as follows:

$$
\begin{aligned}
WACC &= k_d(1 - T)(D/A) + k_s(1 - D/A) \\
&= 0.09(1 - 0.4)(4/9) + 0.11(5/9) \\
&= 0.024 + 0.061 = 0.085 = 8.5\%.
\end{aligned}
$$

The cost of capital is 8.5 percent, while the expansion project's rate of return is 11.0 percent. Since the expected return is 2.5 percentage points higher than the cost, the expansion should be undertaken.

3.   b.   The cost of common stock is as follows:

$$k_s = \frac{D_0(1+g)}{P_0} + g = \frac{\$0.90(1.05)}{\$7.73} + 0.05 = 0.1723 = 17.23\%.$$

Now, determine the weighted average cost of capital.

$$
\begin{aligned}
WACC &= w_d(k_d)(1 - T) + w_c(k_s) \\
&= 0.4(14\%)(0.6) + 0.6(17.23\%) = 13.70\%.
\end{aligned}
$$

To determine FPI's optimal capital budget, we must determine those projects whose returns > WACC. (Note that all projects being considered are independent.) Since Projects A, B, and C all have returns > WACC, they should be accepted. Therefore, the optimal capital budget is $42,000.

4.   c.   GPC's WACC = 14%. Therefore,

$$
\begin{aligned}
14\% &= w_d(k_d)(1 - T) + w_c(k_e) \\
14\% &= 0.3(12\%)(0.6) + 0.7(k_e) \\
11.84\% &= 0.7(k_e) \\
k_e &= 16.91\%.
\end{aligned}
$$

Now, at equilibrium:

$$\hat{k}_e = k_e = \frac{D_1}{P_0(1-F)} + g$$

$$0.1691 = \frac{\$2.00}{P_0(1-0.10)} + 0.06$$

$$0.1091 = \frac{\$2.222}{P_0}$$

$$P_0 = \$20.37.$$

5. a. $k_s = [\$2.40(1.05)]/\$24 + 5\% = 0.1050 + 0.05 = 0.1550 = 15.50\%$.

6. c. $k_d = 12\%$; $k_d(1 - T) = 12\%(0.6) = 7.2\%$.

    $k_s = [\$2.40(1.05)]/\$24 + 5\% = 15.50\%$.

    WACC $= 0.45(7.2\%) + 0.55(15.50\%) = 11.77\%$.

7. c. Since all projects are equally risky and are independent, those projects whose returns > WACC should be chosen. Projects A and B have returns > 11.77%; therefore, the firm's optimal capital budget is $365 million.

8. d.

Project	Cost (Millions)	Return	Risk Level	Risk-Adjusted Cost of Capital
A	$240	13%	High	13.77%
B	125	12	Average	11.77
C	200	11	Low	9.77
D	150	10	Low	9.77

From Self-Test Problem 6 we know that SPC's WACC is 11.77%. We adjust the firm's WACC up by 2% for high-risk projects and lower it by 2% for low-risk projects. Note that once the WACC is risk-adjusted, Projects B, C, and D are acceptable as their returns are greater than the risk-adjusted WACC. Therefore, the firm's optimal capital budget is $475 million.

9. b. If the firm's dividend yield is 4.5% and its stock price is $50.00, the next expected annual dividend can be computed.

Dividend yield $= D_1/P_0$

$4.5\% = D_1/\$50.00$

$D_1 = \$2.25.$

Next, the firm's cost of new common stock can be determined from the DCF approach for the cost of equity.

$k_e = D_1/[P_0(1 - F)] + g$

$k_e = \$2.25/[\$50.00(1 - 0.10)] + 0.065$

$k_e = 11.50\%.$

10.   e.   Examining the DCF approach to the cost of retained earnings, the expected growth rate can be determined from the cost of common equity, price, and expected dividend. However, first, this problem requires that the formula for WACC be used to determine the cost of common equity.

$\text{WACC} = w_d(k_d)(1 - T) + w_c(k_s)$

$12.0\% = 0.45(9\%)(1 - 0.4) + 0.55(k_s)$

$9.57\% = 0.55(k_s)$

$k_s = 0.1740 \text{ or } 17.40\%.$

From the cost of common equity, the expected growth rate can now be determined.

$k_s = D_1/P_0 + g$

$0.1740 = \$4/\$40 + g$

$g = 0.0740 \text{ or } 7.40\%.$

11.   c.   From the formula for the long-run growth rate:

$g = (1 - \text{Div. payout ratio}) \times \text{ROE} = (1 - \text{Div. payout ratio}) \times (\text{NI/Equity})$

$0.0740 = (1 - \text{Div. payout ratio}) \times [\$500 \text{ million}/(0.55 \times 5,000 \text{ million})]$

$0.0740 = (1 - \text{Div. payout ratio}) \times 0.181818$

$0.407 = (1 - \text{Div. payout ratio})$

Div. payout ratio $= 0.5930 \text{ or } 59.30\%.$

12.   a.   If the investment requires \$2.6 million, that means that it requires \$1.43 million (55%) of equity capital and \$1.17 million (45%) of debt capital. In this scenario, the firm would exhaust its \$0.5 million of retained earnings and be forced to raise new stock at a cost of 14%. Needing \$1.17 million in debt capital, the firm could get by raising debt at only 10%. Therefore, its weighted average cost of capital is: WACC = $0.45(10\%)(1 - 0.4) + 0.55(14\%) = 10.4\%.$

LEARNING OBJECTIVES

- Define capital budgeting, explain why it is important, and state how project proposals are generally classified.

- List the steps involved in evaluating a capital budgeting project.

- Calculate payback period, discounted payback period, Net Present Value (NPV), and Internal Rate of Return (IRR) for a given project and evaluate each method.

- Define NPV profiles, and explain the rationale behind the NPV and IRR methods, their reinvestment rate assumptions, and which method is better when evaluating independent versus mutually exclusive projects.

- Briefly explain the problem of multiple IRRs and when this situation could occur.

- Calculate the Modified Internal Rate of Return (MIRR) for a given project and evaluate this method.

- Identify at least one relevant piece of information provided to decision makers for each capital budgeting decision method discussed in the chapter.

- Identify and explain the purposes of the post-audit in the capital budgeting process.

- Identify a number of different types of decisions that use the capital budgeting techniques developed in this chapter.

OVERVIEW

Capital budgeting is similar in principle to security valuation in that future cash flows are estimated, risks are appraised and reflected in a cost of capital discount rate, and all cash flows are evaluated on a present value basis. Five primary methods can be used to determine which projects should be included in a firm's capital budget: (1) payback, (2) discounted payback, (3) Net Present Value (NPV), (4) Internal Rate of Return (IRR), and (5) Modified IRR (MIRR). Both payback methods have deficiencies, and thus should not be used as the sole criterion for making capital budgeting decisions. The NPV, IRR, and MIRR methods all lead to the same accept/reject decisions on independent projects. However, the methods may conflict when ranking mutually exclusive projects that differ in scale or timing. Under these circumstances, the NPV method should be used to make the final decision.

OUTLINE

Capital budgeting is the process of planning expenditures on assets whose cash flows are expected to extend beyond one year.

- A number of factors combine to make capital budgeting perhaps the most important function financial managers and their staffs must perform.
  - ☐ Since the results of capital budgeting decisions continue for many years, the firm loses some of its flexibility.
  - ☐ A firm's capital budgeting decisions define its strategic direction.
  - ☐ Timing is also important since capital assets must be available when they are needed.

- The same general concepts that are used in security valuation are also involved in capital budgeting; however, whereas a set of stocks and bonds exists in the securities market from which investors select, capital budgeting projects are created by the firm.
  - ☐ A firm's growth, and even its ability to remain competitive and to survive, depends on a constant flow of ideas for new products, for ways to make existing products better, and for ways to operate at a lower cost.

- Analyzing capital expenditure proposals has a cost, so firms classify projects into different categories to help differentiate the level of analysis required.
  - ☐ Replacement: maintenance of business.
  - ☐ Replacement: cost reduction.
  - ☐ Expansion of existing products or markets.
  - ☐ Expansion into new products or markets.
  - ☐ Safety and/or environmental projects.
  - ☐ Other miscellaneous projects.

- Normally, a more detailed analysis is required for cost-reduction replacements, expansion, and new product decisions than for simple replacement and maintenance decisions.

□ Projects requiring larger investments will be analyzed more carefully than smaller projects.

□ Decisions to invest in intangible assets are analyzed in the same way as decisions related to tangible assets.

■ Once a potential capital budgeting project has been identified, its evaluation involves the same steps that are used in security analysis.

□ The cost of the project must be determined.

□ Cash flows from the project are estimated.

□ The riskiness of these projected cash flows is determined.

□ Given the riskiness of the projected cash flows, the appropriate cost of capital at which cash flows are to be discounted is determined.

□ Cash inflows are discounted to their present value to obtain an estimate of the asset's value to the firm.

□ The present value of the expected cash inflows is compared with the required outlay, or cost. If the PV of the cash flows exceeds the cost, the project should be accepted; otherwise, it should be rejected.

■ There is a direct link between capital budgeting and stock values: The more effective the firm's capital budgeting procedures, the higher its stock price.

Five key methods are used to rank projects and to decide whether or not they should be accepted for inclusion in the capital budget: (1) payback, (2) discounted payback, (3) Net Present Value (NPV), (4) Internal Rate of Return (IRR), and (5) Modified Internal Rate of Return (MIRR). The MIRR is discussed in a later section.

■ The *payback period* is defined as the expected number of years required to recover the original investment in the project, and it was the first formal method used to evaluate capital budgeting projects. Payback is a type of "breakeven" calculation in the sense that if cash flows come in at the expected rate until the payback year, then the project will break even.

□ The payback method's flaws are that cash flows beyond the payback period are ignored and it does not take into account the cost of capital.

□ Although the payback method has some serious faults as a project ranking criterion, it does provide information on how long funds will be tied up in a project. The shorter the payback period, other things held constant, the greater the project's *liquidity*.

□ Since cash flows expected in the distant future are generally riskier than near-term cash flows, the payback is often used as an indicator of a project's riskiness.

■ A variant of the regular payback, the *discounted payback period* discounts the expected cash flows by the project's cost of capital, thus taking into account the cost of capital.

The discounted payback period is defined as the number of years required for an investment's cash flows, discounted at the investment's cost of capital, to cover its cost.

■ The *Net Present Value (NPV)* method of evaluating investment proposals is a discounted cash flow (DCF) technique that accounts for the time value of all cash flows from a project.

☐ To implement the NPV, proceed as follows: (a) Find the present value of each cash flow, including both inflows and outflows, discounted at the project's cost of capital, (b) sum these discounted cash flows to obtain the project's NPV, and (c) accept the project if the NPV is positive.

☐ The NPV is defined as follows:

$$NPV = \sum_{t=0}^{n} \frac{CF_t}{(1+k)^t}.$$

Here, CF_t is the expected net cash flow in Period t and k is the project's cost of capital. Cash outflows are treated as negative cash flows.

☐ If the NPV is positive, the project should be accepted; if negative, it should be rejected.

● If two projects are *mutually exclusive* (that is, only one can be accepted), the one with the higher positive NPV should be chosen. If both projects have negative NPVs, neither should be chosen.

☐ Finding the NPV with a financial calculator is efficient and easy. Simply enter the different cash flows into the "cash flow register" along with the value of k = i, and then press the NPV key for the solution.

☐ Financial analysts generally use spreadsheets when dealing with capital budgeting projects. Once a spreadsheet has been set up, it is easy to change input values to see what would happen if inputs are changed.

☐ An NPV of zero signifies that the project's cash flows are exactly sufficient to repay the invested capital and to provide the required rate of return on that capital. If a project has a positive NPV, then it is generating more cash than is needed to service its debt and to provide the required return to shareholders. This excess cash accrues to the firm's stockholders.

☐ There is a direct relationship between NPV and EVA. NPV is equal to the present value of the project's future EVAs. Therefore, accepting positive NPV projects should result in a positive EVA and a positive MVA.

■ The *Internal Rate of Return (IRR)* is defined as the discount rate that equates the present value of a project's expected cash inflows to the present value of its costs.

☐ The equation for calculating the IRR is shown below:

$$\sum_{t=0}^{n} \frac{CF_t}{(1+IRR)^t} = 0.$$

This equation has one unknown, the IRR, and we can solve for the value of the IRR that will make the equation equal to zero. The solution value of IRR is defined as the internal rate of return.

☐ The IRR formula is simply the NPV formula solved for the particular discount rate that causes the NPV to equal zero.

☐ To find the IRR with a financial calculator, simply enter the different cash flows into the cash flow register, making sure to input the $t = 0$ cash flow, and then press the IRR key for the solution.

☐ The IRR rule indicates that a project with an IRR greater than its cost of capital should be accepted.

☐ If the internal rate of return exceeds the cost of the funds used to finance the project, a surplus remains after paying for the capital, and this surplus accrues to the firm's stockholders. Taking on a project with an IRR that exceeds its cost of capital increases shareholders' wealth.

■ The same basic equation is used for both the NPV and the IRR methods, but in the NPV method, the discount rate, k, is specified and the NPV is found, whereas in the IRR method the NPV is specified to equal zero, and the value of IRR that forces this equality is determined.

■ The NPV and IRR methods will always lead to the same accept/reject decisions for independent projects. This occurs because if NPV is positive, IRR must exceed k.

☐ NPV and IRR can give conflicting rankings for mutually exclusive projects.

■ Taking on a project whose IRR exceeds its cost of capital increases shareholders' wealth. On the other hand, if the internal rate of return is less than the cost of capital, then taking on the project imposes a cost on current stockholders.

☐ It is this "breakeven" characteristic that makes the IRR useful in evaluating capital projects.

■ In many respects the NPV method is better than the IRR method. However, the IRR is widely used in business. Therefore, it is important to understand the IRR method including its problems.

■ A *net present value profile* is a graph that plots a project's NPV against different discount rates.

☐ The NPV profile crosses the Y-axis at the *undiscounted* NPV, while it crosses the X-axis at the IRR.

☐ If an *independent* project is being evaluated, then the NPV and IRR criteria always lead to the same accept/reject decision.

☐ If two *mutually exclusive* projects have NPV profiles that intersect in the upper right-hand quadrant, then there may be a conflict in rankings between NPV and IRR methods. Two basic conditions can lead to conflicts between NPV and IRR:

- Project size (or scale) differences exist; that is, the cost of one project is larger than that of the other.
- Timing differences exist such that cash flows from one project come in the early years and most of the cash flows from the other project come in the later years.

☐ The *crossover rate* is the cost of capital at which the NPV profiles of two projects cross and, thus, at which the projects' NPVs are equal.

☐ The critical issue in resolving conflicts between mutually exclusive projects is to determine how useful it is to generate cash flows earlier rather than later. Thus, the value of early cash flows depends on the rate at which we can reinvest these cash flows.

- The NPV method implicitly assumes that project cash flows are reinvested at the project's cost of capital.
- The IRR method implicitly assumes that project cash flows are reinvested at the project's IRR.
- The opportunity cost of a project's cash flows is the project's cost of capital. If these cash flows were not available to the firm and if the firm needed capital to invest in new projects, then the funds would be obtained from the firm's capital suppliers; the cost would be the overall cost of capital. Thus, the assumption of reinvestment at the cost of capital is the correct assumption, and NPV is the preferred method.

☐ When evaluating mutually exclusive projects, especially those that differ in scale and/or timing, the NPV method should be used.

Multiple IRRs can result when the IRR criterion is used with a project that has nonnormal cash flows.

■ Projects with nonnormal cash flows call for a large cash outflow either sometime during or at the end of its life.

☐ In these cases, the NPV criterion can be easily applied, and this method leads to conceptually correct capital budgeting decisions.

Business executives often prefer to work with percentage rates of return, such as IRR, rather than dollar amounts of NPV when analyzing investments. To overcome some of the IRR's limitations a Modified IRR, or MIRR, has been devised.

■ The MIRR is defined as the discount rate that forces PV costs = PV terminal value, where *terminal value (TV)* is the future value of the inflows compounded at the project's cost of capital. Thus,

$$\sum_{t=0}^{n} \frac{COF_t}{(1+k)^t} = \frac{\sum_{t=0}^{n} CIF_t (1+k)^{n-t}}{(1+MIRR)^n}$$

$$PV \text{ costs} = \frac{TV}{(1+MIRR)^n}.$$

■ MIRR assumes that cash flows are reinvested at the cost of capital rather than the project's own IRR, making it a better indicator of a project's true profitability.

■ NPV and MIRR will lead to the same project selection decision if the two projects are of equal size and have the same life.
　□ If the projects are of equal size but differ in lives, the MIRR will always lead to the same decision as the NPV, if the MIRRs are both calculated using as the terminal year the life of the longer project.
　　● Fill in zeros for the shorter project's missing cash flows.
　□ Conflicts can still occur when projects differ in scale, and in this case, NPV should be used. The NPV method is still the best way to choose among competing projects because it provides the best indication of how much each project will increase the value of the firm.

■ MIRR is superior to the regular IRR as an indicator of a project's "true" rate of return, or "expected long-term rate of return."
　□ MIRR can also overcome the multiple IRR problem because there is only one MIRR for any set of cash flows.

In making the accept/reject decision, each of the five capital budgeting decision methods provides decision makers with a somewhat different piece of relevant information. Since it is easy to calculate all of them, all should be considered in the decision process. For most decisions, the greatest weight should be given to the NPV.

■ Payback and discounted payback provide an indication of both the risk and the liquidity of a project.

■ NPV is important because it gives a direct measure of the dollar benefit (on a present value basis) of the project to the firm's shareholders, so it is regarded as the best single measure of profitability.

■ IRR also measures profitability, but expressed as a percentage rate of return, which many decision makers seem to prefer. IRR also contains information regarding a project's "safety margin."

■ The modified IRR has all the virtues of the IRR; however, it incorporates the correct reinvestment rate assumption, and it avoids problems the IRR can have when applied to projects with nonnormal cash flows.

An important aspect of the capital budgeting process is the post-audit, which involves comparing actual results with those predicted by the project's sponsors and explaining why any differences occurred. The results of the post-audit help to improve forecasts and to increase efficiency of the firm's operations.

■ The *post-audit* is not a simple process—a number of factors can cause complications.
   ☐ Each element of the cash flow forecast is subject to uncertainty, so a percentage of all projects undertaken by any reasonably aggressive firm will necessarily go awry.
   ☐ Projects sometime fail to meet expectations for reasons beyond the control of the operating executives and for reasons that no one could realistically be expected to anticipate.
   ☐ It is often difficult to separate the operating results of one investment from those of a larger system.
   ☐ It is often hard to hand out blame or praise, because the executives who were responsible for launching a given long-term investment may have moved on by the time the results are known.

■ Observations of both businesses and governmental units suggest that the best-run and most successful organizations are the ones that put the greatest emphasis on post-audits. Post-audits are regarded as being one of the most important elements in a good capital budgeting system.

The techniques developed in this chapter can help managers make a number of different types of decisions.

■ Two examples of decisions that use capital budgeting techniques are evaluating corporate mergers and deciding whether to downsize personnel or to sell off particular assets or divisions.

■ Most decisions should be based on whether they contribute to shareholder value, and that, in turn, can be determined by estimating the net present value of a set of cash flows.

SELF-TEST QUESTIONS

Definitional

1. A firm's _____ _____ outlines its planned expenditures on fixed assets.

2. The number of years necessary to return the original investment in a project is known as the _____ _____.

3. The shorter the payback period, other things held constant, the greater the project's _____.

4. The primary advantage of payback analysis is its _____.

5. One important weakness of payback analysis is the fact that _____ _____ beyond the payback period are _____.

6. The Net Present Value (NPV) method of evaluating investment proposals is a(n) _____ cash flow technique.

7. A capital investment proposal should be accepted if its NPV is _____.

8. If two projects are _____ _____, the one with the _____ positive NPV should be selected.

9. In the IRR approach, a discount rate is sought that makes the NPV equal to _____.

10. A net present value profile plots a project's _____ against different _____ _____.

11. If an independent project's _____ is greater than the project's cost of capital, it should be accepted.

12. If two mutually exclusive projects are being evaluated and one project has a higher NPV while the other project has a higher IRR, the project with the higher _____ should be preferred.

13. The NPV method implicitly assumes reinvestment at the project's _____ ____ _____, while the IRR method implicitly assumes reinvestment at the _____ _____ ____ _____.

14. The MIRR method assumes reinvestment at the _____ ____ _____, making it a better indicator of a project's profitability than IRR.

15. The process of comparing a project's actual results with its projected results is known as a(n) _____-_____.

16. The objective of the post-audit is to improve both _____ and _____.

17. The internal rate of return (IRR) is the _____ rate that equates the present value of future _____ _____ with the project's _____.

18. The MIRR is defined as the discount rate that forces the present value of costs to equal the present value of the _____ _____.

19. Taking on a project whose IRR exceeds its cost of capital increases _____ _____.

20. The NPV profile crosses the Y-axis at the _____ NPV, while it crosses the X-axis at the _____.

21. If a(n) _____ project is being evaluated, then the NPV and IRR criteria always lead to the same accept/reject decisions.

22. Two basic conditions can lead to conflicts between NPV and IRR: _____ and _____ differences.

23. _____ _____ can result when the IRR criterion is used with a project that has nonnormal cash flows.

24. The _____ _____ is the cost of capital at which the NPV profiles of two projects cross and, thus, at which the projects' NPVs are equal.

25. _____ is superior to the regular IRR as an indicator of a project's "true" rate of return, or "expected long-term rate of return."

Conceptual

26. The NPV of a project with cash flows that accrue relatively slowly is *more sensitive* to changes in the discount rate than is the NPV of a project with cash flows that come in more rapidly.

    a. True   b. False

27. The NPV method is preferred over the IRR method because the NPV method's reinvestment rate assumption is better.

   a. True   **b.** False

28. When you find the yield to maturity on a bond, you are finding the bond's net present value (NPV).

   a. True   **b.** False

29. Other things held constant, a decrease in the cost of capital (discount rate) will cause an *increase* in a project's IRR.

   a. True   **b.** False

30. The IRR method can be used in place of the NPV method for all independent projects.

   a. True   **b.** False

31. The NPV and MIRR methods lead to the same decision for mutually exclusive projects regardless of the projects' relative sizes.

   a. True   **b.** False

32. Projects with nonnormal cash flows sometimes have multiple MIRRs.

   a. True   **b.** False

33. Projects A and B each have an initial cost of $5,000, followed by a series of positive cash inflows. Project A has total undiscounted cash inflows of $12,000, while B has total undiscounted inflows of $10,000. Further, at a discount rate of 10 percent, the two projects have identical NPVs. Which project's NPV will be *more sensitive* to changes in the discount rate? (Hint: Projects with steeper NPV profiles are more sensitive to discount rate changes.)

   a. Project A.
   b. Project B.
   c. Both projects are equally sensitive to changes in the discount rate since their NPVs are equal at all costs of capital.
   d. Neither project is sensitive to changes in the discount rate, since both have NPV profiles which are horizontal.
   e. The solution cannot be determined unless the timing of the cash flows is known.

34. Which of the following statements is most correct?

    a. The IRR of a project whose cash flows accrue relatively rapidly is more sensitive to changes in the discount rate than is the IRR of a project whose cash flows come in more slowly.

    b. There are many conditions under which a project can have more than one IRR. One such condition is where an otherwise normal project has a negative cash flow at the end of its life.

    c. The phenomenon called "multiple internal rates of return" arises when two or more mutually exclusive projects that have different lives are being compared.

    d. The modified IRR (MIRR) method has wide appeal to professors, but most business executives prefer the NPV method to either the regular or modified IRR.

    e. Each of the above statements is false.

35. Which of the following statements is most correct?

    a. If a project has an IRR greater than zero, then taking on the project will increase the value of the company's common stock because the project will make a positive contribution to net income.

    b. If a project has an NPV greater than zero, then taking on the project will increase the value of the firm's stock.

    c. Assume that you plot the NPV profiles of two mutually exclusive projects with normal cash flows and that the cost of capital is greater than the rate at which the profiles cross one another. In this case, the NPV and IRR methods will lead to contradictory rankings of the two projects.

    d. For independent (as opposed to mutually exclusive) normal projects, the NPV and IRR methods will generally lead to conflicting accept/reject decisions.

    e. Statements b, c, and d are true.

36. Which of the following statements is most correct?

    a. Underlying the MIRR is the assumption that cash flows can be reinvested at the firm's cost of capital.

    b. Underlying the IRR is the assumption that cash flows can be reinvested at the firm's cost of capital.

    c. Underlying the NPV is the assumption that cash flows can be reinvested at the firm's cost of capital.

    d. The discounted payback method always leads to the same accept/reject decisions as the NPV method.

    e. Statements a and c are correct.

SELF-TEST PROBLEMS

1. Your firm is considering a fast-food concession at the World's Fair. The cash flow pattern is somewhat unusual since you must build the stands, operate them for 2 years, and then tear the stands down and restore the sites to their original conditions. You estimate the net cash flows to be as follows:

Time	Expected Net Cash Flows
0	($800,000)
1	700,000
2	700,000
3	(400,000)

What is the approximate IRR of this venture?

a. 5%   **b.** 15%   **c.** 25%   **d.** 35%   **e.** 45%

(The following data apply to the next three Self-Test Problems.)

Toya Motors needs a new machine for production of its new models. The financial vice president has appointed you to do the capital budgeting analysis. You have identified two different machines that are capable of performing the job. You have completed the cash flow analysis, and the expected net cash flows are as follows:

Year	Expected Net Cash Flows	
	Machine B	Machine O
0	($5,000)	($5,000)
1	2,085	0
2	2,085	0
3	2,085	0
4	2,085	9,677

2. What is the payback period for Machine B?

a. 1.0 year   **b.** 2.0 years   **c.** 2.4 years   **d.** 2.6 years   **e.** 3.0 years

3. The cost of capital is uncertain at this time, so you construct NPV profiles to assist in the final decision. The profiles for Machines B and O cross at what cost of capital?

a. 6%

b. 10%

c. 18%

d. 24%

e. They do not cross in the upper righthand quadrant.

4. If the cost of capital for both projects is 14 percent at the time the decision is made, which project would you choose?

   a. Project B; it has the higher positive NPV.
   b. Project O; it has the higher positive NPV.
   c. Neither; both have negative NPVs.
   d. Either; both have the same NPV.
   e. Project B; it has the higher IRR.

(The following data apply to the next six Self-Test Problems.)

The director of capital budgeting for Giant Inc. has identified two mutually exclusive projects, L and S, with the following expected net cash flows:

	Expected Net Cash Flows	
Year	Project L	Project S
0	($100)	($100)
1	10	70
2	60	50
3	80	20

Both projects have a cost of capital of 10 percent.

5. What is the payback period for Project S?

   a. 1.6 years   b. 1.8 years   c. 2.1 years   d. 2.5 years   e. 2.8 years

6. What is Project L's NPV?

   a. $50.00   b. $34.25   c. $22.64   d. $18.78   e. $10.06

7. What is Project L's IRR?

   a. 18.1%   b. 19.7%   c. 21.4%   d. 23.6%   e. 24.2%

8. What is Project L's MIRR?

   a. 15.3%   b. 16.5%   c. 16.9%   d. 17.1%   e. 17.4%

9. What is Project S's MIRR?

   a. 15.3%   b. 16.5%   c. 16.9%   d. 17.1%   e. 17.4%

10. Plot the NPV profiles for the two projects. At what cost of capital do the two NPV profiles cross?

   a. 6.9%   **b.** 7.8%   **c.** 8.7%   **d.** 9.6%   **e.** 9.9%

11. Your company is considering two mutually exclusive projects, X and Y, whose costs and cash flows are shown below:

Year	Project X	Project Y
0	($2,000)	($2,000)
1	200	2,000
2	600	200
3	800	100
4	1,400	100

The projects are equally risky, and their cost of capital is 10 percent. You must make a recommendation, and you must base it on the modified IRR. What is the MIRR of the better project?

   a. 11.50%   **b.** 12.00%   **c.** 11.70%   **d.** 12.50%   **e.** 13.10%

12. A company is analyzing two mutually exclusive projects, S and L, whose cash flows are shown below:

Year	Project S	Project L
0	($2,000)	($2,000)
1	1,800	0
2	500	500
3	20	800
4	20	1,600

The company's cost of capital is 9 percent, and it can get an unlimited amount of capital at that cost. What is the regular IRR (not MIRR) of the better project? (Hint: Note that the better project may or may not be the one with the higher IRR.)

   a. 11.45%   **b.** 11.74%   **c.** 13.02%   **d.** 13.49%   **e.** 12.67%

13. The stock of Barkley Inc. and "the market" provided the following returns over the last 5 years:

Year	Barkley	Market
1998	-5%	-3%
1999	21	10
2000	9	4
2001	23	11
2002	31	15

Barkley finances only with retained earnings, and it uses the CAPM with a historical beta to determine its cost of equity. The risk-free rate is 7 percent, and the market risk premium is 5 percent. Barkley is considering a project that has a cost at t = 0 of $2,000 and is expected to provide cash inflows of $1,000 per year for 3 years. What is the project's MIRR?

a. 23.46%   **b.** 18.25%   **c.** 22.92%   **d.** 20.95%   **e.** 21.82%

14. CDH Worldwide's stock returns versus the market were as follows, and the same relative volatility is expected in the future:

Year	CDH	Market
1999	12%	15%
2000	-6	-3
2001	25	19
2002	18	12

The T-bond rate is 6 percent; the market risk premium is 7 percent; CDH finances only with equity from retained earnings; and it uses the CAPM to estimate its cost of equity. Now CDH is considering two alternative trucks. Truck S has a cost of $12,000 and is expected to produce cash flows of $4,500 per year for 4 years. Truck L has a cost of $20,000 and is expected to produce cash flows of $7,500 per year for 4 years. By how much would CDH's value rise if it buys the better truck, and what is the MIRR of the better truck?

a. $803.35; 17.05%   **d.** $1,338.91; 16.06%
b. $1,338.91; 17.05%   **e.** $803.35; 14.41%
c. $1,896.47; 16.06%

15.   Assume that your company has a cost of capital of 14 percent and that it is analyzing the following project:

Project M:

0	1	2	3	4
-250	140	140	170	-100

14%

What are the project's IRR and MIRR?

a. 24.26%; 16.28%   d. 24.26%; 17.19%
b. 23.12%; 17.19%   e. None of the above.
c. 23.12%; 16.28%

16.   You are evaluating a project that is expected to produce cash flows of $5,000 each year for the next 10 years and $7,000 each year for the following 10 years. The IRR of this 20-year project is 12%. If the firm's WACC is 8%, what is the project's NPV?

a. $10,989.95   b. $12,276.33   c. $14,321.21   d. $15,100.50   e. $16,000.00

17.   A project has the following cash flows:

Year	Cash Flow
0	($250)
1	100
2	(X)
3	150
4	275
5	300

Notice this project requires two cash outflows at Years 0 and 2, and produces positive cash inflows in the remaining periods. The project's appropriate WACC is 10% and its modified internal rate of return (MIRR) is 13.50%. What is the value of the project's cash outflow in Year 2?

a. $295.20   b. $243.96   c. $375.00   d. $493.96   e. $288.75

ANSWERS TO SELF-TEST QUESTIONS

1.   capital budget   4.   simplicity
2.   payback period   5.   cash flows; ignored
3.   liquidity   6.   discounted

7. positive
8. mutually exclusive; higher
9. zero
10. NPV; discount rates
11. IRR
12. NPV
13. cost of capital; internal rate of return
14. cost of capital
15. post-audit
16. forecasts; operations

17. discount; cash inflows; cost (or initial cost)
18. terminal value
19. shareholders' wealth
20. undiscounted; IRR
21. independent
22. scale; timing
23. Multiple IRRs
24. crossover rate
25. MIRR

26. a. The more the cash flows are spread over time, the greater is the effect of a change in discount rate. This is because the compounding process has a greater effect as the number of years increases.

27. a. Project cash flows are substitutes for outside capital. Thus, the opportunity cost of these cash flows is the firm's cost of capital, adjusted for risk. The NPV method uses this cost as the reinvestment rate, while the IRR method assumes reinvestment at the IRR.

28. b. The yield to maturity on a bond is the bond's IRR.

29. b. The computation of IRR is independent of the project's cost of capital.

30. a. Both the NPV and IRR methods lead to the same accept/reject decisions for independent projects. Thus, the IRR method can be used as a proxy for the NPV method when choosing independent projects.

31. b. NPV and MIRR may not lead to the same decision when the projects differ in scale.

32. b. Multiple IRRs occur in projects with nonnormal cash flows, but there is only one MIRR for each project.

33. a. If we were to begin graphing the NPV profiles for each of these projects, we would know two of the points for each project. The Y-intercepts for Projects A and B would be $7,000 and $5,000, respectively, and the crossover rate would be 10 percent. Thus, from this information we can conclude that Project A's NPV profile would have the steeper slope and would be more sensitive to changes in the discount rate.

34. b. Statement a is false because the IRR is independent of the discount rate. Statement b is true; the situation identified is that of a project with nonnormal cash flows, which has multiple IRRs. Statement c is false; multiple IRRs occur with projects with

nonnormal cash flows, not with mutually exclusive projects with different lives. Statement d is false; business executives tend to prefer the IRR because it gives a measure of the project's safety margin.

35. b. Statement b is true; the others are false. Note that IRR must be greater than the cost of capital; that conflicts arise if the cost of capital is less than the crossover rate; and that for some projects with nonnormal cash flows there are two IRRs, so NPV and IRR could lead to conflicting accept/reject decisions, depending on which IRR we examine.

36. e. Statement e is correct, because both statements a and c are true. The IRR assumes reinvestment at the IRR, and since the discounted payback ignores cash flows beyond the payback period, it could lead to rejections of projects with high late cash flows and hence NPV > 0.

SOLUTIONS TO SELF-TEST PROBLEMS

1. c. Calculator solution: Input CF_0 = -800000, CF_{1-2} = 700000, CF_3 = -400000. Output: IRR = 25.48%. Note that this project actually has multiple IRRs, with a second IRR at about -53 percent.

2. c. After Year 1, there is $5,000 – $2,085 = $2,915 remaining to pay back. After Year 2, only $2,915 – $2,085 = $830 is remaining. In Year 3, another $2,085 is collected. Assuming that the Year 3 cash flow occurs evenly over time, then payback occurs $830/$2,085 = 0.4 of the way through Year 3. Thus, the payback period is 2.4 years.

3. b. To solve graphically you could solve for different NPVs at different discount rates by entering each project's cash flows and a different k and solving for NPV. The graph below would be drawn.

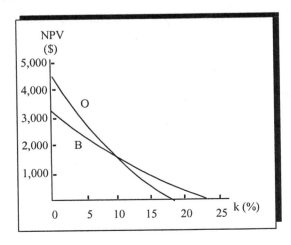

Using a financial calculator, enter the Project Δ cash flows into the cash flow register and solve for the IRR.

			Project Δ
Year	B	O	(B – O)
0	($5,000)	($5,000)	$ 0
1	2,085	0	2,085
2	2,085	0	2,085
3	2,085	0	2,085
4	2,085	9,677	(7,592)

The IRR of Project Δ, 10.00 percent, is the crossover rate.

4. a. Refer to the NPV profiles. When k = 14%, we are to the right of the crossover rate and Project B has the higher NPV. You can verify this fact by calculating the NPVs. When k = 14%, NPV_B = $1,075 and NPV_O = $730. Note that Project B also has the higher IRR. However, the NPV method should be used when evaluating mutually exclusive projects. Note that had the project cost of capital been 8 percent (which is less than the crossover rate), then Project O would be chosen on the basis of the higher NPV.

5. a. After the first year, there is only $30 remaining to be repaid, and $50 is received in Year 2. Assuming an even cash flow throughout the year, the payback period is 1 + $30/$50 = 1.6 years.

6. d. NPV_L = -$100 + $10/1.10 + $60/(1.10)^2 + $80/(1.10)^3 = -$100 + $9.09 + $49.59 + $60.11 = $18.79. Financial calculator solution: Input the cash flows into the cash flow register, I = k = 10, and solve for NPV = $18.78.

7. a. Input the cash flows into the cash flow register and solve for IRR = 18.1%.

8. b. $$\sum_{t=0}^{n} \frac{COF_t}{(1+k)^t} = \frac{\sum_{t=0}^{n} CIF_t (1+k)^{n-t}}{(1+MIRR)^n}.$$

$$PV \text{ cost} = \frac{TV}{(1 + MIRR_L)^n}$$

$$\$100 = \frac{\$10(1.10)^2 + \$60(1.10)^1 + \$80(1.10)^0}{(1 + MIRR_L)^3}$$

$$\$100 = \frac{\$12.10 + \$66.00 + \$80.00}{(1 + MIRR_L)^3}$$

$$\$100 = \frac{\$158.10}{(1 + MIRR_L)^3}$$

$$MIRR_L = 16.50\%.$$

Alternatively, input N = 3, PV = -100, PMT = 0, FV = 158.10, and solve for I = $MIRR_L$ = 16.50%.

9.   c. $$\$100 = \frac{\$70(1.10)^2 + \$50(1.10)^1 + \$20(1.10)^0}{(1 + MIRR_S)^3}$$

$$\$100 = \frac{\$84.70 + \$55.00 + \$20.00}{(1 + MIRR_S)^3}$$

$$\$100 = \frac{\$159.70}{(1 + MIRR_S)^3}$$

$$MIRR_S = 16.89\% \approx 16.9\%.$$

Alternatively, input N = 3, PV = -100, PMT = 0, FV = 159.70, and solve for I = $MIRR_S$ = 16.89%.

10.   c.   The NPV profiles plot as follows:

k	NPV_L	NPV_S
0%	$50	$40
5	33	29
10	19	20
15	7	12
20	(4)	5
25	(13)	(2)

By looking at the graph, the approximate crossover rate is between 8 and 9 percent. Now, to find the precise crossover rate, determine the cash flows

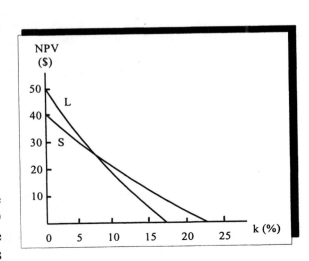

for Project Δ, which is the project whose cash flows represent the differences between the two projects' cash flows:

Year	L	S	Project Δ (L − S)
0	($100)	($100)	$ 0
1	10	70	(60)
2	60	50	10
3	80	20	60

The crossover rate is the IRR of Project Δ, or 8.7 percent.

11. e. Project X:

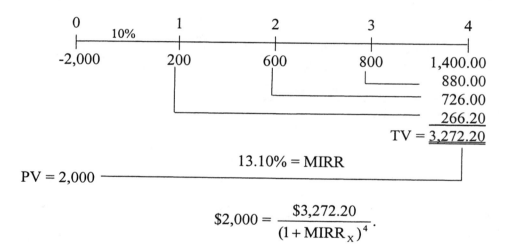

$$\$2,000 = \frac{\$3,272.20}{(1 + MIRR_X)^4}.$$

Project Y:

$$\$2,000 = \frac{\$3,114.000}{(1 + MIRR_Y)^4}.$$

Project X has the higher MIRR; $MIRR_X = 13.10\%$.

Alternate step: You could calculate NPVs, see that X has the higher NPV, and just calculate $MIRR_X$. $NPV_X = \$234.96$ and $NPV_Y = \$126.90$.

12. b. Put the cash flows into the cash flow register, and then calculate NPV at 9% and IRR:

Project S: $NPV_S = \$101.83$; $IRR_S = 13.49\%$.

Project L: $NPV_L = \$172.07$; $IRR_L = 11.74\%$.

Because $NPV_L > NPV_S$, it is the better project. $IRR_L = 11.74\%$.

13. d. First, calculate the beta coefficient. Barkley's stock has been exactly twice as volatile as the market; thus, beta = 2.0. This can be calculated as $[21 - (-5)]/[10 - (-3)] = 26/13 = 2.0$. (Alternatively, you could use a calculator with statistical functions to determine the beta.)

Next, enter the known values in the CAPM equation to find the required rate of return, or the cost of equity capital. Since the company finances only with equity, this is the cost of capital:

$CAPM = k_{RF} + (k_M - k_{RF})b = 7\% + (5\%)b = 7\% + 5\%(2.0) = 17\% = k_s$.

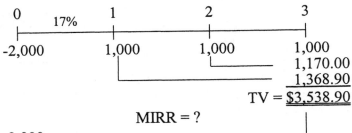

Find TV: N = 3; I = 17; PV = 0; PMT = -1000; FV = $3,538.90.

Find MIRR: N = 3; PV = -2000; PMT = 0; FV = 3538.90; I = MIRR = 20.95%.

14. b. First, we must find the cost of capital. Run a regression between the market and CDH stock returns to get beta = 1.31. Then apply the SML:

$$k_{CDH} = 6\% + (7\%)1.31 = 15.17\%.$$

(1) Now set up the time lines, insert the proper data into the cash flow register of the calculator, and find the NPVs and IRRs for the trucks.

Truck S: NPV = $803.35; IRR = 18.45%.

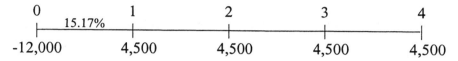

Truck L: NPV = $1,338.91; IRR = 18.45%.

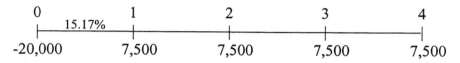

$NPV_L > NPV_S$, thus Truck$_L$ is the better truck.

(2) To find Truck L's MIRR, compound its cash inflows at 15.17 percent to find the TV, then find the MIRR = I that causes PV of TV = $20,000:

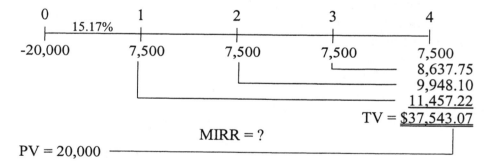

Find TV: Enter N = 4; I = 15.17; PV = 0; PMT = -7500; and solve for FV = $37,543.07.

Find MIRR: Enter N = 4; PV = -20000; PMT = 0; FV = 37543.07; and solve for I = MIRR = 17.05%.

It is interesting to note that both trucks have the same IRR and MIRR; however, the NPV rule should be used so Truck L is the better truck. This problem shows that the NPV method is superior when choosing among competing projects that differ in size.

15.   d.   IRR = 24.26%; MIRR = 17.19%.

To calculate the IRR, enter the given values into the cash flow register and press the IRR key to get IRR = 24.26%.

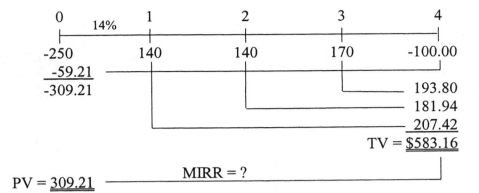

Enter N = 4; PV = -309.21; PMT = 0; FV = 583.16; and solve for MIRR = I = 17.19%.

16. c. Since the IRR is the cost of capital at which the NPV of a project equals zero, the projects inflows can be evaluated at the IRR and the present value of these inflows must equal the initial investment.

Using a financial calculator enter the following:

$CF_0 = 0$
$CF_1 = 5000$
$N_j = 10$
$CF_1 = 7000$
$N_j = 10$

I = 12; NPV = $40,985.66.

Therefore, the initial investment for this project is $40,985.66. Using a calculator, the project's NPV can now be solved at a WACC of 8%.

$CF_0 = -40985.66$
$CF_1 = 5000$
$N_j = 10$
$CF_1 = 7000$
$N_j = 10$

I = 8; NPV = $14,321.21.

17. a. The MIRR can be solved with a financial calculator by finding the terminal future value of the cash inflows and the initial present value of cash outflows, and solving for the discount rate that equates these two values. In this instance, the MIRR is given, but a cash outflow is missing and must be calculated. Therefore, if the terminal future value of the cash inflows is found, it can be entered into a financial calculator, along with the number of years the project lasts and the MIRR, to solve for the initial present value of the cash outflows. One of these cash outflows occurs in Year 0 and the remaining value must be the present value of the missing cash outflow in Year 2.

Cash inflows	Compounding Rate	FV in Year 5 @ 10%
$CF_1 = 100$	$\times (1.10)^4$	146.41
$CF_3 = 150$	$\times (1.10)^2$	181.50
$CF_4 = 275$	$\times 1.10$	302.50
$CF_5 = 300$	$\times 1.00$	300.00
		930.41

Using the financial calculator to solve for the present value of cash outflows:

$N = 5$
$I = 13.50$
$PV = ?$
$PMT = 0$
$FV = 930.41$

The total present value of cash outflows is $493.96, and since the outflow for Year 0 is $250, the present value of the Year 2 cash outflow is $243.96. Therefore, the missing cash outflow for Year 2 is $243.96 $\times (1.1)^2 = $295.20.

LEARNING OBJECTIVES

● Discuss difficulties and relevant considerations in estimating net cash flows, and explain the four major ways that project cash flow differs from accounting income.

● Define the following terms: relevant cash flow, incremental cash flow, sunk cost, opportunity cost, externalities, and cannibalization.

● Identify the three categories to which incremental cash flows can be classified.

● Analyze an expansion project and make a decision whether the project should be accepted on the basis of standard capital budgeting techniques.

● Explain three reasons why corporate risk is important even if a firm's stockholders are well diversified.

● Identify two reasons why stand-alone risk is important.

● Demonstrate sensitivity and scenario analyses, and explain Monte Carlo simulation.

● Discuss the two methods used to incorporate risk into capital budgeting decisions.

OVERVIEW

One of the most critical steps in capital budgeting analysis is cash flow estimation. The key to correct cash flow estimation is to consider only incremental cash flows. However, the process is complicated by such factors as sunk costs, opportunity costs, externalities, net operating working capital changes, and salvage values. Cash flow estimation for replacement projects is similar to that for expansion projects, except that there are more cash flows to consider when analyzing replacement projects. Adjustments to the analysis must be made for the effects of inflation.

Project risk analysis focuses on three issues: (1) the effect of a project on the firm's beta coefficient (market risk), (2) the project's effect on the probability of bankruptcy (corporate risk), and (3) the risk of the project independent of both the firm's other projects and investors' diversification (stand-alone risk). Market risk directly affects the value of the firm's stock. Corporate risk affects the financial strength of the firm, and this, in turn, influences its ability to use debt, and to maintain smooth operations over time. Stand-alone risk is measured by the variability of a project's expected returns. Techniques for measuring stand-alone risk include sensitivity analysis, scenario analysis, and Monte Carlo simulation.

Two methods are used to incorporate project risk into capital budgeting. The certainty equivalent approach scales down all cash flows that are not known with certainty, while the risk-adjusted discount rate method incorporates differential project risk, and is used by most firms.

OUTLINE

The most important, and also the most difficult, step in the analysis of a capital project is estimating its cash flows—the investment outlays and the annual net cash inflows after a project goes into operation. Two key issues to recognize are: (1) capital decisions must be based on cash flows, not accounting income, and (2) only incremental cash flows are relevant.

- *Relevant cash flows* are the specific set of cash flows that should be considered in the decision at hand.
  - ☐ The relevant cash flow for a project is the additional free cash flow that the company expects if it implements the project.
  - ☐ The value of a project depends on its free cash flow, the cash flow available for distribution to investors.

- There are four major ways that project cash flows differ from accounting income:
  - ☐ *Costs of fixed assets.* This is a negative project cash flow; however, accountants do not show the purchase of fixed assets as a deduction from accounting income. Instead, they deduct a depreciation expense each year throughout the asset's life.
  - ☐ *Noncash charges.* In calculating net income, accountants usually subtract some noncash charges from revenues.
    - • One example is depreciation. Depreciation is added back when estimating project cash flow.
  - ☐ *Changes in net operating working capital.* The difference between the required increase in current assets and the spontaneous increase in current liabilities is the change in net operating working capital.
    - • If this change is positive, then additional financing, over and above the cost of fixed assets, will be needed.

- The investment in operating working capital will be returned by the end of the project's life.
- ☐ *Interest expenses are not included in project cash flows.* In calculating accounting income, interest expenses are subtracted because accountants attempt to measure the profit available for stockholders. Project cash flow is the cash flow available for all investors, so interest expenses are not subtracted.

■ In evaluating a capital project, we focus on those cash flows that result directly from the project. These *incremental cash flows* represent the change in the firm's total cash flow that occurs as a direct result of accepting the project. There are three special problems in determining incremental cash flows:
- ☐ A *sunk cost* is an outlay that has already been incurred and that cannot be recovered regardless of whether the project is accepted or rejected. Sunk costs are not incremental, and hence should not be included in the analysis.
- ☐ *Opportunity costs*, which are cash flows that could be generated from assets the firm already owns provided they are not used for the project in question, must be included in the capital budgeting analysis.
- ☐ *Externalities* involve the effects of a project on other parts of the firm, and their effects need to be considered in the incremental cash flows. Externalities are often difficult to quantify, and they can be either positive or negative.
  - *Cannibalization* occurs when the introduction of a new product causes sales of existing products to decline. This is an externality that must be considered in the analysis.

■ We must account properly for the timing of cash flows.
- ☐ In most cases, we simply assume that all cash flows occur at the end of every year.

■ A potential project creates value for the firm's shareholders if and only if the net present value of the incremental cash flows from the project is positive.

■ Incremental cash flows from a typical project can be classified into three categories:
- ☐ The *initial investment outlay* includes the up-front cost of fixed assets associated with the project plus any increases in net operating working capital.
- ☐ The *operating cash flows* are the incremental cash inflows over the project's economic life.
  - Annual operating cash flows equal after-tax operating income plus depreciation.
- ☐ At the end of a project's life, some extra cash flows called *terminal year cash flows* are received.
  - These include the after-tax salvage value of the fixed assets plus the return of the net operating working capital.

■   For each year of the project's life, the net cash flow is determined as the sum of the cash flows from each of the three categories. These annual net cash flows are then plotted on a time line, and used to calculate the project's NPV and IRR.

Two types of capital budgeting decisions are (1) expansion project analysis and (2) replacement project analysis. Despite some differences, the principles for evaluating expansion and replacement projects are the same.

■   A *new expansion project* is defined as one in which the firm invests in new assets to increase sales. Steps in the capital budgeting analysis for the project include:

    ☐ Summarize the investment outlays required for the project. Changes in net operating working capital should be included as an outflow here; however, they should be considered as an inflow at the end of the project.

    ☐ Estimate the cash flows that will occur once production begins, including effects of depreciation and salvage values.

    ☐ Summarize the data by combining all the net cash flows on a time line and evaluate the project by payback period, IRR, MIRR, and NPV (at the appropriate cost of capital). If the project has a positive NPV, the project should be accepted.

    ☐ The cost of capital may need to be increased if the project is deemed riskier than the firm's average project.

    ☐ Cash flows need to be adjusted for inflation because the cost of capital includes inflation.

■   A *replacement project* is defined as one in which the firm replaces an existing asset with a new asset.

    ☐ The incremental cash flows are the additional inflows and outflows from the new asset, relative to the cash flows from the existing asset.

    ☐ The company is effectively comparing its value with the new asset to its value if it stays with the existing asset.

Three separate and distinct types of risk can be identified in capital budgeting: (1) stand-alone risk, (2) corporate (within-firm) risk, and (3) market (beta) risk.

■   Given that the firm's primary objective is to maximize stockholder value, what ultimately matters is the risk that a project imposes on stockholders. Because stockholders are generally diversified, market risk is theoretically the most relevant measure of risk. Market, or beta, risk is important because beta affects the cost of capital which, in turn, affects stock price.

■   Corporate risk is also important for three reasons.

    ☐ Undiversified stockholders are more concerned about corporate risk than about market risk.

☐ Empirical studies of the determinants of required rates of return generally find that both market and corporate risk affect stock prices.

☐ The firm's stability is important to its managers, workers, customers, suppliers, and creditors, as well as to the community in which it operates. Firms that are in serious danger of bankruptcy, or even suffering low profits and reduced output have difficulty attracting and retaining good managers and workers. These factors tend to reduce risky firms' profitability and hence their stock prices, and this makes corporate risk significant.

Stand-alone risk is by far the easiest to measure and may be done so in a number of ways. Because all three types of risk are usually highly correlated, stand-alone risk is generally a good proxy for hard-to-measure corporate and market risk. The starting point for analyzing a project's stand-alone risk involves determining the uncertainty inherent in its cash flows. The nature of the individual cash flow distributions, and their correlations with one another, determine the nature of the NPV probability distribution and, thus, the project's stand-alone risk. Three techniques for assessing a project's stand-alone risk are: (1) sensitivity analysis, (2) scenario analysis, and (3) Monte Carlo simulation.

■ *Sensitivity analysis* is a technique that indicates how much a project's NPV will change in response to a given change in an input variable, other things held constant.

☐ The analysis begins with expected values for unit sales, sales price, fixed costs, and variable costs to give an expected, or base case, NPV. A series of "what if" questions may then be asked to find the change in NPV, given a change in one of the input variables.

● The *base-case NPV* is the NPV when sales and other input variables are set equal to their most likely (or base-case) values.

☐ Each variable is changed by several percentage points above and below the expected value, holding all other variables constant. The resulting set of NPVs is plotted against the variable that was changed to show how sensitive NPV is to changes in each variable.

☐ The steeper the slope, the more sensitive NPV is to changes in each of the inputs.

☐ When comparing two projects, the one with the steeper sensitivity lines would be riskier, because for that project a relatively small error in estimating an input variable would produce a large error in the project's expected NPV.

☐ Sensitivity analysis can provide useful insights into the riskiness of a project.

☐ Spreadsheet computer programs are ideally suited for performing sensitivity analysis.

■ *Scenario analysis* provides a more complete analysis, because in addition to the sensitivity of NPV to changes in key variables, it considers the range of likely values of these variables (the probability distributions of the inputs). It is a risk analysis technique in which bad and good sets of financial circumstances are compared with a most likely, or base-case situation.

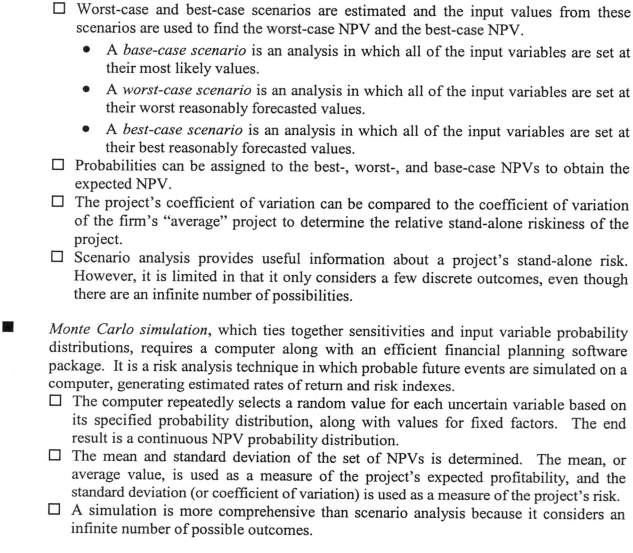

☐ Worst-case and best-case scenarios are estimated and the input values from these scenarios are used to find the worst-case NPV and the best-case NPV.

- A *base-case scenario* is an analysis in which all of the input variables are set at their most likely values.
- A *worst-case scenario* is an analysis in which all of the input variables are set at their worst reasonably forecasted values.
- A *best-case scenario* is an analysis in which all of the input variables are set at their best reasonably forecasted values.

☐ Probabilities can be assigned to the best-, worst-, and base-case NPVs to obtain the expected NPV.

☐ The project's coefficient of variation can be compared to the coefficient of variation of the firm's "average" project to determine the relative stand-alone riskiness of the project.

☐ Scenario analysis provides useful information about a project's stand-alone risk. However, it is limited in that it only considers a few discrete outcomes, even though there are an infinite number of possibilities.

■ *Monte Carlo simulation*, which ties together sensitivities and input variable probability distributions, requires a computer along with an efficient financial planning software package. It is a risk analysis technique in which probable future events are simulated on a computer, generating estimated rates of return and risk indexes.

☐ The computer repeatedly selects a random value for each uncertain variable based on its specified probability distribution, along with values for fixed factors. The end result is a continuous NPV probability distribution.

☐ The mean and standard deviation of the set of NPVs is determined. The mean, or average value, is used as a measure of the project's expected profitability, and the standard deviation (or coefficient of variation) is used as a measure of the project's risk.

☐ A simulation is more comprehensive than scenario analysis because it considers an infinite number of possible outcomes.

From a theoretical standpoint, well-diversified investors should be concerned only with market risk, managers should be concerned only with stock price maximization, and these two factors should lead to the conclusion that market (beta) risk ought to be given virtually all the weight in capital budgeting decisions. However, if investors are not well diversified, if the CAPM does not operate exactly as theory says it should, or if measurement problems keep managers from having confidence in the CAPM approach in capital budgeting, it may be appropriate to give stand-alone and corporate risk more weight than financial theory suggests.

■ CAPM ignores bankruptcy costs and the probability of bankruptcy depends on a firm's corporate risk, not on its beta risk. Therefore, one can easily conclude that even well-diversified investors should want a firm's management to give at least some consideration to a project's corporate risk instead of concentrating entirely on market risk.

■ The best we can do in practice is to estimate project risk in a somewhat nebulous, relative sense.

It is difficult to develop a really good quantitative measure of project risk. This makes it difficult to incorporate differential risk into capital budgeting decisions. Two methods are used to incorporate project risk into capital budgeting: the certainty equivalent approach and risk-adjusted discount rates.

■ With the *certainty equivalent approach* all cash flows that are not known with certainty are scaled down, and the riskier the cash flows, the lower their certainty equivalent values.

■ Most firms use *risk-adjusted discount rates* to incorporate differential project risk in the capital budgeting process. The risk-adjusted discount rate is the discount rate that applies to a particular risky stream of income; the riskier the project's income stream, the higher the discount rate.

☐ A firm's cost of capital may be estimated with a fair degree of accuracy.

☐ Increasing the discount rate for high-risk projects and lowering it for low-risk projects is a somewhat arbitrary and judgmental process, but it does force managers to at least consider a project's riskiness.

☐ Diversified companies with divisions of varying risk may use a two-step process to determine a project's risk-adjusted discount rate.

 • First, divisional costs of capital are established for each of the major operating divisions.

 • Then, within the division, projects classified as high-risk would have an increased discount rate, while low-risk projects would have a lowered discount rate.

☐ Capital structure must also be taken into account if a firm finances different assets in different ways. As a result, a division with real estate might have a higher debt capacity than a division with specialized machinery, hence an optimal capital structure that contains a higher percentage of debt.

Web Appendix 11A reviews depreciation concepts covered in accounting courses. The MACRS classes and asset lives are given, as well as the recovery allowance percentages for 3-year, 5-year, 7-year, and 10-year class personal property. Web Appendix 11B discusses replacement project analysis in more detail and Web Appendix 11C discusses refunding operations.

SELF-TEST QUESTIONS

Definitional

1. An increase in net operating working capital would show up as a cash _____ at time 0 and then again as a cash _____ at the _____ of the project's life.

2. A(n) _____ _____ is a cash outlay that has already been incurred and that cannot be recovered regardless of whether the project is accepted or rejected.

3. A(n) _____ cash flow represents the change in the firm's total cash flow that occurs as a direct result of accepting the project.

4. One of the most critical steps in capital budgeting analysis is _____ _____ _____.

5. _____ _____ are cash flows that could be generated from assets the firm already owns provided they are not used for the project in question, and they must be included in capital budgeting analysis.

6. _____ involve the effects of a project on other parts of the firm, and their effects need to be considered in the incremental cash flows.

7. When a new project takes sales from an existing product, this is often called _____.

8. A(n) _____ _____ project is defined as one where the firm invests in new assets to increase sales.

9. _____ payments are not reflected in the estimated cash flows for a capital budgeting project because the effects of debt financing are reflected in the cost of capital used to discount the cash flows.

10. Incremental cash flows from a typical project can be classified into three categories: (1) the initial _____ _____, (2) _____ cash flows, and (3) _____ _____ cash flows.

11. The difference between the required increase in current assets and the spontaneous increase in current liabilities needed to support a new operation is the change in _____ _____ _____ _____.

12. Three separate and distinct types of risk have been identified in capital budgeting decisions: market risk, _____-_____ risk, and _____ risk.

13. A commonly used method of risk analysis based on constructing optimistic, pessimistic, and expected value estimates for key variables is called _____ _____.

14. In project analysis, changing one key variable at a time and determining the effect on its NPV is known as _____ _____.

15. One purpose of sensitivity analysis is to determine which of the _____ _____ have the greatest influence on the project's NPV.

16. _____ _____ _____ ties together sensitivities and input variable probability distributions, and requires a computer along with an efficient financial planning software package.

17. The _____ _____ approach is one method used to incorporate project risk into capital budgeting, where all cash flows that are not known with certainty are scaled down.

18. _____ cash flows are the specific set of cash flows that should be considered in the decision at hand.

19. A(n) _____ project is defined as one in which the firm replaces an existing asset with a new asset.

20. Three techniques for assessing a project's stand-alone risk are: _____ analysis, _____ analysis, and _____ _____ _____.

21. The _____-_____ NPV is the NPV when sales and other input variables are set equal to their most likely values.

22. A(n) _____-_____ _____ is an analysis in which all of the input variables are set at their worst reasonably forecasted values.

23. A(n) _____-_____ _____ is an analysis in which all of the input variables are set at their most likely values.

24. A(n) _____-_____ _____ is an analysis in which all of the input variables are set at their best reasonably forecasted values.

25. The _____-_____ _____ rate is the rate that applies to a particular risky stream of income; the riskier the project's income stream, the higher the discount rate.

26. The _____ the slope, the more sensitive NPV is to changes in each of the input variables.

27. Capital decisions must be based on _____ _____, not accounting income.

28. The _____ _____ _____ includes the up-front cost of fixed assets associated with the project plus any increases in net operating working capital.

29. Annual _____ _____ _____ equal after-tax operating income plus depreciation.

30. Terminal year cash flows include the after-tax _____ _____ of the fixed assets plus the return of _____ _____ _____ _____.

Conceptual

31. In general, the value of land currently owned by a firm is irrelevant to a capital budgeting decision because the cost of that property is a sunk cost.

    a. True   b. False

32. McDonald's is planning to open a new store across from the student union. Annual revenues are expected to be $5 million. However, opening the new location will cause annual revenues to drop by $3 million at McDonald's existing stadium location. The relevant sales revenues for the capital budgeting analysis are $2 million per year.

    a. True   b. False

33. In capital budgeting decisions, corporate risk will be of least interest to:

    a. Employees.   d. Creditors.
    b. Stockholders with few shares. e. The local community.
    c. Institutional investors.

34. Two corporations are formed. They are identical in all respects except for their methods of depreciation. Firm A uses MACRS depreciation, while Firm B uses the straight-line method. The applicable MACRS depreciation rates are 20 percent, 32 percent, 19 percent, 12 percent, 11 percent, and 6 percent. Both plan to depreciate their assets for tax purposes over a 5-year life (6 calendar years), which is equal to the useful life, and both pay a 35 percent tax rate. (Note: The half-year convention will apply, so the firm using the straight-line method will take 10 percent depreciation in Year 1 and 10 percent in Year 6.) Which of the following statements is *false*?

    a. Firm A will generate higher cash flows from operations in the first year than B.

    b. Firm A will pay more Federal corporate income taxes in the first year than B.

    c. If there is no change in tax rates over the 6-year period, and if we disregard the time value of money, the total amount of funds generated from operations by these projects for each corporation will be the same over the 6 years.

    d. Firm B will pay the same amount of federal corporate income taxes, over the 6-year period, as A.

    e. Firm A could, if it chose to, use straight-line depreciation for stockholder reporting even if it used MACRS for tax purposes.

SELF-TEST PROBLEMS

1. Franklin Corporation is considering an expansion project. The necessary equipment could be purchased for $15 million and shipping and installation costs are another $500,000. The project will also require an initial $2 million investment in net operating working capital. If the company's tax rate is 40 percent, what is the project's initial investment outlay (in millions)?

    a. $15.0   **b.** $15.5   **c.** $16.5   **d.** $17.0   **e.** $17.5

2. Hobart Industries is trying to estimate its first-year operating cash flow (at t = 1) for a proposed project. The financial staff has collected the following information:

Projected sales	$3,000,000
Operating costs	1,200,000
Depreciation	450,000
Interest expense	330,000

The company faces a 40 percent tax rate. What is the project's operating cash flow for the first year (t = 1)?

    a. $1,260,000   **b.** $810,000   **c.** $1,080,000   **d.** $1,500,000   **e.** $1,800,000

3. The capital budgeting director of National Products Inc. is evaluating a new 3-year project that would decrease operating costs by $30,000 per year without affecting revenues. The project's cost is $50,000. The project will be depreciated using the MACRS method over its 3-year class life. The applicable MACRS depreciation rates are 33 percent, 45 percent, 15 percent, and 7 percent. It will have a *zero salvage value* after 3 years. The marginal tax rate of National Products is 35 percent, and the project's cost of capital is 12 percent. What is the project's NPV?

 a. $7,068   b. $8,324   c. $10,214   d. $11,010   e. $12,387

4. Your firm has a marginal tax rate of 40 percent and a cost of capital of 14 percent. You are performing a capital budgeting analysis on a new project that will cost $500,000. The project is expected to have a useful life of 10 years, although its MACRS class life is only 5 years. The applicable MACRS depreciation rates are 20 percent, 32 percent, 19 percent, 12 percent, 11 percent, and 6 percent. The project is expected to increase the firm's net income by $61,257 per year and to have a salvage value of $35,000 at the end of 10 years. What is the project's NPV?

 a. $95,356   b. $108,359   c. $135,256   d. $162,185   e. $177,902

5. The Board of Directors of National Brewing Inc. is considering the acquisition of a new still. The still is priced at $600,000 but would require $60,000 in transportation costs and $40,000 for installation. The still has a useful life of 10 years but will be depreciated over its 5-year MACRS life. The applicable MACRS depreciation rates are 20 percent, 32 percent, 19 percent, 12 percent, 11 percent, and 6 percent. It is expected to have a salvage value of $10,000 at the end of 10 years. The still would increase revenues by $120,000 per year and increase yearly operating costs by $20,000 per year. Additionally, the still would require a $30,000 increase in net operating working capital. The firm's marginal tax rate is 40 percent, and the project's cost of capital is 10 percent. What is the NPV of the still?

 a. $18,430   b. -$12,352   c. -$65,204   d. -$130,961   e. -$203,450

6. Consolidated Inc. uses a weighted average cost of capital of 12 percent to evaluate average-risk projects and adds/subtracts two percentage points to evaluate projects of greater/lesser risk. Currently, two mutually exclusive projects are under consideration. Both have a net cost of $200,000 and last four years. Project A, which is riskier than average, will produce annual after-tax net cash flows of $71,000. Project B, which has less-than-average risk, will produce an after-tax net cash flow of $146,000 in Years 3 and 4 only. What should Consolidated do?

 a. Accept Project B with an NPV of $9,412.
 b. Accept both projects since both NPVs are greater than zero.
 c. Accept Project A with an NPV of $6,874.
 d. Accept neither project since both NPVs are less than zero.
 e. Accept Project A with an NPV of $15,652.

(The following data apply to the next three Self-Test Problems.)

The Carlisle Corporation is considering a proposed project for its capital budget. The company estimates that the project's NPV is $5 million. This estimate assumes that the economy and market conditions will be average over the next few years. The company's CFO, however, forecasts that there is only a 40 percent chance that the economy will be average. Recognizing this uncertainty, she has also performed the following scenario analysis:

Economic Scenario	Probability of Outcome	(NPV)
Recession	0.05	($28 million)
Below Average	0.25	(10 million)
Average	0.40	5 million
Above Average	0.25	8 million
Boom	0.05	15 million

7. What is the project's expected NPV (in millions)?

   a. $0.25   **b.** $0.85   **c.** $1.20   **d.** $1.50   **e.** $2.00

8. What is the project's standard deviation?

   a. $10.04   **b.** $12.78   **c.** $15.65   **d.** $21.37   **e.** $29.43

9. What is the project's coefficient of variation?

   a. 5.02   **b.** 2.75   **c.** 6.39   **d.** 1.25   **e.** 11.81

(The following data apply to the next two Self-Test Problems.)

You are evaluating a capital budgeting project for your company that is expected to last for six years. The project begins with the purchase of a $1,200,000 investment in equipment. You are unsure what method of depreciation to use in your analysis, straight-line depreciation or the 5-year MACRS accelerated method. Straight-line depreciation results in the cost of the equipment depreciated evenly over its life. The 5-year MACRS depreciation rates are 20 percent, 32 percent, 19 percent, 12 percent, 11 percent, and 6 percent. Your company's WACC is 10.5% and it has a tax rate of 35%. For purposes of this question, we are ignoring the half-year convention for the straight-line depreciation method.

10. Under the straight-line and MACRS depreciation methods, what would the depreciation expense be for the second year?

   a. $200,000; $132,000
   b. $200,000; $228,000
   c. $200,000; $384,000
   d. $200,000; $144,000
   e. $200,000; $240,000

11. What is the NPV of the project given by the better depreciation method, i.e., the method that gives the higher NPV?

    a. $16,333.33   **b.** $17,500.00   **c.** $18,182.88   **d.** $20,473.06   **e.** $21,250.75

ANSWERS TO SELF-TEST QUESTIONS

1.	outflow; inflow; end		**17.**	certainty equivalent
2.	sunk cost		**18.**	Relevant
3.	incremental		**19.**	replacement
4.	cash flow estimation		**20.**	sensitivity; scenario; Monte Carlo simulation
5.	Opportunity costs			
6.	Externalities		**21.**	base-case
7.	cannibalization		**22.**	worst-case scenario
8.	new expansion		**23.**	base-case scenario
9.	Interest		**24.**	best-case scenario
10.	investment outlay; operating; terminal year		**25.**	risk-adjusted discount
			26.	steeper
11.	net operating working capital		**27.**	cash flows
12.	stand-alone; corporate (within-firm)		**28.**	initial investment outlay
13.	scenario analysis		**29.**	operating cash flows
14.	sensitivity analysis		**30.**	salvage value; net operating working capital
15.	input variables			
16.	Monte Carlo simulation			

31. b. The net market value of land currently owned is an opportunity cost of the project. If the project is not undertaken, the land could be sold to realize its current market value less any taxes and expenses. Thus, project acceptance means forgoing this cash inflow.

32. a. Incremental revenues, which are relevant in a capital budgeting decision, must consider the effects on other parts of the firm.

33. c. Institutional investors are well diversified and, therefore, more concerned with beta risk.

34. b. Statement a is true; MACRS is an accelerated depreciation method, so Firm A will have a higher depreciation expense than Firm B. We are also given that both firms are identical except for depreciation methods used. Net cash flow is equal to net income plus depreciation. In Year 1, Firm A's depreciation expense is twice as great as Firm B's; however, Firm A's lower net income is more than compensated for by the addition of depreciation (which is twice as high as Firm B's). Thus, in Year 1, Firm A's net cash flow is greater than Firm B's. Statement b is false; because Firm A's depreciation expense is larger, it's earnings before taxes will be lower, and thus it will pay less income taxes than Firm B. Statements c, d, and e are all true.

SOLUTIONS TO SELF-TEST PROBLEMS

1.   e.   Initial investment outlay:

Purchase price	$15,000,000
Shipping/Installation	500,000
Net operating working capital	2,000,000
Total investment outlay	$17,500,000

2.   a.   Operating cash flow:

Sales	$3,000,000
Operating costs	1,200,000
Depreciation	450,000
Oper. income before taxes	$1,350,000
Taxes (40%)	540,000
Oper. income after taxes	$ 810,000
Add: Depreciation	450,000
Operating cash flow	$1,260,000

3.   d.   Cash flow = Net income + Depreciation. The first step is to set up the income statement for Years 1 through 3. (Note that a reduction in operating costs increases revenues.)

	1	2	3
Revenues	$30,000	$30,000	$30,000
Depreciation[a]	16,500	22,500	7,500
Oper. income before taxes	$13,500	$ 7,500	$22,500
Taxes (35%)	4,725	2,625	7,875
Oper. income after taxes	$ 8,775	$ 4,875	$14,625
+ Depreciation	16,500	22,500	7,500
Oper. cash flow	$25,275	$27,375	$22,125
SV tax savings[b]			1,225
Net cash flow	$25,275	$27,375	$23,350

[a]Depreciation schedule: Cost basis = $50,000.

Year	Allowance Percentage	Depreciation	Ending Book Value
1	0.33	$16,500	$33,500
2	0.45	22,500	11,000
3	0.15	7,500	3,500
4	0.07	3,500	0
		$50,000	

[b]At the end of Year 3, the project will not be fully depreciated to its book value of $3,500; however, its salvage value is zero. Thus, National can reduce its taxable income by $3,500, producing a 0.35($3,500) = $1,225 tax savings.

The project's cash flows are then placed on a time line as follows and discounted at the project's cost of capital:

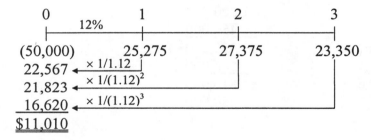

Alternatively, input the cash flows into the cash flow register, input I = 12, and then solve for NPV = $11,010.

4. e. In this case, the *net income* of the project is $61,257. Net cash flow = Net income + Depreciation = $61,257 + Depreciation. The depreciation allowed in each year is calculated as follows:

Dep_1 = $500,000(0.20) = $100,000.
Dep_2 = $500,000(0.32) = $160,000.
Dep_3 = $500,000(0.19) = $95,000.
Dep_4 = $500,000(0.12) = $60,000.
Dep_5 = $500,000(0.11) = $55,000.
Dep_6 = $500,000(0.06) = $30,000.
Dep_{7-10} = $0.

In the final year (Year 10), the firm receives $35,000 from the sale of the machine. However, the book value of the machine is $0. Thus, the firm would have to pay

0.4($35,000) = $14,000 in taxes; and the net salvage value is $35,000 − $14,000 = $21,000. The time line is as follows:

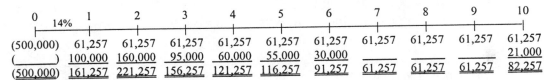

0	14%	1	2	3	4	5	6	7	8	9	10
(500,000)		61,257	61,257	61,257	61,257	61,257	61,257	61,257	61,257	61,257	61,257
( )		100,000	160,000	95,000	60,000	55,000	30,000				21,000
(500,000)		161,257	221,257	156,257	121,257	116,257	91,257	61,257	61,257	61,257	82,257

The project's NPV can be found by discounting each of the cash flows at the firm's 14 percent cost of capital. The project's NPV, found by using a financial calculator, is $177,902.

5.   d. Net cash flow = Net income + Depreciation. The first step to this problem is to set up the income statement for Years 1 through 10.

	1	2	3	4	5	6	7 – 9	10
Revenues	120,000	120,000	120,000	120,000	120,000	120,000	120,000	120,000
Operating costs	20,000	20,000	20,000	20,000	20,000	20,000	20,000	20,000
Depreciation[a]	140,000	224,000	133,000	84,000	77,000	42,000		
Oper. inc. bef. taxes	(40,000)	(124,000)	(33,000)	16,000	23,000	58,000	100,000	100,000
Taxes (40%)	(16,000)	(49,600)	(13,200)	6,400	9,200	23,200	40,000	40,000
Oper. inc. after taxes	(24,000)	(74,400)	(19,800)	9,600	13,800	34,800	60,000	60,000
+ Depreciation	140,000	224,000	133,000	84,000	77,000	42,000		
Oper. cash flow	116,000	149,600	113,200	93,600	90,800	76,800	60,000	60,000
SV (AT)[b]								6,000
Recovery of NOWC								30,000
Net cash flow	116,000	149,600	113,200	93,600	90,800	76,800	60,000	96,000

[a]Depreciation schedule: Cost basis = Price + Transportation + Installation.
                                    = $600,000 + $60,000 + $40,000 = $700,000

Year	Percentage	Allowance Depreciation	Ending Book Value
1	0.20	$140,000	$560,000
2	0.32	224,000	336,000
3	0.19	133,000	203,000
4	0.12	84,000	119,000
5	0.11	77,000	42,000
6	0.06	42,000	0
		$700,000	

[b]At the end of Year 10 the still has a salvage value of $10,000; however, it has been fully depreciated so the firm must pay taxes of 0.4($10,000) = $4,000. Therefore, the still's after-tax salvage value is $10,000 - $4,000 = $6,000. The still's cash flows are then placed on a time line as follows and discounted at the project's cost of capital:

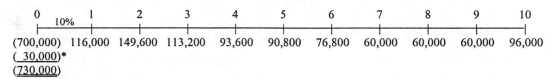

*An increase in net operating working capital is required in Year 0, and this must be added back to the cash flow at the end of the project's life. This amount is included in the Year 10 cash flow shown.

With a financial calculator enter the cash flows into the cash flow register and enter I = 10 and then solve for NPV = -$130,961.

6. a. Look at the time lines:

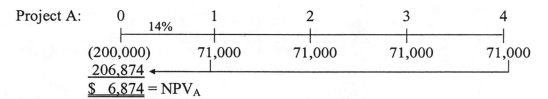

Alternatively, input the cash flows in the cash flow register, enter I = 14, and then solve for NPV_A = $6,873.57.

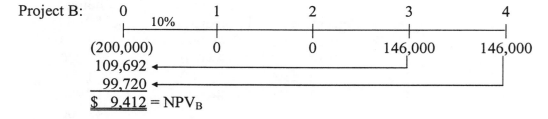

Alternatively, input the cash flows in the cash flow register, enter I = 10, and then solve for NPV_B = $9,411.93.

Note that both discount rates are adjusted for risk. Since the projects are mutually exclusive, the project with the higher NPV is chosen.

7. b. $E(NPV) = 0.05(-\$28) + 0.25(-\$10) + 0.40(\$5) + 0.25(\$8) + 0.05(\$15)$
$= -\$1.40 + -\$2.50 + \$2.00 + \$2.00 + \$0.75$
$= \$0.85$ million.

8. a. $\sigma = [0.05(-\$28 - \$0.85)^2 + 0.25(-\$10 - \$0.85)^2 + 0.40(\$5 - \$0.85)^2 + 0.25(\$8 - \$0.85)^2$
$+ 0.05(\$15 - \$0.85)^2]^{1/2}$
$\sigma = [\$41.62 + \$29.43 + \$6.89 + \$12.78 + \$10.01]^{1/2}$
$\sigma = [\$100.73]^{1/2}$
$\sigma = \$10.04.$

9. e. $CV = \dfrac{\$10.04}{\$0.85}$
$CV = 11.81.$

10. c. The applicable depreciation values are as follows for the two scenarios:

Year	Scenario 1 (Straight-Line)	Scenario 2 (MACRS)
1	$200,000	$240,000
2	200,000	384,000
3	200,000	228,000
4	200,000	144,000
5	200,000	132,000
6	200,000	72,000

11. d. To find the difference in net present values under these two methods, we must determine the difference in incremental cash flows each method provides. The depreciation expenses cannot simply be subtracted from each other, as there are tax ramifications due to depreciation expense. The full depreciation expense is subtracted from revenues to get operating income, and then taxes due are computed. Then, depreciation is added to after-tax operating income to get the project's operating cash flow. Therefore, if the tax rate is 35%, only 65% of the depreciation expense is actually subtracted out during the after-tax operating income calculation and the full depreciation expense is added back to get operating income. So, there is a tax benefit associated with the depreciation expense that amounts to 35% of the depreciation expense. Therefore, the differences between depreciation expenses under each scenario should be computed and multiplied by 0.35 to determine the benefit provided by the depreciation expense.

Year	Depr. Exp. Difference (2 – 1)	Depr. Exp. Diff. × 0.35
1	$ 40,000	$14,000
2	184,000	64,400
3	28,000	9,800
4	-56,000	-19,600
5	-68,000	-23,800
6	-128,000	-44,800

Now to find the difference in NPV to be generated under these scenarios, just enter the cash flows that represent the benefit from depreciation expense and solve for net present value based upon a WACC of 10.5%.

$CF_0 = 0$
$CF_1 = 14000$
$CF_2 = 64400$
$CF_3 = 9800$
$CF_4 = -19600$
$CF_5 = -23800$
$CF_6 = -44800$

$I = 10.5$; NPV = $20,473.06.

So, all else equal the use of the accelerated depreciation method will result in a higher NPV by $20,473.06 than would the use of the straight-line depreciation method.

CHAPTER 12
OTHER TOPICS IN CAPITAL BUDGETING

LEARNING OBJECTIVES

- Use the replacement chain method to compare projects with unequal lives.

- Explain why conventional NPV analysis may not capture a project's impact on the firm's opportunities.

- Define the term option value, and identify four different types of embedded real options.

- Explain what an abandonment option is, and give an example of a project that includes one.

- Explain what a decision tree is and provide an example of one.

- Explain what an investment timing option is, and give an example of a project that includes one.

- Explain what a growth option is, and give an example of a project that includes one.

- Explain what a flexibility option is, and give an example of a project that includes one.

- List the steps a firm goes through when establishing its optimal capital budget in practice.

OVERVIEW

Capital budgeting analysis is in many respects straightforward. A project is deemed acceptable if it has a positive NPV, where the NPV is calculated by discounting the estimated cash flows at the project's risk-adjusted cost of capital. However, things often get more complicated in the real world.

One complication is that many projects include a variety of "embedded options" that dramatically affect their value.

Positive option values expand a firm's opportunities. Opportunities to respond to changing circumstances are called managerial options because they give managers the option to influence the outcome of a project. These options are also called strategic, or real, options.

A typical corporation considers many projects each year, and each project may contain one or more different types of embedded real options. Examples include abandonment/shutdown options, investment timing options, growth/expansion options, and flexibility options.

The replacement chain (common life) approach is a method of comparing projects of unequal lives that assumes that each project can be repeated as many times as necessary to reach a common life span; the NPVs over this life span are then compared, and the project with the higher common life NPV is chosen. We can also consider replacement chain analysis as a real option. The shorter-term project is really less risky than the longer-term project because the second investment can be made or not made depending on what is happening in the future. This chapter discusses both replacement chain analysis and real options.

OUTLINE

If a company is choosing between two mutually exclusive alternatives with significantly different lives, an adjustment may be necessary.

- The *replacement chain (common life) approach* is a method of comparing projects of unequal lives that assumes that each project can be repeated as many times as necessary to reach a common life span; the NPVs over this life span are then compared, and the project with the higher common life NPV is chosen.
  - ☐ As a general rule, the unequal life issue (1) does not arise for independent projects but (2) can arise if mutually exclusive projects with significantly different lives are being compared.
    - Even for mutually exclusive projects, it is not always appropriate to extend the analysis to a common life. This should only be done if there is a high probability that the projects will actually be repeated at the end of their initial lives.
  - ☐ There are 3 potentially serious weaknesses inherent in this type of analysis:
    - If inflation is expected, static conditions built into the analysis would be invalid.
    - Replacements that occur down the road will probably employ new technology, which in turn might change the cash flows.
    - It is difficult enough to estimate the lives of most projects, so estimating the lives of a series of projects is often just a speculation.
  - ☐ Inflation and/or possible efficiency gains can be built into the cash flow estimates using the replacement chain approach.

In recent years a growing number of academics and practitioners have demonstrated that DCF valuation techniques do not always tell the complete story about a project's value and that rote use of DCF can, at times, lead to incorrect capital budgeting decisions.

- ■ DCF techniques were originally developed to value securities such as stocks and bonds. These securities are passive investments—once they have been purchased, most investors have *no* influence over the cash flows the assets produce.

- ■ Real assets are not passive investments—managerial actions can influence their results.
  - ☐ Investing in a new project often brings with it a potential increase in the firm's future opportunities.
  - ☐ Opportunities are *options*, the right but not the obligation to take some action in the future.

- ■ Any project that expands the firm's set of opportunities has positive *option value*. Option value is the value that is not accounted for in a conventional NPV analysis.
  - ☐ Any project that reduces a firm's set of future opportunities has negative option value.

- ■ Traditional capital budgeting theory says nothing about actions that can be taken after the project has been accepted and placed in operation that might cause the cash flows to change.
  - ☐ Chance plays a continuing role throughout the life of a project and managers can respond to changing market conditions and to competitors' actions.

- ■ Opportunities to respond to changing circumstances are called *managerial options* because they give managers the option to influence the outcome of a project.
  - ☐ They are also called *strategic options* because they are often associated with large, strategic projects rather than routine maintenance projects.
  - ☐ They are also called *real options* and are differentiated from financial options because they involve real, rather than financial, assets.
    - Unequal life analysis is a type of real option. The shorter investment contains an "embedded option" to make another investment in the future.

- ■ Examples of real options include abandonment/shutdown options, investment timing options, growth/expansion options, and flexibility options.

An abandonment option is the option of abandoning (or shutting down) a project if operating cash flows turn out to be lower than expected. This option can both raise expected profitability and lower project risk.

- ■ A *decision tree* is a diagram that shows all possible outcomes that result from a decision. Each possible outcome is shown as a "branch" on the tree.
  - ☐ Decision trees are especially useful to analyze the effects of real options in investment decisions.

■ The difference between the expected NPV with and without abandonment represents the value of the option to abandon.

■ It often turns out that if we fail to consider abandonment, the bad case is so bad that the expected NPV is negative, but when abandonment is considered, the expected NPV becomes positive. Clearly, abandonment must be considered to obtain valid assessments for different projects.

■ In general, the opportunity to abandon projects allows companies to limit downside losses.

A conventional NPV analysis implicitly assumes that projects will either be accepted or rejected, which implies that they will be undertaken now or never. However, in practice companies sometimes have a third choice—delay the decision until later, when more information is available. An investment timing option is an option as to when to begin a project. Often, if a firm can delay a decision, it can increase a project's expected NPV.

■ In many respects, the investment timing decision is similar to choosing among mutually exclusive projects. The mutually exclusive choice is between investing in the project today and waiting a year before deciding whether or not to make the investment. The company should select the strategy with the higher expected net present value.

■ With an investment timing option there is a "wait case" NPV and a "proceed immediately" NPV. To make the NPVs comparable, the wait NPV must be discounted back to find the project's value in today's dollars.

■ If the firm chooses to accept the project today, it is effectively giving up the option to pursue the project next year. In such cases, decision makers should insist on an NPV that is both positive and also large enough to offset the value of the lost option. For this reason, some companies deliberately set hurdle rates that are above the calculated cost of capital when evaluating projects that contain timing options.

■ When making "go now" versus "wait" decisions, financial managers need to consider several factors:
   ☐ If a firm decides to wait, it may lose any strategic advantages associated with being the first competitor to enter a new line of business, and this could alter the cash flows.
   ☐ Waiting may enable the company to avoid a costly mistake.

■ In general, the more uncertainty there is about future market conditions, the more attractive it becomes to wait, but this risk reduction may be offset by the loss of the "first mover advantage."

If an investment creates the opportunity to make other potentially profitable investments that would not otherwise be possible, then the investment is said to contain a growth option.

■ The true value of a project that includes an embedded option may exceed the project's NPV as calculated in the conventional manner. Therefore, it is critically important that managers identify any such options and include them in the analysis.

■ Decision trees provide one method of dealing formally with embedded options. Also, option pricing models can be used in certain situations.

■ One should recognize that as a result of embedded options some projects have more or less value than is indicated by their NPVs, and this value should, at a minimum, be subjectively considered when making capital budgeting decisions.

A flexibility option is the option to modify operations depending on how conditions develop during a project's life, especially the type of output produced or the inputs used.

For planning purposes, managers also need to forecast the total amount of investment that will be made, because it is necessary to know how much capital must be raised.

■ Typically, there are four main steps for estimating the optimal capital budget.
   ☐ An estimate of the firm's overall composite WACC is obtained.
   ☐ The corporate WACC is scaled up or down for each of the firm's divisions to reflect the division's capital structure and risk characteristics.
   ☐ Financial managers within each of the firm's divisions estimate the relevant cash flows and risk of each of their potential projects. Within each division, projects are classified into one of three groups—high risk, average risk, and low risk.
   ☐ Each project's NPV is then determined, using its risk-adjusted cost of capital. The optimal capital budget consists of all independent projects with positive NPVs plus those mutually exclusive projects with the highest positive NPVs.

■ Smaller firms, new firms, and firms with dubious track records may have difficulties raising capital, even for projects that the firm concludes have positive NPVs.
   ☐ In such circumstances, the size of the firm's capital budget may be constrained.
   ☐ This circumstance is called *capital rationing*.
      • In such situations capital is scarce, and it should be used in the most efficient way possible.

■ The four steps discussed above force the firm to think carefully about each division's relative risk, about the risk of each project within each division, and about the relationship between the total amount of capital raised and the cost of that capital.

□ This procedure forces the firm to adjust its capital budget to reflect capital market conditions.

□ If the costs of debt and equity increase, this fact will be reflected in the cost of capital used to evaluate projects, and projects that would be marginally acceptable when capital costs were low would correctly be ruled unacceptable when capital costs become high.

SELF-TEST QUESTIONS

Definitional

1. The _____ _____ _____ is a method of comparing projects of unequal lives that assumes that each project can be repeated as many times as necessary to reach a common life span; the NPVs over this life span are then compared, and the project with the higher common life NPV is chosen.

2. As a general rule, the unequal life issue does not arise for _____ projects but can arise if _____ _____ projects with significantly different lives are being compared.

3. _____ assets are not passive investments—managerial actions can influence their results.

4. _____ value is the value that is not accounted for in a conventional NPV analysis.

5. Opportunities to respond to changing circumstances are called _____ _____ because they give managers the option to influence the outcome of a project.

6. Opportunities are _____, the right but not the obligation to take some action in the future.

7. _____ _____, another name for real options, are often associated with large, strategic projects rather than routine maintenance projects.

8. Examples of real options include _____/shutdown options, _____ _____ options, _____/expansion options, and _____ options.

9. A(n) _____ _____ is a diagram that shows all possible outcomes that result from a decision. Each possible outcome is shown as a(n) _____ on the tree.

10. A(n) _____ _____ is the option of shutting down a project if operating cash flows turn out to be lower than expected.

11. The difference between the expected NPV with and without abandonment represents the _____ of the option to abandon.

12. A(n) _____ _____ _____ is an option as to when to begin a project.

13. To make the NPVs comparable, the wait NPV must be _____ back to find the project's value in today's dollars.

14. If a firm decides to wait to invest in a project, it may lose any _____ _____ associated with being the first competitor to enter a new line of business, and this could alter the cash flows.

15. In general, the more uncertainty there is about future market conditions, the more attractive it becomes to wait, but this risk reduction may be offset by the loss of the _____ _____ _____.

16. If an investment creates the opportunity to make other potentially profitable investments that would not otherwise be possible, then the investment is said to contain a(n) _____ _____.

17. A(n) _____ _____ is the option to modify operations depending on how conditions develop during a project's life, especially the type of output produced or the inputs used.

18. _____ _____ is a situation in which a constraint is placed on the total size of the firm's capital budget.

19. _____ option values expand a firm's investment opportunities, while _____ option values reduce the firm's future opportunities.

20. Unequal life analysis is a type of _____ _____. The shorter investment contains a(n) _____ _____ to make another investment in the future.

21. One potentially serious weakness of the replacement chain approach occurs if _____ is expected, static conditions built into the analysis would be invalid.

22. Chance plays a continuing role throughout the life of a project and managers can respond to changing _____ _____ and to _____ actions.

23. An abandonment option can both raise a project's expected _____ and lower project _____.

24.   In general, the opportunity to abandon projects allows companies to limit _____ _____.

25.   In many respects, the investment timing decision is similar to choosing among _____ _____ projects.

Conceptual

26.   Inflation and/or possible efficiency gains cannot be built into the cash flow estimates using the replacement chain approach.

   a. True   **b.** False

27.   Option value is the value that is not accounted for in a conventional NPV analysis.

   a. True   **b.** False

28.   In general, the opportunity to abandon projects allows companies to limit downside losses.

   a. True   **b.** False

29. Which of the following is *not* a weakness inherent in replacement chain analysis?

   a. If inflation is expected, static conditions built into the analysis would be invalid.
   b. Replacements that occur down the road will probably employ new technology, which in turn might change the cash flows.
   c. Estimating the lives of a series of projects is often just a speculation.
   d. None of the statements above is a weakness inherent in the replacement chain analysis.
   e. Statements a, b, and c are all weaknesses inherent in replacement chain analysis.

30.   The Hatfield Company is deciding whether it makes sense to invest in a project today, or to postpone this decision for one year. Which of the following statements best describes the issues that Hatfield faces when considering this investment timing option?

   a. If the project has a positive expected NPV today, this means that its expected NPV will be even higher if it chooses to wait a year.
   b. The investment timing option does not affect the expected cash flows and should therefore have no impact on the project's risk.
   c. The more uncertainty about the project's future cash flows the more likely it is that Hatfield will wait to undertake the project.
   d. All of the statements above are correct.
   e. None of the statements above are correct.

SELF-TEST PROBLEMS

1. The Vetter Corporation has the opportunity to invest in one of two mutually exclusive machines that will produce a product it will need for the foreseeable future. Machine A costs $37 million but realizes after-tax inflows of $14.80 million per year for 4 years. After 4 years, the machine must be replaced. Machine B costs $55.50 million and realizes after-tax inflows of $12.95 million per year for 8 years, after which it must be replaced. Assume that machine prices are not expected to rise because inflation will be offset by cheaper components used in the machines. If the cost of capital is 12 percent, how much is shareholder value increased (in millions of dollars) by using the better machine?

    a. $3.43   **b.** $7.95   **c.** $8.83   **d.** $10.51   **e.** $13.01

    (The following data apply to the next two Self-Test Problems.)

    Vacation Resorts Inc. (VRI) is interested in developing a new hotel in Spain. The company estimates that the hotel would require an initial investment of $32 million. VRI expects that the hotel will produce positive cash flows of $5.25 million a year at the end of each of the next 20 years. The project's cost of capital is 14 percent.

2. What is the project's net present value today (in millions of dollars)?

    a. $1.44   **b.** $2.15   **c.** $2.77   **d.** $3.25   **e.** $4.05

3. While VRI expects the cash flows to be $5.25 million a year, it recognizes that the cash flows could, in fact, be much higher or lower, depending on whether the Spanish government imposes a large hotel tax. One year from now, VRI will know whether the tax will be imposed. There is a 25 percent chance that the tax will be imposed, in which case the yearly cash flows will be only $4.2 million. At the same time, there is a 75 percent chance that the tax will not be imposed, in which case the yearly cash flows will be $5.6 million. VRI is deciding whether to proceed with the hotel today or to wait 1 year to find out whether the tax will be imposed. If VRI waits a year, the initial investment will remain at $32 million. Assume that all cash flows are discounted at 14 percent. Should VRI proceed with the project today or should it wait a year before deciding?

    a. Proceed with the project today, its NPV is $2.77 million.
    b. Wait one year, since the NPV of waiting one year is $3.3484 million and this is larger than its NPV of undertaking the project today.
    c. It doesn't matter whether you go ahead and proceed with the project today or wait one year because their NPVs are identical.
    d. Don't accept the project at all—its NPV today and its NPV if you wait one year are both negative.
    e. Wait one year, since the NPV of waiting one year is $4.4645 million and this is larger than its NPV of undertaking the project today.

4. Haverford Industries recently purchased a new delivery truck. The new truck costs $56,250 and it is expected to generate net after-tax operating cash flows, including depreciation, of $15,625 per year. The truck has a 5-year expected life. The expected year-end abandonment values (salvage values after tax adjustments) for the truck are given below. The company's cost of capital is 11 percent.

Year	Annual Operating Cash Flow	Abandonment Value
0	($56,250)	--
1	15,625	$43,750
2	15,625	35,000
3	15,625	27,500
4	15,625	12,500
5	15,625	0

Should the firm operate the truck until the end of its 5-year physical life; if not, what is its optimal economic life?

a. No; the firm should operate the truck for 3 years because the NPV of doing so is $2,041, and this maximizes the truck's NPV.

b. Yes; the firm should operate the truck for 5 years because the NPV of doing so is $1,498, and this maximizes the truck's NPV.

c. No; the firm should operate the truck for 4 years because the NPV of doing so is $4,600, and this maximizes the truck's NPV.

d. No; the firm should operate the truck for only 1 year because the NPV of doing so is $2,759, and this maximizes the truck's NPV.

e. Yes; the firm should operate the truck for 5 years because the NPV of doing so is $3,500, and this maximizes the truck's NPV.

5. Martinez Manufacturing estimates that its WACC is 11 percent if equity comes from retained earnings. However, if the company issues new stock to raise new equity, it estimates that its WACC will rise to 11.6 percent. The company believes that it will exhaust its retained earnings due to the number of highly profitable projects available to the firm. The company is considering the following seven investment projects:

Project	Size	IRR
A	$250,000	13.0%
B	420,000	12.5
C	420,000	12.2
D	420,000	12.0
E	250,000	11.5
F	250,000	11.3
G	250,000	11.1

Assume that each of these projects is independent and that each is just as risky as the firm's existing assets. Which set of projects should be accepted, and what is the firm's optimal capital budget?

a. Projects A, B, C, D, and E are all acceptable, and the firm's optimal capital budget is $1,760,000.
b. All the projects are acceptable, and the firm's optimal capital budget is $2,260,000.
c. Projects A, B, C, D, E, and F are all acceptable, and the firm's optimal capital budget is $2,010,000.
d. Projects A, B, C, and D are all acceptable, and the firm's optimal capital budget is $1,510,000.
e. There is not enough information given in the problem to arrive at an answer.

ANSWERS TO SELF-TEST QUESTIONS

1. replacement chain (common life) approach
2. independent; mutually exclusive
3. Real
4. Option
5. managerial options
6. options
7. Strategic options
8. abandonment; investment timing; growth; flexibility
9. decision tree; branch

10. abandonment option
11. value
12. investment timing option
13. discounted
14. strategic advantages
15. first mover advantage
16. growth option
17. flexibility option
18. Capital rationing
19. Positive; negative
20. real option; embedded option

21. inflation

22. market conditions; competitors'

23. profitability; risk

24. downside losses

25. mutually exclusive

26. b. Inflation and/or possible efficiency gains can be built into the replacement chain analysis.

27. a. This statement is correct.

28. a. This statement is correct.

29. e. Statements a, b, and c are all weaknesses of the replacement chain analysis, so statement e is the correct choice.

30. c. Statement a is false; just because a project has a positive NPV today doesn't mean that the NPV will be even higher if you wait a year. Statement b is false; investment timing options do impact a project's cash flow and corresponding risk. Statement c is correct.

SOLUTIONS TO SELF-TEST PROBLEMS

1. e. A:

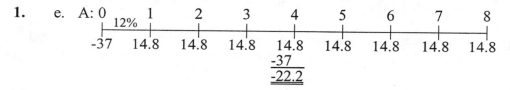

Machine A's simple NPV is calculated as follows: Enter $CF_0 = -37$ and $CF_{1-4} = 14.8$. Then enter I = 12, and press the NPV key to get $NPV_A = \$7.953$ million. However, this does not consider the fact that the project can be repeated again. Enter these values into the cash flow register: $CF_0 = -37$; $CF_{1-3} = 14.8$; $CF_4 = -22.2$; $CF_{5-8} = 14.8$. Then enter I = 12, and press the NPV key to get Extended $NPV_A = \$13.0069 \approx \$13.01$ million.

B:

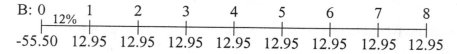

Enter these cash flows into the cash flow register, along with the interest rate, and press the NPV key to get $NPV_B = \$8.831 \approx \$8.83$ million.

Machine A is the better project and will increase the company's value by $13.01 million.

2. **c.**

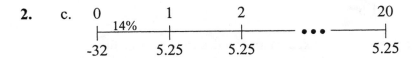

$$NPV = \$2.7714 \approx \$2.77 \text{ million.}$$

3. **b.** Wait 1 year:

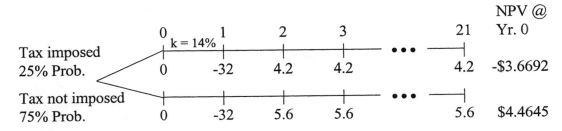

Note though, that if the tax is imposed, the NPV of the project is negative and therefore would not be undertaken. The value of this option of waiting one year is evaluated as $0.25(\$0) + (0.75)(\$4.4645) = \$3.3484$ million.

Since the NPV of waiting one year is greater than going ahead and proceeding with the project today, it makes sense to wait.

4. **a.** NPV of abandonment after Year t:

Using a financial calculator, input the following: $CF_0 = -56250$, $CF_1 = 59375$, and $I = 11$ to solve for $NPV_1 = -\$2,759.01 \approx -\$2,759$.

Using a financial calculator, input the following: $CF_0 = -56250$, $CF_1 = 15625$, $CF_2 = 50625$, and $I = 11$ to solve for $NPV_2 = -\$1,085.04 \approx -\$1,085$.

Using a financial calculator, input the following: $CF_0 = -56250$, $CF_1 = 15625$, $N_j = 2$, $CF_3 = 43125$, and $I = 11$ to solve for $NPV_3 = \$2,040.81 \approx \$2,041$.

Using a financial calculator, input the following: $CF_0 = -56250$, $CF_1 = 15625$, $N_j = 3$, $CF_4 = 28125$, and $I = 11$ to solve for $NPV_4 = \$459.85 \approx \$460$.

Using a financial calculator, input the following: $CF_0 = -56250$, $CF_1 = 15625$, $N_j = 5$, and $I = 11$ to solve for $NPV_5 = \$1,498.39 \approx \$1,498$.

The firm should operate the truck for 3 years, $NPV_3 = \$2,041$.

5.   d. $WACC_1 = 11\%$; $WACC_2 = 11.6\%$.

Because the firm believes that it will exhaust retained earnings, the firm's WACC = 11.6%. Since each project is independent and of average risk, all projects whose IRR > WACC will be accepted. Consequently, Projects A, B, C, and D will be accepted and the optimal capital budget is $1,510,000.

CHAPTER 13
CAPITAL STRUCTURE AND LEVERAGE

LEARNING OBJECTIVES

- Explain why capital structure policy involves a trade-off between risk and return, and list the four primary factors that influence capital structure decisions.

- Distinguish between a firm's business risk and its financial risk.

- Explain how operating leverage contributes to a firm's business risk and conduct a breakeven analysis, complete with a breakeven chart.

- Define financial leverage and explain its effect on expected ROE, expected EPS, and the risk borne by stockholders.

- Briefly explain what is meant by a firm's optimal capital structure.

- Specify the effect of financial leverage on beta using the Hamada equation, and transform this equation to calculate a firm's unlevered beta, b_U.

- Illustrate through a graph the premiums for financial risk and business risk at different debt levels.

- List the assumptions under which Modigliani and Miller proved that a firm's value is unaffected by its capital structure, then explain trade-off theory, signaling theory, and the effect of taxes and bankruptcy costs on capital structure.

- List a number of factors or practical considerations firms generally consider when making capital structure decisions.

- Briefly explain the extent that capital structure varies across industries, individual firms in each industry, and different countries.

OVERVIEW

Capital structure theory suggests that some optimal capital structure exists that simultaneously maximizes a firm's stock price and minimizes its cost of capital. The use of debt tends to increase earnings per share, which will lead to a higher stock price; but, at the same time, the use of debt also increases the risk borne by stockholders, which lowers the stock price. The optimal capital structure strikes a balance between these risk and return effects. While it is difficult to determine the optimal capital structure with precision, it is possible to identify the factors that influence it. A firm's target capital structure is generally set equal to the estimated optimal capital structure. The target may change over time as conditions vary, but, at any given moment, a well-managed firm's management has a specific structure in mind; and financing decisions are made so as to be consistent with this target capital structure.

OUTLINE

Capital structure policy involves a tradeoff between risk and return: Using more debt raises the riskiness of the firm's earnings stream and the risk borne by stockholders; however, a higher debt ratio generally leads to a higher expected rate of return on equity.

- The *target capital structure* is the mix of debt, preferred stock, and common equity with which the firm plans to raise capital.
  - ☐ This target may change over time as conditions change.
  - ☐ A firm's target capital structure is generally set equal to the estimated optimal capital structure.

- The *optimal capital structure* is the one that strikes the optimal balance between risk and return so as to maximize the firm's stock price.

- Four primary factors influence target capital structure decisions; however, operating conditions can cause the actual capital structure to vary from target.
  - ☐ *Business risk* is the riskiness inherent in the firm's operations if no debt is used. The greater the firm's business risk, the lower its optimal debt ratio.
  - ☐ The firm's *tax position* is a major reason for using debt. Interest is tax deductible, which lowers the effective cost of debt.
    - • The higher a firm's tax rate, the more advantageous debt is to the firm.
  - ☐ *Financial flexibility*, which is the ability to raise capital on reasonable terms under adverse conditions, is another consideration. The potential future availability of funds and the consequences of a funds shortage influence the target capital structure.

- The greater the probable future need for capital, and the worse the consequences of a capital shortage, the stronger the balance sheet should be.
☐ *Managerial conservatism or aggressiveness* influences the target capital structures firms actually establish.
  - This factor does not affect the true optimal, or value-maximizing, capital structure, but it does influence the manager-determined target capital structure.

Business risk in a stand-alone sense is a function of the uncertainty inherent in projections of a firm's return on invested capital (ROIC). ROIC is defined as net operating profit after taxes divided by the firm's capital.

■ The business risk of a leverage-free firm can be measured by the standard deviation of its ROE.

■ Business risk varies from one industry to another and also among firms in a given industry. It can also change over time.

■ Business risk depends on a number of factors, the more important of which are: (1) demand variability, (2) sales price variability, (3) input cost variability, (4) ability to adjust output prices for changes in input costs, (5) ability to develop new products in a timely, cost-effective manner, (6) foreign risk exposure, and (7) operating leverage (the extent to which costs are fixed).
☐ Each of these factors is determined partly by the firm's industry characteristics, but each is also controllable to some extent by management.
☐ Many firms use hedging techniques to reduce business risk.

■ *Operating leverage* is the extent to which a firm uses fixed costs in its operations.
☐ Higher fixed costs are generally associated with more highly automated, capital intensive firms and industries.
☐ High operating leverage means that a relatively small change in sales will result in a large change in ROE.
☐ The higher a firm's degree of operating leverage, the higher its operating breakeven point tends to be.
  - The *operating breakeven point* is defined as the output quantity at which EBIT = 0.
  - The breakeven point is calculated as fixed costs divided by the difference in sales price and variable cost per unit: $Q_{BE} = F/(P - V)$.
☐ The higher a firm's operating leverage, the higher its business risk (as measured by variability of EBIT and ROE), other things held constant.
☐ In general, holding other factors constant, the higher the degree of operating leverage, the greater the firm's business risk.

    ☐ Technology limits control over the amount of fixed costs and operating leverage. However, firms do have some control over the type of production processes they employ, and so the firm's capital budgeting decisions will have an impact on its operating leverage and business risk.

Financial leverage refers to the firm's use of fixed-income securities such as debt and preferred stock in the firm's capital structure, and financial risk is the additional risk placed on the common stockholders as a result of the decision to finance with debt.

■   The degree to which a firm employs financial leverage will affect its expected earnings per share (EPS) and the riskiness of these earnings.
    ☐ Financial leverage will cause EPS to rise; however, the degree of risk associated with the firm will also increase as leverage increases.

The optimal capital structure is the one that maximizes the price of the firm's stock, and this generally calls for a debt ratio that is lower than the one that maximizes expected EPS.

■   At first, EPS will rise as the use of debt increases. Interest charges rise, but the number of outstanding shares will decrease as equity is replaced by debt. At some point EPS will peak. Beyond this point interest rates will rise so fast that EPS is depressed in spite of the fact that the number of shares outstanding is decreasing.

■   Risk, as measured by the coefficient of variation of EPS, rises continuously as the use of debt increases.

■   Managers should choose the capital structure that maximizes the firm's stock price.
    ☐ The capital structure that maximizes the stock price is also the one that minimizes the WACC.

■   An increase in the debt/assets ratio raises the costs of both debt and equity.
    ☐ Bondholders recognize that if a firm has a higher debt ratio, this increases the risk of financial distress, and more risk leads to higher interest rates.
    ☐ Sophisticated financial managers use their forecasted ratios to predict how bankers and other lenders will judge their firms' risks and thus determine their cost of debt. Thus, they can judge quite accurately the effects of capital structure on the cost of debt.

■   An increase in the debt ratio also increases the risk faced by shareholders, and this has an effect on the cost of equity, k_s.
    ☐ It has been demonstrated, both theoretically and empirically, that beta increases with financial leverage.

■ The *Hamada equation* specifies the effect of financial leverage on beta:

$$b = b_U[1 + (1 - T)(D/E)].$$

☐ The Hamada equation shows how increases in the debt/equity ratio increase beta.
  • D/E is the measure of financial leverage used in the Hamada equation.
☐ b_U is the firm's unlevered beta coefficient, the beta the firm would have if it has no debt.
  • When the firm has not debt, beta would depend entirely upon business risk and thus be a measure of the firm's "basic business risk."

■ Beta is the only variable under management's control in the CAPM cost of equity equation.
  ☐ Both the risk-free rate and the rate of return on the market are determined by market forces that are beyond the firm's control.
  ☐ Beta is determined by the firm's operating decisions and by its capital structure decisions as reflected in its debt/assets (or debt/equity) ratio.

■ Once b_U is determined, the Hamada equation can be used to estimate how changes in the debt/equity ratio would affect the leveraged beta and the cost of equity.

$$k_s = k_{RF} + \text{Premium for business risk} + \text{Premium for financial risk.}$$

■ Although the component cost of equity is generally higher than that of debt, using only lower-cost debt would not maximize value because of the feedback effects of debt on the costs of debt and equity.

■ The expected stock price will at first increase with financial leverage, will then reach a peak, and finally will decline as financial leverage becomes excessive due to the importance of potential bankruptcy costs.

■ The financial structure that maximizes EPS usually has more debt than the one that results in the highest stock price.

Modern capital structure theory began in 1958, when Professors Franco Modigliani and Merton Miller (MM) published what has been called the most influential finance article ever written.

■ MM proved, under a very restrictive set of assumptions, that a firm's value is unaffected by its capital structure. MM's results suggest that it doesn't matter how a firm finances its operations, hence capital structure is irrelevant. Their theory produces what is often referred to as the "irrelevance result."

■ By indicating the conditions under which capital structure is irrelevant, MM provided us with some clues about what is required for capital structure to be relevant and hence to have an effect on a firm's value. Consequently, MM's work was only the beginning of capital structure research.

☐ Subsequent research has focused on relaxing the MM assumptions in order to develop a more realistic theory of capital structure.

■ MM published a follow-up paper in 1963 in which they relaxed the assumption that there are no corporate taxes. MM demonstrated that if all of their other assumptions hold, the asymmetry of the tax deductibility of interest versus the non-deductibility of dividend payments leads to a situation that calls for 100 percent debt financing.

■ Merton Miller then analyzed the effects of personal taxes. While an increase in the corporate tax rate makes debt look better to corporations, an increase in the personal tax rate encourages additional equity financing.

☐ All income from bonds is generally interest, which is taxed as personal income at rates going up to 38.6 percent.

☐ Income from stocks generally comes partly from dividends and partly from capital gains.

  ● Long-term capital gains are generally taxed at a rate of 20 percent.

  ● Capital gains tax is deferred until the stock is sold and the gain realized.

  ● If stock is held until the owner dies, no capital gains tax must be paid.

☐ On balance, returns on common stocks are taxed at lower effective rates than returns on debt.

■ The deductibility of interest favors the use of debt financing, but the more favorable tax treatment of income from stocks lowers the required rate of return on stock and thus favors the use of equity financing.

☐ It is difficult to say what the net effect of these two factors is. Most observers believe that interest deductibility has the stronger effect, hence that our tax system still favors the corporate use of debt. However, that effect is certainly reduced by the lower long-term capital gains tax rate.

  ● John Graham has estimated the overall tax benefits of debt financing to equal about 7 percent of the average firm's value. Graham's analysis leads him to conclude that some very conservative firms may be overly reluctant to use debt financing.

■ Bankruptcy-related problems are more likely to arise when a firm includes more debt in its capital structure. Therefore, bankruptcy costs discourage firms from pushing their use of debt to excessive levels.

☐ Bankruptcy-related costs have two components: the probability of their occurrence and the costs they would produce given that financial distress has arisen.

☐ Firms whose earnings are more volatile, all else equal, face a greater chance of bankruptcy and, therefore, should use less debt than more stable firms.

- ☐ Firms with high operating leverage, and thus greater business risk, should limit their use of financial leverage.
- ☐ Likewise, firms that would face high costs in the event of financial distress should rely less heavily on debt.
  - For example, firms whose assets are illiquid and thus would have to be sold at "fire sale" prices should limit their use of debt financing.

- ■ The *trade-off theory of leverage* recognizes that firms trade off the *benefits* of debt financing (favorable corporate tax treatment) against the *costs* of debt financing (higher interest rates and bankruptcy costs).
  - ☐ In effect, the government pays part of the cost of debt capital; debt provides tax shelter benefits.

- ■ Many large, successful firms use far less debt than the trade-off theory suggests. This led to the development of signaling theory.

- ■ *Signaling theory* recognizes the fact that investors and managers do *not* have the same information regarding a firm's prospects, as was assumed by the trade-off theory. This is called *asymmetric information,* and it has an important effect on the optimal capital structure.
  - ☐ *Symmetric information* is the situation in which investors and managers have identical information about firms' prospects.
  - ☐ Because of asymmetric information one would expect a firm with very favorable prospects to try to avoid selling stock and to attempt to raise any required new capital by other means, including using debt beyond the normal target capital structure.
    - A firm with unfavorable prospects would want to sell stock, which would mean bringing in new investors to share the losses.
  - ☐ The announcement of a stock offering by a mature firm that seems to have financing alternatives is taken as a *signal* that the firm's prospects as seen by its management are not bright. This, in turn, suggests that when a firm announces a new stock offering, more often than not, the price of its stock will decline.
    - Empirical studies have shown that this situation does indeed exist.
  - ☐ The implication of the signaling theory for capital structure decisions is that firms should, in normal times, maintain a *reserve borrowing capacity* that can be used in the event that some especially good investment opportunity comes along. This means that firms should, in normal times, use more equity and less debt than is suggested by the tax benefit/bankruptcy cost trade-off model.

- ■ Agency conflicts are particularly likely when the firm's managers have too much cash at their disposal. Managers with limited *free cash flow* are less able to make wasteful expenditures. Firms can reduce excess cash flow in a variety of ways:
  - ☐ Funnel cash back to shareholders through higher dividends or stock repurchases.

☐ Shift the capital structure toward more debt in the hope that higher debt service requirements will force managers to become more disciplined.

☐ A leveraged buyout (LBO) is one way to reduce excess cash flow.

- In an LBO, debt is used to finance the purchase of a company's shares, after which the firm "goes private."

■ Increasing debt and reducing free cash flow has its downside: It increases the risk of bankruptcy, which can be costly.

☐ Adding debt to a firm's capital structure is like putting a dagger into the steering wheel of a car.

☐ The dagger motivates you to drive more carefully, but you may get stabbed if someone runs into you, even if you're being careful.

☐ Higher debt forces managers to be more careful with shareholders' money, but even well-run firms could face bankruptcy (get stabbed) if some event beyond their control occurs.

☐ The capital structure decision comes down to deciding how big a dagger stockholders should use to keep managers in line.

■ In practice, capital structure decisions must be made using a combination of judgment and numerical analysis.

The following factors will all have some influence on the firm's choice of a target capital structure.

■ *Sales stability.* If sales are stable, a firm will be more likely to take on increased debt and higher fixed charges than a company with unstable sales.

■ *Asset structure.* Firms whose assets can readily be pledged as collateral for loans will tend to operate with a higher degree of financial leverage.

■ *Operating leverage.* Less operating leverage generally permits a firm to employ more debt.

■ *Growth rate.* Firms that are growing rapidly generally need large amounts of external capital. The flotation costs associated with debt are generally less than those for common stock, so rapidly growing firms tend to use more debt. At the same time, however, rapidly growing firms often face greater uncertainty, which tends to reduce their willingness to use debt.

■ *Profitability.* A high degree of profitability would indicate an ability to carry a high level of debt. However, many profitable firms are able to meet most of their financing needs with retained earnings, and do so.

■ *Taxes.* Interest charges are tax deductible, while dividend payments are not. This factor favors the use of debt over equity for firms in high tax brackets.

■   *Control.* Management control issues such as voting, job security, and fear of takeover, all influence the capital structure of a firm in various ways.

■   *Management attitudes.* Managements vary in their attitudes toward risk. More conservative managers will use stock rather than debt for financing, while less conservative managers will use more debt.

■   *Lender and rating agency attitudes.* This factor will penalize firms that go beyond the average for their industry in the use of financial leverage.

■   *Market conditions.* At any point in time, securities markets may favor either debt or equity.

■   *Firms' internal conditions.* Expected future earnings patterns and internal factors will influence managements' choices of debt versus equity.

■   *Financial flexibility.* Most treasurers have as a goal to always be in a position to raise the capital needed to support operations, even under bad conditions. Therefore, they want to always maintain adequate reserve borrowing capacity.

There are wide variations in the use of financial leverage both among industries and among individual firms within each industry.

■   The times-interest-earned ratio is a good tool to gauge the degree of financial leverage used by a particular firm.
    ☐ It gives a measure of how safe the debt is and how vulnerable the company is to financial distress.
    ☐ TIE ratios depend on three factors: (1) the percentage of debt, (2) the interest rate on debt, and (3) the company's profitability.
    ☐ Generally, the least leveraged industries have the highest coverage ratios, while those industries that finance more heavily with debt have low coverage ratios.

SELF-TEST QUESTIONS

Definitional

1.   The _____ capital structure is the one that strikes the balance between _____ and _____ and thereby maximizes the firm's _____ _____.

2.   A firm's _____ capital structure is generally set equal to the estimated optimal structure.

3. _____ _____ in a stand-alone sense is a function of the uncertainty inherent in projections of a firm's return on invested capital.

4. Some of the factors that influence a firm's business risk include: (1) _____ variability, (2) sales price variability, and (3) _____ leverage.

5. Business risk represents the riskiness of the firm's operations if it uses no _____; financial risk represents the additional risk borne by common stockholders as a result of using _____.

6. Common stockholders are compensated for bearing financial risk by a higher _____ _____.

7. Expected EPS generally _____ as the debt/assets ratio increases.

8. As financial leverage increases, the stock price will first begin to rise, but it will then decline as financial leverage becomes excessive because potential _____ _____ become increasingly important.

9. _____ _____ refers to the use of debt financing.

10. Debt has a(n) _____ advantage over equity in that _____ is a deductible expense while _____ are not.

11. Management may prefer additional _____ as opposed to common stock in order to help maintain _____ of the company.

12. _____ _____ is the ability to raise capital on reasonable terms under adverse conditions.

13. The _____ _____ _____ is defined as the output quantity at which $EBIT = 0$.

14. The _____-_____ theory of leverage recognizes that firms balance the benefits of debt financing against the costs of debt financing.

15. _____ theory recognizes the fact that investors and managers do not have the same information regarding a firm's prospects.

16. The fact that investors and managers do not have the same information regarding a firm's prospects is called _____ information.

17. The implication of the signaling theory for capital structure decisions is that firms should, in normal times, maintain a(n) _____ _____ _____ that can be used in the event that some especially good investment opportunity comes along.

18. The _____-_____-_____ ratio gives a measure of how safe the debt is and how vulnerable the company is to financial distress.

19. TIE ratios depend on three factors: (1) the _____ of debt, (2) the _____ _____ on debt, and (3) the company's _____.

20. _____ ____ _____ _____ is defined as net operating profit after taxes divided by the firm's capital.

21. _____ _____ is the extent to which a firm uses fixed costs in its operations.

22. The higher the degree of operating leverage, the _____ the firm's business risk.

23. The optimal capital structure is the one that maximizes the price of the firm's stock, and this generally calls for a debt ratio that is _____ than the one that maximizes expected EPS.

24. _____, as measured by the coefficient of EPS, rises continuously as the use of debt increases.

25. The capital structure that maximizes the stock price is also the one that _____ the WACC.

26. The _____ _____ specifies the effect of financial leverage on beta.

27. Beta is determined by the firm's _____ decisions and by its _____ _____ decisions as reflected in its debt/assets (or debt/equity) ratio.

28. MM's results suggest that it doesn't matter how a firm finances its operations, hence capital structure is _____.

29. _____ _____ is the situation in which investors and managers have identical information about firms' prospects.

30. _____ _____ are likely when the firm's managers have too much cash at their disposal.

31. The tax deductibility of interest _____ the effective cost of debt.

32. The greater the probable future need of capital, and the worse the consequences of a capital shortage, the _____ the balance sheet should be.

33. Higher fixed costs are generally associated with more highly automated, _____ _____ firms and industries.

34. Bondholders recognize that if a firm has a higher debt ratio, this increases the risk of financial distress, and more risk leads to higher _____ _____.

35. When the firm has no debt, beta would depend entirely upon _____ risk.

Conceptual

36. Firm A has a higher degree of business risk than Firm B. Firm A can offset this by increasing its operating leverage.

   a. True   **b.** False

37. Two firms operate in different industries, but they have the same expected EPS and the same standard deviation of expected EPS. Thus, the two firms must have the same financial risk.

   a. True   **b.** False

38. Two firms could have identical financial and operating leverage yet have different degrees of business risk.

   a. True   **b.** False

39. As a general rule, the capital structure that maximizes stock price also

   a. Maximizes the weighted average cost of capital.
   b. Maximizes EPS.
   c. Maximizes bankruptcy costs.
   d. Minimizes the weighted average cost of capital.
   e. Minimizes the required rate of return on equity.

40. A decrease in the debt ratio will normally have no effect on

   a. Financial risk.   **d.** Systematic risk.
   b. Total risk.   **e.** Firm-unique risk.
   c. Business risk.

41. Which of the following statements is most correct?

a. If a firm is exposed to a high degree of business risk as a result of its high operating leverage, then it probably should offset this risk by using a larger-than-average amount of financial leverage. This follows because debt has a lower after-tax cost than equity.

b. Financial risk can be reduced by replacing common equity with preferred stock.

c. The Hamada equation specifies the effect of financial leverage on beta. It shows how increases in the debt/equity ratio lowers beta.

d. In the text it was stated that the capital structure that minimizes the WACC also maximizes the firm's stock price and its total value, but generally not its expected EPS. One reason given for why debt is beneficial is that it shelters operating income from taxes, while it was stated that a disadvantage of excessive debt has to do with costs associated with bankruptcy and financial distress generally.

e. All of the above statements are false.

SELF-TEST PROBLEMS

1. The Fisher Company will produce 50,000 10-gallon aquariums next year. Variable costs will equal 40 percent of dollar sales, while fixed costs total $100,000. At what price must each aquarium be sold for the firm's EBIT to be $90,000?

    a. $5.00   **b.** $5.33   **c.** $5.50   **d.** $6.00   **e.** $6.33

2. Hairston Industries has $25 million in assets, which is financed with $5 million of debt and $20 million in equity. If Hairston's beta is currently 1.75 and its tax rate is 40 percent, what is its unlevered beta, b_U?

    a. 0.7564   **b.** 1.0000   **c.** 1.2525   **d.** 1.5217   **e.** 2.0125

3. The Hampton Hardware Company is trying to estimate its optimal capital structure. Hampton's current capital structure consists of 20 percent debt and 80 percent equity; however, management believes the firm should use more debt. The risk-free rate, k_{RF}, is 7 percent, the market risk premium, $k_M - k_{RF}$, is 5 percent, and the firm's tax rate is 35 percent. Currently, Hampton's cost of equity is 16 percent, which is determined on the basis of the CAPM. What would be Hampton's estimated cost of equity if it were to change its capital structure from its present capital structure to 40 percent debt and 60 percent equity?

    a. 14.93%   **b.** 15.45%   **c.** 18.10%   **d.** 19.25%   **e.** 20.33%

4. Brown Products is a new firm just starting operations. The firm will produce backpacks that will sell for $22.00 each. Fixed costs are $500,000 per year, and variable costs are $2.00 per unit of production. The company expects to sell 50,000 backpacks per year, and its effective federal-plus-state tax rate is 40 percent. Brown needs $2 million to build facilities, obtain working capital, and start operations. If Brown borrows part of the money, the interest charges will depend on the amount borrowed as follows:

Amount Borrowed	Percentage of Debt in Capital Structure	Interest Rate on Total Amount Borrowed
$ 200,000	10%	9.00%
400,000	20	9.50
600,000	30	10.00
800,000	40	15.00
1,000,000	50	19.00
1,200,000	60	26.00

Assume that stock can be sold at a price of $20 per share on the initial offering, regardless of how much debt the company uses. Then after the company begins operating, its price will be determined as a multiple of its earnings per share. The multiple (or the P/E ratio) will depend upon the capital structure as follows:

Debt/Assets	P/E	Debt/Assets	P/E
0.0%	12.5×	40.0%	8.0×
10.0	12.0	50.0	6.0
20.0	11.5	60.0	5.0
30.0	10.0		

What is Brown's optimal capital structure, which maximizes stock price, as measured by the debt/assets ratio?

a. 10%   **b.** 20%   **c.** 30%   **d.** 40%   **e.** 50%

5. Tapley Dental Supplies Inc. is in a stable, no-growth situation. Its $1,000,000 of debt consists of perpetuities that have a 10 percent coupon and sell at par. Tapley's EBIT is $500,000, its cost of equity is 15 percent, it has 100,000 shares outstanding, all earnings are paid out as dividends, and its federal-plus-state tax rate is 40 percent. Tapley could borrow an additional $500,000 at an interest rate of 13 percent without having to retire the original debt, and it would use the proceeds to repurchase stock *at the current price*, not at the new equilibrium price. The increased risk from the additional leverage will raise the cost of equity to 17 percent. If Tapley does recapitalize, what will be the new stock price?

a. $17.20   **b.** $16.00   **c.** $16.50   **d.** $17.00   **e.** $16.75

6. Backroads Sporting Goods is trying to determine its optimal capital structure, which now consists of only debt and common equity. The firm does not currently use preferred stock in its capital structure, and it does not plan to do so in the future. To estimate how much its debt would cost at different debt levels, the company's treasury staff has consulted with investment bankers and, on the basis of those discussions, has created the following table:

Debt-to-Assets Ratio (w_d)	Equity-to-Assets Ratio (w_c)	Debt-to-Equity Ratio (D/E)	Bond Rating	Before-Tax Cost of Debt (k_d)
0.0	1.0	0.00	A	6.5%
0.2	0.8	0.25	BBB	7.5
0.4	0.6	0.67	BB	9.5
0.6	0.4	1.50	C	11.5
0.8	0.2	4.00	D	14.5

Backroads uses the CAPM to estimate its cost of common equity, k_s. The company estimates that the risk-free rate is 6 percent, the market risk premium is 5 percent, and its tax rate is 40 percent. Backroads estimates that if it had no debt, its "unlevered" beta, b_U, would be 1.25. On the basis of this information, what would be the weighted average cost of capital at the optimal capital structure?

a. 9.56%   b. 10.48%   c. 11.13%   d. 11.45%   e. 12.25%

(The following data apply to the next six Self-Test Problems.)

Currently, Pam's Petals Inc. (PPI) has a capital structure consisting of 30 percent debt and 70 percent equity. PPI's debt currently has a 7 percent yield to maturity. The risk-free rate (k_{RF}) is 5.5 percent and the market risk premium $(k_M - k_{RF})$ is 5 percent. Using the CAPM, PPI estimates that its cost of equity is currently 11.75 percent. The company has a 35 percent tax rate.

7. What is PPI's current WACC?

a. 8.33%   b. 8.67%   c. 9.00%   d. 9.59%   e. 10.25%

8. What is the current beta on PPI's common stock?

a. 1.3350   b. 1.2500   c. 1.0000   d. 1.1000   e. 0.9777

9. What would PPI's beta be if the company had no debt in its capital structure? (That is, what is PPI's unlevered beta, b_U?)

a. 1.3350   b. 1.2500   c. 1.0000   d. 1.1000   e. 0.9777

(The following data apply to the next three Self-Test Problems.)

PPI's financial staff is considering changing its capital structure to 45 percent debt and 55 percent equity. If the company went ahead with the proposed change, the yield to maturity on the company's bonds would rise to 8.75 percent. The proposed change will have no effect on the company's tax rate.

10. What would be the company's new cost of equity if it adopted the proposed change in capital structure?

    a. 12.99%   **b.** 12.25%   **c.** 11.75%   **d.** 13.35%   **e.** 14.00%

11. What would be the company's new WACC if it adopted the proposed change in capital structure?

    a. 8.76%   **b.** 11.20%   **c.** 9.70%   **d.** 10.10%   **e.** 9.33%

12. On the basis of your answer to Self-Test Problem 11, would you advise PPI to adopt the proposed change in capital structure?

    a. Yes, the firm's new WACC after the proposed capital structure change is made declines from 9.59% to 9.33%.
    b. No, the firm's new WACC after the proposed capital structure change is made increases from 9.59% to 9.70%.
    c. A decision cannot be made because there is insufficient information.
    d. Yes, the firm's new WACC after the proposed capital structure change is made declines from 9.00% to 8.76%.
    e. No, the firm's new WACC after the proposed capital structure change is made increases from 10.25% to 11.20%.

ANSWERS TO SELF-TEST QUESTIONS

1. optimal; risk; return; stock price
2. target
3. Business risk
4. demand; operating
5. debt; debt
6. expected return
7. increases
8. bankruptcy costs
9. Financial leverage
10. tax; interest; dividends
11. debt; control
12. Financial flexibility
13. operating breakeven point
14. trade-off
15. Signaling
16. asymmetric
17. reserve borrowing capacity
18. times-interest-earned
19. percentage; interest rate; profitability
20. Return on invested capital

21.	Operating leverage		29.	Symmetric information
22.	greater		30.	Agency conflicts
23.	lower		31.	lowers
24.	Risk		32.	stronger
25.	minimizes		33.	capital intensive
26.	Hamada equation		34.	interest rates
27.	operating; capital structure		35.	business
28.	irrelevant			

36. b. Increasing operating leverage will increase Firm A's business risk; therefore, Firm A should use less operating leverage.

37. b. The two firms would have the same total risk. However, they could have different combinations of business and financial risk.

38. a. Business risk consists of several elements in addition to operating leverage, for example, sales variability, and it does not depend on financial risk at all.

39. d. The optimal capital structure balances risk and return to maximize the stock price. The capital structure that maximizes stock price also minimizes the firm's cost of capital.

40. c. Business risk measures the riskiness of a firm's operations assuming no debt is used.

41. d. Statement a is false; if a firm is exposed to a high degree of business risk this implies that it should offset this risk by using a lower amount of financial leverage. Statement b is false; preferred stock is a fixed-income security, and as such, would increase financial risk. Statement c is false; an increase in the debt/equity ratio increases beta. Statement d is the correct choice.

SOLUTIONS TO SELF-TEST PROBLEMS

1. e. $EBIT = PQ - VQP - F$
$$\$90,000 = P(50,000) - 0.4(50,000)P - \$100,000$$
$$30,000P = \$190,000$$
$$P = \$6.33.$$

2. d. From the Hamada Equation, $b = b_U[1 + (1 - T)(D/E)]$, we can calculate b_U as $b_U = b/[1 + (1 - T)(D/E)]$.

$b_U = 1.75/[1 + (1 - 0.4)(\$5,000,000/\$20,000,000)]$
$b_U = 1.75/1.15$
$b_U = 1.5217.$

3. c. Facts as given: Current capital structure: 20%D, 80%E; k_{RF} = 7%; $k_M - k_{RF}$ = 5%; T = 35%; k_s = 16%.

Step 1: Determine the firm's current beta.
$$k_s = k_{RF} + (k_M - k_{RF})b$$
$$16\% = 7\% + (5\%)b$$
$$9\% = 5\%b$$
$$1.8 = b.$$

Step 2: Determine the firm's unlevered beta, b_U.
$$b_U = b/[1 + (1 - T)(D/E)]$$
$$b_U = 1.8/[1 + (1 - 0.35)(0.20/0.80)]$$
$$b_U = 1.8/1.1625$$
$$b_U = 1.5484.$$

Step 3: Determine the firm's beta under the new capital structure.
$$b = b_U[1 + (1 - T)(D/E)]$$
$$b = 1.5484[1 + (1 - 0.35)(0.4/0.6)]$$
$$b = 1.5484(1.4333)$$
$$b = 2.2194.$$

Step 4: Determine the firm's new cost of equity under the changed capital structure.
$$k_s = k_{RF} + (k_M - k_{RF})b$$
$$k_s = 7\% + (5\%)2.2194$$
$$k_s = 18.1\%.$$

4. b. The first step is to calculate EBIT:

Sales in dollars [50,000($22)]	$1,100,000
Less: Fixed costs	500,000
Variable costs [50,000($2)]	100,000
EBIT	$ 500,000

The second step is to calculate the EPS at each debt/assets ratio using the formula:

$$EPS = \frac{(EBIT - I)(1 - T)}{Shares\ outstanding}.$$

Recognize (1) that I = Interest charges = (Dollars of debt)(Interest rate at each D/A ratio), and (2) that shares outstanding = (Assets – Debt)/Initial price per share = ($2,000,000 – Debt)/$20.00.

D/A	EPS	D/A	EPS
0%	$3.00	40%	$3.80
10	3.21	50	3.72
20	3.47	60	2.82
30	3.77		

Finally, the third step is to calculate the stock price at each debt/assets ratio using the following formula: Price = (P/E)(EPS).

D/A	Price	D/A	Price
0%	$37.50	40%	$30.40
10	38.52	50	22.32
20	39.91	60	14.10
30	37.70		

Thus, a debt/assets ratio of 20 percent maximizes stock price. This is the optimal capital structure.

5. a. Value of stock = [$500,000 - 0.1($1,000,000)](0.6)/0.15 = $1,600,000.
    P_0 = $1,600,000/100,000 = $16.

    After the recapitalization, value of stock is equal to [$500,000 - 0.1($1,000,000) − 0.13($500,000)](0.6)/0.17 = $1,182,353.

    P_0 = $1,182,353/[100,000 - ($500,000/$16)] = $17.20.

6. c. Tax rate = 40% k_{RF} = 6.0%
        b_U = 1.25 $k_M - k_{RF}$ = 5.0%

    From data given in the problem and table we can develop the following table:

D/A	E/A	D/E	k_d	$k_d(1-T)$	Leveraged beta[a]	k_s[b]	WACC[c]
0.00	1.00	0.0000	6.5%	3.90%	1.2500	12.2500%	12.25%
0.20	0.80	0.2500	7.5	4.50	1.4375	13.1875	11.45
0.40	0.60	0.6667	9.5	5.70	1.7500	14.7500	11.13
0.60	0.40	1.5000	11.5	6.90	2.3750	17.8750	11.29
0.80	0.20	4.0000	14.5	8.70	4.2500	27.2500	12.41

Notes:
[a] These beta estimates were calculated using the Hamada equation:
$b = b_U[1 + (1 - T)(D/E)]$.

[b] These k_s estimates were calculated using the CAPM: $k_s = k_{RF} + (k_M - k_{RF})b$.
[c] These WACC estimates were calculated with the following equation:
$WACC = w_d(k_d)(1 - T) + (w_c)(k_s)$.

The firm's optimal capital structure is that capital structure which minimizes the firm's WACC. Backroads' WACC is minimized at a capital structure consisting of 40% debt and 60% equity. At that capital structure, the firm's WACC is 11.13%.

7.   d.   Using the standard formula for the weighted average cost of capital, we find:

$$WACC = w_d k_d (1 - T) + w_c k_s$$
$$WACC = (0.3)(7\%)(1 - 0.35) + (0.7)(11.75\%)$$
$$WACC = 1.365\% + 8.225\%$$
$$WACC = 9.59\%.$$

8.   b.   The firm's current levered beta at 30% debt can be found using the CAPM formula.

$$k_s = k_{RF} + (k_M - k_{RF})b$$
$$11.75\% = 5.5\% + (5\%)b$$
$$6.25\% = (5\%)b$$
$$b = 1.25.$$

9.   e.   To "unlever" the firm's beta, the Hamada Equation is used.

$$b_L = b_U[1 + (1 - T)(D/E)]$$
$$1.25 = b_U[1 + (1 - 0.35)(0.3/0.7)]$$
$$1.25 = b_U(1.278571)$$
$$b_U = 0.9777.$$

10.   a.   To determine the firm's new cost of common equity, one must find the firm's new beta under its new capital structure. Consequently, you must "relever" the firm's beta using the Hamada Equation:

$$b_{L,45\%} = b_U[1 + (1 - T)(D/E)]$$
$$b_{L,45\%} = 0.9777 [1 + (1 - 0.35)(0.45/0.55)]$$
$$b_{L,45\%} = 0.9777 (1.5318)$$
$$b_U = 1.4977.$$

The firm's cost of equity, as stated in the problem, is derived using the CAPM equation.

$$k_s = k_{RF} + (k_M - k_{RF})b$$
$$k_s = 5.5\% + (5\%)1.4977$$
$$k_s = 12.99\%.$$

11.   c.   Again, the standard formula for the weighted average cost of capital is used. Remember, the WACC is a marginal, after-tax cost of capital and hence the relevant before-tax cost of debt is now 8.75% and the cost of equity is 12.99%.

$$WACC = w_d k_d(1 - T) + w_c k_s$$
$$WACC = (0.45)(8.75\%)(1 - 0.35) + (0.55)(12.99\%)$$
$$WACC = 9.70\%.$$

12.   b.   The firm should be advised not to proceed with the recapitalization because it causes the WACC to increase from 9.59% to 9.70%. If the recapitalization were made, it would lead to a decrease in firm value.

LEARNING OBJECTIVES

- Define target payout ratio and optimal dividend policy.

- Discuss the three theories of investors' dividend preference: (1) the dividend irrelevance theory, (2) the "bird-in-the-hand" theory, and (3) the tax preference theory; and whether empirical evidence has determined which theory is best.

- Explain the information content, or signaling, hypothesis and the clientele effect.

- Identify the two components of dividend stability, and briefly explain what a "stable dividend policy" means.

- Explain the logic of the residual dividend policy, and state why firms are more likely to use this policy in setting a long-run target than as a strict determination of dividends in a given year.

- Explain the use of dividend reinvestment plans, distinguish between the two types of plans, and discuss why the plans are popular with certain investors.

- List a number of factors that influence dividend policy in practice.

- Discuss why the dividend decision is made jointly with capital structure and capital budgeting decisions.

- Specify why a firm might split its stock or pay a stock dividend.

- Discuss stock repurchases, including advantages and disadvantages, and effects on EPS, stock price, and the firm's capital structure.

OVERVIEW

Dividend policy involves the decision to pay out earnings as dividends or to retain and reinvest them in the firm. Any change in dividend policy has both favorable and unfavorable effects on the firm's stock price: higher dividends mean higher immediate cash flows to investors, which is good, but lower future growth, which is bad. The optimal dividend policy balances these opposing forces and maximizes stock price. Three theories regarding the relationship between dividend payout and stock price have been proposed: (1) dividend irrelevance, which states that dividend policy has no effect on the firm's stock price; (2) the "bird-in-the-hand" theory, which states that investors prefer dividends because they are less risky than potential capital gains; and (3) the tax preference theory, which states that investors prefer to have companies retain earnings rather than pay them out as dividends because capital gains are subject to less taxes than dividends. In addition, dividend policy is further complicated due to signaling and clientele effects. It is simply not possible to state that any one dividend policy is correct, and hence it is impossible to develop a precise model for use in establishing dividend policy. Thus, financial managers must consider a number of factors when setting their firms' dividend policies.

OUTLINE

Dividend policy involves the decision to pay out earnings or to retain them for reinvestment in the firm.

- The *target payout ratio* is defined as the percentage of net income to be paid out as cash dividends as desired by the firm, and it should be based in large part on investors' preferences for dividends versus capital gains.

- The constant growth stock model, $P_0 = D_1/(k_s - g)$, shows that paying out more dividends will increase stock price. However, if D_1 is raised then less money will be available for reinvestment, that will cause the expected growth rate to decline, and that would tend to lower the stock's price.

- The *optimal dividend policy* strikes a balance between investors' desire for current cash flows (dividends) and future expected growth so as to maximize the firm's stock price.

A number of theories have been proposed to explain how factors interact to determine a firm's optimal dividend policy. These theories include: (1) the dividend irrelevance theory, (2) the "bird-in-the-hand" theory, and (3) the tax preference theory.

■ Modigliani and Miller (MM), the principal proponents of the *dividend irrelevance theory*, argue that the value of the firm depends only on the income produced by its assets, not on how this income is split between dividends and retained earnings.

  ☐ MM prove their proposition, but only under a set of restrictive assumptions including the absence of taxes and brokerage costs.

  ☐ Obviously, taxes and brokerage costs do exist, so the MM conclusions on dividend irrelevance may not be valid under real-world conditions. The validity of a theory must be judged by empirical tests, not by the realism of its assumptions.

■ The principal conclusion of MM's dividend irrelevance theory is that dividend policy does not affect the required rate of return on equity, k_s. Relaxing this assumption provides the basis for the "bird-in-the-hand" theory.

  ☐ Myron Gordon and John Lintner argue that k_s decreases as the dividend payout is increased because investors are less certain of receiving income from capital gains that presumably result from retained earnings than they are of receiving dividend payments.

  ☐ MM call the Gordon-Lintner argument the *"bird-in-the-hand" fallacy* because Gordon and Lintner believe that investors view dividends in the hand as being less risky than capital gains in the bush. In MM's view, however, most investors plan to reinvest their dividends in the stock of the same or similar firms, and the riskiness of the firm's cash flows to investors in the long run is determined by the riskiness of operating cash flows, not by dividend payout policy.

■ The *tax preference theory* states that investors may prefer to have companies retain most of their earnings because of various tax advantages. Investors then would be willing to pay more for low-payout companies than for otherwise similar high-payout companies. There are three tax-related reasons for thinking that investors might prefer a low dividend payout to a high payout.

  ☐ Long-term capital gains are generally taxed at a rate of 20 percent, whereas dividend income is taxed at effective rates that go up to 38.6 percent. Therefore, wealthy investors might prefer to have companies retain and plow earnings back into the business. Earnings growth would presumably lead to stock price increases, and lower-taxed capital gains would be substituted for higher-taxed dividends.

  ☐ Taxes are not paid on the gain until a stock is sold. Due to time value effects, a dollar of taxes paid in the future has a lower effective cost than a dollar paid today.

  ☐ If a stock is held by someone until he or she dies, no capital gains tax is due at all.

Empirical testing of the dividend theories has not produced definitive results regarding which theory is correct. We cannot find a set of publicly owned firms that differ only in their dividend policies, nor can we obtain precise estimates of the cost of equity. Finally, even if we could solve these two problems, it might turn out that bird-in-the-hand and tax preference investors were evenly balanced, causing the aggregate results to indicate that

MM's indifference theory is correct, whereas in actuality there are no indifferent investors. However, a consideration of dividend theory does make a few things clear.

- Since some investors prefer more dividends while others prefer less, it makes sense for different companies to follow different dividend policies and thus to provide different investors with what they want.

- Some companies are more logical candidates for high-payout policies and others for low payouts.

- Investors like to know what a company's payout policy is, and they prefer companies whose dividend policies are relatively stable.

- Investors' preferences change over time, as do companies' fundamental positions, so, while stable dividends are desirable, dividend policy should not be set in stone. As conditions change, it may become desirable to change the dividend policy.

There are two other issues that have a bearing on optimal dividend policy: (1) the information content, or signaling, hypothesis and (2) the clientele effect.

- It has been observed that a dividend increase announcement is often accompanied by an increase in the stock price, while a dividend cut generally leads to a stock price decline.
  - ☐ This might be interpreted by some to mean that investors prefer dividends over capital gains, thus supporting the Gordon-Lintner hypothesis.
  - ☐ However, MM argue that a dividend increase is a signal to investors that the firm's management forecasts good future earnings. Thus, MM argue that investors' reactions to dividend announcements do not necessarily show that investors prefer dividends to retained earnings. Rather, the fact that the stock price changes merely indicates that there is an important information content in dividend announcements. This is referred to as the *information content, or signaling, hypothesis.*

- MM also suggest that a *clientele effect* might exist.
  - ☐ Some stockholders (for example, retirees) prefer current income; therefore, they would want the firm to pay out a high percentage of its earnings as dividends.
  - ☐ Other stockholders have no need for current income (for example, doctors in their peak earning years) and they would simply reinvest any dividends received, after first paying income taxes on the dividend income. Therefore, they would want the firm to retain most of its earnings.
  - ☐ Thus, a firm establishes a dividend policy and then attracts a specific clientele that is drawn to this dividend policy. Those who do not like the dividend policy can simply sell their shares to those that do.

☐ To the extent that stockholders can switch firms, a firm can change from one dividend payout policy to another and then let stockholders who do not like the new policy sell to other investors who do.

- However, frequent switching would be inefficient because of brokerage costs, the likelihood that stockholders who are selling will have to pay capital gains taxes, and a possible shortage of investors who like the firm's newly adopted dividend policy.

- Management should be hesitant to change its dividend policy, because a change might cause current shareholders to sell their stock, forcing the stock price down. Such a price decline might be temporary, but it might also be permanent. If few new investors are attracted by the new dividend policy, then the stock price would remain depressed.

Dividend stability is important.

■ Profits and cash flows vary over time, as do investment opportunities. Taken alone, this suggests that corporations should vary their dividends over time, increasing them when cash flows are large and the need for funds is low and lowering them when cash is in short supply relative to investment opportunities.

☐ However, many stockholders rely on dividends to meet expenses, and they would be seriously inconvenienced if the dividend stream were unstable.

☐ Reducing dividends to make funds available for capital investment could send incorrect signals to investors who may push down the stock price because they interpret the dividend cut to mean that the company's future earnings prospects have been diminished.

■ Maximizing its stock price requires a firm to balance its internal needs for funds against the needs and desires of its stockholders.

■ Dividend stability has two components.
☐ How dependable is the growth rate?
☐ Can we count on at least receiving the current dividend in the future?

■ The most stable policy, from an investor's standpoint, is that of a firm whose dividend growth rate is predictable.
☐ Such a company's total return (dividend yield plus capital gains yield) would be relatively stable over the long run, and its stock would be a good hedge against inflation.

■ The second most stable policy is one in which stockholders can be reasonably sure that the current dividend will not be reduced—it may not grow at a steady rate, but management will probably be able to avoid cutting the dividend.

■ The least stable policy is one in which earnings and cash flows are so volatile that investors cannot count on the company to maintain the current dividend over a typical business cycle.

■ Investors prefer stocks that pay more predictable dividends to stocks that pay the same average amount of dividends but in a more erratic manner. The cost of equity will be minimized, and the stock price maximized, if a firm stabilizes its dividends as much as possible.

When deciding how much cash should be distributed to stockholders, two points should be kept in mind: (1) The overriding objective is to maximize shareholder value, and (2) the firm's cash flows really belong to its shareholders, so management should refrain from retaining income unless it can be reinvested to produce returns higher than shareholders could themselves earn by investing the cash in investments of equal risk.

■ When establishing a dividend policy, one size does not fit all.
  □ Over the past few decades, there has been an increasing number of young, high-growth firms trading on the stock exchanges. A recent study by Fama and French shows that the proportion of firms paying dividends has fallen sharply over this time period.

■ The optimal payout ratio is a function of four factors: (1) investors' preferences for dividends versus capital gains, (2) the firm's investment opportunities, (3) its target capital structure, and (4) the availability and cost of external capital.
  □ The last three elements are combined in the residual dividend model.

■ The *residual dividend model* is based on the premise that investors prefer to have a firm retain and reinvest earnings rather than pay them out in dividends if the rate of return the firm can earn on reinvested earnings exceeds the rate of return investors can obtain for themselves on other investments of comparable risk. Further, it is less expensive for the firm to use retained earnings than it is to issue new common stock. The word residual implies "leftover," and the residual policy implies that dividends are paid out of leftover earnings. A firm using the residual model would follow these four steps:
  □ Determine the optimal capital budget.
  □ Determine the amount of equity required to finance the optimal capital budget given its target capital structure, recognizing that the funds used will consist of both equity and debt to preserve the optimal capital structure.
  □ To the extent possible, use retained earnings to supply the equity required.
  □ Pay dividends only if more earnings are available than are needed to support the optimal capital budget.

■ If a firm rigidly follows the residual dividend policy, then dividends paid in any given year can be expressed as follows:

$$\text{Dividends} = \text{Net Income} - [(\text{Target Equity Ratio})(\text{Total Capital Budget})].$$

■ Since investment opportunities and earnings will surely vary from year to year, strict adherence to the residual dividend policy would result in unstable dividends. Firms should use the residual policy to help set their *long-run target payout ratios*, but not as a guide to the payout in any one year.

■ Companies use the residual dividend model to help understand the determinants of an optimal dividend policy, but they typically use a computerized financial forecasting model when setting the target payout ratio.
  ☐ Most companies use the computer model to find a dividend pattern over the forecast period that will provide sufficient equity to support the capital budget without having to sell new common stock or move the capital structure ratio outside the optimal range.

■ Some companies, especially those in cyclical industries, have difficulty maintaining in bad times a dividend that is really too low in good times. Such companies set a very low "regular" dividend and then supplement it with an "extra" dividend when times are good. This is called a *low-regular-dividend-plus-extras* policy.
  ☐ Investors recognize that the extras might not be maintained in the future, so they do not interpret them as a signal that the companies' earnings are increasing permanently, nor do they take the elimination of the extra as a negative signal.
  ☐ In recent years, companies following this policy have replaced the "extras" with stock repurchases.

■ Dividends clearly depend more on cash flows, which reflect the company's ability to pay dividends, than on current earnings, which are heavily influenced by accounting practices and which do not necessarily reflect the ability to pay dividends.

Firms usually pay dividends on a quarterly basis in accordance with the following payment procedures:

■ *Declaration date.* This is the day on which the board of directors declares the dividend. At this time they set the amount of the dividend to be paid, the holder-of-record date, and the payment date.

■ *Holder-of-record date.* This is the date the stock transfer books of the corporation are closed. Those shareholders who are listed on the company's books on this date are the holders of record and they receive the announced dividend.

■ *Ex-dividend date.* This date is two business days prior to the holder-of-record date. Shares purchased after the ex-dividend date are not entitled to the dividend. This practice is a convention of the brokerage business that allows sufficient time for stock transfers to be made on the books of the corporation.

- *Payment date.* This is the day when dividend checks are actually mailed to the holders of record.

Many firms have instituted dividend reinvestment plans (DRIPs) whereby stockholders can automatically reinvest dividends received in the stock of the paying corporation. Income taxes on the amount of the dividends must be paid even though stock rather than cash is received.

- There are two types of DRIPs.
  - ☐ Plans that involve only "old stock" that is already outstanding.
  - ☐ Plans that involve newly issued stock. Hence, this type of plan raises new capital for the firm.

- Stockholders choose between continuing to receive dividend checks or having the company use the dividends to buy more stock in the corporation.

- One interesting aspect of DRIPs is that they are forcing corporations to reexamine their basic dividend policies.
  - ☐ A high participation rate in a DRIP suggests that stockholders might be better off if the firm simply reduced cash dividends, which would save stockholders some personal income taxes.

- Companies start or stop using new stock DRIPs depending on their need for equity capital.

- Some companies have expanded their DRIPs by moving to *open enrollment* whereby anyone can purchase the firm's stock directly and bypass brokers' commissions.

Regardless of the debate on the relevancy of dividend policy, it is possible to identify several factors that influence dividend policy. These factors are grouped into four broad categories.

- Constraints: (1) Bond indentures, (2) preferred stock restrictions, (3) impairment of capital rule, (4) availability of cash, and (5) penalty tax on improperly accumulated earnings.

- Investment opportunities: (1) Number of profitable investment opportunities and (2) ability to accelerate or postpone projects.

- Alternative sources of capital: (1) Cost of selling new stock, (2) ability to substitute debt for equity, and (3) control.

■ Effects of dividend policy on k_s: (1) Stockholders' desire for current versus future income, (2) perceived riskiness of dividends versus capital gains, (3) the tax advantage of capital gains over dividends, and (4) the information content of dividends (signaling).

Dividend policy decisions are exercises in informed judgment, not decisions that can be based on a precise mathematical model.

■ Dividend policy is not an independent decision—the dividend decision is made jointly with capital structure and capital budgeting decisions. The underlying reason for this joint process is asymmetric information, which influences managerial actions in two ways.
  ☐ In general, managers do not want to issue new common stock. Managers strongly prefer to use retained earnings as their primary source of new equity.
  ☐ Dividend changes provide signals about managers' beliefs as to their firms' future prospects. Thus, dividend reductions, or worse yet, omissions, generally have a significant negative effect on a firm's stock price.

■ In setting dividend policy, managers should begin by considering the firm's future investment opportunities relative to its projected internal sources of funds.

■ Managers should use the residual dividend model to set dividends, but in a long-term framework.

■ The current dollar dividend should be set so that there is an extremely low probability that the dividend, once set, will have to be lowered or omitted.

■ In general, firms with superior investment opportunities should set lower payouts, hence retain more earnings, than firms with poor investment opportunities. The degree of uncertainty also influences the decision.
  ☐ If there is a great deal of uncertainty in the forecasts of free cash flows, then it is best to be conservative and to set a lower current dollar dividend.
  ☐ Firms with postponable investment opportunities can afford to set a higher dollar dividend, because, in times of stress, investments can be postponed for a year or two, thus increasing the cash available for dividends.
  ☐ Firms whose cost of capital is largely unaffected by changes in the debt ratio can also afford to set a higher payout ratio, because they can, in times of stress, more easily issue additional debt to maintain the capital budgeting program without having to cut dividends or issue stock.

■ Today's dividend decisions are constrained by policies that were set in the past, hence setting a policy for the next five years necessarily begins with a review of the current situation.

■ Because dividend policy still remains one of the most judgmental decisions that firms must make, it is always set by the board of directors. The financial staff analyzes the situation and makes a recommendation, but the board makes the final decision.

Stock dividends and stock splits are often used to lower a firm's stock price and, at the same time, to conserve its cash resources.

■ The effect of a *stock split* is an increase in the number of shares outstanding and a reduction in the par, or stated, value of the shares. For example, if a firm had 1,000 shares of stock outstanding with a par value of $100 per share, a 2-for-1 split would reduce the par value to $50 and increase the number of shares to 2,000.
   □ The total net worth of the firm remains unchanged.
   □ The stock split does not involve any cash payment, only additional certificates representing new shares.
   □ Stock splits often occur due to the widespread belief that there is an *optimal price range* for each stock.
   □ Stock splits are generally used after a sharp price run-up to produce a large price reduction.

■ A *stock dividend* requires an accounting entry transfer from retained earnings to common stock.
   □ Again, no cash is involved with this "dividend." Net worth remains unchanged, and the number of shares is increased.
   □ Stock dividends used on a regular annual basis will keep the stock price more or less constrained.

■ Unless the total amount of dividends paid on shares is increased, any upward movement in the stock price following a stock split or dividend is likely to be temporary. The price will normally fall in proportion to the dilution in earnings and dividends unless earnings and dividends rise.

Stock repurchases are an alternative to dividends for transmitting cash to stockholders.

■ There are three principal types of repurchases: (1) Situations in which the firm has cash available for distribution to its stockholders, and it distributes this cash by repurchasing shares rather than by paying cash dividends; (2) situations in which the firm concludes that its capital structure is too heavily weighted with equity, and then it sells debt and uses the proceeds to buy back its stock; and (3) situations in which a firm has issued options to employees and then uses open market repurchases to obtain stock for use when the options are exercised.

■ Stock repurchased by the issuing firm is called *treasury stock*.

■ Assuming that the repurchase does not adversely affect the firm's future earnings, the earnings per share on the remaining shares will increase, resulting in a higher market price per share. As a result, capital gains will have been substituted for dividends.

■ Advantages of repurchases include:
   ☐ The repurchase is often motivated by management's belief that the firm's shares are undervalued.
   ☐ The stockholder is given a choice of whether or not to sell his stock to the firm.
   ☐ The repurchase can remove a large block of stock overhanging the market.
   ☐ If an increase in cash flow is temporary, the cash can be distributed to stockholders as a repurchase rather than as a dividend, which could not be maintained in the future.
   ☐ The company has more flexibility in adjusting the total distribution than it would if the entire distribution were in the form of cash dividends, because repurchases can be varied from year to year without giving off adverse signals.
   ☐ Repurchases can be used to produce large-scale changes in capital structures.
   ☐ Companies that use stock options as an important component of employee compensation can repurchase shares and then use those shares when employees exercise their options.

■ Disadvantages of repurchases include:
   ☐ Repurchases are not as dependable as cash dividends; therefore, the stock price may benefit more from cash dividends. A dependable repurchase program may not be practical due to the improper accumulation tax.
   ☐ Selling stockholders may not be aware of all the implications of the repurchase; therefore, repurchases are usually announced in advance.
   ☐ If a firm pays too high a price for the repurchased stock, it is to the disadvantage of the remaining stockholders.

■ Increases in the size and frequency of repurchases in recent years suggest that companies are doing more repurchases and paying out less cash as dividends.

SELF-TEST QUESTIONS

Definitional

1.   MM argue that a firm's dividend policy has ____ _____ on a stock's price.

2. Gordon and Lintner hypothesize that investors value a dollar of _____ more highly than a dollar of expected _____ _____.

3. A company may be forced to increase its _____ ratio in order to avoid a tax on retained earnings deemed to be unnecessary for the conduct of the business.

4. Some stockholders prefer dividends to _____ _____ because of a need for current _____.

5. If the _____ of a firm's stock increases with the announcement of an increase in dividends, it may be due to the _____ content in the dividend announcement rather than to a preference for dividends over capital gains.

6. A firm with _____ earnings is most appropriate for using the policy of "extra" dividends.

7. The stock transfer books of a corporation are closed on the _____-____-_____ date.

8. The ____-_____ date occurs two business days prior to the _____-____-_____ date and provides time for stock transfers to be recorded on the firm's books.

9. Actual payment of a dividend is made on the _____ date as announced by the _____ ____ _____.

10. Many firms have instituted _____ _____ plans whereby stockholders can use their dividends to purchase additional shares of the company's stock.

11. A stock split involves a reduction in the _____ _____ of the common stock, but no accounting transfers are made between accounts.

12. The assumption that some investors prefer a high dividend payout while others prefer a low payout is called the _____ effect.

13. The residual dividend policy is based on the fact that new common stock is _____ _____ than retained earnings.

14. Stock repurchased by the firm that issued it is called _____ _____.

15. _____ _____ involves the decision to pay out earnings or to retain them for reinvestment in the firm.

16. The _____ _____ _____ is defined as the percentage of net income to be paid out as cash dividends as desired by the firm, and it should be based in large part on investors' preferences for dividends versus capital gains.

17. The _____ _____ theory states that investors may prefer to have companies retain most of their earnings because of various tax advantages.

18. Dividend _____ has two components: (1) How dependable is the growth rate, and (2) can we count on at least receiving the current dividend in the future?

19. The _____ _____ _____ is based on the premise that investors prefer to have a firm retain and reinvest earnings rather than to pay them out as dividends, if the rate of return the firm can earn on reinvested earnings exceeds the rate of return investors can obtain for themselves on other investments of comparable risk.

20. Some companies have expanded their DRIPs by moving to _____ _____ whereby anyone can purchase the firm's stock directly and bypass brokers' commissions.

21. The dividend decision is made jointly with _____ _____ and _____ _____ decisions.

22. _____ _____ are an alternative to dividends for transmitting cash to stockholders.

23. The _____-_____-_____-_____ theory states that investors prefer dividends because they are less risky than potential capital gains.

24. The _____ _____ _____ strikes a balance between investors' desire for current cash flows and future expected growth so as to maximize the firm's stock price.

25. Modigliani and Miller, the principal proponents of the _____ _____ theory, argue that the value of the firm depends only on the income produced by its assets, not on how income is split between dividends and retained earnings.

26. A(n) _____ _____ requires an accounting entry transfer from retained earnings to common stock.

27. The optimal payout ratio is a function of four factors: (1) investors' preferences for dividends versus capital gains, (2) the firm's _____ opportunities, (3) its target _____ _____, and (4) the _____ and _____ of external capital.

Conceptual

28. An increase in cash dividends will always result in an increase in the price of the common stock because D_1 will increase in the stock valuation model.

    a. True   **b.** False

29. A stock split will affect the amounts shown in which of the following balance sheet accounts?

    a. Common stock   **d.** Cash
    b. Paid-in capital   **e.** None of the above accounts.
    c. Retained earnings

30. If investors prefer dividends to capital gains, then

    a. The required rate of return on equity, k_s, will not be affected by a change in dividend policy.
    b. The cost of capital will not be affected by a change in dividend policy.
    c. k_s will increase as the payout ratio is reduced.
    d. k_s will decrease as the retention rate increases.
    e. A policy conforming to the residual dividend model will maximize stock price.

31. Which of the following statements is most correct?

    a. Modigliani and Miller's theory of the effect of dividend policy on the value of a firm has been called the "bird-in-the-hand" theory, because MM argued that a dividend in the hand is less risky than a potential capital gain in the bush. After extensive empirical tests, this theory is now accepted by most financial experts.
    b. According to proponents of the "dividend irrelevance theory," if a company's stock price rises after the firm announces a greater-than-expected dividend increase, the price increase occurs because of signaling effects, not because of investors' preferences for dividends over capital gains.
    c. The tax preference theory states that the value of the firm depends only on the income produced by its assets, not on how this income is split between dividends and retained earnings.
    d. Statements a, b, and c are correct.
    e. Statements a, b, and c are false.

32. Which of the following statements is most correct?

    a. The residual dividend model calls for the establishment of a fixed, stable dividend (or dividend growth rate) and then for the level of investment each year to be determined as a residual equal to net income minus the established dividends.

    b. According to the residual dividend model, if a firm has a large number of profitable investment opportunities this will tend to produce a lower optimal dividend payout ratio.

    c. According to the text, a firm would probably maximize its stock price if it established a specific dividend payout ratio, say 40 percent, and then paid that percentage of earnings out each year because stockholders would then know exactly how much dividend income to count on when they planned their spending for the coming year.

    d. If you buy a stock after the ex-dividend date but before the dividend has been paid, then you, and not the seller, will receive the next dividend check the company sends out.

    e. All of the statements above are false.

33. Which of the following statements is most correct?

    a. According to the asymmetric information, or signaling, theory of capital structure, the announcement of a new stock issue by a mature firm would generally lead to an *increase* in the price of the firm's stock.

    b. According to the asymmetric information, or signaling, theory of capital structure, the announcement of a new stock issue by a mature firm would generally lead to a *decrease* in the price of the firm's stock.

    c. If Firm A's managers believe in the asymmetric information theory, but Firm B's managers do not, then, other things held constant, Firm A would probably have the *higher* normal target debt ratio.

    d. There is no such thing as the asymmetric information theory of capital structure, at least according to the text.

    e. Statements b and c are true.

34. Which of the following statements is most correct?

   a. According to the tax preference theory, investors prefer dividends and, as a result, the higher the payout ratio, the higher the value of the firm.

   b. According to the "bird-in-the-hand" theory, investors prefer cash to paper (stock), so if a company announces that it plans to repurchase some of its stock, this causes the price of the stock to increase.

   c. According to the dividend irrelevance theory developed by Modigliani and Miller, stock dividends (but not cash dividends) are irrelevant because they "merely divide the pie into thinner slices."

   d. According to the information content, or signaling, hypothesis, the fact that stock prices generally increase when an increase in the dividend is announced demonstrates that investors prefer higher to lower payout ratios.

   e. According to the text, the residual dividend model is more appropriate for setting a company's long-run target payout ratio than for determining the payout ratio on a year-to-year basis.

35. Which of the following statements is most correct?

   a. Stock prices generally rise on the ex-dividend date, and that increase is especially great if the company increases the dividend.

   b. Dividend reinvestment plans are popular with investors because investors who do not need cash income can have their dividends reinvested in the company's stock and thereby avoid having to pay income taxes on the dividend income until they sell the stock.

   c. In the past, stock dividends and stock splits were frequently used by corporations that wanted to lower the prices of their stocks to an "optimal trading range." However, recent empirical studies have demonstrated that stock dividends and stock splits generally cause stock prices to decline, so companies today rarely split their stock or pay stock dividends.

   d. Statements a, b, and c are false.

   e. Statements a, b, and c are true.

SELF-TEST PROBLEMS

1. Express Industries' expected net income for next year is $1 million. The company's target and current capital structure is 40 percent debt and 60 percent common equity. The optimal capital budget for next year is $1.2 million. If Express uses the residual theory of dividends to determine next year's dividend payout, what is the expected payout ratio?

   a. 0%   **b.** 10%   **c.** 28%   **d.** 42%   **e.** 56%

2. Amalgamated Shippers has a current and target capital structure of 30 percent debt and 70 percent equity. This past year Amalgamated, which uses the residual dividend model, had a dividend payout ratio of 47.5 percent and net income of $800,000. What was Amalgamated's capital budget?

   a. $400,000   **b.** $500,000   **c.** $600,000   **d.** $700,000   **e.** $800,000

3. The Aikman Company's optimal capital structure calls for 40 percent debt and 60 percent common equity. The interest rate on its debt is a constant 12 percent; its cost of common equity is 18 percent; and its federal-plus-state tax rate is 40 percent. Aikman has the following investment opportunities:

   Project A: Cost = $5 million; IRR = 22%.
   Project B: Cost = $5 million; IRR = 14%.
   Project C: Cost = $5 million; IRR = 11%.

   Aikman expects to have net income of $7 million. If Aikman bases its dividends on the residual policy, what will be its payout ratio?

   a. 22.62%   **b.** 14.29%   **c.** 31.29%   **d.** 25.62%   **e.** 18.75%

4. Hiers Automotive Supply Inc.'s stock trades at $100 a share. The company is contemplating a 4-for-3 stock split. Assuming that the stock split will have no effect on the market value of its equity, what will be the company's stock price following the stock split?

   a. $50.00   **b.** $62.50   **c.** $70.00   **d.** $75.00   **e.** $80.00

5. Ridgdill Corporation has net income of $8,000,000 and it has 1,000,000 shares of common stock outstanding. The company's stock currently trades at $30 a share. Ridgdill is considering a plan in which it will use available cash to repurchase 15 percent of its shares in the open market. The repurchase is expected to have no effect on either net income or the company's P/E ratio. What will be its stock price following the stock repurchase?

   a. $35.29   **b.** $32.00   **c.** $36.89   **d.** $35.15   **e.** $31.43

(The following data apply to the next five Self-Text Problems.)

Hammond Industries is expecting to pay an annual dividend per share of $1.50 out of annual earnings per share of $4.50. Currently, Hammond's stock is selling for $40 per share. Adhering to the company's target capital structure, the firm has $20 million in assets, of which 45 percent is funded by debt. Assume that the firm's book value of equity equals its market value. In past years, the firm has earned a return on equity (ROE) of 15 percent, which is expected to continue this year and into the foreseeable future.

6. On the basis of the above information, what long-run growth rate can the firm be expected to maintain? [Hint: g = Retention rate × ROE.]

   a. 5.0%   **b.** 6.5%   **c.** 7.3%   **d.** 8.2%   **e.** 10.0%

7. What is the stock's required return?

   a. 10.00%   **b.** 11.50%   **c.** 12.60%   **d.** 13.75%   **e.** 14.00%

8. If the firm were to change its dividend policy and pay an annual dividend of $3.00 per share, financial analysts predict that the change in policy will have no effect upon the firm's stock price or ROE. Therefore, what must be the firm's new expected long-run growth rate and required return?

   a. 10.7%   **b.** 12.5%   **c.** 13.0%   **d.** 14.2%   **e.** 14.8%

9. Suppose instead that the firm has decided to proceed with its original plan of disbursing $1.50 per share to shareholders, but the firm intends to do so in the form of a stock dividend rather than a cash dividend. The firm will allot new shares based on the current stock price of $40. In other words, for every $40 in dividends due to shareholders, a share of stock will be issued. How large will the stock dividend be relative to the firm's current market capitalization? [Hint: Remember market capitalization = P_0 × number of shares outstanding.]

   a. 3.75%   **b.** 4.00%   **c.** 2.50%   **d.** 4.50%   **e.** 5.00%

10. If the plan in Self-Test Problem 9 is implemented, how many new shares of stock will be issued, and by how much will the company's earnings per share be diluted?

   a. 13,750; $0.10   **d.** 15,000; $0.16
   b. 15,000; $0.12   **e.** 17,500; $0.25
   c. 13,750; $0.16

ANSWERS TO SELF-TEST QUESTIONS

1. no effect
2. dividends; capital gains
3. payout
4. capital gains; income
5. price (or value); information

6. volatile (fluctuating)
7. holder-of-record
8. ex-dividend; holder-of-record
9. payment; board of directors
10. dividend reinvestment

11.	par value	20.	open enrollment
12.	clientele	21.	capital structure; capital budgeting
13.	more costly	22.	Stock repurchases
14.	treasury stock	23.	bird-in-the-hand
15.	Dividend policy	24.	optimal dividend policy
16.	target payout ratio	25.	dividend irrelevance
17.	tax preference	26.	stock dividend
18.	stability	27.	investment; capital structure; availability; cost
19.	residual dividend model		

28. b. A dividend increase could be perceived by investors as signifying poor investment opportunities and hence lower growth in future earnings, thus reducing g in the DCF model. The net effect on stock price is uncertain.

29. e. A stock split will affect the par value and number of shares outstanding. However, no dollar values will be affected.

30. c. This is the Gordon-Lintner hypothesis. If investors view dividends as being less risky than potential capital gains, then the cost of equity is inversely related to the payout ratio.

31. b. Statement a is false; the proponents of this theory were Gordon and Lintner and empirical tests have not proven any of the dividend theories. Statement b is correct. Statement c is false; the theory discussed here is the dividend irrelevance theory.

32. b. Statement a is false; the residual dividend model calls for the determination of the optimal capital budget and then the dividend is established as a residual of net income minus the amount of retained earnings necessary for the capital budget. Statement b is correct. Statement c is false; a constant payout policy would lead to uncertainty of dividends due to fluctuating earnings. Statement d is false; if a stock is bought after the ex-dividend date the dividend remains with the seller of the stock.

33. b. The asymmetric information theory suggests that investors regard the announcement of a stock sale as bad news: If the firm had really good investment opportunities, it would use debt financing so that existing stockholders would receive all the benefits from the good projects. Therefore, the announcement of a stock sale leads to a decline in the firm's stock price. To reduce the chances of issuing stock, firms set low target debt ratios, which give them "reserve borrowing capacity."

34. e. Statements a, b, c, and d are false, but statement e is true.

35. d. The statements are false.

SOLUTIONS TO SELF-TEST PROBLEMS

1. c. The $1,200,000 capital budget will be financed using 40 percent debt and 60 percent equity. Therefore, the equity requirement will be 0.6($1,200,000) = $720,000. Since the expected net income is $1,000,000, $280,000 will be available to pay as dividends. Thus, the payout ratio is expected to be $280,000/$1,000,000 = 0.28 = 28%.

2. c. Of the $800,000 in net income, 0.475($800,000) = $380,000 was paid out as dividends. Thus, $420,000 was retained in the firm for investment. This is the equity portion of the total capital budget, or 70 percent of the total capital budget. Therefore, the total capital budget was $420,000/0.7 = $600,000.

3. b. WACC = 0.4(12%)(0.6) + 0.6(18%) = 13.68%.

   We see that the capital budget should be $10 million, since only Projects A and B have IRRs > WACC. We know that 60 percent of the $10 million should be equity. Therefore, the company should pay dividends of:

   Dividends = NI – Needed equity = $7,000,000 – $6,000,000 = $1,000,000.
   Payout ratio = $1,000,000/$7,000,000 = 0.1429 = 14.29%.

4. d. $P_0 = \$100$; Split = 4 for 3; New $P_0 = ?$ $P_{0 \text{ New}} = \dfrac{\$100}{4/3} = \$75.00$.

5. a. NI = $8,000,000; Shares = 1,000,000; $P_0 = \$30$; Repurchase = 15%; New $P_0 = ?$

   Repurchase = 0.15 × 1,000,000 = 150,000 shares.

   Repurchase amount = 150,000 × $30.00 = $4,500,000.

   $$EPS_{Old} = \frac{NI}{Shares} = \frac{\$8,000,000}{1,000,000} = \$8.00.$$

   $$P/E = \frac{\$30}{\$8} = 3.75\times.$$

   $$EPS_{New} = \frac{\$8,000,000}{1,000,000 - 150,000} = \frac{\$8,000,000}{850,000} = \$9.41.$$

   $Price_{New} = EPS_{New} \times P/E = \$9.41 \times 3.75 = \$35.29.$

6. e. Before finding the long-run growth rate, the dividend payout ratio must be determined.

Dividend payout ratio = DPS/EPS = $1.50/$4.50 = 0.3333.

The firm's long-run growth rate can be found by multiplying the portion of a firm's earnings that are retained times the firm's return on equity.

g = ROE × Retention ratio
  = (Net income/Equity capital) × (1 − Dividend payout ratio)
  = 15% × (1 − 0.3333) = 10%.

7. d. The required return can be calculated using the DCF approach.

$k_s = D_1/P_0 + g$
$k_s = \$1.50/\$40.00 + 0.10$
$k_s = 0.1375$ or 13.75%.

8. b. The new payout ratio can be calculated as:

$3.00/$4.50 = 0.6667.

The new long-run growth rate can now be calculated as:

g = ROE × (1 − Dividend payout ratio)
g = 15% × (1 − 0.6667) = 5%.

The firm's required return would be:

$k_s = D_1/P_0 + g$
$k_s = \$3.00/\$40.00 + 0.05$
$k_s = 0.125$ or 12.5%.

9. a. The firm's original plan was to issue a dividend equal to $1.50 per share, which equates to a total dividend of $1.50 times the number of shares outstanding. So, first the number of shares outstanding must be determined from the EPS.

Amount of equity capital = Total assets × Equity ratio
              = $20 million × 0.55 = $11 million.

Net income = Equity capital × ROE = $11 million × 0.15 = $1.65 million.

$$EPS = \text{Net income/Number of shares}$$
$$\$4.50 = \$1.65 \text{ million/Number of shares}$$
Number of shares $= 366,667$.

With 366,667 shares outstanding, the total dividend that would be paid would be $1.50 × 366,667 shares = $550,000. The firm's current market capitalization is $14,666,680, determined by 366,667 shares at $40 per share. If the stock dividend is implemented, it shall account for 5% of the firm's current market capitalization ($550,000/$14,666,680 = 0.0375).

10. c. If the total amount of value to be distributed to shareholders is $550,000, at a price of $40 per share, then the number of new shares issued would be:

Number of new shares $=$ Dividend value/Price per share
Number of new shares $= \$550,000/\$40$
Number of new shares $= 13,750$ shares.

The stock dividend will leave the firm's net income unchanged, therefore the firm's new EPS is its net income divided by the new total number of shares outstanding.

New EPS $=$ Net income/(Old shares outstanding + New shares outstanding)
New EPS $= \$1,650,000/(366,667 + 13,750)$
New EPS $= \$4.3373 \approx \$4.34$.

The dilution of earnings per share is the difference between old EPS and new EPS.

Dilution of EPS $=$ Old EPS $-$ New EPS
Dilution of EPS $= \$4.50 - \$4.34$
Dilution of EPS $= \$0.16$ per share.

CHAPTER 15
MANAGING CURRENT ASSETS

LEARNING OBJECTIVES

- Define basic working capital terminology.

- Calculate the inventory conversion period, the receivables collection period, and the payables deferral period to determine the cash conversion cycle.

- Briefly explain the basic idea of zero working capital.

- Briefly explain how a negative cash conversion cycle works.

- Distinguish among relaxed, restricted, and moderate current asset investment policies, and explain the effect of each on risk and expected return.

- Explain how EVA methodology provides a useful way of thinking about working capital.

- List the reasons for holding cash.

- Construct a cash budget, and explain its purpose.

- Briefly explain useful tools and procedures for effectively managing cash inflows and outflows.

- Explain why firms are likely to hold marketable securities.

- State the goal of inventory management and identify the three categories of inventory costs.

- Identify and briefly explain the use of several inventory control systems.

- Monitor a firm's receivables position by calculating its DSO and reviewing aging schedules.

- List and explain the four elements of a firm's credit policy, and identify other factors influencing credit policy.

OVERVIEW

About 60 percent of a typical financial manager's time is devoted to working capital management, and many students' first jobs will involve working capital. This is particularly true of smaller businesses, where new job creation is especially rapid. Therefore, working capital is an essential topic.

Working capital policy involves two basic questions: (1) What is the appropriate amount of current assets for the firm to carry, both in total and for each specific account, and (2) how should current assets be financed? This chapter addresses the first question, while Chapter 16 addresses the second question.

Sound working capital management goes beyond finance. Indeed, most of the ideas for improving working capital management often stem from other disciplines.

OUTLINE

It is useful to begin by reviewing some basic definitions and concepts.

■ *Working capital*, sometimes called *gross working capital*, is defined as current assets used in operations, while *net working capital* is defined as current assets minus current liabilities.

■ *Net operating working capital* is defined as current assets minus non-interest bearing current liabilities.

■ The *current ratio*, which is calculated as current assets divided by current liabilities, is intended to measure liquidity.

■ The *quick ratio*, which also attempts to measure liquidity, is calculated as current assets less inventories, divided by current liabilities.
  □ The quick ratio is an "acid test" of a company's ability to meet its current obligations.

■ The most comprehensive picture of a firm's liquidity is obtained by examining its *cash budget*, which forecasts a firm's cash inflows and outflows, and thus focuses on what really counts, the firm's ability to generate sufficient cash inflows to meet its required cash outflows.

■ *Working capital policy* refers to the firm's policies regarding target levels for each category of current assets and how current assets will be financed.

■ *Working capital management* involves both setting working capital policy and carrying out that policy in day-to-day operations.

Firms typically follow a cycle in which they purchase inventory, sell goods on credit, and then collect accounts receivable. This cycle is referred to as the cash conversion cycle, and it highlights the strengths and weaknesses of the company's working capital policy. It focuses on the length of time between when the company makes payments and when it receives cash inflows.

■ Sound working capital policy is designed to minimize the time between cash expenditures on materials and the collection of cash on sales.

■ The following terms and definitions are used:
  □ *Inventory conversion period* is the average time required to convert materials into finished goods and then to sell these goods.

$$\text{Inventory conversion period} = \frac{\text{Inventory}}{\text{Sales per day}}.$$

  □ *Receivables collection period* is the average length of time required to convert the firm's receivables into cash, that is, to collect cash following a sale. It is also called the days sales outstanding (DSO).

$$\text{Receivables collection period} = \text{DSO} = \frac{\text{Receivables}}{\text{Sales/365}}.$$

  □ *Payables deferral period* is the average length of time between the purchase of materials and labor and the payment of cash for them.

$$\text{Payables deferral period} = \frac{\text{Payables}}{\text{Cost of goods sold/365}}.$$

  □ The *cash conversion cycle* equals the length of time between the firm's actual cash expenditures to pay for productive resources (materials and labor) and its own cash receipts from the sale of products (that is, the length of time between paying for labor and materials and collecting on receivables). Thus, the cash conversion cycle equals the average length of time a dollar is tied up in current assets.

■ Using these definitions, the cash conversion cycle is defined as follows:

$$\begin{array}{ccccc} \text{Inventory} & & \text{Receivables} & & \text{Payables} & & \text{Cash} \\ \text{conversion} & + & \text{collection} & - & \text{deferral} & = & \text{conversion}. \\ \text{period} & & \text{period} & & \text{period} & & \text{cycle} \end{array}$$

- To illustrate, suppose it takes a firm an average of 72 days to convert materials and labor to widgets and to sell them, and it takes another 24 days to collect on receivables, while 30 days normally lapse between receipt of materials (and work done) and payments for materials and labor. In this case, the cash conversion cycle is 72 days + 24 days − 30 days = 66 days.

- The firm's goal should be to shorten its cash conversion cycle as much as possible without hurting operations. This would maximize profits, because the longer the cash conversion cycle, the greater the need for external financing, and that financing has a cost.
  - ☐ The cash conversion cycle can be shortened (1) by reducing the inventory conversion period by processing and selling goods more quickly, (2) by reducing the receivables collection period by speeding up collections, or (3) by lengthening the payables deferral period by slowing down the firm's own payments.
  - ☐ To the extent that these actions can be taken without increasing costs or depressing sales, they should be carried out.

- Results of a recent study of over 2,900 companies during a recent 20-year period found a strong relationship between a company's cash conversion cycle and its performance.

In today's world of intense global competition, working capital management is receiving increasing attention from managers striving for peak efficiency. In fact, the goal of many leading companies today is zero working capital.

- Proponents of *zero working capital* claim that a movement toward this goal not only generates cash but also speeds up production and helps businesses make more timely deliveries and operate more efficiently.

- The concept has its own definition of working capital: Inventories + Receivables − Payables.
  - ☐ The rationale here is (1) inventories and receivables are the keys to making sales, but (2) inventories can be financed by suppliers through accounts payable.

- Reducing working capital and thus increasing turnover has two major financial benefits.
  - ☐ Every dollar freed up by reducing inventories or receivables, or by increasing payables, results in a one-time contribution to cash flow.
  - ☐ A movement toward zero working capital permanently raises a company's earnings.

- Like all capital, funds invested in working capital cost money, so reducing those funds yields permanent savings in capital costs.

■ Reducing working capital forces a company to produce and deliver faster than its competitors, which helps it gain new business and charge premium prices for providing good service.

■ The most important factor in moving toward zero working capital is increased speed. The best companies are able to start production after an order is received yet still meet customer delivery requirements. This system is known as *demand flow,* or *demand-based management*, and it builds on the just-in-time method of inventory control.
☐ Demand flow management is broader than just-in-time, because it requires that all elements of a production system operate quickly and efficiently.

■ A focus on minimizing receivables and inventories while maximizing payables will help a firm lower its investment in working capital and achieve financial and production economies.

A firm's current asset levels rise and fall with business cycles and seasonal trends. At the peak of such cycles, businesses carry their maximum amounts of current assets.

■ There are three alternative policies regarding the total amount of current assets carried. Each policy differs with regard to the amount of current assets carried to support any given level of sales, hence in the turnover of those assets.
☐ A *relaxed current asset investment policy* is one in which relatively large amounts of cash, marketable securities, and inventories are carried, and sales are stimulated by the use of a credit policy that provides liberal financing to customers and a corresponding high level of receivables.
☐ A *restricted current asset investment policy* is one in which holdings of cash, securities, inventories, and receivables are minimized. Current assets are turned over more frequently, so each dollar of current assets is forced to "work harder."
☐ A moderate current asset investment policy is between the two extremes.
☐ Generally, the decision on the current assets level involves a risk/return tradeoff. The relaxed policy minimizes risk, but it also has the lowest expected return. On the other hand, the restricted policy offers the highest expected return coupled with the highest risk. The moderate policy falls in between the two extremes in terms of expected risk and return.
☐ Changing technology can lead to dramatic changes in the optimal current asset investment policy.

■ Working capital consists of four main components: cash, marketable securities, inventory, and accounts receivable.

■ For each type of asset, firms face a fundamental tradeoff: Current assets are necessary to conduct business, and the greater the holdings of current assets, the smaller the danger of running out, hence the lower the firm's operating risk. However, holding working capital is costly; so, there is pressure to hold the amount of working capital to the minimum consistent with running the business without interruption.

Approximately 1.5 percent of the average industrial firm's assets are held in the form of cash, which is defined as demand deposits plus currency. Cash is a nonearning asset. Excessive cash balances reduce the rate of return on equity and hence the value of a firm's stock. Thus, the goal of cash management is to minimize the amount of cash the firm must hold in order to conduct its normal business activities, yet at the same time, to have sufficient cash (1) to take trade discounts, (2) to maintain its credit rating, and (3) to meet unexpected cash needs.

- ■ Firms hold cash for two primary reasons:
  - ☐ *Transactions balances* are held to provide the cash needed to conduct normal business operations.
  - ☐ *Compensating balances* are often required by banks for providing loans and services.

- ■ Two secondary reasons are also cited:
  - ☐ *Precautionary balances* are held in reserve for random, unforeseen fluctuations in cash inflows and outflows.
    - The less predictable the firm's cash flows, the larger such balances should be.
    - Firms that would otherwise need large precautionary balances tend to hold highly liquid marketable securities rather than cash per se.
  - ☐ *Speculative balances* are held to enable the firm to take advantage of bargain purchases.

- ■ Firms do not segregate funds for each of these motives, because the same money often serves more than one purpose, but firms do consider all four factors in setting their overall cash positions.

- ■ An ample cash balance should be maintained to take advantage of *trade discounts* and favorable business opportunities, to help the firm maintain its credit rating, and to meet emergency needs.

A cash budget projects cash inflows and outflows over some specified period of time.

- ■ The basis for a cash budget is the sales forecast, the level of fixed assets and inventory that will be required to meet the forecasted sales level, and the times when payment must be made.

■ Cash budgets can be created for any interval, but firms typically use a monthly cash budget for the coming year, a weekly budget for the coming month, and a daily budget for the coming week, or something similar.
  ☐ The monthly cash budgets are used for planning purposes, and the daily or weekly budgets for actual cash control.

■ A typical cash budget consists of three sections.
  ☐ The *collections and purchases worksheet* summarizes the firm's cash collections from sales and cash purchases for materials.
  ☐ The *cash gain or loss section* lays out the cash inflows and outflows, and the "bottom line" of this section is the net cash gain or loss.
  ☐ The *loan requirement* or *cash surplus section* summarizes the firm's cumulative need for loans and cumulative surplus cash.

■ If the firm's inflows and outflows are not uniform over the budget interval, say monthly, the cash budget will overstate or understate the firm's cash needs.

■ The cash budget can be used to help set the firm's *target cash balance*, the desired cash balance that a firm plans to maintain in order to conduct business. This is accomplished by incorporating uncertainty into the budget, and then setting a target balance that provides a cushion against adverse conditions.

■ Note that the cash budget focuses on the physical movement of cash, and hence depreciation cash flow does not appear directly in the budget. It does, however, affect the amount of taxes paid.

■ Since the cash budget represents a forecast, all the values in the table are *expected* values.

■ Spreadsheet programs are particularly well suited for constructing and analyzing cash budgets, especially with respect to the sensitivity of cash flows to changes in sales levels, collection periods, and the like.

■ The target cash balance probably will be adjusted over time, rising and falling with seasonal patterns and with long-term changes in the scale of the firm's operations.

Cash management has changed significantly over the last two decades as a result of an upward trend in interest rates and technological developments.

■ From the early 1970s to the mid-1980s, there was a clear upward trend in interest rates that increased the opportunity cost of holding cash. This encouraged financial managers to search for more efficient ways of managing the firm's cash.

■ Technological developments, particularly computerized electronic funds transfer mechanisms, changed the way cash is managed.

■ Effective cash management encompasses proper management of cash inflows and outflows, which entails (1) synchronizing cash flows, (2) using float, (3) accelerating collections, (4) getting available funds to where they are needed, and (5) controlling disbursements.

■ Synchronizing cash inflows and outflows enables firms to reduce cash balances, decrease bank loans, lower interest expenses, and increase profits.

■ *Check clearing* is the process of converting a check that has been written and mailed into cash in the payee's account.

■ *Net float* is the difference between the balance shown in a firm's checkbook and the balance on the bank's records.
  □ A firm's net float is a function of its ability to speed up collections on checks received (*collections float*) and to slow down collections on checks written (*disbursement float*).

Several techniques are now used to speed collections and to get funds where they are needed.

■ A *lockbox plan* is a procedure that speeds up collections and reduces float through the use of post office boxes in payers' local areas.
  □ Customers mail checks to a post office box in a specified city. A local bank then collects the checks, deposits them, starts the clearing process, and notifies the selling firm that payment has been received.
  □ Processing time is further reduced because it takes less time for banks to collect local checks.

■ Firms are increasingly demanding payments of larger bills by wire, or even by automatic electronic debits, whereby funds are automatically deducted from one account and added to another.
  □ Computer technology is making such a process increasingly feasible and efficient.

Marketable securities typically provide much lower yields than a firm's operating assets, yet they are often held in sizable amounts.

■ In many cases companies hold marketable securities for the same reasons they hold cash.

■ While these securities are not as liquid as cash, in most cases they can be converted to cash on very short notice.

■ Marketable securities provide at least a modest return, while cash yields nothing.

■ Marketable securities can be used as a substitute for transactions balances, for precautionary balances, for speculative balances, or for all three. In most cases, marketable securities are held primarily for precautionary purposes.

■ William Baumol first recognized that the trade-off between cash and marketable securities is similar to the one firms face when setting the optimal inventory level.
   ☐ He applied the EOQ inventory model to determine the optimal level of cash balances.
   ☐ He suggested that cash holdings should be higher if costs are high and the time to liquidate marketable securities is long, but that those cash holdings should be lower if interest rates are high.
      ● If it is expensive and time consuming to convert securities to cash, and if securities do not earn much because interest rates are low, then it does not pay to hold securities as opposed to cash. It does pay to hold securities if interest rates are high and the securities can be converted to cash quickly and cheaply.

■ There are both benefits and costs associated with holding cash and marketable securities. Thus, firms face a trade-off between benefits and costs.
   ☐ The benefits are (1) the firm reduces transactions costs because it won't have to issue securities or borrow as frequently to raise cash and (2) it will have ready cash to take advantage of bargain purchases or growth opportunities.
   ☐ The primary disadvantage is that the after-tax return on cash and short-term securities is very low.

■ Recent research supports the benefit/cost trade-off hypothesis as an explanation for firms' cash holdings.
   ☐ Firms with high growth opportunities suffer the most if they don't have ready cash, so these firms do hold relatively high levels of cash and marketable securities.
   ☐ Firms with volatile cash flows are the ones most likely to run low on cash, so they are the ones that hold the highest levels of cash.
   ☐ In contrast, cash holdings are less important to large firms with high credit ratings, because they have quick and inexpensive access to capital markets.
   ☐ Volatile firms with good growth opportunities are still the ones with the highest cash balances, on average.

Inventories, which may be classified as supplies, raw materials, work-in-process, and finished goods, is an essential part of virtually all business operations.

■ Inventory levels depend heavily upon sales. Since inventories are acquired before sales can take place, an accurate sales forecast is critical to effective inventory management.

■ Errors in the establishment of inventory levels quickly lead either to lost sales or to excessive carrying costs.

■ Since financial managers have a responsibility both for raising the capital needed to carry inventory and for the firm's overall profitability, it's important for them to understand the financial aspects of inventory management.

■ Proper inventory management requires close coordination among the sales, purchasing, production, and finance departments. Lack of coordination among departments, poor sales forecasts, or both, can lead to disaster.

The twin goals of inventory management are (1) to ensure that the inventories needed to sustain operations are available, but (2) to hold costs of ordering and carrying inventories to the lowest possible level.

■ Inventory costs are divided into three categories: carrying costs, ordering and receiving costs, and costs that are incurred if the firm runs short of inventory.
   □ *Carrying costs* generally rise in direct proportion to the average amount of inventories held. Carrying costs associated with inventories include cost of the capital tied up, storage and handling costs, insurance, property taxes, and depreciation and obsolescence.
   □ *Ordering costs*, which are considered to be fixed costs, decline as average inventories increase, that is, as the number of orders decrease. Ordering costs include the costs of placing and receiving orders.
   □ The *costs of running short* include loss of sales, loss of customer goodwill, and disruption of production schedules.

Inventory management requires the establishment of an inventory control system. These systems vary from the extremely simple to the very complex.

■ One simple control procedure is the *red-line method*. A red line is drawn inside the bin where the inventory is stocked. When the red line shows, an order is placed.

■ The *two-bin method* has inventory items stocked in two bins. When the working bin is empty, an order is placed and inventory is drawn from the second bin.

■ Large companies employ much more sophisticated *computerized inventory control systems*. A good inventory control system is dynamic, not static. The computer starts with an inventory count in memory. As withdrawals are made, they are recorded by the computer, and the inventory balance is revised. Orders are automatically placed once the reorder point is reached.

■ The *just-in-time (JIT) system* coordinates a manufacturer's production with suppliers' production so that raw materials arrive from suppliers just as they are needed in the production process. It also requires that component parts be perfect; therefore, JIT inventory management has been developed in conjunction with total quality management (TQM).

■ Another important development related to inventory is *out-sourcing*, which is the practice of purchasing components rather than making them in-house. Out-sourcing is often combined with just-in-time systems to reduce inventory levels.

■ Inventory policy must be coordinated with the firm's manufacturing and procurement policies, because the ultimate goal is to minimize total production and distribution costs, and inventory costs are just one part of total costs.

Carrying receivables has both direct and indirect costs, but it also has an important benefit—granting credit will increase sales.

■ *Accounts receivable* are created when a firm sells goods or performs services on credit rather than on a cash basis. When cash is received, accounts receivable are reduced by the same amount.

■ The total amount of accounts receivable outstanding is determined by (1) the volume of credit sales and (2) the average length of time between sales and collections.

■ The investment in receivables, like any asset, must be financed in some manner. However, the entire amount of receivables does not have to be financed because the profit portion does not represent a cash outflow.

Receivables must be actively managed to ensure that the firm's receivables policy is effective. There are two commonly used methods to monitor a firm's receivables.

■ The *days sales outstanding (DSO)*, sometimes called the average collection period (ACP), measures the average length of time it takes a firm's customers to pay off their credit purchases.
　□ The DSO is calculated by dividing the receivables balance by average daily credit sales.

❑ The DSO can be compared with the industry average and the firm's own credit terms to get an indication of how well customers are adhering to the terms prescribed and how customers' payments, on average, compare with the industry average.

■ An *aging schedule* breaks down a firm's receivables by the ages of the accounts, and it points out the percentage of receivables due that are attributable to late paying customers.
   ❑ Aging schedules cannot be constructed from the type of summary data reported in financial statements; they must be developed from the firm's accounts receivable ledger.

■ Management should constantly monitor both the DSO and the aging schedule to detect trends, to see how the firm's collection experience compares with its credit terms, and to see how effectively the credit department is operating in comparison with other firms in the industry.
   ❑ If the DSO starts to lengthen, or if the aging schedule begins to show an increasing percentage of past-due accounts, then the firm's credit policy may need to be tightened.

■ Both the DSO and aging schedule can be distorted if sales are seasonal or if a firm is growing rapidly.
   ❑ A deterioration in either the DSO or the aging schedule should be taken as a signal to investigate further, but not necessarily as a sign that the firm's credit policy has weakened.
   ❑ DSO and the aging schedule are useful tools for reviewing the credit department's performance.

The major controllable determinants of demand are sales prices, product quality, advertising, and the firm's credit policy. The credit policy consists of (1) the credit period, (2) discounts, (3) credit standards, and (4) collection policy.

■ The *credit period* is the length of time buyers are given to pay for their purchases.
   ❑ Increasing the credit period often stimulates sales, but there is a cost involved in carrying the increased receivables.
   ❑ A firm's regular *credit terms* include the credit period and discount.

■ *Credit standards* refer to the financial strength and creditworthiness a customer must exhibit in order to qualify for credit.
   ❑ Setting credit standards requires a measurement of *credit quality*, which is defined in terms of the probability of a customer's default.
   ❑ Credit evaluation is a well-established practice, and a good credit manager can make reasonably accurate judgments of the probability of default by different classes of customers.

☐ Computerized information systems can assist in making better credit decisions, but in the final analysis, most credit decisions are really exercises in informed judgment.

■ *Collection policy* refers to the procedures the firm follows to collect past-due accounts.
   ☐ The collection process can be expensive in terms of both out-of-pocket expenditures and lost goodwill, but at least some firmness is needed to prevent an undue lengthening of the collection period and to minimize outright losses.
   ☐ A balance must be struck between the costs and benefits of different collection policies.

■ Discounts attract customers and encourage early payment but reduce the dollar amount received on each discount sale.
   ☐ Offering discounts should cause a reduction in the days sales outstanding, because some existing customers will pay more promptly in order to get the discount.
   ☐ The optimal discount percentage is established at the point where marginal costs and benefits are exactly offsetting.
   ☐ If sales are seasonal, a firm may use *seasonal dating* on discounts.
      ● Seasonal dating is the offering of terms to induce customers to buy early by not requiring payment until the purchaser's selling season, regardless of when the goods are shipped.
      ● By offering seasonal dating, the company induces some of its customers to stock up early, saving the firm storage costs and also "nailing down sales."

■ Other factors may also influence a firm's overall credit policy.
   ☐ It is sometimes possible to sell on credit and assess a carrying charge on the receivables that are outstanding, making credit sales more profitable than cash sales.
   ☐ It is illegal for a firm to charge prices or to set credit terms that discriminate between customers unless these differential prices are cost-justified.

SELF-TEST QUESTIONS

Definitional

1. Current assets are also referred to as _____ _____.

2. _____ working capital is defined as _____ assets minus current _____.

3. The goal of cash management is to _____ the amount of _____ the firm must hold in order to conduct its normal business activities.

4. Precautionary balances are maintained in order to allow for random, unforeseen fluctuations in cash _____ and _____ .

5. _____ balances are maintained to pay banks for services they perform.

6. Efficient cash management is often concerned with speeding up the _____ of checks received and slowing down the _____ of checks issued.

7. One method for speeding the collection process (through the use of post office boxes in payers' local areas) is the use of a(n) _____ system.

8. The difference between a firm's balance on its own books and its balance as carried on the bank's books is known as net _____ .

9. Inventory is usually classified as _____ , _____ _____ , _____-_____-_____ , and _____ _____ .

10. The twin goals of inventory management are to provide the inventory needed to sustain operations at the _____ _____ .

11. Storage costs, obsolescence, and other costs that _____ with larger inventory are known as _____ costs.

12. Ordering and receiving costs are _____ related to average inventory size.

13. Inventory control systems that require suppliers to deliver items as they are needed are called _____-____-_____ systems.

14. _____ _____ are created when goods are sold or services are performed on credit.

15. A firm's outstanding accounts receivable will be determined by the _____ of credit sales and the length of time between _____ and _____ .

16. Sales volume and the collection period will be affected by a firm's _____ _____ .

17. Extremely strict credit standards will result in lost _____ .

18. Credit terms generally specify the _____ for which credit is granted and any _____ _____ that is offered for early payment.

19.   The optimal credit terms involve a trade-off between increased _____ and the cost of carrying additional _____ _____.

20.   _____ policy refers to the manner in which a firm tries to obtain payment from past-due accounts.

21.   Two popular methods for monitoring receivables are _____ _____ and the _____ _____ _____.

22.   Credit sales may be especially profitable if a(n) _____ charge is assessed on accounts receivable.

23.   The most comprehensive picture of a firm's liquidity is obtained by examining its _____ _____, which forecasts a firm's cash inflows and outflows.

24.   _____ _____ _____ refers to the firm's policies regarding target levels for each category of current assets and how current assets will be financed.

25.   A(n) _____ current asset investment policy is one in which relatively large amounts of cash, marketable securities, and inventories are carried, and sales are stimulated by the use of a credit policy that provides liberal financing to customers and a corresponding high level of receivables.

26.   A(n) _____ current asset investment policy is one in which holdings of cash, securities, inventories, and receivables are minimized.

27.   Firms hold cash for two primary reasons: _____ and _____ balances.

28.   _____ _____ _____ defines working capital as inventories plus receivables less payables.

29.   _____ _____ management is a system in which firms are able to start production after an order is received, yet still meet customer delivery requirements, and it builds on the just-in-time method of inventory control.

30.   A typical cash budget consists of three sections: the _____ and _____ worksheet, the cash _____ or _____ section, and the loan requirement or cash surplus section.

31.   The _____ cash balance is the desired cash balance that a firm plans to maintain in order to conduct business.

32. _____ _____ typically provide much lower yields than a firm's operating assets, yet they are often held in sizable amounts and are held for the same reasons firms hold cash.

33. _____-_____ is the practice of purchasing components rather than making them in-house.

34. _____ _____ is defined in terms of the probability of a customer's default.

Conceptual

35. A firm changes its credit policy from 2/10, net 30, to 3/10, net 30. The change is to meet competition, so no increase in sales is expected. The firm's average investment in accounts receivable will probably increase as a result of the change.

    a. True   **b.** False

36. An aging schedule is constructed by a firm to keep track of when its accounts payable are due.

    a. True   **b.** False

37. If a credit policy change increases the firm's accounts receivable, the entire increase must be financed by some source of funds.

    a. True   **b.** False

38. Which of the following actions would not be consistent with good cash management?

    a. Increasing the synchronization of cash flows.
    b. Using lockboxes in funds collection.
    c. Maintaining an average cash balance equal to that required as a compensating balance or that which minimizes total cost.
    d. Minimizing the use of float.
    e. None of the above; all are consistent with good cash management.

39. The costs of a stock-out do *not* include

    a. Disruption of production schedules.
    b. Loss of customer goodwill.
    c. Depreciation and obsolescence.
    d. Loss of sales.
    e. Answers c and d above.

40. The goal of credit policy is to

    a. Minimize bad debt losses.
    b. Minimize DSO.
    c. Maximize sales.
    d. Minimize collection expenses.
    e. Extend credit to the point where marginal profits equal marginal costs.

SELF-TEST PROBLEMS

1. The Mill Company has a daily average collection of checks of $250,000. It takes the company 4 days to convert the checks to cash. Assume a lockbox system could be employed that would reduce the cash conversion period to 3 days. The lockbox system would have a net cost of $25,000 per year, but any additional funds made available could be invested to net 8 percent per year. Should Mill adopt the lockbox system?

    a. Yes; the system would free $250,000 in funds.
    b. Yes; the benefits of the lockbox system exceed the costs.
    c. No; the benefit is only $10,000.
    d. No; the firm would lose $5,000 per year if the system were used.
    e. The benefits and costs are equal; hence the firm is indifferent toward the system.

(The following data apply to the next three Self-Test Problems.)

Simmons Brick Company sells on terms of 3/10, net 30. Gross sales for the year are $1,216,667 and the collections department estimates that 30 percent of the customers pay on the tenth day and take discounts; 40 percent pay on the thirtieth day; and the remaining 30 percent pay, on average, 40 days after the purchase.

2. What is the days sales outstanding?

    a. 10 days   **b.** 13 days   **c.** 20 days   **d.** 27 days   **e.** 40 days

3. What is the current receivables balance?

    a. $60,000   **b.** $70,000   **c.** $75,000   **d.** $80,000   **e.** $90,000

4. What would be the new receivables balance if Simmons toughened up on its collection policy, with the result that all nondiscount customers paid on the thirtieth day?

    a. $60,000   **b.** $70,000   **c.** $75,000   **d.** $80,000   **e.** $90,000

5. Haberdash Inc. last year reported sales of $12 million and an inventory turnover ratio of 3. The company is now adopting a just-in-time inventory system. If the new system is able to reduce the firm's inventory level and increase the firm's inventory turnover ratio to 7.5, while maintaining the same level of sales, how much cash will be freed up?

   a. $2,400,000   **b.** $1,600,000   **c.** $4,000,000   **d.** $3,000,000   **e.** $5,250,000

(The following data apply to the next four Self-Test Problems)

Tauscher Textiles Corporation has an inventory conversion period of 45 days, a receivables collection period of 36 days, and a payables deferral period of 35 days.

6. What is the length of the firm's cash conversion cycle?

   a. 35 days   **b.** 46 days   **c.** 52 days   **d.** 81 days   **e.** 117 days

7. If Tauscher's sales are $4,309,028 and all sales are on credit, what is the firm's investment in accounts receivable?

   a. $325,000   **b.** $375,000   **c.** $425,000   **d.** 500,000   **e.** $575,000

8. How many times per year does Tauscher turn over its inventory?

   a. 3.0   **b.** 5.3   **c.** 7.5   **d.** 8.1   **e.** 9.2

9. If the firm's sales are $4,309,028, how much inventory is on the firm's balance sheet?

   a. $531,250   **b.** $350,175   **c.** $410,225   **d.** $500,790   **e.** $480,000

(The following data apply to the next two Self-Test Problems.)

Ridgdill Industries currently has $30,250 in cash, $60,000 in accounts receivable, $85,000 in inventories, $12,500 in accrued liabilities, and $90,000 in accounts payable on its balance sheet. The firm's production manager has determined that cost of goods sold account for 75% of the sales revenue produced. Furthermore, the firm has determined that the length of the firm's cash conversion cycle is 20 days.

10. What is Ridgdill's annual sales?

   a. $400,000   **b.** $428,333   **c.** $456,250   **d.** $478,125   **e.** $500,000

11. The firm's production manager has determined that through negotiation with it suppliers, the firm could reduce the ratio of the cost of goods sold to sales down to 65%, and thus reduce its cash conversion cycle time. However, the firm would then take this opportunity to use cash to reduce its accounts payable. The firm realizes that reducing accounts payable increases the cash conversion cycle time, but it is more concerned with pleasing its creditors, who are unhappy with the firm's liquidity position. None of these changes is expected to have any impact upon sales. If the firm reduces accounts payable enough to improve the current ratio to 2.25, what would be the length of the firm's cash conversion cycle?

a. 32.00 **b.** 35.52 **c.** 25.00 **d.** 28.75 **e.** 23.25

ANSWERS TO SELF-TEST QUESTIONS

1.	working capital	18.	period; cash discount
2.	Net; current; liabilities	19.	sales; accounts receivable
3.	minimize; cash	20.	Collection
4.	inflows; outflows	21.	aging schedules; days sales outstanding
5.	Compensating		
6.	collection; payment	22.	carrying
7.	lockbox	23.	cash budget
8.	float	24.	Working capital policy
9.	supplies; raw materials; work-in-process; finished goods	25.	relaxed
		26.	restricted
10.	lowest cost	27.	transactions; compensating
11.	increase; carrying	28.	Zero working capital
12.	inversely	29.	Demand flow (based)
13.	just-in-time	30.	collections; purchases; gain; loss
14.	Accounts receivable	31.	target
15.	volume; sales; collections	32.	Marketable securities
16.	credit policy	33.	Out-sourcing
17.	sales	34.	Credit quality

35. b. No new customers are being generated. The current customers pay either on Day 10 or Day 30. The increase in trade discount will induce some customers who are now paying on Day 30 to pay on Day 10. Thus, the days sales outstanding is shortened which, in turn, will cause a decline in accounts receivable.

36. b. The aging schedule breaks down accounts receivable according to how long they have been outstanding.

37. b. Receivables are based on sales price, which presumably includes some profit. Only the actual cash outlays associated with receivables must be financed. The remainder, or profit, appears on the balance sheet as an increase in retained earnings.

38. d. Management should try to maximize float.

39. c. Depreciation and obsolescence are inventory carrying costs.

40. e. The goal of credit policy is to maximize overall profits. This is achieved when the marginal profits equal the marginal costs.

SOLUTIONS TO SELF-TEST PROBLEMS

1. d. Currently, Mill has 4($250,000) = $1,000,000 in unavailable collections. If lockboxes were used, this could be reduced to $750,000. Thus, $250,000 would be available to invest at 8 percent, resulting in an annual return of 0.08($250,000) = $20,000. If the system costs $25,000, Mill would lose $5,000 per year by adopting the system.

2. d. 0.3(10 days) + 0.4(30 days) + 0.3(40 days) = 27 days.

3. e. Receivables = (DSO)(Sales/365) = 27($1,216,667/365) = $90,000.

4. d. New days sales outstanding = 0.3(10) + 0.7(30) = 24 days.
Sales per day = $1,216,667/365 = $3,333.33.
Receivables = $3,333.33(24 days) = $80,000.00.

Thus, the average receivables would drop from $90,000 to $80,000. Furthermore, sales may decline as a result of the tighter credit and reduce receivables even more. Also, some additional customers may now take discounts, which would further reduce receivables.

5. a. Inventory turnover ratio$_{Old}$ = Sales/Inventory
$$3 = \$12,000,000/I$$
$$3I = \$12,000,000$$
$$I = \$4,000,000.$$

$$\text{Inventory turnover ratio}_{New} = \text{Sales/Inventory}$$
$$7.5 = \$12,000,000/I$$
$$I = \$12,000,000/7.5$$
$$I = \$1,600,000.$$

Cash freed up = $4,000,000 − $1,600,000 = $2,400,000.

6. b. Cash conversion cycle = 45 + 36 − 35 = 46 days.

7. c. $$\text{DSO} = \frac{\text{AR}}{\text{Sales/365}}$$
$$36 = \frac{\text{AR}}{\$4,309,028/365}$$
$$\text{AR} = \$425,000.$$

8. d. Inventory turnover $= 365/45$
$$= 8.1\times.$$

9. a. Inventory conversion period $= \dfrac{\text{Inventory}}{\text{Sales/365}}$
$$45 = \frac{I}{\$4,309,028/365}$$
$$I = \$531,250.$$

10. c. Setting up the formula for the cash conversion cycle, sales can be calculated as follows:

$$\text{CCC} = \frac{\text{Acct. Rec.}}{\text{Avg. Daily Sales}} + \frac{\text{Inv.}}{\text{Avg. Daily Sales}} - \frac{\text{Acct. Pay.}}{\text{Avg. Daily COGS}}$$
$$20 = (\$60,000/\text{ADS}) + (\$85,000/\text{ADS}) - (\$90,000/0.75\text{ADS})$$
$$20 = (\$60,000/\text{ADS}) + (\$85,000/\text{ADS}) - (\$120,000/\text{ADS})$$
$$20 = \$25,000/\text{ADS}$$
$$20(\text{ADS}) = \$25,000$$
$$\text{ADS} = \$1,250.00.$$

Therefore, annual sales equal $456,250 ($1,250 × 365 = $456,250).

11.   b.   On the basis of the information given, the firm's current assets equal $175,250 ($30,250 + $60,000 + $85,000). Therefore, for its current ratio to increase to 2.25, it must reduce accounts payable to a level such that current liabilities total $77,889 ($175,250/2.25). If accrued liabilities on the balance sheet equal $12,500, accounts payable must be reduced to $65,389 ($77,889 − $12,500). The firm's new average daily cost of goods sold would equal $1,250 × 0.65 = $812.50. Combined with the original information, the new CCC can be determined as follows:

CCC = (AR/Avg. Daily Sales) + (Inv/Avg. Daily Sales) − (AP/Avg. Daily COGS)
CCC = ($60,000/$1,250) + ($85,000/$1,250) − ($65,389/$812.50)
CCC = 48.00 + 68.00 − 80.48
CCC = 35.52 days.

CHAPTER 16
FINANCING CURRENT ASSETS

LEARNING OBJECTIVES

● Identify and distinguish among the three different current asset financing policies.

● Briefly explain the advantages and disadvantages of short-term financing.

● List the four major types of short-term funds.

● Distinguish between free and costly trade credit, calculate both the nominal and effective annual percentage costs of not taking discounts, given specific credit terms, and explain what stretching accounts payable is and how it reduces the cost of trade credit.

● Describe the importance of short-term bank loans as a source of short-term financing and discuss some of the key features of bank loans.

● Calculate the effective interest rate for (1) simple interest, (2) discount interest, (3) add-on interest loans; and explain the effect of compensating balances on the effective cost of a loan.

● List some factors that should be considered when choosing a bank.

● Explain why large, financially strong corporations issue commercial paper, and why this source of short-term credit is typically less reliable than bank loans if the firm gets into financial difficulties.

● Define what a "secured" loan is and what type of collateral can be used to secure a loan.

OVERVIEW

Working capital policy involves decisions relating to current assets, including decisions about financing them. Since about half of the typical firm's capital is invested in current assets, working capital policy and management are important to the firm and its shareholders.

In fact, about 60 percent of a financial manager's time is devoted to working capital policy and management, and many finance students' first assignments on the job will involve working capital. For these reasons, working capital policy is a vitally important topic.

OUTLINE

A firm's current asset levels and financing requirements rise and fall with business cycles and seasonal trends. At the peak of such cycles, businesses carry their maximum amounts of current assets. Similar fluctuations in financing needs can occur over these cycles, typically, financing needs contract during recessions, and they expand during booms.

■ Current assets rarely drop to zero, and this fact has led to the development of the idea of *permanent current assets*. These are the current assets on hand at the low point of the cycle.

■ *Temporary current assets* are current assets that fluctuate with seasonal or cyclical variations in sales.

■ The manner in which the permanent and temporary current assets are financed is called the firm's *current asset financing policy*.
   □ The *maturity matching, or "self-liquidating," approach* matches asset and liability maturities.
      • Defined as a moderate current asset financing policy, this would use permanent financing for permanent assets (permanent current assets and fixed assets), and use short-term financing to cover seasonal and/or cyclical temporary assets (fluctuating current assets).
      • This strategy minimizes the risk that the firm will be unable to pay off its maturing obligations.
      • Two factors prevent exact maturity matching: (1) there is uncertainty about the lives of assets, and (2) some common equity must be used, and common equity has no maturity.
      • In practice, firms don't finance each specific asset with a type of capital that has a maturity equal to the asset's life. However, academic studies do show that most firms tend to finance short-term assets from short-term sources and long-term assets from long-term sources.
   □ The *aggressive approach* is used by a firm that finances all of its fixed assets with long-term capital but part of its permanent current assets with short-term, nonspontaneous credit.

☐ A *conservative approach* would be to use permanent capital to meet some of the cyclical demand, and then hold the temporary surpluses as marketable securities at the trough of the cycle (storing liquidity). Here, the amount of permanent financing exceeds permanent assets.

● The firm uses a small amount of short-term, nonspontaneous credit to meet its peak requirements, but it also meets a part of its seasonal needs by storing liquidity in the form of marketable securities.

☐ The three possible financing policies above are distinguished by the relative amounts of short-term debt used under each policy.

There are advantages and disadvantages to the use of short-term financing.

■ A short-term loan can be obtained much faster than long-term credit.

■ Short-term debt is more flexible since it may be repaid if the firm's financing requirements decline. If its needs for funds are seasonal or cyclical, a firm may not want to commit itself to long-term debt for three reasons.

☐ Long-term debt can be retired, but this will probably involve a prepayment penalty.

☐ Flotation costs are higher for long-term debt than for short-term credit.

☐ Long-term loan agreements always contain provisions, or covenants, that constrain the firm's future actions.

■ Short-term interest rates are normally lower than long-term rates, since the yield curve is normally upward sloping. Financing with short-term credit usually results in lower interest costs.

■ Short-term debt is generally more risky than long-term debt for two reasons.

☐ Short-term interest rates fluctuate widely, while long-term rates tend to be more stable and predictable. The interest rate on short-term debt could increase dramatically over a short period.

☐ Short-term debt comes due every few months. If a firm does not have the cash to repay debt when it comes due, and if it cannot refinance the loan, it may be forced into bankruptcy.

Different types of short-term funds have different characteristics. One source of short-term funds is accrued wages and taxes, which increase and decrease spontaneously as a firm's operations expand and contract.

■ This type of debt is "free" in the sense that no interest is paid on funds raised through accrued liabilities.

■ A firm cannot ordinarily control its accrued liabilities.
  ☐ The timing of wage payments is set by economic forces and industry custom, while tax payment dates are established by law.

Accounts payable, or trade credit, is the largest single category of short-term debt. Trade credit is a "spontaneous" source of funds because it arises from ordinary business transactions. Most firms make purchases on credit, recording the debt as an account payable.

■ Lengthening the credit period, as well as expanding sales and purchases, generates additional financing.

■ The cost of trade credit is made up of discounts lost by not paying invoices within the discount period.
  ☐ For example, if credit terms are 2/10, net 30, the cost of 20 additional days' credit is 2 percent of the dollar value of the purchases made.
  ☐ The following equation may be used to calculate the nominal percentage cost, on an annual basis, of not taking discounts:

$$\frac{\text{Nominal annual}}{\text{percentage cost}} = \frac{\text{Discount \%}}{100 - \text{Discount \%}} \times \frac{365\,\text{days}}{\text{Days credit is}\ -\ \text{Discount}} .$$
$$\text{outstanding}\quad\text{period}$$

  ☐ For example, the nominal cost of not taking the discount when the credit terms are 2/10, net 30, is

$$\frac{\text{Nominal annual}}{\text{percentage cost}} = \frac{2}{98} \times \frac{365}{30-10} = 0.0204(18.25) = 0.3724 = 37.24\%.$$

  ☐ The nominal annual cost formula does not consider compounding so, in effective annual interest terms, the rate is even higher. Note that the first term on the right-hand side of the nominal cost equation is the periodic cost, and the second term is the number of periods per year. Thus, the effective annual rate is:

$$(1.0204)^{18.25} - 1.0 = 1.4459 - 1.0 = 44.59\%.$$

■ Trade credit can be divided into two components: *Free trade credit* is that credit received during the discount period. *Costly trade credit* is obtained by foregoing discounts. This costly component should be used only when it is less expensive than funds obtained from other sources.
  ☐ Financial managers should always use the free component, but they should use the costly component only after analyzing the cost of this capital to make sure that it is less than the cost of funds that could be obtained from other sources.

- ☐ The cost of not taking discounts is relatively expensive, so stronger firms will avoid using it.
- ☐ Competitive conditions may permit firms to do better than the stated credit terms by taking discounts beyond the discount period or by simply paying late. Such practices, called *stretching accounts payable*, reduce the cost of trade credit, but they also result in poor relationships with suppliers.

Bank loans appear on a firm's balance sheet as notes payable and represent another important source of short-term financing. Bank loans are not generated spontaneously but must be negotiated and renewed on a regular basis.

- ■ About two-thirds of all bank loans mature in a year or less, although banks do make longer-term loans.

- ■ When a firm obtains a bank loan, a *promissory note* specifying the following items is signed: the amount borrowed, the interest rate, the repayment schedule, any collateral offered as security, and other terms and conditions to which the bank and the borrower have agreed.
  - ☐ When the note is signed, the bank credits the borrower's checking account with the funds, so on the borrower's balance sheet both cash and notes payable increase.

- ■ Banks normally require regular borrowers to maintain *compensating balances* equal to 10 to 20 percent of the face amount of the loan. Such required balances increase the effective interest rate on the loan.

- ■ A *line of credit* is an informal agreement between a bank and a borrower indicating the maximum credit the bank will extend to the borrower.

- ■ A *revolving credit agreement* is a formal line of credit often used by large firms. Normally, the borrower will pay the bank a commitment fee to compensate the bank for guaranteeing that the funds will be available. This fee is paid in addition to the regular interest charge on funds actually borrowed.
  - ☐ As a general rule, the interest rate on "revolvers" is pegged to the prime rate, the T-bill rate, or some other market rate, so the cost of the loan varies over time as interest rates change.
  - ☐ Note that a revolving credit agreement is very similar to an informal line of credit, but with an important difference: The bank has a *legal obligation* to honor a revolving credit agreement, and for this it receives a commitment fee.
    - ● Neither the legal obligation nor the fee exists under the informal line of credit.
  - ☐ Often, a line of credit will have a *clean-up clause* that requires the borrower to reduce the loan balance to zero at least once a year.

- A line of credit typically is designed to help finance negative operating cash flows that are incurred as a natural part of a company's business cycle, not as a source of permanent capital.

The interest cost of loans will vary for different types of borrowers and for all borrowers over time. Rates charged will vary depending on economic conditions, the risk of the borrower, and the size of the loan. If a firm can qualify as a "prime credit" because of its size and financial strength, it can borrow at the prime rate, which at one time was the lowest rate banks charged. Interest charges on bank loans can be calculated in one of several ways listed below.

- *Regular, or simple, interest.* The nominal interest rate is divided by the number of days in the year to get the rate per day. This rate is then multiplied by the actual number of days during the specific payment period, and then times the amount of the loan.

$$\text{Interest rate per day} = \frac{\text{Nominal rate}}{\text{Days in year}}.$$

Interest charge for period = (Days in period)(Rate per day)(Amount of loan).

- ☐ The effective rate on the loan depends on how frequently interest must be paid—the more frequently, the higher the effective rate.
  - The best procedure to use is to lay out all the cash flows on a time line and solve for the interest rate.

- *Discount interest.* Under this method, the bank deducts interest in advance (*discounts* the loan). The effective annual rate of interest on a discount loan is always higher than the rate on an otherwise simple interest loan.
  - ☐ To find the effective interest rate on a discount loan, lay out all the cash flows on a time line (remembering to subtract out the interest paid in advance) and solve for the interest rate.
  - ☐ The firm actually receives less than the face amount of the loan.

  Funds received = Face amount of loan (1.0 − Nominal interest rate).

  - ☐ The face amount of the loan can be calculated as follows:

$$\text{Face amount of loan} = \frac{\text{Funds received}}{1.0 - \text{Nominal rate (decimal)}}.$$

  - ☐ Shortening the period of a discount loan lowers the effective rate of interest. This occurs because there is a delay in paying interest relative to a longer-term discount loan.

■ If the bank requires a compensating balance, and if the amount of the required balance exceeds the amount the firm would normally hold on deposit, this has the effect of raising the effective rate on the loan.

■ *Installment loans: add-on interest.* Interest charges are calculated and then added on to the amount received to determine the loan's face value, which is paid off in equal installments.

    ☐ The borrower has use of the full amount of the funds received only until the first installment is paid.

    ☐ The approximate annual rate is double the stated rate, because the average amount of the loan outstanding is only about half the face amount borrowed.

$$\text{Approximate annual rate}_{\text{Add-on}} = \frac{\text{Interest paid}}{(\text{Amount received})/2}.$$

    ☐ To determine the effective rate of an add-on loan, lay out all the cash flows on a time line and solve for the interest rate.

    ☐ The payments are calculated as the total amount to be repaid, which consists of principal plus the total interest divided by 12.

■ *Annual percentage rate (APR)* is a rate reported by banks and other lenders on loans when the effective rate exceeds the nominal rate of interest.

$$\text{APR rate} = (\text{Periods per year})(\text{Rate per period}).$$

Choosing a bank involves an analysis of the following variables:

■ *Willingness to assume risks.* Some banks are quite conservative, while others are more willing to make risky loans.

■ *Advice and counsel.* A bank's ability to provide counsel is particularly important to firms in their formative years.

■ *Loyalty to customers.* This variable deals with a bank's willingness to support customers during difficult economic times.

■ *Specialization.* A bank may specialize in making loans to a particular type of business. Firms should seek out a bank which is familiar with their particular type of business.

■ *Maximum loan size.* This is an important consideration for large companies when establishing a borrowing relationship because most banks cannot lend to a single customer more than 15 percent of the bank's capital accounts.

- *Merchant banking.* Originally the term applied to banks that not only loaned depositors' money but also provided its customers with equity capital and financial advice. In recent years, commercial banks have been attempting to get back into merchant banking, in part because their foreign competitors offer such services, and U. S. banks compete with foreign banks for multinational corporations' business.

- *Other services.* The availability of services such as providing cash management services, assisting with electronic funds transfers, and helping firms obtain foreign exchange should also be taken into account when selecting a bank.

Commercial paper, another source of short-term credit, is an unsecured promissory note. It is generally sold to other business firms, to insurance companies, to banks, and to money market mutual funds. Only large, financially strong firms are able to tap the commercial paper market.

- Maturities of commercial paper range from a few days to nine months, with an average of about five months.
  - □ Interest rates on prime commercial paper generally range from 1 1/2 to 3 percentage points below the stated prime rate, and about 1/8 to 1/2 of a percentage point above the T-bill rate. However, rates fluctuate daily with supply and demand conditions in the marketplace.
  - □ Using commercial paper permits a corporation to tap a wide range of credit sources, including financial institutions outside its own area and industrial corporations across the country, and this can reduce interest costs.
  - □ A disadvantage of the commercial paper market vis-a-vis bank loans is that the impersonal nature of the market makes it difficult for firms to use commercial paper at times when they are in temporary financial distress.

For a strong firm, borrowing on an unsecured basis is generally cheaper and simpler than on a secured loan basis because of the administrative costs associated with the use of security. However, firms often find that they can borrow only if they put up some type of collateral to protect the lender, or that by using security they can borrow at a much lower rate. Most secured short-term business borrowing involves the use of accounts receivable and inventories as collateral. Web Appendix 16A discusses secured short-term financing in more detail.

SELF-TEST QUESTIONS

Definitional

1. In the maturity matching approach to working capital financing, permanent assets should be financed with _____ capital, while _____ assets should be financed with short-term credit.

2. Some firms use short-term financing to finance permanent assets. This approach maximizes _____ _____, but also has the _____ _____.

3. Short-term borrowing provides more _____ for firms that are uncertain about their _____ borrowing needs.

4. Short-term borrowing will be less expensive than borrowing long-term if the yield curve is _____ sloping.

5. Short-term interest rates fluctuate _____ than long-term rates.

6. _____ wages and taxes are a common source of short-term credit. However, most firms have little control over the _____ of these accounts.

7. Accounts payable, or _____ _____, is the largest single source of short-term credit for most businesses.

8. Trade credit is a(n) _____ source of funds in the sense that it automatically increases when sales increase.

9. Trade credit can be divided into two components: _____ trade credit and _____ trade credit.

10. Free trade credit is that credit received during the _____ period.

11. _____ trade credit should only be used when the cost of the trade credit is less than the cost of alternative sources.

12. The instrument signed when bank credit is obtained is called a(n) _____ _____.

13. Many banks require borrowers to keep _____ _____ on deposit with the bank equal to 10 or 20 percent of the loan's face value.

14. Maturities on commercial paper generally range from a few days to _____ months, with interest rates set about 1 1/2 to 3 percentage points _____ the _____ rate.

15. A(n) _____ loan is one in which collateral such as _____ or _____ have been pledged in support of the loan.

16. A(n) _____ ____ _____ is an informal agreement between a bank and a borrower as to the maximum loan that will be permitted.

17. The fee paid to a bank to secure a revolving credit agreement is known as a(n) _____ fee.

18. If interest charges are deducted in advance, this is known as _____ interest, and the effective rate is higher than the _____ interest rate.

19. With a(n) _____ loan, the average amount of the usable funds during the loan period is equal to approximately _____-_____ of the face amount of the loan.

20. Commercial paper can only be issued by _____, _____ _____ firms.

21. _____ current assets are those current assets on hand at the low point of a business cycle.

22. Seasonal current assets are defined as _____ current assets.

23. Competitive conditions may permit firms to do better than the stated credit terms by taking discounts beyond the discount period or by simply paying late; such practices are called _____ _____ _____.

24. A(n) _____ _____ _____ is a formal line of credit often used by large firms.

25. _____ the period of a discount loan lowers the effective rate of interest.

26. _____ _____ _____ is a rate reported by banks and other lenders on loans when the effective rate exceeds the nominal rate of interest, and it is calculated as the number of periods per year times the rate per period.

27. A(n) _____ _____ to financing is used by a firm that finances all of its fixed assets with long-term capital but part of its permanent current assets with short-term, nonspontaneous credit.

28.   A(n) _____ _____ to financing would be to use permanent capital to meet some of the cyclical demand, and then hold the temporary surpluses as marketable securities at the trough of the cycle.

29.   The manner in which the permanent and temporary current assets are financed is called the firm's _____ _____ _____ _____.

30.   _____ _____ appear on a firm's balance sheet as notes payable and represent another important source of short-term financing.

Conceptual

31.   The matching of asset and liability maturities is considered desirable because this strategy minimizes interest rate risk.

   a. True   **b.** False

32.   Accrued liabilities are "free" in the sense that no interest must be paid on these funds.

   a. True   **b.** False

33.   The effect of compensating balances is to decrease the effective interest rate of a loan.

   a. True   **b.** False

34.   Which of the following statements concerning commercial paper is most correct?

   a. Commercial paper is secured debt of large, financially strong firms.
   b. Commercial paper is sold primarily to individual investors.
   c. Maturities of commercial paper generally exceed nine months.
   d. Commercial paper interest rates are typically 1 1/2 to 3 percentage points above the stated prime rate.
   e. None of the above statements is correct.

35. Which of the following statements is most correct?

a. If you had just been hired as Working Capital Manager for a firm with but one stockholder, and that stockholder told you that she had all the money she could possibly use, hence that her primary operating goal was to avoid even the remotest possibility of bankruptcy, then you should set the firm's working capital financing policy on the basis of the "Maturity Matching, or Self-Liquidating, Approach."

b. Due to the existence of positive maturity risk premiums, at most times short-term debt carries lower interest rates than long-term debt. Therefore, if a company finances primarily with short-term as opposed to long-term debt, its expected TIE ratio, hence its overall riskiness, will be lower than if it finances with long-term debt. Therefore, the more conservative the firm, the greater its reliance on short-term debt.

c. If a firm buys on terms of 2/10, net 30, and pays on the 30th day, then its accounts payable may be thought of as consisting of some "free" and some "costly" trade credit. Since the percentage cost of the costly trade credit is lowered if the payment period is reduced, the firm should try to pay earlier than on Day 30, say on Day 25.

d. Suppose a firm buys on terms of 2/10, net 30, but it normally pays on Day 60. Disregarding any "image" effects, it should, if it can borrow from the bank at an effective rate of 14 percent, take out a bank loan and start taking discounts.

e. Each of the above statements is false.

SELF-TEST PROBLEMS

(The following data apply to the next three Self-Test Problems.)

A firm buys on terms of 2/10, net 30, but generally does not pay until 40 days after the invoice date. Its purchases total $1,095,000 per year.

1. How much "non-free" trade credit does the firm use on average each year?

a. $120,000   b. $90,000   c. $60,000   d. $30,000   e. $20,000

2. What is the nominal cost of the "non-free" trade credit?

a. 16.2%   b. 19.4%   c. 21.9%   d. 24.8%   e. 27.9%

3. What is the effective cost rate of the costly credit?

a. 16.2%   b. 19.4%   c. 21.9%   d. 24.8%   e. 27.9%

4. Lawton Pipelines Inc. has developed plans for a new pump that will allow more economical operation of the company's oil pipelines. Management estimates that $2,400,000 will be required to put this new pump into operation. Funds can be obtained from a bank at 10 percent discount interest, or the company can finance the expansion by delaying payment to its suppliers. Presently, Lawton purchases under terms of 2/10, net 40, but management believes payment could be delayed 30 additional days without penalty; that is, payment could be made in 70 days. Which means of financing should Lawton use? (Use the nominal cost of trade credit.)

    a. Trade credit, since the cost is about 12.41 percent.
    b. Trade credit, since the cost is about 3.30 percentage points less than the bank loan.
    c. Bank loan, since the cost is about 1.30 percentage points less than trade credit.
    d. Bank loan, since the cost is about 3.30 percentage points less than trade credit.
    e. The firm could use either since the costs are the same.

    (The following data apply to the next four Self-Test Problems.)

    You plan to borrow $10,000 from your bank, which offers to lend you the money at a 10 percent nominal, or stated, rate on a 1-year loan.

5. What is the effective interest rate if the loan is a discount loan?

    a. 11.1%   b. 13.3%   c. 15.0%   d. 17.5%   e. 20.0%

6. What is the approximate interest rate if the loan is an add-on interest loan with 12 monthly payments?

    a. 11.1%   b. 13.3%   c. 15.0%   d. 17.5%   e. 20.0%

7. What is the effective interest rate if the loan is a discount loan with a 15 percent compensating balance?

    a. 11.1%   b. 13.3%   c. 15.0%   d. 17.5%   e. 20.0%

8. Under the terms of the previous problem, how much would you have to borrow to have the use of $10,000?

    a. $10,000   b. $11,111   c. $12,000   d. $13,333   e. $15,000

9. Gibbs Corporation needs to raise $1,000,000 for one year to supply working capital to a new store. Gibbs buys from its suppliers on terms of 4/10, net 90, and it currently pays on the 10th day and takes discounts, but it could forego discounts, pay on the 90th day, and get the needed $1,000,000 in the form of costly trade credit. Alternatively, Gibbs could borrow from its bank on a 15 percent discount interest rate basis. What is the effective annual cost rate of the lower cost source?

a. 20.17%　　　**b.** 18.75%　　　**c.** 17.65%　　　**d.** 18.25%　　　**e.** 19.50%

ANSWERS TO SELF-TEST QUESTIONS

1.	permanent (long-term); temporary		16.	line of credit
2.	expected return; greatest risk		17.	commitment
3.	flexibility; future		18.	discount; simple (or nominal or stated)
4.	upward		19.	installment; one-half
5.	more		20.	large; financially strong
6.	Accrued; size (amount)		21.	Permanent
7.	trade credit		22.	temporary
8.	spontaneous		23.	stretching accounts payable
9.	free; costly		24.	revolving credit agreement
10.	discount		25.	Shortening
11.	Costly		26.	Annual percentage rate
12.	promissory note		27.	aggressive approach
13.	compensating balances		28.	conservative approach
14.	nine; below; prime		29.	current asset financing policy
15.	secured; receivables; inventory		30.	Bank loans

31. b. The matching of maturities minimizes default risk, or the risk that the firm will be unable to pay off its maturing obligations, and reinvestment rate risk, or the risk that the firm will have to roll over the debt at a higher rate.

32. a. Neither workers nor the IRS require interest payments on wages and taxes that are not paid as soon as they are earned.

33. b. Compensating balances increase the effective rate because the firm is required to maintain excess non-interest-bearing balances.

34. e. Commercial paper is the unsecured debt of strong firms. It generally has a maturity from a few days to nine months and is sold primarily to other corporations and financial institutions. Rates on commercial paper are typically below the prime rate.

35. d. Statement a is false; the conservative approach would be the safest current asset financing policy. Statement b is false; short-term debt fluctuates more than long-term debt, thus, the greater the firm's reliance on short-term debt, the riskier the firm. Statement c is false; it makes no difference in the cost if the firm pays on Day 25 versus Day 30 in this instance. Statement d is true; if the firm can "stretch" its payables the nominal cost is 14.90% (the effective cost is 15.89%). Thus, the firm should obtain the 14% bank loan to take discounts as this is the lowest cost to the firm.

SOLUTIONS TO SELF-TEST PROBLEMS

1. b. $1,095,000/365 = $3,000 in purchases per day. Typically, there will be $3,000(40) = $120,000 of accounts payable on the books at any given time. Of this, $3,000(10) = $30,000 is "free" credit, while $3,000(30) = $90,000 is "non-free" credit.

2. d. $$\text{Nominal cost} = \frac{\text{Discount \%}}{100 - \text{Discount}} \times \frac{365}{\text{Days credit is } - \text{Discount}}$$
$$\text{outstanding} \quad \text{period}$$

$$= \frac{2}{100 - 2} \times \frac{365}{40 - 10} = \frac{2}{98} \times \frac{365}{30} = 24.8\%.$$

3. e. The periodic rate is 2/98 = 2.04%, and there are 365/30 = 12.1667 periods per year. Thus, the effective annual rate is 27.9 percent:

$$\left(1 + \frac{k_{\text{Nom}}}{m}\right)^{12} - 1.0 = (1.0204)^{12.1667} - 1.0$$

$$= 1.2786 - 1.0 = 0.2786 = 27.9\%.$$

4. c. $$\text{Face amount} = \frac{\$2,400,000}{1 - 0.10}$$
$$= \$2,666,667.$$

Interest to be deducted in advance = $0.10 \times \$2,666,667 = \$266,667.$

```
        0                                    1
        ├────────────────────────────────────┤
   2,666,667                            -2,666,667
    -266,667
   2,400,000
```

Using a financial calculator, enter N = 1, PV = 2400000, PMT = 0, and FV = -2666667; and then solve for I to get the effective cost of the loan, 11.11%.

Credit terms are 2/10, net 40, but delaying payments 30 additional days is the equivalent of 2/10, net 70. Assuming no penalty, the nominal cost is as follows:

$$\text{Nominal cost} = \frac{\text{Discount \%}}{100 - \text{Discount \%}} \times \frac{365}{\text{Days credit is} - \text{Discount}}$$
$$\text{outstanding} \quad \text{period}$$

$$= \frac{2}{100 - 2} \times \frac{365}{70 - 10} = \frac{2}{98} \times \frac{365}{60} = 0.0204(6.0833) = 12.41\%.$$

Therefore, the loan cost is 1.30 percentage points less than trade credit.

5. a. Face amount $= \dfrac{\$10,000}{1 - 0.10}$
$= \$11,111.$

Interest to be deducted in advance $= 0.1 \times \$11,111 = \$1,111.$

```
        0                                    1
        ├────────────────────────────────────┤
     11,111                              -11,111
     -1,111
     10,000
```

Using a financial calculator, enter N = 1, PV = 10000, PMT = 0, and FV = -11111; and then solve for I to get the effective cost of the loan, 11.11%.

6. e. Approximate annual rate $= \$1,000/\$5,000 = 20.0\%.$

7. b. Face amount of loan $= \dfrac{\$10,000}{1 - 0.10 - 0.15}$
$= \$13,333.$

Interest to be deducted in advance $= 0.1 \times \$13,333 = \$1,333.$
Compensating balance $= 0.15 \times \$13,333 = \$2,000.$

```
      0                                      1
      ├──────────────────────────────────────┤
   13,333                                 -13,333
   -1,333                                  +2,000
   -2,000                                 -11,333
   10,000
```

Using a financial calculator, enter N = 1, PV = 10000, PMT = 0, and FV = -11333; and then solve for I to get the effective cost of the loan, 13.33%.

8. d. $\dfrac{\$10,000}{1-0.15-0.10} = \$13,333.$

0.15($13,333) = $2,000 is required for the compensating balance, and 0.10($13,333) = $1,333 is required for the immediate interest payment.

9. c. Accounts payable:
Nominal cost = (4/96)(365/80) = 0.04167(4.5625) = 19.01%.
EAR cost = $(1.04167)^{4.5625} - 1.0 = 20.47\%.$

Cost of notes payable:

Face amount of loan $= \dfrac{\$1,000,000}{1-0.15}$

$= \$1,176,471.$

Interest to be deducted in advance = 0.15 × $1,176,471 = $176,471.

```
      0                                      1
      ├──────────────────────────────────────┤
  1,176,471                              -1,176,471
   -176,471
  1,000,000
```

Using a financial calculator, enter N = 1, PV = 1000000, PMT = 0, and FV = -1176471; and then solve for I to get the effective cost of the loan, 17.65%.

- Briefly explain the following terms: mission statement, corporate scope, corporate purpose, corporate objectives, and corporate strategies.

- Briefly explain what operating plans are.

- Identify the six steps in the financial planning process.

- List the advantages of computerized financial planning models over "pencil-and-paper" calculations.

- Discuss the importance of sales forecasts in the financial planning process, and why managers construct pro forma financial statements.

- Briefly explain the steps involved in the percent of sales method.

- Calculate additional funds needed (AFN), using both the projected financial statement approach and the formula method.

- Identify other techniques for forecasting financial statements discussed in the text and explain when they should be used.

OVERVIEW

Managers and investors need to understand how to forecast future results. Managers use pro forma, or projected, statements and use them in four ways. First, by looking at projected statements, managers can assess whether the firm's anticipated performance is in line with the firm's own internal targets and with investors' expectations. Second, pro forma statements can be used to estimate the impact of proposed operating changes. Third, managers use pro forma statements to anticipate the firm's future financing needs, and then arrange the necessary financing. Finally, projected financial statements are used to estimate free cash flows, which determine the company's overall value. Managers forecast free cash flows under different operating plans, forecast their capital requirements, and then choose the plan that maximizes shareholder value. Security analysts make the same types of projections as managers, and influence investors, who determine the future of managers.

In this chapter we explain how to create and use pro forma statements, beginning with the strategic plan, the foundation for pro forma statements. We discuss how firms use computerized financial planning models in the financial planning process. Then we focus on three key elements of the financial plan: (1) the sales forecast, (2) pro forma financial statements, and (3) the external financing plan.

OUTLINE

Value creation is impossible unless a company has a well-articulated plan. Most companies have a mission statement, a condensed version of a firm's strategic plan.

■   *Strategic plans* and *mission statements* usually begin with a statement of the overall *corporate purpose.*
  □ It is increasingly common for U.S. companies to state that their key corporate purpose is to maximize stockholder value.

■   The *corporate scope* defines a firm's lines of business and geographic area of operations.
  □ Several recent studies have found that the market tends to value focused firms more highly than it does diversified firms.

■   *Corporate objectives* set forth specific goals for management to attain, which can be specified both in qualitative and quantitative terms.
  □ Most companies have multiple objectives, and revise these as business conditions change.

■   Once a firm has defined its purpose, scope, and objectives, it must develop a strategy for achieving its goals.
  □ *Corporate strategies* are broad approaches rather than detailed plans.
  □ Corporate strategies should be both attainable and compatible with the firm's purpose, scope, and objectives.

Operating plans can be developed for any time horizon, but most companies use a five-year horizon. The plan is intended to provide detailed implementation guidance, based on the corporate strategy, to help meet the corporate objectives. It explains in considerable detail who is responsible for a particular function, when specific tasks are to be accomplished, sales and profit targets, and the like.

■ Large multidivisional companies break down their operating plans by division. Each division has its own goals, mission, and plan for meeting its objectives, and these plans are then consolidated to form the corporate plan.

The financial planning process can be divided into six steps: (1) Development of projected financial statements and analysis of effects on ratios, (2) determination of the funds needed to support the five-year plan, (3) forecast of funds availability over the next five years, (4) establishment and maintenance of a system of controls governing the allocation and use of funds within the firm, (5) development of procedures for adjusting the basic plan, and (6) establishment of a performance-based management compensation system.

Although the type of financial forecasting described in this chapter can be done with a hand calculator, virtually all corporate forecasts are made using computerized forecasting models. Most models are based on spreadsheet programs, such as *Microsoft Excel*.

■ Spreadsheets have two major advantages over pencil-and-paper calculations.
  ☐ It is much faster to construct a spreadsheet model than to make a "by-hand" forecast if the forecast period extends beyond a year or two.
  ☐ A spreadsheet model can recalculate the projected financial statements and ratios almost instantaneously when one of the input variables is changed, thus making it easy for managers to determine the effects of changes in variables such as sales.

The sales forecast generally begins with a review of sales during the past five to ten years.

■ The *sales forecast* is a forecast of a firm's unit and dollar sales for some future period, and it is generally based on recent sales trends plus forecasts of the economic prospects for the nation, region, industry, and so forth.

■ If the sales forecast is off, the consequences can be serious. An accurate sales forecast is critical to the firm's well being.

Once sales have been forecasted, future balance sheets and income statements must be forecast. The most commonly used technique is the percent of sales method, which begins with the sales forecast, expressed as an annual growth rate in dollar sales revenues.

■ The *percent of sales method* is a method of forecasting future financial statements that expresses each account as a percentage of sales. These percentages can be constant or they can change over time.
  ☐ The forecasted sales over a period of time is called the explicit forecast period, with the last year being the *forecast horizon*.
  ☐ Population growth and inflation determine the *long-term growth rate* for most companies.

    ☐ Companies often have a *competitive advantage period*, during which they can grow at rates higher than the long-term growth rate.

    ☐ Many items on the income statement and balance sheet are often assumed to increase proportionally with sales.

        ● Items that are not tied directly to sales depend on the company's policies and its managers' decisions.

■ The first step in using the percent of sales method is to forecast the next year's income statement to estimate income and the addition to retained earnings.

    ☐ A sales forecast is needed.

    ☐ The percent of sales method assumes initially that all costs except depreciation are a specified percentage of sales.

    ☐ In the simplest case, costs are assumed to increase at the same rate as sales; in more complicated situations, specific costs are forecasted separately.

    ☐ Interest and preferred dividend amounts are simply prior year amounts carried over to the forecast period. These amounts are changed when external financing requirements are analyzed in a later step.

■ The second step is to forecast next year's balance sheet.

    ☐ All asset accounts can be assumed to increase directly as a percentage of sales unless the firm is operating at less than full capacity.

        ● If the firm is not operating at full capacity, then fixed assets will not vary directly with sales, but the cash, receivables, and inventory accounts will increase as a percentage of sales.

    ☐ Liabilities, equity, or both must also increase if assets increase—asset expansions must be financed in some manner.

    ☐ Certain liability accounts, such as accounts payable and accrued liabilities, can be expected to increase spontaneously with sales. These are *spontaneously generated funds* obtained automatically from routine business transactions.

    ☐ Retained earnings will increase, but not at the same rate as sales. The new retained earnings will be determined from the projected income statement.

        ● The new balance for retained earnings will be the old level plus the addition to retained earnings.

    ☐ Other financing accounts, such as notes payable, long-term debt, preferred stock, and common stock, are not directly related to sales.

        ● Changes in these accounts result from managerial financing decisions; they do not increase spontaneously as sales increase.

    ☐ The difference between projected total assets and projected liabilities and capital is the amount of *additional funds needed (AFN)*.

        ● AFN are funds that a firm must raise externally through borrowing or by selling new common or preferred stock.

■   The third step is the decision on how to finance the additional funds required.

    □   Sometimes contractual agreements, such as a limit on the debt ratio, will restrict the firm's financing decisions.

    □   Other factors that the financial staff must consider are the firm's target capital structure, the effect of short-term borrowing on its current ratio, and conditions in the debt and equity markets.

■   One complexity that arises in financial forecasting relates to *financing feedbacks*, which are the effects on the income statement and balance sheet of actions taken to finance asset increases. In view of the fact that all of the data are based on forecasts, and since the adjustments add substantially to the work but relatively little to the accuracy of the forecasts, we leave them to later finance courses.

■   Once the pro forma financial statements have been developed, the key ratios can be analyzed to determine whether the forecast meets the firm's financial targets as set forth in its financial plan. If the statements do not meet the targets, then elements of the forecast must be changed.

    □   A spreadsheet model can be run using different sales growth rates, with the results analyzed to see how the ratios would change under different growth scenarios.

    □   A spreadsheet model can also be used to evaluate dividend policy, financing alternatives, and alternative working capital policies.

■   Forecasting is an iterative process, both in the way the financial statements are generated and the way the financial plan is developed.

    □   For planning purposes, the financial staff develops a preliminary forecast based on a continuation of past policies and trends. This provides a starting point, or "baseline" forecast.

    □   Projections are modified to see what effects alternative operating plans would have on the firm's earnings and financial condition. This results in a revised forecast.

    □   Alternative operating plans are examined under different sales growth scenarios, and the model is used to evaluate both dividend policy and capital structure decisions.

■   Free cash flow is calculated as follows:

$$\text{FCF} = \text{Operating cash flow} - \text{Gross investment in operating capital.}$$

Alternatively, free cash flow can be calculated as:

$$\text{FCF} = \text{NOPAT} - \text{Net investment in operating capital.}$$

    □   Free cash flow represents the amount of cash generated in a given year minus the amount of cash needed to finance the additional capital expenditures and working capital needed to support the firm's growth.

- ☐ Forecasts of free cash flows are used by investors and financial managers to estimate the firm's stock price.
- ☐ Managers measure the expected changes in the determinants of value under different strategic and operating alternatives.

Although forecasts of capital requirements are always made by constructing pro forma financial statements as described above, if the ratios are expected to remain constant an approximation can be obtained by using a simple forecasting formula. The formula is useful to obtain a quick "back of the envelope" estimate of external financing requirements for nonconstant ratio companies.

- ■   The formula is as follows:

$$\begin{array}{cccc} \text{Additional} & \text{Required} & \text{Spontaneous} & \text{Increase in} \\ \text{funds} & = \text{increase} & - \text{increase in} & - \text{retained} \\ \text{needed} & \text{in assets} & \text{liabilities} & \text{earnings} \end{array}$$

or $$\text{AFN} = (A^*/S_0)\Delta S - (L^*/S_0)\Delta S - MS_1(RR).$$

- ☐ A^*/S_0 = assets that must increase if sales are to increase, assets that are tied directly to sales.
- ☐ L^*/S_0 = liabilities that increase spontaneously as a percentage of sales, or spontaneously generated financing per \$1 increase in sales.
- ☐ S_1 = total expected sales for the year in question. S_0 = last year's sales.
- ☐ ΔS = change in sales = $S_1 - S_0$.
- ☐ M = profit margin, or profit per \$1 of sales.
- ☐ RR is the retention ratio, which is the percentage of net income that is retained.
  - ●   RR is also equal to 1 − payout ratio.
  - ●   The retention ratio and the payout ratio must total to 1.0 = 100%.

- ■   This equation shows that external financing requirements depend on five factors:
  - ☐ Rapidly growing companies require large increases in assets, other things held constant, so sales growth is an important factor.
  - ☐ The amount of assets required per dollar of sales, or *capital intensity ratio,* has a major effect on capital requirements. Companies with higher assets-to-sales ratios require more assets for a given increase in sales, hence a greater need for external financing.
  - ☐ Companies that spontaneously generate a large amount of liabilities from accounts payable and accrued liabilities will have a relatively small need for external financing.
  - ☐ The higher the profit margin, the larger the net income available to support increases in assets, hence the lower the need for external financing.

☐ Companies that retain more of their earnings as opposed to paying them out as dividends will generate more retained earnings and have less need for external financing.

If the A^*/S_0 ratio is not constant, then constant growth forecasting methods as discussed should not be used. Rather, other techniques must be used to forecast asset levels to determine additional financing requirements. Two of these methods include linear regression and excess capacity adjustments.

■ If one assumes that the relationship between a certain type of asset and sales is linear, then one can use *simple linear regression* techniques to estimate the requirements for that type of asset for any given sales increase. An estimated regression equation is determined that provides an estimated relationship between a given asset account and sales.

■ If a firm's fixed assets are not operating at full capacity, then the calculation for the required level of fixed assets will need to be adjusted.

☐ Full capacity sales are actual sales divided by the percentage of capacity at which the fixed assets were operated to achieve these sales:

$$\text{Full capacity sales} = \frac{\text{Actual sales}}{\substack{\text{Percentage of capacity at which} \\ \text{fixed assets were operated}}}.$$

☐ The target fixed assets to sales ratio is equal to the current year's fixed assets divided by full capacity sales:

$$\text{Target fixed assets to sales ratio} = \frac{\text{Actual fixed assets}}{\text{Full capacity sales}}.$$

☐ The required level of fixed assets is equal to the target fixed assets to sales ratio times projected sales:

$$\substack{\text{Required level} \\ \text{of fixed assets}} = (\text{Target fixed assets to sales ratio})(\text{Projected sales}).$$

● When excess capacity exists, sales can grow to the capacity sales with no increase whatever in fixed assets, but sales beyond that level will require fixed asset additions.

● Excess capacity can occur with other types of assets. However, as a practical matter excess capacity normally exists only with respect to fixed assets and inventories.

Web Appendix 17B

Both the AFN formula and the projected financial statement method as used initially in the text assume that the ratios of assets and liabilities to sales remain constant over time. This, in turn, requires the assumption that each "spontaneous" asset and liability item increases at the same rate as sales. The assumption of constant ratios and identical growth rates is appropriate at times, but there are times when it is incorrect.

- Where *economies of scale* occur in asset use, the ratio of that asset to sales will change as the size of the firm increases.

- Technological considerations sometimes dictate that fixed assets be added in large, discrete units, often referred to as *lumpy assets*. This automatically creates excess capacity immediately after a plant expansion.

- *Forecasting errors* can cause the actual asset/sales ratio for a given period to be quite different from the planned ratio, resulting in excess capacity.

SELF-TEST QUESTIONS

Definitional

1. The most important element in financial planning is the _____ forecast.

2. Those asset items that typically increase proportionately with higher sales are _____, _____, and _____. _____ assets are frequently not used to full capacity, and when that occurs, do not increase as a percentage of sales.

3. If various asset categories increase, _____ and/or _____ must also increase.

4. Typically, certain liabilities will rise _____ with sales. These include accounts _____ and _____ _____.

5. Short-term and long-term _____, _____ stock, _____ stock, and _____ earnings are examples of accounts that do not increase proportionately with higher levels of sales.

6. As the dividend _____ ratio is increased, the amount of earnings available to finance new assets is _____.

7. Retained earnings depend not only on next year's sales level and dividend payout ratio but also on the _____ _____.

8. The amount of assets that are tied directly to sales, A^*/S_0, is often called the _____ _____ ratio.

9. A capital intensive industry will require large amounts of _____ capital to finance increased growth.

10. The _____ ____ _____ method is a method of forecasting future financial statements that expresses each account as a percentage of sales. These percentages can be constant, or they can change over time.

11. _____ _____ _____ are funds that a firm must raise externally through borrowing or by selling new common or preferred stock.

12. Two methods can be used to estimate external funding requirements: the _____ ____ _____ and the _____ methods.

13. One complexity that arises in financial forecasting relates to _____ _____, which are the effects on the income statement and balance sheet of actions taken to finance asset increases.

14. Forecasting is a(n) _____ process, both in the way financial statements are generated and the way the financial plan is developed.

15. The faster a firm's growth rate in sales, the _____ its need for additional financing.

16. If the capital intensity ratio is not constant, then the percent of sales method should not be used. Other techniques such as linear _____ and _____ _____ adjustment should be used.

17. _____ _____ _____ is defined as actual sales divided by the percentage of capacity at which fixed assets were operated to achieve those sales.

18. The _____ _____ _____ to _____ ratio is equal to the current year's fixed assets divided by full capacity sales.

19. The _____ level of _____ _____ is equal to the target fixed assets to sales ratio times projected sales.

20. _____ _____ set forth specific goals for management to attain, which can be specified both in qualitative and quantitative terms.

Conceptual

21. An increase in a firm's inventory will call for additional financing unless the increase is offset by an equal or larger *decrease* in some other asset account.

    a. True   **b.** False

22. If the capital intensity ratio of a firm actually decreases as sales increase, use of the formula method will typically *overstate* the amount of additional funds required, other things held constant.

    a. True   **b.** False

23. If the dividend payout ratio is 100 percent, all ratios are held constant, and the firm is operating at full capacity, then any increase in sales will require additional financing.

    a. True   **b.** False

24. One of the first steps in the percent of sales method of forecasting is to identify those asset and liability accounts that increase spontaneously with retained earnings.

    a. True   **b.** False

25. Which of the following would *reduce* the additional funds required if all other things are held constant?

    a. An increase in the dividend payout ratio.
    b. A decrease in the profit margin.
    c. An increase in the capital intensity ratio.
    d. An increase in the expected sales growth rate.
    e. A decrease in the firm's tax rate.

SELF-TEST PROBLEMS

1. United Products Inc. has the following balance sheet:

Current assets	$ 5,000	Accounts payable	$ 1,000
		Notes payable	1,000
Net fixed assets	5,000	Long-term debt	4,000
		Common equity	4,000
Total assets	$10,000	Total liabilities and equity	$10,000

Business has been slow; therefore, fixed assets are vastly underutilized. Management believes it can double sales next year with the introduction of a new product. No new fixed assets will be required, and management expects that there will be no earnings retained next year. What is next year's additional financing requirement?

a. $0 **b.** $4,000 **c.** $6,000 **d.** $13,000 **e.** $19,000

2. The 2002 balance sheet for American Pulp and Paper is shown below (in millions of dollars):

Cash	$ 3.0	Accounts payable	$ 2.0
Accounts receivable	3.0	Notes payable	1.5
Inventories	5.0		
Total current assets	$11.0	Total current liabilities	$ 3.5
Fixed assets	3.0	Long-term debt	3.0
		Common equity	7.5
Total assets	$14.0	Total liabilities and equity	$14.0

In 2002, sales were $60 million. In 2003, management believes that sales will increase by 20 percent to a total of $72 million. The profit margin is expected to be 5 percent, and the dividend payout ratio is targeted at 40 percent. No excess capacity exists. What is the additional financing requirement (in millions) for 2003 using the formula method?

a. $0.36 **b.** $0.24 **c.** $0 **d.** -$0.24 **e.** -$0.36

3. Refer to Self-Test Problem 2. How much can sales grow above the 2002 level of $60 million without requiring any additional funds?

a. 12.28% **b.** 14.63% **c.** 15.75% **d.** 17.65% **e.** 18.14%

4. Smith Machines Inc. has a net income this year of $500 on sales of $2,000 and is operating its fixed assets at full capacity. Management expects sales to increase by 25 percent next year and is forecasting a dividend payout ratio of 30 percent. The profit margin is not expected to change. If spontaneous liabilities are $500 this year and no excess funds are expected next year, what are Smith's total assets this year?

    a. $1,000   **b.** $1,500   **c.** $2,250   **d.** $3,000   **e.** $3,500

5. Wilson Widgets Company has $500 million in sales. The company expects that its sales will increase 8 percent this year. Wilson's CFO uses a simple linear regression to forecast the company's inventory level for a given level of projected sales. On the basis of recent history, the estimated relationship between inventories and sales (in millions of dollars) is

    $$\text{Inventories} = \$42 + 0.136(\text{Sales}).$$

    Given the estimated sales forecast and the estimated relationship between inventories and sales, what is your forecast of the company's year-end inventory turnover ratio?

    a. 3.33   **b.** 4.68   **c.** 1.57   **d.** 2.44   **e.** 3.50

    (The following data apply to the next three Self-Test Problems.)

    Holden Industries has $3 billion in sales and $1.25 billion in fixed assets. Currently, the company's fixed assets are operating at 80 percent of capacity.

6. What level of sales (in billions of dollars) could Holden Industries have obtained if it had been operating at full capacity?

    a. $3.25   **b.** $4.50   **c.** $3.75   **d.** $4.80   **e.** $5.23

7. What is Holden's target fixed asset/sales ratio?

    a. 33.33%   **b.** 25.00%   **c.** 10.50%   **d.** 18.75%   **e.** 41.67%

8. If Holden's sales increase 25 percent, how large of an increase in fixed assets (in millions of dollars) would the company need in order to meet its target fixed asset/sales ratio?

    a. $312.50   **b.** $250.00   **c.** $75.50   **d.** $3.00   **e.** $0

(The following financial statements apply to the next three Self-Test Problems.)

Crossley Products Company's 2002 financial statements are shown below:

Crossley Products Company
Balance Sheet as of December 31, 2002
(Thousands of Dollars)

Cash	$ 600	Accounts payable	$ 2,400
Receivables	3,600	Notes payable	1,157
Inventories	4,200	Accrued liabilities	840
Total current assets	$ 8,400	Total current liabilities	$ 4,397
		Mortgage bonds	1,667
		Common stock	667
Net fixed assets	7,200	Retained earnings	8,869
Total assets	$15,600	Total liabilities and equity	$15,600

Crossley Products Company
Income Statement for December 31, 2002
(Thousands of Dollars)

Sales	$12,000
Operating costs	10,261
EBIT	$ 1,739
Interest	339
EBT	$ 1,400
Taxes (40%)	560
Net income	$ 840
Dividends (60%)	$ 504
Addition to retained earnings	$ 336

9. Assume that the company was operating at full capacity in 2002 with regard to all items except fixed assets; fixed assets in 2002 were utilized to only 75 percent of capacity. By what percentage could 2003 sales increase over 2002 sales without the need for an increase in fixed assets?

   a. 33%   **b.** 25%   **c.** 20%   **d.** 44%   **e.** 50%

10. Now suppose 2003 sales increase by 25 percent over 2002 sales. Assume that Crossley cannot sell any fixed assets. Use the percent of sales method to develop a pro forma balance sheet and income statement. Assume that any required financing is borrowed as notes payable. Use a pro forma income statement to determine the addition to retained earnings. How much additional external capital (in thousands) will be required?

a. $825   b. $925   c. $750   d. $900   e. $850

11. Refer to Self-Test Problem 10. After the required financing is borrowed as notes payable, what is the firm's current and debt ratios?

a. 1.73; 38.84%   d. 1.73; 43.64%
b. 2.02; 38.84%   e. 2.02; 43.64%
c. 1.73; 44.06%

(The following financial statement applies to the next two Self-Test Problems.)

Tatum Toys recently reported the following income statement (in millions of dollars):

Sales	$875
Operating costs	625
EBIT	$250
Interest	50
EBT	$200
Taxes (40%)	80
Net income	$120
Dividends (33.3%)	$40
Addition to retained earnings	$80

This year the company is forecasting a 20 percent increase in sales, and it expects that its year-end operating costs will decline to 65 percent of sales. Tatum's tax rate, interest expense, and dividend payout ratio are all expected to remain constant.

12. What is Tatum's projected 2003 net income (in millions of dollars)?

a. $75.75   b. $151.50   c. $225.25   d. $190.50   e. $300.00

13. What is the expected growth rate in Tatum's dividends?

a. 25.00%   b. 33.33%   c. 58.75%   d. 15.50%   e. 42.25%

14. At the end of last year, Heuser Industries reported the following income statement (in thousands of dollars):

Sales	$6,000
Operating costs excluding depreciation	4,900
EBITDA	$1,100
Depreciation	500
EBIT	$ 600
Interest	250
EBT	$ 350
Taxes (40%)	140
Net income	$ 210

Looking ahead to the following year, the company's CFO has assembled the following information:

- Year-end sales are expected to be 15 percent higher than the $6 million in sales generated last year.
- Year-end operating costs excluding depreciation are expected to equal 80 percent of year-end sales.
- Depreciation is expected to increase at the same rate as sales.
- Interest costs are expected to remain unchanged.
- The tax rate is expected to remain at 40 percent.

On the basis of this information, what will be the forecast for Heuser's net income (in thousands of dollars) at the end of the year?

a. $175　　　　b. $333　　　　c. $125　　　　d. $215　　　　e. $288

(The following financial statements apply to the next two Self-Test Problems.)

Taylor Technologies Inc.'s 2002 financial statements are shown below:

Taylor Technologies Inc.
Balance Sheet as of December 31, 2002

Cash	$ 90,000	Accounts payable	$ 180,000
Receivables	180,000	Notes payable	78,000
Inventories	360,000	Accrued liabilities	90,000
Total current assets	$ 630,000	Total current liabilities	$ 348,000
		Common stock	900,000
Net fixed assets	720,000	Retained earnings	102,000
Total assets	$1,350,000	Total liabilities and equity	$1,350,000

Taylor Technologies Inc.
Income Statement for December 31, 2002

Sales	$ 1,800,000
Operating costs	1,639,860
EBIT	$ 160,140
Interest	10,140
EBT	$ 150,000
Taxes (40%)	60,000
Net income	$ 90,000
Dividends (60%)	$ 54,000
Addition to retained earnings	$ 36,000

15. Suppose that in 2003, sales increase by 10 percent over 2002 sales. Construct the pro forma financial statements using the percent of sales method. Assume the firm operated at full capacity in 2002. How much additional capital will be required?

a. $72,459   b. $70,211   c. $68,157   d. $66,445   e. $63,989

16. Refer to Self-Test Problem 15. Assume now that fixed assets are only being operated at 95 percent of capacity. Construct the proforma financial statements using the percent of sales method. How much additional capital will be required?

a. $28,557   b. $32,400   c. $39,843   d. $45,400   e. $50,000

17. Your company's sales were $2,000 last year, and they are forecasted to rise by 50 percent during the coming year. Here is the latest balance sheet:

Cash	$ 100	Accounts payable	$ 200
Receivables	300	Notes payable	200
Inventories	800	Accrued liabilities	20
Total current assets	$ 1,200	Total current liabilities	$ 420
		Long-term debt	780
		Common stock	400
Net fixed assets	800	Retained earnings	400
Total assets	$2,000	Total liabilities and equity	$2,000

Fixed assets were used to only 80 percent of capacity last year, and year-end inventory holdings were $100 greater than were needed to support the $2,000 of sales. The other current assets (cash and receivables) were at their proper levels. All assets would be a constant percentage of sales if excess capacity did not exist; that is, all assets would increase at the same rate as sales if no excess capacity existed. The company's after-tax profit margin will be 3 percent, and its payout ratio will be 80 percent. If all additional funds needed (AFN) are raised as notes payable, what will be the current ratio at the end of the coming year?

a. 2.47 **b.** 1.44 **c.** 1.21 **d.** 1.00 **e.** 1.63

18. The Bouchard Company's sales are forecasted to increase from $500 in 2002 to $1,000 in 2003. Here is the December 31, 2002, balance sheet:

Cash	$ 50	Accounts payable	$ 25
Receivables	100	Notes payable	75
Inventories	100	Accrued liabilities	25
Total current assets	$250	Total current liabilities	$125
		Long-term debt	200
		Common stock	50
Net fixed assets	250	Retained earnings	125
Total assets	$500	Total liabilities and equity	$500

Bouchard's fixed assets were used to only 50 percent of capacity during 2002, but its current assets were at their proper levels. All assets except fixed assets should be a constant percentage of sales, and fixed assets would also increase at the same rate if the current excess capacity did not exist. Bouchard's after-tax profit margin is forecasted to be 8 percent, and its payout ratio will be 40 percent. What is Bouchard's additional funds needed (AFN) for the coming year?

a. $102 **b.** $152 **c.** $197 **d.** $167 **e.** $183

(The following financial statements apply to the next two Self-Test Problems.)

Tillman Tractor Company recently reported the following income statement and balance sheet.

Income Statement

Sales	$2,100
Operating costs	1,890
EBIT	$ 210
Interest	60
EBT	$ 150
Taxes (40%)	60
Net income	$ 90

Dividends paid	$ 0
Addition to retained earnings	$ 90

Balance Sheet

Cash and marketable securities	$ 21	Accounts payable and accrued liab.	$ 84
Accounts receivable	168	Notes payable	125
Inventories	220	Current liabilities	$ 209
Current assets	$ 409	Long-term debt	350
		Common stock	200
Net fixed assets	1,281	Retained earnings	931
Total assets	$1,690	Total liabilities and equity	$1,690

In constructing its forecast for the upcoming year, the company has put together the following information:

- Sales are expected to increase 12 percent this upcoming year.
- Operating costs are expected to remain at 90 percent of sales.
- Cash and marketable securities are expected to remain at 1 percent of sales.
- Accounts receivable are expected to remain at 8 percent of sales.
- Because of excess capacity, the company expects that its year-end inventory will remain at current levels.
- Fixed assets are expected to remain at 61 percent of sales.
- Spontaneous liabilities (accounts payable and accrued liabilities) are expected to increase at the same rate as sales.
- The company will continue to pay a zero dividend, and its tax rate will remain at 40 percent.
- The company anticipates that any additional funds needed will be raised in the following manner: 30 percent notes payable, 30 percent long-term debt, and 40 percent common stock.

19. On the basis of assumptions listed above, construct Tillman's pro forma income statement and balance sheet. Assume that there are no financial feedback effects. (That is, assume interest will remain unchanged even though the company may increase its debt.) What is Tillman's notes payable balance after external funds have been raised?

    a. $94.08   **b.** $55.75   **c.** $188.75   **d.** $237.44   **e.** $143.36

20. On the basis of this forecast and after external funds have been raised, what is the firm's return on equity (ROE)? Assume there are no financial feedback effects.

    a. 7.96%   **b.** 8.25%   **c.** 8.34%   **d.** 8.50%   **e.** 9.10%

ANSWERS TO SELF-TEST QUESTIONS

1. sales
2. cash; receivables; inventories; Fixed
3. liabilities; equity
4. spontaneously; payable; accrued liabilities
5. debt; preferred; common; retained
6. payout; decreased
7. profit margin
8. capital intensity
9. external
10. percent of sales

11. Additional Funds Needed
12. percent of sales; formula
13. financing feedbacks
14. iterative
15. greater
16. regression; excess capacity
17. Full capacity sales
18. target fixed assets; sales
19. required; fixed assets
20. Corporate objectives

21. a. When an increase in one asset account is not offset by an equivalent decrease in another asset account, then financing is needed to reestablish equilibrium on the balance sheet. Note, though, that this additional financing may come from a spontaneous increase in accounts payable/accrued liabilities or from retained earnings.

22. a. A decreasing capital intensity ratio, $A*/S_0$, means that fewer assets are required, proportionately, as sales increase. Thus, the external funding requirement is overstated. Always keep in mind that the formula method assumes that the asset/sales ratio is constant regardless of the level of sales.

23. a. With a 100 percent payout ratio, there will be no retained earnings. When operating at full capacity, *all* assets are spontaneous, but *all* liabilities cannot be spontaneous since a firm must have common equity. Thus, the growth in assets cannot be matched

by a growth in spontaneous liabilities, so additional financing will be required in order to keep the financial ratios (the debt ratio in particular) constant.

24. b. The first step is to identify those accounts that increase spontaneously with sales.

25. e. Answers a through d would increase the additional funds required, but a decrease in the tax rate would raise the profit margin and thus increase the amount of available retained earnings.

SOLUTIONS TO SELF-TEST PROBLEMS

1. b. Look at next year's balance sheet:

Current assets	$10,000	Accounts payable	$ 2,000
Net fixed assets	5,000	Notes payable	1,000
		Current liabilities	$ 3,000
		Long-term debt	4,000
		Common equity	4,000
			$11,000
		AFN	4,000
Total assets	$15,000	Total liabilities and equity	$15,000

With no retained earnings next year, the common equity account remains at $4,000. Thus, the additional financing requirement is $15,000 − $11,000 = $4,000.

2. b. None of the items on the right side of the balance sheet rises spontaneously with sales except accounts payable. Therefore,

$$AFN = (A^*/S_0)(\Delta S) - (L^*/S_0)(\Delta S) - MS_1(RR)$$
$$= (\$14/\$60)(\$12) - (\$2/\$60)(\$12) - (0.05)(\$72)(0.6)$$
$$= \$2.8 - \$0.4 - \$2.16 = \$0.24 \text{ million.}$$

The firm will need $240,000 in additional funds to support the increase in sales.

3. d. Note that g = Sales growth = $\Delta S/S_0$ and $S_1 = S_0(1 + g)$. Then,

$$AFN = A^*g - L^*g - M[(S_0)(1 + g)](RR) = 0$$
$$\$14g - \$2g - 0.05[(\$60)(1 + g)](0.60) = 0$$
$$\$12g - [(\$3 + \$3g)(0.60)] = 0$$
$$\$12g - \$1.8 - \$1.8g = 0$$
$$\$10.20g = \$1.80$$
$$g = 0.1765 = 17.65\%.$$

4. c.
$$0 = (A^*/S_0)(\Delta S) - (L^*/S_0)(\Delta S) - MS_1(RR)$$
$$0 = (A^*/\$2,000)(\$500) - (\$500/\$2,000)(\$500) - (\$500/\$2,000)(\$2,500)(0.7)$$
$$0 = (\$500A^*/\$2,000) - \$125 - \$437.50$$
$$0 = (\$500A^*/\$2,000) - \$562.50$$
$$\$562.50 = 0.25A^*$$
$$A^* = \$2,250.$$

5. b. Sales = $500,000,000; g_{Sales} = 8%; Inv. = $42 + 0.136$(Sales).

$S_1 = \$500,000,000 \times 1.08 = \$540,000,000.$

Inv. = $42 + 0.136(\$540)$
$\qquad = \$115.44$ million.

Sales/Inv. = $540,000,000/\$115,440,000 = 4.68.$

6. c. Sales = $3,000,000,000; FA = $1,250,000,000; FA are operated at 80% capacity.

Full capacity sales = $3,000,000,000/0.80 = \$3,750,000,000.$

7. a. Target FA/S ratio = $1,250,000,000/\$3,750,000,000 = 33.33\%.$

8. e. Sales increase = 25%; ΔFA = ?

$S_1 = \$3,000,000,000 \times 1.25 = \$3,750,000,000.$

No increase in FA for sales up to $3,750,000,000.

9. a.
$$\text{Full capacity sales} = \frac{\text{Actual sales}}{\text{\% of capacity at which FA were operated}} = \frac{\$12,000}{0.75} = \$16,000.$$

$$\text{Percent increase} = \frac{\text{New sales} - \text{Old sales}}{\text{Old sales}} = \frac{\$16,000 - \$12,000}{\$12,000} = 0.33 = 33\%.$$

Therefore, sales could expand by 33 percent before Crossley Products would need to add fixed assets.

10.   e.

Crossley Products Company
Pro Forma Income Statement
December 31, 2003
(Thousands of Dollars)

	2002	Forecast Basis[a]	2003 Forecast
Sales	$12,000	1.25	$15,000
Operating costs	10,261	0.8551	12,826
EBIT	$ 1,739		$ 2,174
Interest	339		339
EBT	$ 1,400		$ 1,835
Taxes (40%)	560		734
Net income	$ 840		$ 1,101
Dividends (60%)	$ 504		$ 661
Addition to RE	$ 336		$ 440

Crossley Products Company
Pro Forma Balance Sheet
December 31, 2003
(Thousands of Dollars)

	2002	Forecast Basis[a]	2003 Forecast	AFN	2003 After AFN
Cash	$ 600	0.05	$ 750		$ 750
Receivables	3,600	0.30	4,500		4,500
Inventories	4,200	0.35	5,250		5,250
Total current assets	$ 8,400		$10,500		$10,500
Net fixed assets	7,200		7,200[b]		7,200
Total assets	$15,600		$17,700		$17,700
Accts. payable	$ 2,400	0.20	$ 3,000		$ 3,000
Notes payable	1,157		1,157	+850	2,007
Accrued liabilities	840	0.07	1,050		1,050
Total current liab.	$ 4,397		$ 5,207		$ 6,057
Mortgage bonds	1,667		1,667		1,667
Common stock	667		667		667
Retained earnings	8,869	440[c]	9,309		9,309
Total liabilities and equity	$15,600		$16,850		$17,700

$$AFN = \$ \quad 850$$

Notes:

[a]Sales are increased by 25%. Operating costs, all assets except fixed assets, accrued liabilities, and accounts payable are divided by 2002 sales to determine the appropriate ratios to apply to 2003 sales to calculate 2003 account balances.

[b]From Self-Test Problem 9 we know that sales can increase by 33 percent before additions to fixed assets are needed.

[c]See income statement.

11. d. Current ratio $= CA/CL$
$= \$10,500/\$6,057$
$= 1.73\times.$

Debt/Assets ratio $= \dfrac{(\$6,057 + \$1,667)}{\$17,700}$
$= 43.64\%.$

12. d.

	2002	Forecast Basis	2003
Sales	$875	× 1.20	$1,050.00
Oper. costs	625	× 0.65 Sales	682.50
EBIT	$250		$ 367.50
Interest	50		50.00
EBT	$200		$ 317.50
Taxes (40%)	80		127.00
Net income	$120		$ 190.50
Dividends (33.3%)	$ 40		$ 63.50
Addit. to R/E	$ 80		$ 127.00

13. c. ΔDividends $= (\$63.50 - \$40.00)/\$40.00 = 58.75\%.$

14. b.

	Actual	Forecast Basis	Pro Forma
Sales	$6,000	× 1.15	$6,900
Oper. costs excluding depreciation	4,900	× 0.80 Sales	5,520
EBITDA	$1,100		$1,380
Depreciation	500	× 0.0833 Sales	575
EBIT	$ 600		$ 805
Interest	250		250
EBT	$ 350		$ 555
Taxes (40%)	140		222
Net income	$ 210		$ 333

15.   c.   The projected balance sheet indicates that the AFN = $68,157.

Taylor Technologies Inc.
Pro Forma Income Statement
December 31, 2003

	2002	Forecast Basis[a]	2003 Forecast
Sales	$1,800,000	1.10	$1,980,000
Operating costs	1,639,860	0.9110	1,803,846
EBIT	$ 160,140		$ 176,154
Interest	10,140		10,140
EBT	$ 150,000		$ 166,014
Taxes (40%)	60,000		66,406
Net income	$ 90,000		$ 99,608
Dividends (60%)	$ 54,000		$ 59,765
Addition to RE	$ 36,000		$ 39,843

Taylor Technologies Inc.
Pro Forma Balance Sheet
December 31, 2003

	2002	Forecast Basis[a]	2003 Forecast
Cash	$ 90,000	0.05	$ 99,000
Receivables	180,000	0.10	198,000
Inventories	360,000	0.20	396,000
Total current assets	$ 630,000		$ 693,000
Fixed assets	720,000	0.40	792,000
Total assets	$1,350,000		$1,485,000
Accts. payable	$ 180,000	0.10	$ 198,000
Notes payable	78,000		78,000
Accrued liabilities	90,000	0.05	99,000
Total current liabilities	$ 348,000		$ 375,000
Common stock	900,000		900,000
Ret. earnings	102,000	39,843[b]	141,843
Total liabilities and equity	$1,350,000		$1,416,843
		AFN =	$ 68,157

Notes:

[a]Sales are increased by 10%. Operating costs, all assets, accrued liabilities, and accounts payable are divided by 2002 sales to determine the appropriate ratios to apply to 2003 sales to calculate 2003 account balances.

[b]See income statement.

16.   a.   The projected balance sheet indicates that the AFN = $28,557.

Taylor Technologies Inc.
Pro Forma Income Statement
December 31, 2003

	2002	Forecast Basis[a]	2003 Forecast
Sales	$1,800,000	1.10	$1,980,000
Operating costs	1,639,860	0.9110	1,803,846
EBIT	$ 160,140		$ 176,154
Interest	10,140		10,140
EBT	$ 150,000		$ 166,014
Taxes (40%)	60,000		66,406
Net income	$ 90,000		$ 99,608
Dividends (60%)	$ 54,000		$ 59,765
Addition to RE	$ 36,000		$ 39,843

Taylor Technologies Inc.
Pro Forma Balance Sheet
December 31, 2003

	2002	Forecast Basis[a]	2003 Forecast
Cash	$ 90,000	0.05	$ 99,000
Receivables	180,000	0.10	198,000
Inventories	360,000	0.20	396,000
Total current assets	$ 630,000		$ 693,000
Fixed assets	720,000	32,400[b]	752,400
Total assets	$1,350,000		$1,445,400
Accts. payable	$ 180,000	0.10	$ 198,000
Notes payable	78,000		78,000
Accrued liabilities	90,000	0.05	99,000
Total current liabilities	$ 348,000		$ 375,000
Common stock	900,000		900,000
Ret. earnings	102,000	39,843[c]	141,843
Total liabilities and equity	$1,350,000		$1,416,843
		AFN =	$ 28,557

Notes:

[a]Sales are increased by 10%. Operating costs, all assets except fixed assets, accrued liabilities, and accounts payable are divided by 2002 sales to determine the appropriate ratios to apply to 2003 sales to calculate 2003 account balances.

$$^b \frac{\text{Full}}{\text{capacity}} = \frac{\$1,800,000}{0.95} = \$1,894,737.$$

$$\text{Target fixed assets/Sales ratio} = \frac{\$720,000}{\$1,894,737} = 38\%.$$

$$\frac{\text{Required level}}{\text{of fixed assets}} = (0.38)(\$1,980,000)$$

$$= \$752,400.$$

Necessary FA increase = $752,400 - $720,000 = $32,400.

^{c}See income statement.

17. e.

	Actual	Forecast Basis[a]	Pro Forma 1st Pass	AFN	Pro Forma 2nd Pass
Cash	$ 100	0.05	$ 150		$ 150
Receivables	300	0.15	450		450
Inventories	800	+250[b]	1,050		1,050
Total curr. assets	$1,200		$1,650		$1,650
Net fixed assets	800	+160[c]	960		960
Total assets	$2,000		$2,610		$2,610
Accts. payable	$ 200	0.10	$ 300		$ 300
Notes payable	200		200	+ 482	682
Accrued liabilities	20	0.01	30		30
Total curr. liab.	$ 420		$ 530		$1,012
Long-term debt	780		780		780
Common stock	400		400		400
Ret. earnings	400	+ 18[d]	418		418
Total liab./equity	$2,000		$2,128		$2,610
			AFN = $ 482		

Notes:

^{a}Cash, receivables, accounts payable, and accrued liabilities are divided by actual sales to determine the appropriate ratios to apply to next year's sales to calculate next year's account balances.

^{b}Target inventories/assets = ($800 − $100)/$2,000 = 35%.
Target inventory level = 0.35($3,000) = $1,050.
Since we already have $800 of inventories, we need:
Additional inventories = $1,050 − $800 = $250.

^{c}Capacity sales = Sales/Capacity factor = $2,000/0.8 = $2,500.
Target FA/S ratio = FA/Capacity sales = $800/$2,500 = 32%.
Required FA = (Target ratio) (Forecasted sales) = 0.32($3,000) = $960.
Since we already have $800 of fixed assets, we need:
Additional fixed assets = $960 − $800 = $160.

^{d}Addition to RE = $M(S_1)(RR)$ = 0.03($3,000)(0.2) = $18.

The problem asks for the forecasted current ratio, which is calculated as:
Forecasted current ratio = $1,650/$1,012 = 1.6304×.

18. **b.**

	2002	Forecast Basis^a	1st Pass 2003
Cash	$ 50	0.10	$100
Receivables	100	0.20	200
Inventories	100	0.20	200
Total current assets	$250		$500
Net fixed assets	250	+ 0^b	250
Total assets	$500		$750
Accounts payable	$ 25	0.05	$ 50
Notes payable	75		75
Accrued liabilities	25	0.05	50
Total current liabilities	$125		$175
Long-term debt	200		200
Common stock	50		50
Retained earnings	125	+48^c	173
Total claims	$500		$598
			AFN = $152

Notes:

^{a}Cash, receivables, inventories, accounts payable, and accrued liabilities are divided by 2002 sales to determine the appropriate ratios to apply to 2003 sales to calculate 2003 account balances.

^{b}Capacity sales = Actual sales/Capacity factor = $500/0.5 = $1,000.
Target FA/S ratio = $250/$1,000 = 0.25.
Target FA = 0.25($1,000) = $250 = Required fixed assets.
Since Bouchard currently has $250 of FA, no new FA will be required.

^{c}Addition to RE = $M(S_1)(RR)$ = 0.08($1,000)(0.6) = $48.

19. e. Income statement:

	Actual	Forecast Basis	Pro Forma 1st Pass	AFN	2nd Pass
Sales	$2,100	× 1.12	$2,352.00		$2,352.00
Oper. costs	1,890	× 0.9 Sales	2,116.80		2,116.80
EBIT	$ 210		$ 235.20		$ 235.00
Interest	60		60.00		60.00
EBT	$ 150		$ 175.20		175.20
Taxes (40%)	60		70.08		70.08
Net income	$ 90		$ 105.12		$ 105.12
Dividends	$ 0		$ 0.00		$ 0.00
Addit. to R/E	$ 90		$ 105.12		$ 105.12

Balance sheet:

	Actual	Forecast Basis	Pro Forma 1st Pass	AFN	2nd Pass
Cash & mkt. sec.	$ 21	× 0.01 Sales	$ 23.52		$ 23.52
Accts. rec.	168	× 0.08 Sales	188.16		188.16
Inventories	220		220.00		220.00
Total CA	$ 409		$ 431.68		$ 431.68
Net fixed assets	1,281	× 0.61 Sales	1,434.72		1,434.72
Total assets	$1,690		$1,866.40		$1,866.40
A/P & accrued liab.	$ 84	× 0.04 Sales	$ 94.08		$ 94.08
N/P	125		125.00	18.36	143.36
Total CL	$ 209		$ 219.08		237.44
LT debt	350		350.00	18.36	368.36
Common stock	200		200.00	24.48	224.48
RE	931	+105.12	1,036.12		1,036.12
Total liab. & equity	$1,690		$1,805.20		$1,866.40
AFN			$ 61.20		

External Financing:

N/P   0.30 × $61.20 = $18.36.

LT debt   0.30 × $61.20 = $18.36.

Common stock 0.40 × $61.20 = $24.48.

20. c. 2nd-pass pro forma ROE $= \dfrac{\$105.12}{(\$224.48 + \$1,036.12)} = \dfrac{\$105.12}{\$1,260.60} = 8.34\%.$

- Identify several good reasons for companies to manage risk.

- Define the term "natural hedge" and give some examples.

- List three reasons why the derivatives markets have grown more rapidly than any other major market in recent years.

- Explain what an option is, identify some factors that affect the value of a call option, and calculate the exercise value and premium of an option.

- Explain the term riskless hedge and then go through an example to create one.

- Use the Black-Scholes Option Pricing Model to calculate the value of a call option.

- Distinguish between forward and futures contracts and define the following terms: swaps, structured notes, and inverse floaters.

- Briefly explain what risk management involves and identify the steps in the three-step approach to risk management.

- Explain how financial futures can be used to hedge against security price exposure and how commodity futures can be used to hedge against commodity price exposure.

OVERVIEW

Risk management can mean many things, but in business it involves identifying events that could have adverse financial consequences for the firm and then undertaking actions to prevent and/or minimize the damage caused by these events. Years ago, corporate risk managers dealt primarily with insurance—they made sure the firm was adequately insured against fire, theft, and other casualties and that it had adequate liability coverage.

More recently, however, the scope of risk management has been broadened to include such things as controlling the costs of key inputs or protecting against changes in interest rates or exchange rates. In addition, risk managers try to ensure that actions designed to hedge against risks are not actually increasing risks.

Since perhaps the most important aspect of risk management involves derivative securities, we begin the chapter with a discussion of derivatives. Derivatives are securities whose values are determined, in whole or in part, by the market price (or interest rate) of some other asset. Derivatives include options, whose values depend on the price of some underlying stock; interest rate and exchange rate futures and swaps, whose values depend on interest rate and exchange rate levels; and commodity futures, whose values depend on commodity prices.

OUTLINE

Although there is no proof that risk management adds value, there are several good reasons for companies to manage risk.

- *Debt capacity.* Risk management can reduce the volatility of cash flows, and this decreases the probability of bankruptcy. Firms with lower operating risks can use more debt, and this can lead to higher stock prices due to the interest tax savings.

- *Maintaining the optimal capital budget over time.* By smoothing out the cash flows, risk management can alleviate the possibility that internal cash flows will be too low to support the optimal capital budget.

- *Financial distress.* Financial distress is associated with having cash flows fall below expected levels. Risk management can reduce the likelihood of low cash flows, hence of financial distress.

- *Comparative advantages in hedging.* Many investors cannot implement a homemade hedging program as efficiently as can a company.
  - ☐ Firms have lower transactions costs due to a larger volume of hedging activities.
  - ☐ Managers know more about the firm's risk exposure than outside investors, hence managers can create more effective hedges.
  - ☐ Effective risk management requires specialized skills and knowledge that firms are more likely to have.

- *Borrowing costs.* Firms can sometimes reduce input costs, especially the interest rate on debt, through the use of swaps. Any such cost reduction adds value to the firm.

■   *Tax effects.* Companies with volatile earnings pay more taxes than more stable companies due to the treatment of tax credits and the rules governing corporate loss carry-forwards and carry-backs. Therefore, our tax system encourages risk management to stabilize earnings.

■   *Compensation systems.* Many compensation systems establish "floors" and "ceilings" on bonuses or else reward managers for meeting targets. Typically, a manager's bonus is higher if earnings are stable. So, even if hedging does not add much value for stockholders, it may still be beneficial to managers.

A historical perspective is useful when studying derivatives. One of the first formal markets for derivatives was the futures market for wheat.

■   *Hedging* with futures lowered aggregate risk in the economy.

■   The earliest futures dealings were between two parties who arranged transactions between themselves. Soon, though, middlemen came into the picture, and trading in futures was established.
   □ The Chicago Board of Trade was an early marketplace for this dealing, and *futures dealers* helped make a market in futures contracts. This improved the efficiency and lowered the cost of hedging operations.

■   *Speculators* then entered the scene. Speculators add capital and players to the derivatives market, and this stabilizes the market. Derivatives markets are inherently volatile due to the leverage involved, hence risk to the speculators themselves is high. Still, their bearing that risk makes the derivatives markets more stable for the hedgers.

■   *Natural hedges* are situations in which aggregate risk can be reduced by derivatives transactions between two parties (called *counterparties*). These exist for many commodities, for foreign currencies, for interest rates on securities with different maturities, and even for common stocks in which portfolio managers want to "hedge their bets."

■   Hedging can also be done in situations where no natural hedge exists. Here one party wants to reduce some type of risk, and another party agrees to sell a contract that protects the first party from that specific event or situation.
   □ Insurance is an obvious example of this type of hedge.
   □ Note that with nonsymmetric hedges risks are generally transferred rather than eliminated.

■   The derivatives markets have grown more rapidly than any other major market in recent years for a number of reasons.

☐ Analytical techniques have been developed to help establish "fair" prices, and having a better basis for pricing hedges makes the counterparties more comfortable with deals.

☐ Computers and electronic communications make it much easier for counterparties to deal with one another.

☐ Globalization has greatly increased the importance of currency markets and the need for reducing the exchange rate risks brought on by global trade.

☐ The use of derivatives for risk management is bound to grow.

■ Derivatives do have a potential downside. These instruments are highly leveraged, so small miscalculations can lead to huge losses. Also, they are complicated, hence not well understood by most people. This makes mistakes more likely than with less complex instruments, and it makes it harder for a firm's top management to exercise proper control over derivatives transactions.

An option is a contract that gives its holder the right to buy (or sell) an asset at a predetermined price within a specified period of time.

■ The *strike*, or *exercise*, *price* is the price that must be paid for a share of common stock when an option is exercised.

■ A *call option* is an option to buy, or "call," a share of stock at a certain price within a specified period, while a *put option* is an option to sell a share of stock at a certain price within a specified period.

■ The seller of an option is called the *option writer*.

■ An investor who "writes" call options against stock held in his or her portfolio is said to be selling *covered options*. Options sold without the stock to back them up are called *naked options*.

■ When the exercise price exceeds the current stock price, a call option is said to be *out-of-the-money*. When the exercise price is below the current price of the stock, a call option is *in-the-money*.

■ Options can be used to create *hedges* that protect the value of an individual stock or portfolio.

■ Conventional options are generally written for 6 months or less, but a new type of option called a *Long-Term Equity Anticipation Security* (LEAPS) has been trading in recent years.

☐ Like conventional options, LEAPS are listed on exchanges and are tied both to individual stocks and to stock indexes.

☐ LEAPS are long-term options, having maturities of up to 2½ years.

☐ One-year LEAPS cost about twice as much as the matching three-month option, but because of their much longer time to expiration, LEAPS provide buyers with more potential for gains and offer better long-term protection for a portfolio.

■ Corporations on whose stocks options are written have nothing to do with the option market.

☐ Corporations do not raise money in the option market, nor do they have any direct transactions in it.

☐ Option holders do not vote for corporate directors or receive dividends.

■ There are at least three factors that affect a call option's value.

☐ For a given strike price, the higher the stock's market price in relation to the strike price, the higher will be the call option price.

☐ For a given stock price, the higher the strike price, the lower the call option price.

☐ The longer the option period, the higher will be the option price.

   ● This occurs because the longer the time before expiration, the greater the chance that the stock price will climb substantially above the exercise price.

■ A call option's *exercise value* is equal to the current stock price less the strike price.

☐ Realistically, the minimum "true" value of an option is zero, because no one would exercise an out-of-the-money option.

☐ The actual market price of the option lies above the exercise value at each price of the common stock, although the premium declines as the price of the stock increases.

   ● Options enable individuals to gain a high degree of personal leverage when buying securities.

   ● The declining leverage impact and the increasing danger of larger losses help explain why the premium diminishes as the price of the common stock rises.

■ In addition to the stock price and the exercise price, the price of an option depends on three other factors: (1) the option's term to maturity, (2) the variability of the stock price, and (3) the risk-free rate.

☐ The longer a call option has to run, the greater its value and the larger its premium.

☐ An option on an extremely volatile stock is worth more than one on a very stable stock.

☐ The price of a call option always increases as the risk-free rate increases.

   ● The expected growth rate of a firm's stock price increases as interest rates increase, but the present value of future cash flows decreases. The first effect dominates the second one.

All option pricing models are based on the concept of a riskless hedge.

■ A *riskless hedge* is a hedge in which an investor buys a stock and simultaneously sells a call option on that stock and ends up with a riskless position.

■ If an investment is riskless, it must, in equilibrium, yield the riskless rate.

■ Given the price of the stock, its potential volatility, the option's exercise price, the life of the option, and the risk-free rate, there is but one price for the option if it is to meet the equilibrium condition, namely, that a portfolio that consists of the stock and the call option will earn the riskless rate.

The Black-Scholes Option Pricing Model (OPM) is widely used by option traders to estimate the value of a call option. It is based on the creation of a riskless portfolio, but which is applicable to "real-world" option pricing because it allows for a complete range of ending stock prices.

■ The assumptions made in the OPM are:
  ☐ The stock underlying the call option provides no dividends or other distributions during the life of the option.
  ☐ There are no transaction costs for buying or selling either the stock or the option.
  ☐ The short-term, risk-free interest rate is known and is constant during the life of the option.
  ☐ Any purchaser of a security may borrow any fraction of the purchase price at the short-term, risk-free interest rate.
  ☐ Short selling is permitted, and the short seller will receive immediately the full cash proceeds of today's price for a security sold short.
  ☐ The call option can be exercised only on its expiration date.
  ☐ Trading in all securities takes place continuously, and the stock price moves randomly.

■ The Black-Scholes model consists of the following three equations:

$$V = P[N(d_1)] - Xe^{-k_{RF}t}[N(d_2)].$$

$$d_1 = \frac{\ln(P/X) + [k_{RF} + (\sigma^2/2)]t}{\sigma\sqrt{t}}.$$

$$d_2 = d_1 - \sigma\sqrt{t}.$$

  ☐ V = current value of the call option.
  ☐ P = current price of the underlying stock.

☐ $N(d_i)$ = probability that a deviation less than d_i will occur in a standard normal distribution. Thus, $N(d_1)$ and $N(d_2)$ represent areas under a standard normal distribution function.

☐ X = exercise, or strike, price of the option.

☐ $e \approx 2.7183$.

☐ k_{RF} = risk-free interest rate.

☐ t = time until the option expires (the option period).

☐ $\ln(P/X)$ = natural logarithm of P/X.

☐ σ^2 = variance of the rate of return on the stock.

■ If the actual option price is different from the one determined by the Black-Scholes Option Pricing Model, this would provide the opportunity for arbitrage profits, which would force the option price back to the value indicated by the model.

Put and call options represent an important class of derivative securities, but there are other types of derivatives, including forward contracts, futures, swaps, structured notes, inverse floaters, and a host of other "exotic" contracts.

■ *Forward contracts* are agreements under which one party agrees to buy a commodity at a specific price on a specific future date and the other party agrees to make the sale. Physical delivery occurs.

■ A *futures contract* is similar to a forward contract, but with three key differences.

☐ Futures contracts are "marked to market" on a daily basis, meaning that gains and losses are noted and money must be put up to cover losses.

☐ With futures, physical delivery of the underlying asset is virtually never taken—the two parties simply settle up with cash for the difference between the contracted price and the actual price on the expiration date.

☐ Futures contracts are generally standardized instruments that are traded on exchanges, whereas forward contracts are generally tailor-made, are negotiated between two parties, and are not traded after they have been signed.

■ Futures and forward contracts were originally used for commodities, but today more trading is done in foreign exchange and interest rate futures.

☐ Interest rate futures are based on a hypothetical 20-year Treasury bond with a 6 percent semiannual coupon. If interest rates in the economy go up, the value of the hypothetical T-bond will go down, and vice versa.

☐ The primary motivation behind the vast majority of these transactions (forward contracts and futures) is to hedge risks, not to create them.

■ In a *swap* two parties agree to swap something, generally obligations to make specified payment streams. Most swaps today involve either interest payments or currencies.

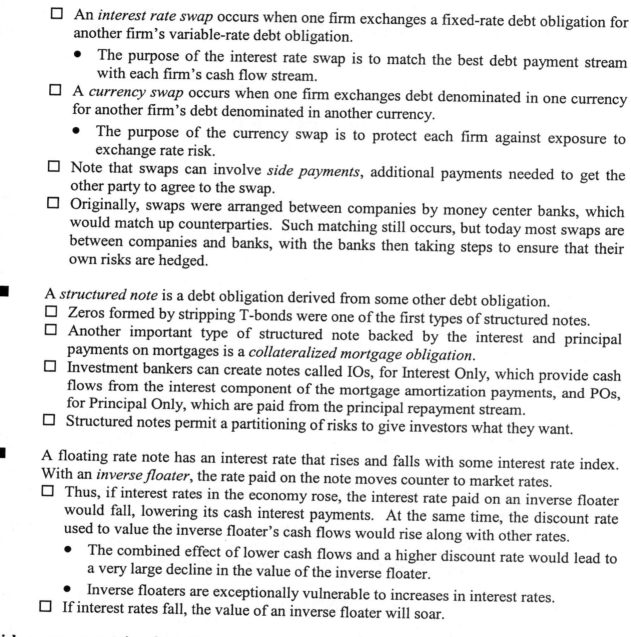

- ☐ An *interest rate swap* occurs when one firm exchanges a fixed-rate debt obligation for another firm's variable-rate debt obligation.
  - • The purpose of the interest rate swap is to match the best debt payment stream with each firm's cash flow stream.
- ☐ A *currency swap* occurs when one firm exchanges debt denominated in one currency for another firm's debt denominated in another currency.
  - • The purpose of the currency swap is to protect each firm against exposure to exchange rate risk.
- ☐ Note that swaps can involve *side payments*, additional payments needed to get the other party to agree to the swap.
- ☐ Originally, swaps were arranged between companies by money center banks, which would match up counterparties. Such matching still occurs, but today most swaps are between companies and banks, with the banks then taking steps to ensure that their own risks are hedged.

- ■ A *structured note* is a debt obligation derived from some other debt obligation.
  - ☐ Zeros formed by stripping T-bonds were one of the first types of structured notes.
  - ☐ Another important type of structured note backed by the interest and principal payments on mortgages is a *collateralized mortgage obligation*.
  - ☐ Investment bankers can create notes called IOs, for Interest Only, which provide cash flows from the interest component of the mortgage amortization payments, and POs, for Principal Only, which are paid from the principal repayment stream.
  - ☐ Structured notes permit a partitioning of risks to give investors what they want.

- ■ A floating rate note has an interest rate that rises and falls with some interest rate index. With an *inverse floater*, the rate paid on the note moves counter to market rates.
  - ☐ Thus, if interest rates in the economy rose, the interest rate paid on an inverse floater would fall, lowering its cash interest payments. At the same time, the discount rate used to value the inverse floater's cash flows would rise along with other rates.
    - • The combined effect of lower cash flows and a higher discount rate would lead to a very large decline in the value of the inverse floater.
    - • Inverse floaters are exceptionally vulnerable to increases in interest rates.
  - ☐ If interest rates fall, the value of an inverse floater will soar.

Risk management involves the management of unpredictable events that have adverse consequences for the firm. Risk can be classified in many ways and different classifications are commonly used in different industries.

- ■ Here's one list that provides an idea of the wide variety of risks to which a firm can be exposed: pure risks, speculative risks, demand risks, input risks, financial risks, property risks, personnel risks, environmental risks, liability risks, and insurable risks.

■   Different classifications are commonly used in different industries.

Firms often use the following three-step approach to risk management: (1) identify the risks faced by the firm; (2) measure the potential effect of the risks identified; and (3) decide how each relevant risk should be handled.

■   There are several techniques to help minimize risk exposure:
- ☐ *Transfer the risk to an insurance company.* Often, it is advantageous to insure against, and hence transfer, a risk.
  - Insurability does not necessarily mean that a risk should be covered by insurance.
  - It might be better for the company to *self-insure*, which means bearing the risk directly rather than paying to have another party bear the risk.
- ☐ *Transfer the function that produces the risk to a third party.* In some situations, risks can be reduced most easily by passing them on to some other company that is not an insurance company.
- ☐ Purchase derivative contracts to reduce risk. Firms use derivatives to hedge risk.
- ☐ *Reduce the probability of occurrence of an adverse event.* In some instances, it is possible to take action to reduce the probability that an adverse event will occur.
- ☐ Reduce the magnitude of the loss associated with an adverse event.
- ☐ Totally avoid the activity that gives rise to the risk.

■   Risk management decisions, like all corporate decisions, should be based on a cost/benefit analysis for each feasible alternative.
- ☐ The same financial management techniques applied to other corporate decisions can also be applied to risk management decisions.

Firms are subject to numerous risks related to interest rate, stock price, and exchange rate fluctuations in the financial markets. For an investor, one of the most obvious ways to reduce financial risks is to hold a broadly diversified portfolio of stocks and debt securities; however, derivatives can also be used to reduce the risks associated with financial and commodity markets.

■   One of the most useful tools for reducing interest rate, exchange rate, and commodity risk is to *hedge* in the futures markets.
- ☐ Futures contracts are divided into two classes, *commodity futures* and *financial futures*.
  - Commodity futures are contracts that are used to hedge against price changes for input materials.
  - Financial futures are contracts that are used to hedge against fluctuating interest rates, stock prices, and exchange rates.

☐ When futures contracts are purchased, the purchaser does not have to put up the full amount of the purchase price; rather, the purchaser is required to post an initial *margin*. However, investors are required to maintain a certain value in the margin account, called a *maintenance margin*.

- If the value of the contract declines, then the owner may be required to add additional funds to the margin account, and the more the contract value falls, the more money must be added.

☐ An *option* is similar to a futures contract, but it merely gives someone the right to buy (call) or sell (put) an asset, but the holder of the option does not have to complete the transaction. A *futures contract*, on the other hand, is a definite agreement on the part of one party to buy something on a specific date and a specific price, and the other party agrees to sell on the same terms. The two parties must settle the contract at the agreed-upon price.

- Options exist both for individual stocks and for "bundles" of stocks such as those in the S&P and *Value Line* indexes, but generally not for commodities.

- Futures, on the other hand, are used for commodities, debt securities, and stock indexes.

■ Firms are exposed to losses due to changes in security prices when securities are held in investment portfolios, and they are also exposed during times when securities are being issued. In addition, firms are exposed to risk when floating rate debt is used to finance an investment that produces a fixed income stream. These types of risk can be reduced by using *derivatives*. *Futures and swaps* are two types of derivatives used to manage security price exposure.

☐ *Futures markets* are used for both speculation and hedging: *Speculation* involves betting on future price movements; *hedging* is done by a firm or individual to protect against a price change that would otherwise negatively affect profits.

- There are two basic types of hedges: (1) *long hedges*, in which futures contracts are bought in anticipation of (or to guard against) price increases, and (2) *short hedges*, where a firm or individual sells futures contracts to guard against price declines.

☐ A *perfect hedge* occurs when the gain or loss on the hedged transaction exactly offsets the loss or gain on the unhedged position.

☐ The futures and options markets permit flexibility in the timing of financial transactions, because the firm can be protected, at least partially, against changes that occur between the time a decision is reached and the time when the transaction will be completed. However, this protection has a cost—the firm must pay commissions.

- A *swap* is another method for reducing financial risks. It is an exchange of cash payment obligations, in which each party to the swap prefers the payment type or pattern of the other party.

- Major changes have occurred over time in the swaps market. Standardized contracts have been developed for the most common types of swaps, and this has had two effects: (1) Standardized contracts lower the time and effort involved in arranging swaps, and thus lower transaction costs. (2) The development of standardized contracts has led to a secondary market for swaps, which has increased the liquidity and efficiency of the swaps market.

While the use of derivatives to hedge risk is an important tool for risk managers, if improperly constructed or if derivatives are used for speculation purposes, they have the potential to create very large losses in very short periods.

■ Hedging allows managers to concentrate on running their core businesses without having to worry about interest rate, currency, and commodity price variability.

■ CFOs, CEOs, and board members should be reasonably knowledgeable about the derivatives their firms use, should establish policies regarding when they can and cannot be used, and should establish audit procedures to ensure that the policies are actually carried out.

■ Moreover, a firm's derivatives position should be reported to stockholders.

SELF-TEST QUESTIONS

Definitional

1. _____ _____ involves the management of unpredictable events that have adverse financial consequences for the firm.

2. Firms often use a three-step approach to risk management: (1) _____ the risks faced by the firm, (2) _____ the potential effect of the risks identified, and (3) decide how each relevant risk should be handled.

3. To _____-_____ means bearing the risk directly rather than paying to have another party bear the risk.

4. Risk management decisions, like all corporate decisions, should be based on a(n) _____/_____ analysis for each feasible alternative.

5. When the exercise price exceeds the current stock price a call option is said to be _____-_____-_____; however, when the exercise price is less than the current price of the underlying stock, a call option is _____-_____-_____.

6.   The _____-_____ _____ _____ _____ is widely used by option traders to estimate the value of a call option.

7.   _____ _____ are generally standardized instruments that are traded on exchanges and that are "marked to market" daily, but where physical delivery of the underlying asset is virtually never taken.

8.   Futures markets are used for both hedging and speculation: _____ involves betting on future price movements, while _____ is done by a firm or individual to protect against price changes that would otherwise negatively affect profits.

9.   _____ are securities whose values are determined, in whole or in part, by the market price (or interest rate) of some other asset.

10.   A(n) _____ is an exchange of cash payment obligations, in which each party to the transaction prefers the payment type or pattern of the other party.

11.   A(n) _____ _____ is a debt obligation derived from some other debt obligation, for example, collateralized mortgage obligations.

12.   The two parties involved in derivatives transactions are called _____.

13.   _____ _____ are situations in which aggregate risk can be reduced by derivatives transactions between two parties.

14.   A(n) _____ is a contract that gives its holder the right to buy (or sell) an asset at a predetermined price within a specified period of time.

15.   The _____, or _____, price is the price that must be paid for a share of common stock when an option is exercised.

16.   The seller of an option is called the option _____.

17.   An investor who writes call options against stock held in his or her portfolio is said to be selling _____ options.

18.   Options sold without the stock to back them up are called _____ options.

19.   An option that gives you the right to sell a stock at a specified price within some future period is called a(n) _____ option.

20. Conventional options are generally written for 6 months or less, but a new type of option called a(n) _____-_____ _____ _____ Security has a maturity of up to 2½ years.

21. A call option's _____ _____ is equal to the current stock price less the strike price.

22. _____ _____ are agreements under which one party agrees to buy a commodity at a specific price on a specific future date and the other party agrees to make the sale. Physical delivery occurs.

23. A floating rate note has an interest rate that rises and falls with some interest rate index. With a(n) _____ _____, the rate paid on the note moves counter to market rates.

24. _____ futures are contracts that are used to hedge against price changes for input materials.

25. _____ futures are contracts that are used to hedge against fluctuating interest rates, stock prices, and exchange rates.

26. There are two basic types of hedges: (1) _____ hedges, in which futures contracts are bought in anticipation of (or to guard against) price increases, and (2) _____ hedges, where a firm or individual sells futures contracts to guard against price declines.

27. A(n) _____ option is an option to buy a share of stock at a certain price within a specified period.

28. A(n) _____ _____ occurs when an investor buys a stock and simultaneously sells a call option on that stock and ends up with a riskless position.

29. A(n) _____ _____ _____ occurs when one firm exchanges a fixed-rate debt obligation for another firm's variable-rate debt obligation.

30. A(n) _____ _____ occurs when the gain or loss on the hedged transaction exactly offsets the loss or gain on the unhedged position.

Conceptual

31. The two basic types of hedges involving the futures market are long hedges and short hedges, where the words "long" and "short" refer to the maturity of the hedging instrument. For example, a long hedge might use stocks, while a short hedge might use 3-month T-bills.

    a. True   **b.** False

32. Speculators add capital and players to the derivatives market; thus, this tends to make the market unstable.

    a. True   **b.** False

33. A swap is a method for reducing financial risk. Which of the following statements about swaps, if any, is *incorrect*?

    a. A swap involves the exchange of cash payment obligations.
    b. The earliest swaps were currency swaps, in which companies traded debt denominated in different currencies, say dollars and pounds.
    c. Swaps are generally arranged by a financial intermediary, who may or may not take the position of one of the counterparties.
    d. A problem with swaps is the lack of standardized contracts, which limits the development of a secondary market.
    e. None of the statements are incorrect; all of the above statements are correct.

34. Which of the following statements regarding futures and forward contracts is most correct?

    a. Futures contracts are similar to forward contracts except for the length of time the contract is outstanding.
    b. Forward contracts are "marked to market" on a daily basis, while futures contracts are not "marked to market."
    c. With forward contracts, physical delivery of the underlying asset is virtually never taken.
    d. Forward contracts are generally standardized instruments that are traded on exchanges, whereas futures contracts are generally tailor-made, are negotiated between two parties, and are not traded after they have been signed.
    e. All of the above statements are false.

35. Which of the following statements is most correct?

    a. Recently, the scope of risk management has been broadened to include things like controlling the costs of key inputs or protecting against changes in interest rates on exchange rates.

    b. Hedging with futures raises the aggregate risk in the economy.

    c. Corporations on whose stocks options are written have nothing to do with the option market.

    d. The actual market price of an option lies below the exercise value at each price of the common stock, although the premium rises as the stock price increases.

    e. Statements a and c are correct.

SELF-TEST PROBLEMS

1. A call option on the stock of Heuser Enterprises has a market price of $15. The stock sells for $38 a share, and the option has an exercise price of $30 a share. What is the exercise value of the call option?

    a. $5.00   **b.** $6.25   **c.** $7.00   **d.** $7.50   **e.** $8.00

2. Refer to Self-Test Problem 1. What is the premium on the option?

    a. $5.00   **b.** $6.25   **c.** $7.00   **d.** $7.50   **e.** $8.00

3. Assume you have been given the following information on Detweiler Industries:

Current stock price = $27.50   Option's exercise price = $27.50

Time to maturity of option = 3 months   Risk-free rate = 8%

Variance of stock price = 0.14 $d_1 = 0.20045$

$d_2 = 0.01336$ $N(d_1) = 0.57942$

$N(d_2) = 0.50533$

Using the Black-Scholes Option Pricing Model, what would be the option's value?

    a. $2.00   **b.** $2.31   **c.** $2.73   **d.** $3.18   **e.** $3.75

4. What is the implied interest rate on a Treasury bond ($100,000) futures contract that settled at 101-2?

    a. 5.91%   **b.** 6.05%   **c.** 6.55%   **d.** 6.73%   **e.** 7.25%

5. Refer to Self-Test Problem 4. If the interest rate were 6.50 percent, what would be the contract's new value?

    a. $101,062.50 **b.** $100,235.33 **c.** $97,875.42 **d.** $94,447.89 **e.** $93,657.44

ANSWERS TO SELF-TEST QUESTIONS

1.	Risk management		**16.**	writer
2.	identify; measure		**17.**	covered
3.	self-insure		**18.**	naked
4.	cost/benefit		**19.**	put
5.	out-of-the-money; in-the-money		**20.**	Long-Term Equity Anticipation
6.	Black-Scholes Option Pricing Model		**21.**	exercise value
7.	Futures contracts		**22.**	Forward contracts
8.	speculation; hedging		**23.**	inverse floater
9.	Derivatives		**24.**	Commodity
10.	swap		**25.**	Financial
11.	structured note		**26.**	long; short
12.	counterparties		**27.**	call
13.	Natural hedges		**28.**	riskless hedge
14.	option		**29.**	interest rate swap
15.	strike; exercise		**30.**	perfect hedge

31. b. Long hedges are futures contracts bought to guard against price increases, while short hedges are futures contracts sold to guard against price declines.

32. b. These very things tend to stabilize the market.

33. d. Standardized contracts have been developed for the most common types of swaps.

34. e. Futures contracts are similar to forward contracts except for three key differences: (1) Futures contracts are "marked to market," (2) physical delivery of the underlying asset is virtually never taken, and (3) futures contracts are standardized instruments that are traded on the exchange.

35. e. Statement b is false because hedging lowers the aggregate risk in the economy. Statement d is false because an option's market value lies above its exercise value at each price of the common stock, although the premium declines as the stock price increases. Since statement a and c are correct, the proper choice is statement e.

SOLUTIONS TO SELF-TEST PROBLEMS

1. e. Exercise value = Current stock price – Strike price
$$= \$38 - \$30$$
$$= \$8.$$

2. c. Premium = Option's market price – Exercise value
$$= \$15 - \$8$$
$$= \$7.$$

3. b. $V = P[N(d_1)] - Xe^{-k_{RF}t}[N(d_2)]$
$$= \$27.50(0.57942) - \$27.50e^{-0.02}[0.50533]$$
$$= \$15.93 - \$13.62$$
$$= \$2.31.$$

4. a. Futures contract settled at 101 2/32% of $100,000 contract value, so PV = 1.010625 × $1,000 = 1,010.625 × 100 bonds = $101,062.50. Using a financial calculator, we can solve for k_d as follows:

   N = 40; PV = -1010.625; PMT = 30; FV = 1000; solve for I = k_d = 2.9544% × 2 = 5.9087% ≈ 5.91%.

5. d. If the interest rate were 6.50%, then we would solve for PV as follows:

   N = 40; I = 6.50/2 = 3.25; PMT = 30; FV = 1000; solve for PV = $944.4789 × 100 = $94,447.89.

CHAPTER 19
MULTINATIONAL FINANCIAL MANAGEMENT

LEARNING OBJECTIVES

- Define the term "multinational corporation" and identify 6 primary reasons why firms go international.

- List six major factors that distinguish financial management in firms operating entirely within a single country from those that operate in several different countries.

- Distinguish between direct and indirect quotations, and calculate exchange rates between any two or three countries.

- Briefly explain the following terms: floating rate system, trade deficit, pegged exchange rate, and convertible currency.

- Differentiate between spot and forward rates, and explain what it means for a forward currency to sell at a discount or premium.

- Briefly explain the concepts of interest rate and purchasing power parity.

- Explain the implications of relative inflation rates, or rates of inflation in foreign countries compared with that in the home country on multinational financial decisions.

- Distinguish between foreign portfolio investments and direct investments, and briefly explain the following terms: Eurodollar, Eurocurrencies, LIBOR, foreign bonds, and Eurobonds.

- Identify some key differences in capital budgeting as applied to foreign versus domestic operations including the following terms: repatriation of earnings, exchange rate risk, and political risk.

- Explain whether international differences in financial leverage exist.

- List some factors that make working capital management especially complicated in a multinational corporation.

OVERVIEW

As the world economy becomes more integrated, the role of multinational firms is increasing. Although the same basic principles of financial management apply to multinational corporations as well as to domestic ones, the financial managers of multinational firms face a much more complex task. The primary problem, from a financial standpoint, is that cash flows must cross national boundaries.

These flows may be constrained in various ways, and, equally important, their values in dollars may rise or fall depending on exchange rate fluctuations. This means that the multinational financial manager must be constantly aware of the many complex interactions among national economies and their effects on international operations.

OUTLINE

A multinational, or global, corporation is one that operates in an integrated fashion in a number of countries. The growth of multinationals has greatly increased the degree of worldwide economic and political interdependence.

- ■ Companies, both U.S. and foreign, go "international" for six primary reasons:
  - ☐ After a company has saturated its home market, growth opportunities are often better in foreign markets.
  - ☐ Many of the present multinational firms began their international operations because raw materials were located abroad.
  - ☐ Because no single nation holds a commanding advantage in all technologies, companies are scouring the globe for leading scientific and design ideas.
  - ☐ Still other firms have moved their manufacturing facilities overseas to take advantage of cheaper production costs in low-cost countries.
  - ☐ Firms can avoid political and regulatory hurdles by moving production to other countries.
  - ☐ Finally, firms go international so that they can diversify, and consequently, cushion the impact of adverse economic trends in any single country.

- ■ Over the past 10 to 15 years, there has been an increasing amount of investment in the U.S. by foreign corporations, and in foreign nations by U.S. corporations. These developments suggest an increasing degree of mutual influence and interdependence among business enterprises and nations, to which the United States is not immune.

In theory, financial concepts and procedures are valid for both domestic and multinational operations. However, there are six major factors that distinguish financial management as

practiced by firms operating entirely within a single country from management by firms that operate globally. These six factors complicate financial management, and they increase the risks faced by multinational firms. However, the prospects for high returns, diversification benefits, and other factors make it worthwhile for firms to accept these risks and learn how to manage them.

- Cash flows will be denominated in different currencies, making exchange rate analysis necessary for all types of financial decisions.

- Economic and legal differences among countries can cause significant problems when the corporation tries to coordinate and control worldwide operations of its subsidiaries.

- The ability to communicate is critical in all business transactions. U.S. citizens are often at a disadvantage because we are generally fluent only in English.

- Values and the role of business in society reflect the cultural differences that may vary dramatically from one country to the next.

- Financial models based on the traditional assumption of a competitive marketplace must often be modified to include political (governmental) and other noneconomic facets of the decision.

- *Political risk,* which is seldom negotiable and may be as extreme as *expropriation,* must be explicitly addressed in financial analysis. Political risk varies from country to country.

An exchange rate specifies the number of units of a given currency that can be purchased for one unit of another currency.

- An *exchange rate* listed as the number of U.S. dollars required to purchase one unit of foreign currency is called a *direct quotation.*
  - ☐ The number of units of foreign currency that can be purchased for one U.S. dollar is called an *indirect quotation.*
    - Indirect quotations often begin with the foreign currency's equivalent to the dollar sign.
  - ☐ Normal practice in the U.S. is to use indirect quotations for all currencies other than British pounds, for which direct quotations are given.

- It is also a universal convention on the world's foreign currency exchanges to state all exchange rates except British pounds on a "dollar basis"—that is, as the foreign currency price of one U.S. dollar.
  - ☐ This convention eliminates confusion when comparing quotations from one trading center with those from another.

■ Converting from one foreign currency to another foreign currency may require the use of *cross rates*. For example, if the direct quotation between pounds and dollars is $1.4428 and the indirect quotation between euros and dollars is 1.1215 euros, the cross rate between pounds and euros can be calculated as follows:

$$\text{Cross rate} = \frac{\text{Dollars}}{\text{Pound}} \times \frac{\text{Euros}}{\text{Dollar}} = \frac{\text{Euros}}{\text{Pound}}$$
$$= 1.4428 \text{ dollars per pound} \times 1.1215 \text{ euros per dollar}$$
$$= 1.6181 \text{ euros per pound.}$$

■ The tie-in with the dollar ensures that all currencies are related to one another in a consistent manner. If this consistency did not exist, currency traders could profit by buying undervalued currencies and selling overvalued currencies. This process, known as *arbitrage*, works to bring about an equilibrium, and that, at any point in time cross rates are all internally consistent.

Every nation has a monetary system and a monetary authority. If countries are to trade with one another, there must be some sort of system designed to facilitate payments between nations.

■ The United States and other major trading nations currently operate under a system of floating exchange rates.
  □ A *floating exchange rate system* is one under which currency prices are allowed to reach their own levels without much governmental intervention.
  □ The present managed floating system permits currency rates to move without any specific limits, but central banks do buy and sell currencies to smooth out exchange rate fluctuations.
   • Each central bank would like to keep its average exchange rate at a level deemed desirable by its government's economic policy. This is important, because exchange rates have a profound effect on the levels of imports and exports, which influence the level of domestic employment. A *trade deficit* occurs when a country imports more than it exports.
   • Market forces will prevail in the long run.

■ The inherent volatility of exchange rates under a floating system increases the uncertainty of the cash flows for a multinational corporation. This uncertainty is known as *exchange rate risk*, and it is a major factor differentiating a global corporation from a purely domestic one.

■ In today's floating-exchange-rate environment, some smaller countries have chosen to peg their currencies to one or more major currencies.
  □ Countries with *pegged exchange rates* establish a fixed exchange rate with another major currency, and then the values of the pegged currencies move together over time.

■ Not all currencies are *convertible*. A currency is convertible when the issuing nation allows it to be traded in the currency markets and is willing to redeem the currency at market rates.
  □ This means that, except for limited central bank influence, the issuing government loses control over the value of its currency.
  □ A lack of convertibility creates major problems for international trade.

Importers, exporters, and tourists, as well as governments, buy and sell currencies in the foreign exchange market, which consists of a network of brokers and banks based in New York, London, Tokyo, and other financial centers. Most buy and sell orders are conducted by computer and telephone.

■ The rate paid for delivery of currency no more than two days after the day of trade is called the *spot rate*.

■ When currency is bought or sold and is to be delivered at some agreed-upon future date, usually 30, 90, or 180 days into the future, a *forward exchange rate* is used.
  □ If one can obtain more of the foreign currency for a dollar in the forward market than in the spot market, then the forward currency is less valuable than the spot currency, and the forward currency is said to be selling at a *discount*.
  □ If a dollar will buy fewer units of a currency in the forward market than in the spot market, then the forward currency is more valuable than the spot currency, and the forward currency is said to be selling at a *premium*.

Market forces determine whether a currency sells at a forward premium or discount, and the general relationship between spot and forward exchange rates is specified in a concept called interest rate parity.

■ *Interest rate parity* holds that investors should expect to earn the same return on security investments in all countries after adjusting for risk.
  □ It recognizes that when you invest in a country other than your home country, you are affected by two forces—returns on the investment itself and changes in the exchange rate.
    ● Your overall return will be higher than the investment's stated return if the currency in which your investment is denominated appreciates relative to your home currency.
    ● Your overall return will be lower if the foreign currency you receive declines in value.

■ Interest rate parity is expressed as follows:

$$\frac{\text{Forward exchange rate}}{\text{Spot exchange rate}} = \frac{(1 + k_h)}{(1 + k_f)}.$$

- □ Both the forward and spot rates are expressed in terms of the amount of home currency received per unit of foreign currency.
- □ k_h and k_f are the periodic interest rates in the home country and foreign country, respectively.

- ■ Interest rate parity shows why a particular currency might be at a forward premium or discount.
    - □ Notice that a currency is at a forward premium whenever domestic interest rates are higher than foreign interest rates ($k_h > k_f$).
    - □ Discounts prevail if domestic interest rates are lower than foreign interest rates.
    - □ If these conditions do not hold, then arbitrage forces interest rates back to parity.

Market forces work to ensure that similar goods sell for similar prices in different countries after taking exchange rates into account. This relationship is known as purchasing power parity (PPP).

- ■ *Purchasing power parity (PPP)*, sometimes referred to as the law of one price, implies that the level of exchange rates adjusts so that identical goods cost the same amount in different countries.

- ■ The equation for purchasing power parity is

$$P_h = (P_f)(\text{Spot rate}) \text{ or Spot rate} = \frac{P_h}{P_f}.$$

    - □ P_h is the price of the good in the home country.
    - □ P_f is the price of the good in the foreign country.
    - □ The spot market exchange rate is expressed as the number of units of home currency that can be exchanged for one unit of foreign currency.

- ■ PPP assumes that market forces will eliminate situations in which the same product sells at a different price overseas.

- ■ PPP assumes there are no transportation or transaction costs, or import restrictions, all of which limit the ability to ship goods between countries. In many cases, these assumptions are incorrect, which explains why PPP is often violated.
    - □ An additional complication is products in different countries are rarely identical. Frequently, there are real or perceived differences in quality, which can lead to price differences in different countries.

- ■ The concepts of interest rate parity and purchasing power parity are critically important to those engaged in international activities. Companies and investors must anticipate changes in interest rates, inflation, and exchange rates, and they often try to hedge the risks of adverse movements in these factors. Parity relationships are extremely useful in judging and anticipating future conditions.

Relative inflation rates, or the rates of inflation in foreign countries compared with that in the home country, have many implications for multinational financial decisions. Relative inflation rates will greatly influence future production costs at home and abroad. Equally important, inflation has a dominant influence on relative interest rates and exchange rates. Both of these factors influence the methods chosen by multinational corporations for financing their foreign investments, and both have an important effect on the profitability of foreign investments.

- A foreign currency, on average, will depreciate at a percentage rate approximately equal to the amount by which its country's inflation rate exceeds the U.S. inflation rate. Conversely, foreign currencies in countries with less inflation than the U.S. will, on average, appreciate relative to the U.S. dollar.

- Countries experiencing higher rates of inflation tend to have higher interest rates. The reverse is true for countries with lower inflation rates.

- Gains from borrowing in countries with low interest rates can be offset by losses from currency appreciation in those countries.

There exists a well developed system of international money and capital markets. It is important for both corporate managers and investors to have an understanding of international markets. These markets often offer better opportunities for raising or investing capital than are available domestically.

- Americans can invest in world markets by investing in the stock of U.S. multinational corporations or by buying the bonds and stocks of large corporations (or governments) headquartered outside the United States.
  - ☐ Investment by U.S. firms in foreign operating assets is called *direct investment.*
  - ☐ Investment in foreign stocks and bonds is called *portfolio investment.*

- The *Eurodollar market* is essentially a short-term market for handling dollar-denominated loans and deposits made outside the United States. Most loans and deposits are for less than one year.
  - ☐ A *Eurodollar* is a U.S. dollar deposited in a bank outside the United States. They are usually held in interest-bearing accounts.
  - ☐ The major difference between a dollar on deposit in Chicago and a dollar on deposit in London is the geographic location. The deposits do not involve different currencies, so

exchange rate considerations do not apply. However, Eurodollars are outside the direct control of the U.S. monetary authorities, so U.S. banking regulations, including reserve requirements and FDIC insurance premiums, do not apply.

☐ Although the dollar is the leading international currency, British pounds, Swiss francs, Japanese yen, and other currencies are also deposited outside their home countries; these *eurocurrencies* are handled in exactly the same way as eurodollars.

☐ If interest rates in the United States are above Eurodollar rates, these funds will be sent back and invested in the United States, while if Eurodollar deposit rates are significantly above U.S. interest rates, more dollars will be sent out of the United States.

☐ Interest rates on Eurodollar deposits (and loans) are tied to a standard rate known as the *London Interbank Offer Rate (LIBOR)*, the rate of interest offered by the largest and strongest London banks on dollar deposits of significant size.

■ Any bond sold outside the country of the borrower is called an *international bond*. However, two international bond markets have developed that trade in long-term funds.

☐ *Foreign bonds* are bonds sold by a foreign borrower but denominated in the currency of the country in which the issue is sold.

☐ *Eurobonds* are bonds sold in a country other than the one in whose currency the issue is denominated.

   ● The institutional arrangements by which Eurobonds are marketed are different than those for most other bond issues, with the most important distinction being a far lower level of required disclosure than is usually found for bonds issued in domestic markets, particularly in the United States.

☐ Eurobonds appeal to investors for several reasons.

   ● Generally, they are issued in bearer form rather than as registered bonds, so the names and nationalities of investors are not recorded.

   ● Most governments do not withhold taxes on interest payments associated with Eurobonds.

■ New issues of stock are sold in international markets for a variety of reasons.

☐ Firms are able to tap a much larger source of capital than their home countries.

☐ Firms want to create an equity market presence to accompany operations in foreign countries.

☐ Large multinational companies also occasionally issue new stock simultaneously in multiple countries.

■ In addition to new issues, outstanding stocks of large multinational companies are increasingly being listed on multiple international exchanges.

■   In addition to direct listing, U.S. investors can invest in foreign companies through *American depository receipts (ADRs)*, which are certificates representing ownership of foreign stock held in trust.

        ☐ About 1,700 ADRs are now available in the United States, with most of them traded on the over-the-counter market.

There are several important differences in the capital budgeting analysis of foreign versus domestic operations.

■   Cash flow estimation is much more complex for overseas investments.

        ☐ Usually a firm will organize a separate subsidiary in each foreign country in which it operates.

        ☐ Any dividends or royalties repatriated by the subsidiary must be converted to the currency of the parent company and thus are subject to exchange rate risk.

            ● *Repatriation of earnings* is the process of sending cash flows from a foreign subsidiary back to the parent company.

        ☐ Dividends and royalties received are normally taxed by both foreign and domestic governments.

        ☐ Some governments place restrictions, or exchange controls, on the amount of cash that may be repatriated to the parent company in order to encourage reinvestment of earnings in the foreign country or to prevent large currency outflows, which might disrupt the exchange rate.

        ☐ The relevant cash flows for analysis of an international investment are the financial cash flows that the subsidiary can legally send back to the parent.

            ● The present value of those cash flows is found by applying an appropriate discount rate, and this present value is then compared with the parent's required investment to determine the project's NPV.

■   The cost of capital may be different for foreign investments because they may be more or less risky than domestic investments. A higher risk could arise from two primary sources: (1) exchange rate risk and (2) political risk. A lower risk might result from international diversification.

        ☐ *Exchange rate risk* relates to the value of the basic cash flows in the parent company's home currency.

            ● An exchange rate risk premium should be added to the domestic cost of capital to reflect this risk.

            ● It is sometimes possible to hedge against exchange rate fluctuations, but not completely. If hedging is used, the costs must be subtracted from the project's cash flows.

☐ *Political risk* refers to potential actions by a host government that would reduce the value of a company's investment.

- It includes at one extreme the *expropriation* without compensation of the subsidiary's assets, but it also includes less drastic actions that reduce the value of the parent firm's investment in the foreign subsidiary, including higher taxes, tighter repatriation or currency controls, and restrictions on prices charged.

■ Companies can take steps to reduce the potential loss from expropriation in three major ways.
☐ Finance the subsidiary with local capital.
☐ Structure operations so that the subsidiary has value only as a part of the integrated corporate system.
☐ Obtain insurance against economic losses from expropriation.

- Insurance premiums would have to be added to the project's cost.

Companies' capital structures vary among the large industrial nations.

■ After adjusting for accounting differences, evidence suggests that companies in Germany and the United Kingdom tend to have less leverage, whereas firms in Canada appear to have more leverage, relative to firms in the United States, France, Italy, and Japan.
☐ This conclusion is supported by the times-interest-earned ratio data. In general, firms with more leverage have a lower times-interest-earned ratio. The data indicate that this ratio is highest in the United Kingdom and Germany and lowest in Canada.

The objectives of working capital management in the multinational corporation are similar to those in the domestic firm but the task is more complex.

■ The objectives of cash management in the multinational corporation are to speed up collections and to slow disbursements to maximize net float, to shift cash rapidly from those parts of the business that do not need it to those parts that do, and to obtain the highest possible risk-adjusted rate of return on temporary cash balances.
☐ The same general procedures are used by multinational firms as those used by domestic firms, but because of longer distances and more serious mail delays, lockbox systems and electronic funds transfers are especially important.

■ Granting credit is more risky in an international context because, in addition to the normal risks of default, the multinational corporation must also worry about exchange rate changes between the time a sale is made and the time a receivable is collected.
☐ Credit policy is generally more important for a multinational firm than for a domestic firm.
☐ Much of the U.S.'s trade is with poorer, less-developed countries; thus, granting credit is generally a necessary condition for doing business.

☐ Nations whose economic health depends upon exports often help their manufacturing firms compete internationally by granting credit to foreign countries.

■ The physical location of inventories is a complex consideration for the multinational firm.
☐ The multinational firm must weigh a strategy of keeping inventory concentrated in a few areas from which they can be shipped, and thus minimize the total amount of inventory needed to operate the global business, with the possibility of delays in getting goods from central locations to user locations around the world.
☐ Exchange rates, import/export quotas or tariffs, the threat of expropriation, and taxes all influence inventory policy.
● Multinational firms may consider the possibility of at-sea storage. This eliminates the danger of expropriation, minimizes the property tax problem, and maximizes flexibility with regard to shipping to areas where needs are greatest or prices highest.

SELF-TEST QUESTIONS

Definitional

1. The _____ _____ specifies the number of units of one currency that can be purchased for one unit of another currency.

2. A(n) _____ _____ rate system is one under which currency prices are allowed to reach their own levels without much governmental intervention.

3. Evaluation of foreign investments involves the analysis of dividend and royalty cash flows that are _____ to the parent company.

4. Some foreign governments restrict, or block, the amount of income that can be repatriated to encourage _____ in the foreign country.

5. _____ risk refers to potential actions by a host government that would reduce the value of a company's investment.

6. A dollar deposited in a non-U.S. bank is often called a(n) _____.

7. Investment by U.S. firms in foreign operations is called _____ investment, while the purchase of foreign bonds and stock by U.S. citizens or firms is called _____ investment.

8. _____ bonds are bonds sold by a foreign borrower but denominated in the currency of the country in which the issue is sold.

9. A(n) _____ corporation is one that operates in an integrated fashion in a number of countries.

10. An exchange rate listed as the number of U.S. dollars required to purchase one unit of foreign currency is called a(n) _____ quotation. The number of units of foreign currency that can be purchased for one U.S. dollar is called a(n) _____ quotation.

11. _____ is the process that works to bring about an equilibrium among exchange rates.

12. A currency is _____ when the issuing nation allows it to be traded in the currency markets and is willing to redeem the currency at market rates.

13. Countries with _____ exchange rates establish a fixed exchange rate with another major currency, and then the values of these currencies move together over time.

14. The rate paid for delivery of currency no more than two days after the day of trade is called the _____ rate.

15. When currency is bought or sold and is to be delivered at some agreed-upon future date a(n) _____ exchange rate is used.

16. _____ _____ _____ holds that investors should expect to earn the same return on security investments in all countries after adjusting for risk.

17. _____ _____ _____, sometimes referred to as the law of one price, implies that the level of exchange rates adjusts so that identical goods cost the same amount in different countries.

18. The _____ _____ _____ _____ is the rate of interest offered by the largest and strongest London banks on dollar deposits of significant size.

19. _____ are bonds sold in a country other than the one in whose currency the issue is denominated.

20. _____ _____ _____ are certificates representing ownership of foreign stock held in trust.

21. If a dollar will buy fewer units of a currency in the forward market than in the spot market, then the forward currency is more valuable than the spot currency, and the forward currency is said to be selling at a(n) _____.

22. Converting from one foreign currency to another foreign currency may require the use of _____ _____.

23. Although the dollar is the leading international currency, British pounds, Swiss francs, Japanese yen, and other currencies are also deposited outside their home countries; these _____ are handled in exactly the same way as eurodollars.

24. Any bond sold outside the country of the borrower is called a(n) _____ bond.

25. _____ ____ _____ is the process of sending cash flows from a foreign subsidiary back to the parent company.

26. Normal practice in the U.S. is to use _____ quotations for all currencies other than British pounds, for which _____ quotations are given.

27. Eurobonds are issued in _____ form rather than as registered bonds, so the names and nationalities of investors are not recorded.

28. A(n) _____ _____ occurs when a country imports more than it exports.

29. If one can obtain more of the foreign currency for a dollar in the forward market than in the spot market, then the forward currency is less valuable than the spot currency, and the forward currency is said to be selling at a(n) _____.

30. Your overall return will be higher than the investment's stated return if the currency in which your investment is denominated _____ relative to your home country.

Conceptual

31. Financial analysis is not able to take into account political risk.

    a. True   **b.** False

32. Over the past 10 to 15 years, there has been an increasing amount of investment in the U.S. by foreign corporations, and in foreign nations by U.S. corporations. These developments suggest an increasing degree of mutual influence and interdependence among business enterprises and nations, to which the United States is not immune.

    a. True   **b.** False

33. A foreign currency will, on average, appreciate at a percentage rate approximately equal to the amount by which its inflation rate exceeds the inflation rate in the United States.

    a. True   **b.** False

34. The cost of capital is generally lower for a foreign project than for an equivalent domestic project since the possibility of exchange gains exists.

    a. True   **b.** False

35. Which of the following statements concerning multinational cash flow analysis is *not* correct?

    a. The relevant cash flows are the dividends and royalties repatriated to the parent company.

    b. The cash flows must be converted to the currency of the parent company and, thus, are subject to future exchange rate changes.

    c. Dividends and royalties received are normally taxed only by the government of the country in which the subsidiary is located.

    d. Foreign governments may restrict the amount of the cash flows that may be repatriated.

SELF-TEST PROBLEMS

1. The "spot rate" for the Danish krone is 0.1263 U.S. dollar per krone. What would the exchange rate be expressed in krones per dollar?

    a. 0.1263 krone per dollar   **d.** 79.1770 krones per dollar
    b. 3.1300 krones per dollar   **e.** 255.2652 krones per dollar
    c. 7.9177 krones per dollar

2. One EMU euro can be exchanged for $1.0173 today. The euro is expected to appreciate by 10 percent tomorrow. What is the expected exchange rate tomorrow expressed in euros per dollar?

    a. 0.7750 euro per dollar   **d.** 0.9830 euro per dollar
    b. 0.8500 euro per dollar   **e.** 1.0813 euros per dollar
    c. 0.8936 euro per dollar

3. You are considering the purchase of a block of stock in Galic Steel, a French steel producer. Galic just paid a dividend of 1.5244 euros per share; that is, $D_0 = 1.5244$ euros. You expect the dividend to grow indefinitely at a rate of 15 percent per year, but because of a higher expected rate of inflation in Europe than in the United States, you expect the euro to depreciate against the dollar at a rate of 5 percent per year. The exchange rate is currently 0.9830 euro per one U.S. dollar, but this ratio will change as the euro depreciates. For a stock with this degree of risk, including exchange rate risk, you feel that a 20 percent rate of return is required. What is the most, in dollars, that you should pay for the stock?

    a. $16.21   **b.** $18.75   **c.** $20.90   **d.** $25.33   **e.** $30.00

4. Refer to Self-Test Problem 3. Now assume that the euro is expected to appreciate against the dollar at the rate of 1 percent per year. All other facts are unchanged. Under these conditions, what should you be willing to pay for the stock?

    a. $33.33   **b.** $35.00   **c.** $38.75   **d.** $43.60   **e.** $46.78

5. A currency trader observes that in the spot exchange market, one U.S. dollar can be exchanged for 114.35 Japanese yen or for 1.0611 EMU euros. How many euros would you receive for every yen exchanged?

    a. 0.00093   **b.** 0.00928   **c.** 0.034389   **d.** 66.506724   **e.** 107.76554

6. A deluxe refrigerator costs $1,300 in the United States. The same refrigerator costs 788 British pounds. If purchasing power parity holds, what is the spot exchange rate between pounds and the dollar? In other words, according to the spot rate calculated, how many pounds would you receive for every dollar exchanged?

    a. 0.5778   **b.** 0.6375   **c.** 0.6062   **d.** 1.2349   **e.** 1.6497

7. 6-month U.S. T-bills have a nominal rate of 8 percent, while default-free German bonds that mature in 6 months have a nominal rate of 6 percent. In the spot exchange market, one euro equals $0.9666. If interest rate parity holds, what is the 6-month forward exchange rate? In other words, how many U.S. dollars would you receive for every euro exchanged 6 months from now?

    a. $0.9760   **b.** $0.9850   **c.** $1.0000   **d.** $1.0053   **e.** $1.0100

(The following data apply to the next three Self-Test Problems.)

Geneva Manufacturing Co. is a Swiss multinational manufacturing company. Currently, Geneva's financial planners are considering undertaking a one-year project in the United States. The project's expected dollar-denominated cash flows consist of an initial investment of $5,000 and a cash inflow the following year of $7,500. Geneva estimates that its risk-adjusted cost of capital is 15%. Currently, 1 U.S. dollar will buy 1.5078 Swiss francs. In addition, one-year risk-free securities in the United States are yielding 5.50%, while similar securities in Switzerland are yielding 3.25%.

8. If this project were instead undertaken by a similar U.S.-based company with the same risk-adjusted cost of capital, what would be the net present value and rate of return generated by this project?

   a. $1,578.85; 50%
   b. $1,521.74; 15%
   c. $1.500.00; 25%

   d. $1,521.74; 50%
   e. $1,578.85; 25%

9. What is the expected forward exchange rate one year from now?

   a. 0.9787 SF per U.S. $
   b. 1.2500 SF per U.S. $
   c. 1.5555 SF per U.S. $

   d. 1.3333 SF per U.S. $
   e. 1.4756 SF per U.S. $

10. If Geneva undertakes the project, what is the project's net present value and rate of return for Geneva?

   a. 2,000.00 SF; 46.80%
   b. 2,084.76 SF; 46.80%
   c. 2,084.76 SF; 45.75%

   d. 1,857.85 SF; 40.00%
   e. 2,000.00 SF; 45.75%

ANSWERS TO SELF-TEST QUESTIONS

1.	exchange rate	8.	Foreign
2.	floating exchange	9.	multinational
3.	repatriated	10.	direct; indirect
4.	reinvestment	11.	Arbitrage
5.	Political	12.	convertible
6.	Eurodollar	13.	pegged
7.	direct; portfolio	14.	spot

15. forward
16. Interest rate parity
17. Purchasing power parity
18. London Interbank Offer Rate
19. Eurobonds
20. American depository receipts
21. premium
22. cross rates

23. eurocurrencies
24. international
25. Repatriation of earnings
26. indirect; direct
27. bearer
28. trade deficit
29. discount
30. appreciates

31. b. Political risk must be explicitly addressed by international financial managers.

32. a. This statement is correct.

33. b. The foreign currency will depreciate if its inflation rate is higher than that of the United States.

34. b. The cost of capital is generally higher because of exchange rate risk and political risk.

35. c. Dividends and royalties received will generally also be taxed by the U.S. government, but the total taxes paid to both governments will not exceed that which would be paid had the earnings occurred in the United States.

SOLUTIONS TO SELF-TEST PROBLEMS

1. c. The exchange rate for krones per dollar would be the reciprocal of the exchange rate of dollars per krone: 1/(0.1263 dollars per krone) = 7.9177 krones per dollar.

2. c. Today: 1 EMU = $1.0173. Tomorrow: 1 EMU = $1.0173 × 1.1 = $1.1190. 1/1.1190 = 0.8936 euro per dollar.

3. a. First, the valuation equation must be modified to convert the expected dividend stream to dollars:

$$D_t = D_0(1 + g)(ER),$$

where ER = exchange ratio. ER = 1/0.9830 today, but if euros depreciate at a rate of 5 percent, it will take more euros to buy a dollar in the future. The value of ER at some future time (t) will be

$$ER_t = \frac{Dollars}{Euros} = \frac{1}{0.9830(1.05)^t}.$$

Therefore, D_t in dollars may be calculated as follows:

$$
\begin{aligned}
D_t \text{ (in dollars)} &= (1.5244 \text{ euros})(1 + g)^t (ER_t) \\
&= \frac{\$1.5244(1.15)^t}{0.9830(1.05)^t} \\
&= \frac{\$1.5508(1.15)^t}{(1.05)^t} \\
&= \$1.5508\left(\frac{1.15}{1.05}\right)^t \\
&= \$1.5508(1.0952)^t.
\end{aligned}
$$

Thus, if the dividend in euros is expected to grow at a rate of 15 percent per year, but the euro is expected to depreciate at a rate of 5 percent per year against the dollar, then the growth rate, in dollars, of dividends received will be 9.52 percent. We can now calculate the value of the stock in dollars:

$$\hat{P}_0 = \frac{D_1}{k_s - g} = \frac{\$1.5508(1.0952)}{0.20 - 0.0952} = \frac{\$1.6984}{0.1048} = \$16.21.$$

4.   e.   Solve the problem as above: $ER_t = 1(1.01)^t/0.9830$.

$$
\begin{aligned}
D_t \text{(in dollars)} &= (1.5244 \text{ euros})(1 + g)^t \left(\frac{(1.01)^t}{0.9830}\right) \\
&= (\$1.5244/0.9830)(1.15)^t(1.01)^t \\
&= \$1.5508(1.1615)^t.
\end{aligned}
$$

Thus, the euro dividend is expected to increase at a rate of 15 percent per year, and the value of these euros is expected to rise at the rate of 1 percent per year, so the expected annual growth rate of the dollar dividend is 16.15 percent. We can now calculate the stock price:

$$\hat{P}_0 = \frac{D_1}{k_s - g} = \frac{\$1.5508(1.1615)}{0.20 - 0.1615} = \frac{\$1.8012}{0.0385} = \$46.78.$$

5. b. $1 = 114.35 Japanese yen; $1 = 1.0611 EMU euros; Euros/Yen = ?

Cross rate: $\dfrac{\text{Dollar}}{\text{Yen}} \times \dfrac{\text{Euros}}{\text{Dollar}} = \dfrac{\text{Euros}}{\text{Yen}}$.

Note that an indirect quotation is given for the Japanese yen; however, the cross rate formula requires a direct quotation. The indirect quotation is the reciprocal of the direct quotation. Since $1 = 114.35 Japanese yen, then 1 yen = $0.00874508.

$\dfrac{\text{Euro}}{\text{Yen}} = 0.00874508 \times 1.0611 = 0.00927941$ euro per yen,

or approximately 0.00928 euro per yen.

6. c. $P_h = (P_f)(\text{Spot rate})$
$1,300 = (788)(\text{Spot rate})$
$\dfrac{1,300}{788} = \text{Spot rate}$
$\text{Spot rate} = \$1.6497.$

1 pound = $1.6497. This is a direct quotation. However, the problem asks for how many pounds would you receive for every dollar exchanged, an indirect quote. To obtain the answer, take the reciprocal of 1.6497 = 1/1.6497 = 0.6062 pound per 1 U.S. dollar.

7. a. $\dfrac{\text{Forward exchange rate}}{\text{Spot exchange rate}} = \dfrac{(1+k_h)}{(1+k_f)} ; k_h = \dfrac{8\%}{2} = 4\%; k_f = \dfrac{6\%}{2} = 3\%;$ Spot rate = $0.9666.

$\dfrac{\text{Forward exchange rate}}{\$0.9666} = \dfrac{1.04}{1.03}$
$(1.03)(\text{Forward exchange rate}) = \$1.0053$
$\text{Forward exchange rate} = \$0.9760.$

8. d. If a U.S.-based company undertakes the project, the rate of return for the project is a simple calculation, as is the net present value.

$\text{NPV} = -\$5,000 + \$7,500/1.15 = \$1,521.74.$

$\text{Rate of return} = \$7,500/\$5,000 - 1 = 50\%.$

9.   e.   According to interest rate parity, the following condition holds:

$$f_t/e_0 = (1 + k_{SWISS})/(1 + k_{US})$$
$$f_t/1.5078 = (1 + 0.0325)/(1 + 0.0550)$$
$$f_t/1.5078 = 0.9787$$
$$f_t = 1.4756 \text{ SF per U.S. \$.}$$

10.   b.   First, we must adjust the cash flows to reflect Geneva's home currency.

Year	CF ($)	CF (SFrancs)
0	-5,000	-7,539.00
1	7,500	11,067.32

Using the Swiss franc-denominated cash flows, the NPV and appropriate rate of return can be found.

NPV = -7,539 + 11,067.32/1.15 = 2,084.76 Swiss francs.

Rate of return = 11,067.32SF/7,539SF – 1 = 46.80%.

CHAPTER 20
HYBRID FINANCING: PREFERRED STOCK, LEASING, WARRANTS, AND CONVERTIBLES

LEARNING OBJECTIVES

- Define preferred stock, describe some of its basic features, and identify its advantages and disadvantages.

- Characterize the various types of leases, discuss the financial statement effects of "off balance sheet financing," and perform the analysis necessary to make lease versus borrow-and-purchase decisions.

- Discuss warrants and the way in which corporations utilize warrants together with bonds as an alternative means of raising investment capital, describe how warrants are valued, the component cost of bonds with warrants, and discuss the wealth effects and dilution due to warrants.

- Explain how convertible securities work, how they are valued, the component cost of convertibles, and how they affect the issuing firm's capital structure.

- Identify differences between warrants and convertibles.

- Explain the three different ways to report earnings per share if warrants or convertibles are outstanding.

OVERVIEW

Firms can use different types of long-term financing other than common stock and debt. Other types of securities include (1) preferred stock, which is a hybrid security that is a cross between debt and equity; (2) leasing, which is an alternative to borrowing; (3) warrants, which are derivative securities that are issued by firms; and (4) convertibles, which are hybrids between debt (or preferred stock) and warrants. All of these methods are widely used today, and an understanding of them is essential for the financial manager and his or her staff.

OUTLINE

Preferred stock is a hybrid type of long-term financing. It is called a hybrid, because it represents an equity investment in a business, yet it has many of the characteristics associated with debt. It imposes a fixed charge and thus increases the firm's financial leverage, yet omitting the preferred dividend does not force a company into bankruptcy.

- Preferred stock has the following basic features.
  - Preferred stock has a *par* (or liquidating) value.
  - The preferred dividend is stated as either a percentage of par, as so many dollars per share, or both ways.
  - If the preferred dividend is not earned, the company does not have to pay it. However, most preferred issues are *cumulative*, meaning that the cumulative total of all unpaid preferred dividends must be paid before dividends can be paid on the common stock.
  - Unpaid preferred dividends are called *arrearages*. Dividends in arrears do not earn interest.
  - Preferred stock normally has no voting rights. However, most preferred issues stipulate that the preferred stockholder can elect a minority of the directors, if the preferred dividend is passed (omitted).

- From the viewpoint of the issuing corporation, preferred stock is less risky than bonds.

- Investors regard preferred stock as being riskier than bonds for two reasons.
  - Preferred stockholders' claims are subordinated to those of bondholders in the event of liquidation.
  - Bondholders are more likely to continue receiving income during hard times than are preferred stockholders.

- Since 70 percent of preferred dividends is exempt from corporate taxes, preferred stock is attractive to corporate investors.
  - As a result, in recent years high-grade preferred stock, on average, has sold on a lower pre-tax yield basis than have high-grade bonds.

- Some preferred stocks are similar to perpetual bonds in that they have no maturity date, but most new issues now have specified maturities.

- Nonconvertible preferred stock is virtually all owned by corporations, which can take advantage of the 70 percent dividend exclusion to obtain a higher after-tax yield on preferred stock than on bonds.

- For issuers, preferred stock has a tax disadvantage relative to debt—interest expense is deductible, but preferred dividends are not.

☐ Firms with low tax rates may have an incentive to issue preferred stock that can be bought by corporate investors with high tax rates, who can take advantage of the 70 percent dividend exclusion.

■ Two important new types of preferred stock have been developed in recent years: (1) floating, or adjustable rate, preferred and (2) money market, or market auction, preferred.

☐ *Adjustable rate preferred stocks (ARPs)* have their dividends tied to the rate on Treasury securities.

● ARPs still have some price volatility due to changes in riskiness of the issues and Treasury yields fluctuate between dividend rate adjustment dates.

● ARPs have too much price instability to be held in the liquid asset portfolios of many corporate investors.

☐ In 1984, investment bankers introduced *money market*, or *market auction, preferred*. Here the underwriter conducts an auction on the issue every seven weeks.

● Holders who want to sell their shares can put them up for auction at par value.

● Buyers submit bids in the form of the yields they are willing to accept over the next 7-week period.

● The yield set on the issue for the coming period is the lowest yield sufficient to sell all the shares being offered at that auction.

● From the holder's standpoint, market auction preferred is a low-risk, largely tax-exempt, 7-week maturity security that can be sold between auction dates at close to par.

■ There are advantages and disadvantages to financing with preferred stock:

☐ In contrast to bonds, the obligation to pay preferred dividends is not contractual, and passing a preferred dividend cannot force a firm into bankruptcy.

☐ By issuing preferred stock, the firm avoids the dilution of common equity that occurs when common stock is sold.

☐ Since preferred stock sometimes has no maturity, and since preferred sinking fund payments, if present, are typically spread over a long period, preferred issues reduce the cash flow drain from repayment of principal that occurs with debt issues.

☐ Preferred stock dividends are not deductible to the issuer, hence the after-tax cost of preferred is typically higher than the after-tax cost of debt. However, the tax advantage of preferreds to corporate purchasers (70 percent dividend exclusion) lowers its pre-tax cost and thus its effective cost.

☐ Although preferred dividends are considered to be a fixed cost, hence their use, like that of debt, increases the firm's financial risk and thus its cost of common equity.

The ownership of assets is not as important as the ability to use them in a profitable manner. Leasing provides the same ability to use capital assets as outright ownership. Leasing is similar to borrowing, and it provides the same type of financial leverage.

- ■ Historically, land and buildings were the types of assets most often leased, but today it is possible to lease almost any kind of fixed asset.
  - □ The *lessor* is the owner of the leased property and receives such tax benefits of ownership as depreciation write-offs.
  - □ The *lessee* buys the right to use the property by making lease payments to the lessor.

- ■ There are three common types of leasing arrangements.
  - □ Under a *sale and leaseback*, a firm owning an asset sells the property and simultaneously leases it back for a specified period at specific terms. This arrangement provides an alternative to taking out a mortgage loan.
  - □ *Operating,* or *service, leases* provide for both financing and maintenance. Ordinarily, these leases call for the lessor to maintain and service the leased equipment, and the cost of providing maintenance is built into the lease payments.
    - These leases are frequently not fully amortized; that is, the payments required under the lease contract are not sufficient to recover the full cost of the equipment.
    - A feature frequently contained in operating leases is a *cancellation clause*, which gives the lessee the right to cancel the lease before the expiration of the basic agreement.
  - □ *Financial,* or *capital, leases* do not provide for maintenance, are not cancelable, and are fully amortized over their life.
    - They differ from a sale and leaseback only in that new equipment is purchased by the lessor from a manufacturer instead of from the user-lessee.
    - A sale and leaseback may be thought of as a special type of financial lease, and both sale and leasebacks and financial leases are analyzed in the same manner.

- ■ Leasing is often referred to as *off balance sheet financing* because under certain conditions neither the leased assets nor the lease liabilities appear on the firm's balance sheet.
  - □ A firm with extensive lease arrangements would have both its assets and its liabilities understated in comparison with a firm that borrowed to purchase the assets. Under this situation the firm that leases would show a lower debt ratio. Thus, the benefits of leasing would accrue to stockholders at the expense of new investors, who were, in effect, being deceived by the fact that the firm's balance sheet did not fully reflect its true liability situation.
  - □ FASB #13 requires firms to *capitalize* certain financial leases and thus to restate their balance sheets to report leased assets as fixed assets and the present value of future lease payments as a liability.

□ A lease must be classified as a capital lease, and hence be capitalized and shown directly on the balance sheet, if any one of the following conditions exists:

- Under the lease terms, ownership of the property is effectively transferred from the lessor to the lessee.

- The lessee can purchase the property or renew the lease at less than a fair market price when the lease expires.

- The lease runs for a period equal to or greater than 75 percent of the asset's life. Thus, if an asset has a 10-year life and if the lease is written for more than 7.5 years, the lease must be capitalized.

- The present value of the lease payments is equal to or greater than 90 percent of the asset's initial value.

■ Leases are recognized to be essentially the same as debt, and they have the same effects as debt on the firm's required rate of return.
   □ Leasing will not generally permit a firm to use more financial leverage than could be obtained with conventional debt.

■ Any prospective lease must be evaluated by both the lessee and the lessor.
   □ The lessee must determine whether leasing an asset is less costly than buying it, and the lessor must decide whether or not the lease will provide a reasonable rate of return.

■ For the lessee, leasing is a substitute for debt financing. In an NPV-type analysis, the lessee estimates the cost of leasing and the cost of owning. If the PV cost of leasing is less than the PV cost of owning, the asset should be leased.
   □ The decision to acquire the asset is based on regular capital budgeting decisions; therefore, its acquisition is a "done deal" before the lease analysis begins.
   □ All cash flows must reflect tax effects.
   □ Since leasing is a substitute for debt financing and since lease cash flows have approximately the same risk as debt cash flows, the *appropriate discount rate is the after-tax cost of debt.*

■ Other factors often arise in leasing decisions.
   □ The value of the leased asset at lease termination is called its *residual value.*

- It might first appear that assets with large residual values would most likely be owned since the owner gets the residual value.

- However, competition among leasing companies forces lease contracts to reflect expected residual values. Thus, the existence of large residual values on equipment is not likely to bias the decision against leasing.
   □ Leasing is sometimes said to have an advantage for firms that are seeking the maximum degree of financial leverage.

- It is sometimes argued that a firm can obtain more money, and for a longer period, under a lease arrangement than under a loan secured by the asset.
- Because some leases do not appear on the balance sheet, lease financing has been said to give the firm a stronger appearance in a superficial credit analysis, thus permitting it to use more leverage than it could if it did not lease. There may be some truth to these claims for smaller firms. However, for larger firms this point is of questionable validity.

A warrant is a long-term option issued by a company that gives the holder the right to buy a stated number of shares of common stock at a specified price for some specified length of time. Thus, warrants are essentially company-issued call options, which have value because their holders can buy the firm's common stock at a fixed price regardless of how high the stock price climbs.

- ■ Generally, warrants are distributed with debt, and they are used to induce investors to buy a firm's long-term debt at a lower interest rate than would otherwise be required.
  - □ Additionally, warrants may eliminate the need for extremely restrictive indenture provisions.

- ■ Warrants were originally used as "sweeteners" by small, rapidly growing firms to help sell either debt or preferred stocks. However, some strong firms have also used warrants.

- ■ A bond with warrants has some characteristics of debt and some characteristics of equity. It is a hybrid security that provides the financial manager with an opportunity to expand the firm's mix of securities and thus to appeal to a broader group of investors.

- ■ The price paid for a bond with warrants is determined as follows:

  Price paid for bond with warrants = Straight-debt value of bond + Value of warrants.

- ■ Virtually all warrants today are *detachable* and can be traded separately from the bond or preferred stock with which they were issued.
  - □ Even after the warrants have been exercised, the bond (with its low coupon rate) remains outstanding.
  - □ When warrants are exercised, the stock provided to the warrant holders are newly issued shares. This means that the exercise of warrants dilutes the value of the original equity.

- ■ The exercise price on warrants is generally set some 20 to 30 percent above the stock's market price on the date the bond is issued.

- There are three conditions that encourage holders to exercise their warrants.
  - ☐ Warrant holders will exercise warrants and buy stock if the warrants are about to expire and the stock's market price is above the exercise price.
  - ☐ Warrant holders will exercise voluntarily if the company raises the dividend on the common stock by a sufficient amount.
    - No dividend is earned on the warrant, so it provides no current income. However, if the common stock pays a high dividend, it provides an attractive dividend yield but limits price growth. This induces warrant holders to exercise their option to buy the stock.
  - ☐ Warrants sometimes have *stepped-up exercise prices*, which prod owners into exercising them.
    - Many warrant holders will exercise their options before the stepped-up price takes effect and the value of the warrants falls.

- Another desirable feature of warrants is that they generally bring in funds only if funds are needed. This occurs because as a company becomes successful and grows, the stock price increases over the exercise price and the warrants are exercised providing an additional inflow of funds. If the company is not successful, and it cannot profitably employ additional money, the price of its stock will probably not rise sufficiently to induce exercise of the warrants.

- When warrants are exercised, a wealth transfer occurs from original stockholders to the warrant holders. However, the original shareholders are willing to trade off the potential dilution from the issuance of new shares for a lower coupon rate on the bonds with warrants.

- The expected rate of return to investors on the bonds with warrants is higher than the return on straight debt. This reflects the fact that the issue is riskier to investors than a straight-debt issue because some of the return is expected in the form of stock price appreciation, and that part of the return is relatively risky.
  - ☐ The expected rate of return to investors is the before-tax cost to the company—this is true of common stocks, straight bonds, and preferred stock, and it is also true of bonds sold with warrants.

Convertible securities are bonds or preferred stocks that, under specified terms and conditions, can be exchanged for common stock at the option of the holder.

- Conversion of a bond or preferred stock, unlike the exercise of a warrant, does not produce additional funds for the firm. The debt or preferred stock is simply replaced on the balance sheet.

❑ Conversion does lower the debt ratio. Of course, this improves the firm's financial strength and makes it easier to raise additional fixed charge capital.

■ The *conversion ratio (CR)* specifies the number of common shares that will be received for each bond or share of preferred stock that is converted.

■ The *conversion price, P_c,* is the effective price paid for the common stock when conversion occurs. For example, if a bond is issued at its par value of $1,000 and can be converted into 40 shares of common stock, the conversion price would be:

$$\frac{\text{Conversion}}{\text{price}} = P_c = \frac{\text{Par value of bond}}{CR} = \frac{\$1,000}{40} = \$25.$$

Someone buying the bond for $1,000 and then converting it would, in effect, be paying $25 per share for the stock.

■ Once the conversion ratio is set, the value of the conversion price is established, and vice versa.

■ The conversion price is typically set at about 20 to 30 percent above the prevailing market price of common stock when the convertible issue is sold. Thus, if the common stock is selling for $20.83 at the time the convertible is issued, the conversion price might be set at 1.2($20.83) = $25. This would produce a conversion ratio of CR = 40:

$$CR = \frac{\$1,000}{P_c} = \frac{\$1,000}{\$25} = 40 \text{ shares.}$$

❑ Generally, the conversion price and conversion ratio are fixed for the bond's life, although sometimes a stepped-up conversion price is used.

❑ A standard feature of almost all convertibles is a clause protecting the convertible against dilution from stock splits, stock dividends, and the sale of common stock at prices below the conversion price.

   ● The typical provision states that if common stock is sold at a price below the conversion price, then the conversion price must be lowered (and the conversion ratio raised) to the price at which the new stock was issued.

■ The bond's conversion value, C_t, is the value of common stock obtained by converting a convertible security. The actual market price of the bond must always be equal to or greater than the higher of its straight-debt value or its conversion value. Therefore, the higher of the bond value and conversion value represents the floor price for the bond.

■ A convertible's expected return is more risky than that of a straight bond, because part of the return is interest income and part of the return is expected capital gain, which is risky. Therefore, the cost of the convertible should be larger than the cost of straight debt.

■ Convertibles have two important advantages from the issuer's standpoint.
  ☐ By giving investors an opportunity to realize capital gains, a firm can sell debt with a lower interest rate.
  ☐ The sale of a convertible issue may be thought of as having the effect of selling common stock at a higher-than-market price at the time the convertible is issued.

■ Convertibles have three important disadvantages from the standpoint of the issuer.
  ☐ Although the use of a convertible bond may give the issuer the opportunity to sell stock at a price higher than the price at which it could be sold currently, if the stock greatly increases in price, the firm would probably find that it would have been better off if it had used straight debt in spite of its higher cost and then later sold common stock and refunded the debt.
  ☐ Convertibles typically have a low coupon interest rate, and the advantage of this low-cost debt will be lost when conversion occurs.
  ☐ If the company truly wants to raise equity capital, and if the stock price does not rise sufficiently after the bond is issued, then the company will be stuck with debt.

■ One of the potential agency problems between bondholders and stockholders is asset substitution. Stockholders have an "option-related" incentive to take on projects with high upside potential even though they increase the riskiness of the firm. When such an action is taken, there is potential for a wealth transfer between bondholders and stockholders.
  ☐ When convertible debt is issued, actions that increase the company's riskiness may also increase the value of the convertible debt.
  ☐ Some of the gains to shareholders from taking on high-risk projects may be shared with convertible bondholders, which lower agency costs.
  ☐ The same general logic applies to warrants.

At first blush, it might appear that debt with warrants and convertible debt are more or less interchangeable. A closer look reveals one major and several minor differences between these securities.

■ The exercise of warrants brings in new equity capital, while the conversion of convertibles results only in an accounting transfer.

■ There is a difference in the flexibility they provide management.
  ◻ Most convertible issues contain a call provision that allows the issuer either to refund the debt or to force conversion. Most warrants are not callable, so firms generally must wait until maturity for the warrants to generate new equity capital.

■ Generally, maturities also differ between warrants and convertibles.
  ◻ Warrants typically have much shorter maturities than convertibles, and warrants typically expire before their accompanying debt matures.

■ Warrants often provide for fewer future common shares than do convertibles because with convertibles all of the debt is converted to common whereas debt remains outstanding when warrants are exercised.

■ In general, firms that issue debt with warrants are smaller and riskier than those that issue convertibles.

■ There is a significant difference in issuance costs between debt with warrants and convertible debt. Bonds with warrants typically require issuance costs that are about 120 basis points more than the flotation cost for convertibles.

If warrants or convertibles are outstanding, a firm can theoretically report earnings per share in one of three ways.

■ *Basic EPS.* Earnings available to common stockholders are divided by the average number of shares actually outstanding during the period.

■ *Primary EPS.* The earnings per share are divided by the average number of shares that would have been outstanding if warrants and convertibles "likely to be converted in the near future" had actually been exercised or converted. Accountants have a formula that basically compares the conversion or exercise price with the actual market value of the stock to determine the likelihood of conversion when deciding on the need to use this adjustment procedure.

■ *Diluted EPS.* This is similar to primary EPS except that all warrants and convertibles are assumed to be exercised or converted, regardless of the likelihood of either occurring.

SELF-TEST QUESTIONS

Definitional

1. Preferred stock is referred to as a hybrid because it is similar to _____ in some respects and to _____ _____ in others.

2. Most preferred stock dividends are _____ and thus must be paid before any dividends can be paid to common stockholders.

3. Preferred stocks are attractive to _____ investors because of the 70 percent dividend exclusion.

4. Issuing preferred stock decreases the danger of _____ if operating income is low.

5. Conceptually, leasing is similar to _____, and it provides the same type of financial _____.

6. Under a(n) _____-_____-_____ arrangement, the seller receives the purchase price of the asset but retains the _____ of the property.

7. _____ leases include both financing and maintenance arrangements.

8. A(n) _____, or _____, lease is similar to a sale-and-leaseback arrangement, but these leases generally apply to the purchase of _____ equipment directly from a manufacturer.

9. Capitalizing a lease requires that the asset be listed under _____ _____, and that the _____ _____ of the future lease payments be shown as a(n) _____.

10. _____ among leasing companies will tend to force leasing rates down to the point where expected _____ values are fully reflected in the lease rates.

11. Since some leases do not appear on the _____ _____, a firm may be able to use more _____ than if it did not lease.

12. A firm with low profits may be able to transfer the depreciation write-off to another firm and be compensated in the form of lower _____ _____.

13. The leasing decision is normally a(n) _____ decision rather than a(n) _____ _____ decision.

14.   Warrants and convertible securities may make a company's securities more attractive to a broader range of _____ and lower its _____ ____ _____.

15.   A(n) _____ is a long-term option sold with a bond or preferred stock permitting the holder the right to buy a stated number of shares of _____ _____ at a specified _____.

16.   When they are exercised, warrants add additional _____ _____ to a firm's capital structure.

17.   Warrants will certainly be exercised if the stock price is above the _____ price and the warrant is about to _____.

18.   Holders of warrants will have an extra incentive to exercise if the company sharply increases the _____ on its common shares.

19.   Almost all warrants are _____ and can be traded separately from the debt or preferred stock with which they were issued.

20.   Convertible bonds may be exchanged for _____ _____ at the option of the _____.

21.   The _____ _____ specifies the number of shares of common stock that will be received for each bond that is converted.

22.   The _____ _____ is the effective price paid for the common stock when conversion occurs.

23.   The _____ is the owner of the leased property and receives such tax benefits of ownership as depreciation write-offs.

24.   The _____ buys the right to use the property by making lease payments.

25.   Unpaid preferred dividends are called _____.

26.   From the viewpoint of the issuing corporation, preferred stock is _____ risky than bonds.

27.   Since leasing is a substitute for debt financing, and since lease cash flows have approximately the same risk as debt cash flows, the appropriate discount rate is the _____-____ _____ ____ _____.

28.   The value of the leased asset at lease termination is called its _____ _____.

29. Most convertible issues contain a(n) _____ _____ that allows the issuer either to refund the debt or to force conversion, while most warrants are not _____.

30. _____ _____ preferred stocks have their dividends tied to the rate on Treasury securities.

31. A feature frequently contained in operating leases is a(n) _____ _____, which gives the lessee the right to terminate the lease before the expiration of the basic agreement.

32. _____ EPS is calculated as earnings available to common stockholders divided by the average number of shares actually outstanding during the period.

33. _____ EPS is similar to primary EPS except that all warrants and convertibles are assumed to be exercised or converted, regardless of the likelihood of either occurring.

34. Preferred stock normally has no _____ rights.

35. _____ _____ requires firms to capitalize certain financial leases.

Conceptual

36. When one is evaluating a lease proposal, cash flows should be discounted at a relatively high rate because lease flows are fairly certain.

    a. True   **b.** False

37. Generally, operating leases are fully amortized, and the lease is written for the expected life of the asset.

    a. True   **b.** False

38. A firm that uses extensive lease financing and does not capitalize its leases will have a substantially lower debt ratio than an otherwise similar firm that borrows to finance its assets.

    a. True   **b.** False

39. Firms may or may not capitalize a financial lease, at their own option.

    a. True   **b.** False

40. The coupon interest rate on convertible bonds is generally higher than the rate on nonconvertible bonds of the same riskiness and rating.

    a. True   **b.** False

41. Primary EPS shows what EPS would have been if all warrants and convertibles outstanding had been converted prior to the reporting date.

    a. True   **b.** False

42. Investors are willing to accept lower interest (or dividend) yields on convertible securities in the hopes of later realizing capital gains.

    a. True   **b.** False

43. The conversion of a convertible bond replaces debt with common equity on a firm's balance sheet, but it does not bring in any additional capital.

    a. True   **b.** False

44. Which of the following statements is most correct?

    a. Adjustable rate preferred stocks, whose dividends are indexed to the rate on Treasury securities, are often used by strong, profitable corporations for two reasons: (1) the fact that the dividend is indexed means that the stock will generally sell at a price close to par, which makes it safe to the purchaser, so its cost to the issuer will be low, and (2) the fact that 70 percent of preferred dividends can be deducted by the issuer for tax purposes lowers the cost even further.

    b. Some years ago leasing was called "off balance sheet financing" because the leased asset and the corresponding lease obligation did not appear directly on the balance sheet. Today, though, that situation has changed materially because *all leases* must be capitalized and reported on the balance sheet, along with the value of the leased asset.

    c. In a lease-versus-purchase analysis, cash flows should generally be discounted at the weighted average cost of capital (WACC).

    d. Each of the above statements is true.

    e. Each of the above statements is false.

SELF-TEST PROBLEMS

(The following data apply to the next three Self-Test Problems.)

Treadmill Trucking Company is negotiating a lease for five new tractor/trailer rigs with International Leasing. Treadmill has received its best offer from Betterbilt Trucks for a total price of $900,000. The terms of the lease offered by International Leasing call for 4 payments of $260,000, with each payment occurring at the beginning of each year. As an alternative to leasing, the firm can borrow from a large insurance company and buy the trucks. The $900,000 would be borrowed on an amortized term loan at a 10 percent interest rate for 4 years. Assume the trucks fall into the MACRS 3-year class and have an expected residual value of $100,000. The applicable depreciation rates are 33 percent, 45 percent, 15 percent, and 7 percent. Maintenance costs would be included in the lease. If the trucks are owned, a maintenance contract would be purchased at the beginning of each year for $10,000 per year. Treadmill plans to buy a new fleet of trucks at the end of the fourth year. Treadmill Trucking has an effective federal-plus-state tax rate of 40 percent.

1. What is Treadmill's present value of the cost of owning?

    a. $515,225   **b.** $533,354   **c.** $583,189   **d.** $601,717   **e.** $552,957

2. What is Treadmill's present value of the cost of leasing?

    a. $592,468   **b.** $605,265   **c.** $572,990   **d.** $629,668   **e.** $535,419

3. Treadmill should lease the trucks.

    a. True   **b.** False

4. White Corporation has just sold a bond issue with 10 warrants attached to each bond. The bonds have a 20-year maturity, an annual coupon rate of 12 percent, and they sold at the $1,000 initial offering price. The current yield to maturity on bonds of equal risk, but without warrants, is 15 percent. What is the value of each warrant?

    a. $22.56   **b.** $21.20   **c.** $20.21   **d.** $19.24   **e.** $18.78

(The following data apply to the next three Self-Test Problems.)

Central Food Brokers is considering issuing a 20-year convertible bond that will be priced at its par value of $1,000 per bond. The bonds have a 12 percent annual coupon interest rate, and each bond could be converted into 40 shares of common stock. The stock currently sells at $20 per share, has an expected annual dividend of $3.00, and is growing at a constant 5 percent rate per year. The bonds are callable after 10 years at a price of $1,050, with the price declining by $5 per year. If, after 10 years, the conversion exceeds the call price by at least 20 percent, management will probably call the bonds.

5. What is the conversion price?

    a. $20   **b.** $25   **c.** $33   **d.** $40   **e.** $50

6. If the yield to maturity on nonconvertible bonds of similar risk is 16 percent, what is the straight-debt value?

    a. $1,000.00   **b.** $907.83   **c.** $812.22   **d.** $762.85   **e.** $692.37

7. If an investor expects the bond issue to be called in Year 10 and if he plans on converting it at that time, what is the investor's expected rate of return upon conversion?

    a. 12.0%   **b.** 12.2%   **c.** 13.6%   **d.** 14.4%   **e.** 15.3%

(The following data apply to the next six Self-Test Problems.)

Travis Corporation wants to issue $50 million in new capital to fund new opportunities. If Travis were to raise the $50 million of new capital in a straight-debt 20-year bond offering, Travis would have to offer a coupon rate of 11 percent. However, Travis' advisors have suggested a 20-year bond offering with stock warrants. According to the advisors, Travis could issue 9 percent coupon-bearing debt with 20 warrants per $1,000 face value bond. Travis has 8 million shares of common stock outstanding, at a current price of $22.50. The stock can be exercised in 10 years (on December 31, 2012), at an exercise price of $26.50. After issuing the bonds and warrants, Travis' operations and investments are expected to grow at a constant rate of 9 percent per year.

8. If investors pay $1,000 for each bond, what is the value of each warrant attached to the bond issue?

    a. $7.96   **b.** $8.25   **c.** $8.75   **d.** $9.33   **e.** $9.50

9. What is the expected total value of Travis Corporation in 10 years?

    a. $230,000,000   **d.** $544,493,645
    b. $325,000,000   **e.** $568,939,775
    c. $476,532,125

10. If there were no warrants, what would be Travis' price per share in 10 years?

    a. $33.33   **b.** $48.75   **c.** $62.55   **d.** $65.00   **e.** $66.67

11. What would be the price per share in 10 years with the warrants?

    a. $58.54   **b.** $31.25   **c.** $65.00   **d.** $61.25   **e.** $55.33

12.   What is the component cost of these bonds with warrants?

   a. 10.75%   **b.** 11.78%   **c.** 11.30%   **d.** 12.10%   **e.** 12.55%

13.   What is the premium to the component cost associated with using the bonds with warrants as compared to straight debt?

   a. 0.30%   **b.** 0.55%   **c.** 1.55%   **d.** 1.10%   **e.** 0.78%

ANSWERS TO SELF-TEST QUESTIONS

1.   debt; common stock
2.   cumulative
3.   corporate
4.   bankruptcy
5.   borrowing; leverage
6.   sale-and-leaseback; use
7.   Operating
8.   financial; capital; new
9.   fixed assets; present value; liability
10.   Competition; residual
11.   balance sheet; leverage
12.   lease payments
13.   financing; capital budgeting
14.   investors; cost of capital
15.   warrant; common stock; price
16.   common equity
17.   exercise (strike); expire
18.   dividend

19.   detachable
20.   common stock; holder
21.   conversion ratio
22.   conversion price
23.   lessor
24.   lessee
25.   arrearages
26.   less
27.   after-tax cost of debt
28.   residual value
29.   call provision; callable
30.   Adjustable rate
31.   cancellation clause
32.   Basic
33.   Diluted
34.   voting
35.   FASB #13

36.   b.   The cash flows are fairly certain, so they should be discounted at a relatively low rate, generally, the after-tax cost of debt.

37.   b.   Operating leases are frequently not fully amortized. The lessor expects to recover all costs either in subsequent leases or through the sale of the used equipment at its residual value.

38.   a.   However, analysts would recognize that leases are as risky as debt financing and thus include the impact of lease financing on the firm's debt costs and capital structure. Also, if the company that leases capitalizes the leases, then the debt ratios will be similar.

39.   b.   FASB #13 spells out in detail the conditions under which leases must be capitalized for an unqualified audit opinion.

40. b. The coupon interest rate is lower because investors expect some capital gains return upon conversion. Note, however, that the overall required rate of return is probably higher for the convertible issue than the straight-debt issue, because the capital gains portion of the convertible's total return is more risky.

41. b. Primary EPS includes only those shares from warrants and convertibles *likely to be converted* in the near future. Diluted EPS includes all shares.

42. a. However, the investor is including the expected capital gain as part of his required return, so the total required return on convertibles is higher than on a straight-debt security.

43. a. The bond is turned in to the company and replaced with common stock. No cash is exchanged. When a warrant is exercised, the firm receives additional capital.

44. e. Statement a is false; preferred dividends are not tax deductible to the issuer. Statement b is false; only certain leases that meet the FASB #13 criteria for capitalization have to be reported on the balance sheet. Statement c is false; the discount rate in a borrow-versus-lease decision is the after-tax cost of debt because the cash flows are fairly certain. Therefore, statement e is the correct choice.

SOLUTIONS TO SELF-TEST PROBLEMS

1. e. Place the cash flows associated with ownership on a time line:

	0	1	2	3	4
		6%			
Purchase price	(900,000)				
Dep. tax savings[a]		118,800	162,000	54,000	25,200
Maintenance payment (AT)[b]	(6,000)	(6,000)	(6,000)	(6,000)	
Salvage value[c]					60,000
Net cash flow	(906,000)	112,800	156,000	48,000	85,200

PV cost of owning at a 6 percent after-tax cost of debt is $552,957.

[a]Depreciable basis = $900,000.

Year	Factor	Depreciation Expense	Tax Savings
1	0.33	$297,000	$118,800
2	0.45	405,000	162,000
3	0.15	135,000	54,000
4	0.07	63,000	25,200
		$900,000	$360,000

[b]After-tax maintenance cash flow = $10,000(1 – T) = $10,000(0.6) = $6,000.
[c]After-tax residual value = $100,000(1 – T) = ($100,000)(0.6) = $60,000.

2. c. Place the cash flows associated with leasing on a time line:

```
        0                 1                 2                 3
              6%
        |-----------------|-----------------|-----------------|
  (156,000)ᵃ        (156,000)ᵃ        (156,000)ᵃ        (156,000)ᵃ
```

[a]$260,000(1 – T) = ($260,000)(0.6) = $156,000.

PV cost of leasing at a 6 percent after-tax cost of debt is $572,990.

3. b. The PV cost of leasing is $572,990 – $552,957 = $20,033 more than the cost of owning.

4. e. First, find the straight-debt value:

Using a financial calculator, input N = 20, I = 15, PMT = 120, FV = 1000, and solve for PV = $812.22.

Thus, the value of the attached warrants is $1,000 – $812.22 = $187.78. Since each bond has 10 warrants, each warrant must have a value of $18.78.

5. b. P_c = Par value/Shares received = $1,000/40 = $25.00.

6. d. Using a financial calculator, input N = 20, I = 16, PMT = 120, FV = 1000, and solve for PV = $762.85.

7.   c.   To receive the convertible bond's cash flows, an investor will pay $1,000. In return, the investor will receive annual interest payments and expects to receive capital gains when conversion occurs.

The investor receives the $120 annual interest on the convertible bond for 10 years.

The stock's expected market value in Year 10 $= (1.05)^{10} \times \$20 \times 40$ shares $= \$1,303.12$, which exceeds the call price by more than 20 percent.

To solve for the investor's expected return upon conversion, we put the cash flows on a time line and solve for the IRR.

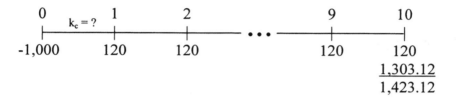

Using a financial calculator, enter the following cash flows into the cash flow register: $CF_0 = -1000$, $CF_{1-9} = 120$, $CF_{10} = 1423.12$, and solve for IRR $= k_c = 13.60\%$.

8.   a.   The value of the 9% coupon bonds, evaluated at 11%, can be found as follows: N = 20; I = 11; PMT = 90; and FV = 1000. Solve for PV = $840.73.

If investors are willing to pay $1,000 for these bonds with warrants attached, then the value of the warrants must be $1,000 − $840.73 = $159.27. Since there are 20 warrants issued with each bond, the value per warrant must be $7.96.

9.   d.   The firm's current market value of equity is $22.50 × 8 million shares = $180 million. Combined with a $50 million bond issue ($1,000 × 50,000 bonds), the firm's current total value is $230 million. The firm's operations and investments are expected to grow at a constant rate of 9%. Hence, the expected total value of the firm in 10 years is:

Total firm value (t = 10) $= \$230,000,000 \times (1.09)^{10}$
Total firm value (t = 10) = $544,493,645.

10.   c.   With 10 years left to maturity, each of the 50,000 bonds will be worth: N = 10; I = 11; PMT = 90; and FV = 1000. Solve for PV = $882.2154.

Thus, the total value of debt would be $882.2154 \times 50,000 = \$44,110,768$. Hence, the value of equity would be $\$544,493,645 - \$44,110,768 = \$500,382,877$. If no warrants were issued, there would still be 8 million shares outstanding, which would each have a value of $62.55.

11. a. With warrants issued and exercised, there would be 20 warrants exercised for each of the 50,000 bonds, resulting in 1 million new shares. Therefore, there will be 9 million shares outstanding if the warrants are exercised, and an additional $26.5 million of equity (1 million warrants $\times$ $26.50 exercise price). The value of each share of stock would be $(\$500,382,877 + \$26,500,000)/9,000,000 = \$58.54$.

12. b. The investors would expect to receive $90 per year and $1,000 in Year 20 (the face value). In addition, if warrants are exercised then the investors will receive a profit of $58.54 - $26.50 = $32.04 per share, or a total cash flow of $640.80 ($32.04 \times 20$) in Year 10. Therefore, in Year 10 investors will receive $90 + $640.80 = $730.80. Hence, the component cost of these bonds can be found by determining the IRR of a cash flow stream consisting of each coupon payment, the face value, and the profit from exercising the warrants.

Input $CF_0 = -1000$, $CF_{1-9} = 90$, $CF_{10} = 730.80$, $CF_{11-19} = 90$, and $CF_{20} = 1090$. Solve for IRR $= 11.778\% \approx 11.78\%$.

13. e. The component cost is 11.78%, and the premium associated with the warrants is $11.78\% - 11\% = 0.78\%$, or roughly 78 basis points.

LEARNING OBJECTIVES

- Define the term merger, and list some motives for mergers.

- Characterize the different types of mergers.

- Identify the five major "merger waves" that have occurred in the United States.

- Differentiate between the merger process in hostile versus friendly takeovers.

- Briefly explain the need to regulate mergers, and whether states play a role in merger regulation.

- Determine the value of a target firm using discounted cash flow analysis and the appropriate discount rate.

- Identify alternative ways of structuring takeover bids.

- Explain the correct financial reporting treatment for mergers.

- Explain the steps for an analysis of a true consolidation.

- Discuss the roles investment bankers play in merger transactions.

- Explain whether corporate acquisitions create value and how the value is shared between the parties.

- Differentiate between a merger and a corporate alliance.

- Explain what a leveraged buyout (LBO) is.

- Define the term divestiture, briefly discuss the major types of divestitures, and give some reasons for divestitures.

OVERVIEW

Most corporate growth occurs by internal expansion, which takes place when a firm's existing divisions grow through normal capital budgeting activities. However, the most dramatic examples of growth, and often the largest increases in stock prices, result from mergers, the first topic covered in this chapter. Mergers are one way for two companies to join forces, but many companies are striking cooperative deals, called corporate, or strategic alliances, which stop far short of merging.

Leveraged buyouts, or LBOs, occur when a firm's stock is acquired by a small group of investors rather than by another operating company. Since LBOs are similar to mergers in many respects, they are also covered in this chapter.

Conditions change over time, and, as a result, firms often find it desirable to sell off, or divest major divisions to other firms that can better utilize the divested assets. Divestitures are also discussed in the chapter.

OUTLINE

Several reasons have been proposed to justify corporate mergers.

■ One major reason for mergers is *synergy,* the condition wherein the whole is greater than the sum of its parts.
  □ If Companies A and B merge to form Company C, and if C's value exceeds that of A and B taken separately, then synergy is said to exist.
  □ Synergism can arise from four sources.

    • Operating economies, which result from economies of scale in management, marketing, production, or distribution.

    • Financial economies, including lower transaction costs and better coverage by security analysts.

    • Differential efficiency, which implies that the management of one firm is more efficient and that the weaker firm's assets will be more productive after the merger.

    • Increased market power due to reduced competition.
  □ Operating and financial economies, as well as increases in managerial efficiency, are socially desirable. However, mergers that reduce competition are both socially undesirable and illegal.

■ *Tax considerations* can provide an incentive for mergers.
  □ A highly profitable firm might merge with a firm that has accumulated tax losses so as to put these losses to immediate use.

☐ A firm with excess cash and a shortage of internal investment opportunities might seek a merger rather than pay the cash out as dividends, which would result in the shareholders paying immediate taxes on the distribution.

■ Occasionally, a firm will merge with another because it thinks it has found a "bargain," that is, *assets can be purchased below their replacement cost.*
   ☐ The true value of any firm is a function of its future earnings power, not the cost of replacing its assets.
   ☐ Acquisitions should be based on the economic value of the acquired assets, not on their replacement cost.

■ *Diversification* is often cited by managers as a rationale for mergers.
   ☐ Diversification may bring some real benefits to the firm, especially by reducing the variability of the firm's earnings stream, which benefits the firm's managers, creditors, and other stakeholders.
   ☐ However, by simply holding portfolios of stocks, stockholders can generally diversify more easily and efficiently than can firms.
   ☐ Research of U. S. firms suggests that in most cases diversification does not increase the firm's value.

■ Financial economists like to think that business decisions are based only on economic considerations. However, some business decisions are based more on managers' personal motivations than on economic factors.
   ☐ Some mergers occur because managers want to increase the size of their firms, and hence gain more power, prestige, and monetary compensation.
   ☐ Other mergers occur because managers want to keep their jobs, so they merge with other firms to make the firm less attractive to hostile suitors. This type of merger is called a *defensive merger*.

■ Firms are generally valued in the markets as ongoing firms. However, some firms are worth more if they are broken up and then sold off in pieces. Thus, some acquisitions are motivated by the fact that a firm's *breakup value* is greater than its current market value.

There are four primary types of mergers.

■ A *horizontal merger* occurs when one firm combines with another in its same line of business.

■ A *vertical merger* occurs between a firm and one of its suppliers or customers.

■ A *congeneric merger* is a merger of firms in the same general industry, but for which no customer or supplier relationship exists.

■ A *conglomerate merger* is a merger of companies in totally different industries.

Five major "merger waves" have occurred in the United States. The high level of merger activity that is still going on has been sparked by several factors.

■ Five major "merger waves" have occurred in the U. S.
  □ In the late 1800s consolidations occurred in the oil, steel, tobacco, and other basic industries.
  □ In the 1920s the stock market boom helped financial promoters consolidate firms in a number of industries.
  □ In the 1960s conglomerate mergers were the rage.
  □ In the 1980s LBO firms and others began using junk bonds to finance all manner of acquisitions.
  □ Currently, strategic alliances are being formed to enable firms to compete better in the global economy.

■ In general, recent mergers have been significantly different from those of the 1980s.
  □ While in the 1980s mergers were financial transactions in which buyers sought to buy companies that were selling at less than their true values, recently most of the mergers have been strategic in nature.
  □ Other differences between mergers in the 1980s and recent mergers are the way the mergers were financed and how the target firms' stockholders were compensated.
  □ Recent mergers involve an increase in cross-border mergers. Many of these mergers have been motivated by large shifts in the value of the world's leading currencies.

In most mergers, one company, the target company, is acquired by another, the acquiring company.

■ In a *friendly merger*, the management of the target company approves the merger and recommends it to their stockholders. In a friendly merger the terms are approved by the managements of both companies.
  □ Under these circumstances a suitable price is determined, and the acquiring company will simply buy the target company's shares through a friendly *tender offer*.
  □ Payment will be made either in cash or in the stock or debt of the acquiring firm.

■ A *hostile merger* is one in which the target firm's management resists the acquisition. The target firm's management either believes the price offered is too low, or it may simply want to remain independent.

- ☐ Under these circumstances, the acquiring company may make a hostile tender offer for the target company's shares. This is a direct appeal to the target firm's stockholders asking them to exchange their shares for cash, bonds, or stock in the acquiring firm.
- ☐ A *proxy fight* is an attempt to gain control of a firm by soliciting stockholders to vote for a new management team.

Mergers are regulated by both the state and federal governments.

- ■ The Williams Act, passed by Congress in 1968, has two main objectives.
  - ☐ To regulate the way acquiring firms can structure takeover offers.
  - ☐ To force acquiring firms to disclose more information about their offers.
    - ● Congress wanted to put target managements in a better position to defend against hostile offers.

- ■ The Williams Act placed four major restrictions on acquiring firms. These restrictions were intended to reduce the acquiring firm's ability to surprise management and to stampede target shareholders into accepting an inadequate offer.
  - ☐ Acquirers must disclose their current holdings and future intentions within 10 days of amassing at least 5 percent of a company's stock.
  - ☐ Acquirers must disclose the source of the funds to be used in the acquisition.
  - ☐ Target shareholders must be given at least 20 days to tender their shares.
  - ☐ If the tender price is increased during the 20-day open period, all shareholders who tendered prior to the new offer must receive the higher price.

- ■ Many states now have merger laws that restrict the actions that can be taken by raiders.
  - ☐ One such law restricts the ability of a raider to vote the shares they have acquired; that is, the merger must be approved by a majority of disinterested shareholders, defined as those who are neither officers nor inside directors of the company, nor associates of the raider.
  - ☐ New state laws also have some features that protect target stockholders from their own managers. These laws limit the use of *golden parachutes,* onerous debt-financing plans, and some types of takeover defenses.

While merger analysis may appear simple, there are a number of complex issues involved.

- ■ The acquiring firm must perform a capital budgeting-type analysis. If it appears that the target firm can be purchased for less than its intrinsic value, then the offer should be made.

- ■ Several methodologies are used to value firms. Two commonly-used methods are *discounted cash flow analysis* and *market multiple analysis.* Regardless of the valuation methodology, two facts must be recognized.

- ☐ Any changes in operations occurring as a result of the proposed merger that will impact the value of the business must be considered in the analysis.
- ☐ The goal of merger valuation is to value the target firm's equity, because a firm is acquired from its owners, not from its creditors.

■ The *discounted cash flow approach* to valuing a business involves the application of capital budgeting procedures to an entire firm rather than to a single project.
- ☐ To apply this method, two key items are needed: (1) a set of pro forma statements that forecast the incremental free cash flows expected to result from the merger, and (2) a discount rate, or cost of capital, to apply to these projected cash flows.
- ☐ In a pure *financial merger*, in which no synergies are expected, the incremental postmerger cash flows are simply the expected cash flows of the target firm.
- ☐ In an *operating merger*, in which the two firms' operations are to be integrated, forecasting future cash flows is more difficult.

■ Merger cash flows, unlike capital budgeting cash flows, *must include* interest expense. This is done for three reasons.
- ☐ The target firm usually has embedded debt that will be assumed by the acquiring company, so old debt at different coupon rates is often part of the deal.
- ☐ The acquisition is often financed partially by debt.
- ☐ If the subsidiary is expected to grow in the future, new debt will have to be issued over time to support its expansion.
  - Thus, debt associated with a merger is typically more complex than the single issue of new debt associated with a normal capital project. Therefore, debt costs must be explicitly included in the cash flow analysis.

■ With debt costs included in the cash flow analysis, the resulting net cash flows accrue solely to the equity holders of the acquiring firm; thus, we are using the *equity residual method* to value the target firm.

■ In a friendly merger, the acquiring firm sends a team consisting of accountants, engineers, etc. to the target firm. Such an investigation, which is called *due diligence*, is an essential part of any merger analysis.

■ The *appropriate discount rate is a cost of equity* rather than an overall cost of capital, because the bottom-line net cash flows are after interest and taxes—hence they represent equity.
- ☐ The cost of equity used must reflect the underlying riskiness of the target company's cash flows and the riskiness of the financing mix used for the acquisition.

■ The value of the target consists of the target's premerger value plus any value created by operating or financial synergies.

■ The present value of the incremental merger cash flows is the maximum price that the acquiring firm should pay for the target company.

■ Another method of valuing a target company is *market multiple analysis*, which applies a market-determined multiple to net income, earnings per share, sales, or book value. The basic premise is that the value of any business depends on the earnings that the business produces.
  □ Note that earnings (or cash flow) measures other than net income can be used in the market multiple approach.
    ● Another commonly used measure is *earnings before interest, taxes, depreciation, and amortization (EBITDA)*.

■ The price to be paid determines whether the shareholders of the acquiring company or the shareholders of the target company reap the greater benefits from the merger.
  □ If there were no synergistic benefits, the maximum bid would be equal to the current value of the target company.
    ● The greater the synergistic gains, the greater the gap between the target's current price and the maximum the acquiring company could pay.
  □ The greater the synergistic gains, the more likely a merger is to be consummated.
  □ The issue of how to divide the synergistic benefits is critically important. Obviously, both parties will want to receive as much as possible.
  □ Where in the range the actual price will be set depends on whether cash or securities is offered, the negotiating skills of the two management teams, and the bargaining positions of the two parties as determined by fundamental economic conditions.
  □ The acquiring firm wants to keep its maximum bid secret, and it would plan its bidding strategy carefully and consistently with the situation.

■ *Post-merger control of the firm* is of great interest to managers due to their concern for their jobs.

Once the value of the target is estimated, the acquiring firm must decide on the structure of the takeover bid.

■ The structure of the bid is extremely important since it affects:
  □ The capital structure of the postmerger firm.
  □ The tax treatment of both the acquiring firm and the target firm's stockholders.
  □ The ability of the target firm's stockholders to benefit from future merger-related gains.
  □ The types of federal and state regulations that apply to the merger.

■ The tax consequences of the merger depend on whether it is classified as a *taxable offer* or a *nontaxable offer*.

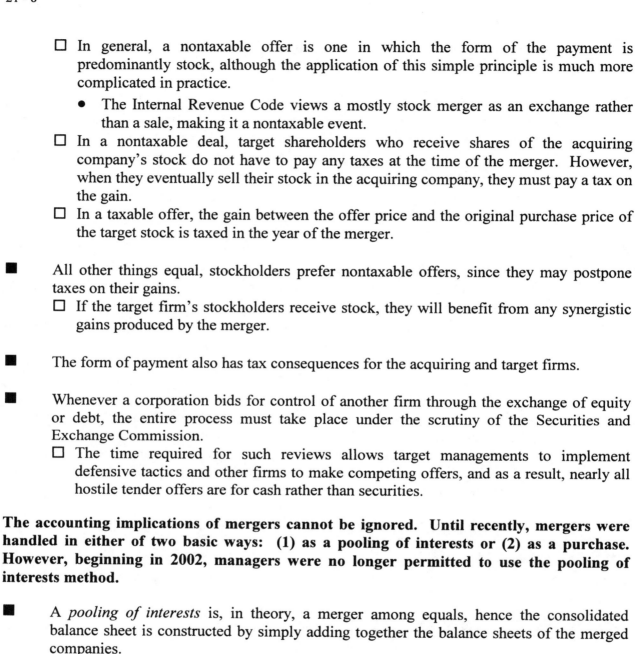

- ☐ In general, a nontaxable offer is one in which the form of the payment is predominantly stock, although the application of this simple principle is much more complicated in practice.
  - ● The Internal Revenue Code views a mostly stock merger as an exchange rather than a sale, making it a nontaxable event.
- ☐ In a nontaxable deal, target shareholders who receive shares of the acquiring company's stock do not have to pay any taxes at the time of the merger. However, when they eventually sell their stock in the acquiring company, they must pay a tax on the gain.
- ☐ In a taxable offer, the gain between the offer price and the original purchase price of the target stock is taxed in the year of the merger.

■ All other things equal, stockholders prefer nontaxable offers, since they may postpone taxes on their gains.
  - ☐ If the target firm's stockholders receive stock, they will benefit from any synergistic gains produced by the merger.

■ The form of payment also has tax consequences for the acquiring and target firms.

■ Whenever a corporation bids for control of another firm through the exchange of equity or debt, the entire process must take place under the scrutiny of the Securities and Exchange Commission.
  - ☐ The time required for such reviews allows target managements to implement defensive tactics and other firms to make competing offers, and as a result, nearly all hostile tender offers are for cash rather than securities.

The accounting implications of mergers cannot be ignored. Until recently, mergers were handled in either of two basic ways: (1) as a pooling of interests or (2) as a purchase. However, beginning in 2002, managers were no longer permitted to use the pooling of interests method.

■ A *pooling of interests* is, in theory, a merger among equals, hence the consolidated balance sheet is constructed by simply adding together the balance sheets of the merged companies.

■ *Purchase accounting* assumes one firm buys another firm in much the same way it would buy any capital asset, paying for it with cash, debt, or stock of the acquiring company.
  - ☐ If the price paid is exactly equal to the acquired firm's *net asset value*, which is defined as its total assets minus its liabilities, then the consolidated balance sheet will be identical to that under pooling.
  - ☐ Otherwise, there is an important difference. If the price paid exceeds the net asset value, then asset values will be increased to reflect the price actually paid, whereas if

the price paid is less than the net asset value, then assets must be written down when preparing the consolidated balance sheet.

- *Goodwill* refers to the excess paid for a firm above the appraised value of the physical and intangible assets purchased.

☐ Significant differences can also arise in reported profits under the two accounting methods.

- If asset values are increased, as they often are under a purchase, this must be reflected in higher depreciation charges (and also in a higher cost of goods sold if inventories are written up). This, in turn, will further reduce reported profits.

- Prior to the recent accounting change, goodwill had to be written off, or "amortized," over a period corresponding to the expected life of the superior earning power, but in no case more than 40 years.

- In many instances these goodwill charges were quite large, and they depressed earnings for a number of years. This explains why most managers preferred pooling to purchase accounting, and why they objected so strongly to the recent guidelines that forbid pooling accounting.

- As part of a compromise designed to soften the blow of banning pooling, companies no longer have to amortize goodwill. Under the new guidelines, each year the company must conduct an impairment test, and goodwill must be written down only if the test indicates that there has been an impairment of value.

In many situations it is hard to identify an "acquirer" and a "target"—the merger appears to be a true "merger of equals." Here are the steps involved in the analysis.

■ Develop pro forma financial statements for the consolidated corporation. The key set of figures is the projected consolidated free cash flows available to stockholders.

■ Estimate the new company's cost of equity, and use that rate to discount the equity flows of the consolidated company. This is the value of the equity of the consolidated company.

■ Decide how to allocate the new company's stock between the two sets of old stockholders.
☐ There is no rule, or formula, that can be applied, but one basis for the allocation is the relative pre-announcement values of the two companies.
☐ Unless a case could be made for giving a higher percentage of the shares to one of the companies because it was responsible for more of the synergistic value, then the premerger value proportions would seem to be a "fair" solution.

Investment bankers play an important role in merger activities.

■ The major investment banking firms have merger and acquisition (M&A) departments that help arrange mergers.
  ☐ Members of these departments identify firms with excess cash that might want to buy other firms, companies that might be willing to be bought, and firms that might be attractive to others.

■ Investment bankers help target companies develop and implement defensive tactics.
  ☐ Sometimes a *white knight*, who is acceptable to the target firm's management, will be lined up to acquire a firm that is trying to avoid being taken over by an unfriendly suitor.
  ☐ In other situations, a *white squire*, who is friendly to current management, may be sought to buy enough of the target firm's shares to block the hostile takeover.
  ☐ Investment bankers can also recommend *poison pills*, which are actions that effectively destroy the value of the firm in the event of a merger, and hence drive off unwanted suitors.
  ☐ *Golden parachutes* are large payments made to the managers of a firm if it is acquired.
  ☐ Another takeover defense that is being used is the *employee stock ownership plan (ESOP)*. ESOPs are designed to give lower-level employees an ownership stake in the firm.

■ Investment bankers are often used to value target companies. Generally, both the acquiring and target firms will use investment bankers to help establish a price and also to participate in the negotiations.

■ Investment bankers help finance mergers.
  ☐ To be successful in mergers and acquisitions, an investment banker must be able to offer a financing package to clients, whether they are acquirers who need capital to take over companies or target companies trying to finance stock repurchase plans or other defenses against takeovers.

■ Investment banking firms invest in the stocks of potential merger candidates. They engage in *risk arbitrage*, which means speculating in the stocks of companies that are likely takeover targets.
  ☐ To be successful, the arbitrageurs need to be able to sniff out likely targets, assess the probability of offers reaching fruition, and move in and out of the market quickly and with low transactions costs.
    • *Arbitrage* generally means simultaneously buying and selling the same commodity or security in two different markets at different prices, and pocketing a risk-free return.

The recent merger activity has sparked a great deal of research to answer two questions: Do corporate acquisitions create value, and if so, how is this value shared between the parties?

■ Most researchers agree that takeovers increase the wealth of the shareholders of target firms, for otherwise they would not agree to the offer. There is a debate as to whether mergers benefit the acquiring firm's shareholders. In particular, managements of acquiring firms may be motivated by factors other than shareholder wealth maximization.

■ Researchers attempt to answer questions such as this by examining abnormal returns associated with merger announcements, where abnormal returns are defined as that part of a stock price change caused by factors other than changes in the general stock market.

■ On average, the stock prices of target firms increase by 30 percent in hostile tender offers, while in friendly mergers the average increase is about 20 percent. However, for both hostile and friendly deals, the stock price of acquiring firms, on average, remains constant.

■ The evidence strongly indicates that acquisitions do create value, but that shareholders of target firms reap virtually all of the benefits. These results are not surprising.
  □ Target firms' shareholders are in the driver's seat.
  □ Takeovers are a competitive game, so if one potential acquiring firm does not offer full value for a potential target, then another firm will generally jump in with a higher bid.
  □ Managements of acquiring firms might well be willing to give up all the value created by the merger, because the merger would enhance the acquiring managers' personal positions without harming their shareholders.

Mergers are one way for two companies to completely join assets and management, but many firms are striking cooperative deals, which fall short of merging. Such cooperative amalgamations are called corporate alliances, and they occur in many forms.

■ *Joint ventures* are an important type of alliance, in which parts of companies are joined to achieve specific, limited objectives.
  □ Joint ventures are controlled by a combined management team consisting of representatives of the two (or more) parent companies.

In a leveraged buyout (LBO), a small group of investors, usually including current management, acquires a firm in a transaction financed largely by debt.

■ The debt is serviced with funds generated by the acquired company's operations and by the sale of some of its assets.

■ Generally, the acquiring group plans to run the acquired company for a number of years, boost its sales and profits, and then take it public again as a stronger company.

Although corporations do more buying than selling of productive assets, selling, or divestiture, does take place.

■ There are four types of *divestitures*.
  ☐ An operating unit may be *sold to another firm*.
  ☐ In a *spin-off*, a division may be set up as a separate corporation with the parent firm's stockholders then being given stock in the new corporation on a pro rata basis.
  ☐ In a *carve-out*, a minority interest in a corporate subsidiary is sold to new shareholders, so the parent gains new equity financing yet retains control. A firm follows the steps for a spin-off but sells only some of the shares.
  ☐ In a *liquidation*, the assets of a division are sold off piecemeal, rather than as an operating entity.

■ There are a variety of reasons cited for divestitures:
  ☐ It appears that, on occasion, investors do not properly value some assets when they are part of a large conglomerate. Thus, divestiture can occur to focus on a firm's core business and enhance firm value.
  ☐ Often, firms will need to raise large amounts of cash to finance expansion in their primary business, or to reduce an onerous debt burden, and divestitures can raise the needed cash.
  ☐ Conditions change, corporate strategies change in response, and as a result firms alter their asset portfolios by divestitures.
  ☐ Sometimes, assets are just no longer profitable and must be liquidated.
  ☐ Firms that are struggling against bankruptcy often have to divest profitable divisions just to stay alive.
  ☐ The government sometimes mandates divestiture on antitrust grounds.

Web Appendix 21A

A holding company is a firm that holds large blocks of stock in other companies and exercises control over those firms. The holding company is often called the parent company and the controlled companies are known as subsidiaries or operating companies. Holding companies may be used to obtain some of the same benefits that could be achieved through mergers and acquisitions. However, the holding company device has some unique disadvantages as well as unique advantages.

■ Advantages of holding companies include the following:
  ☐ *Control with fractional ownership.* Effective control of a company may be achieved with far less than 50 percent ownership of the common stock.
  ☐ *Isolation of risks.* Claims on one unit of the holding company may not be liabilities to the other units. Each element of the holding company organization is a separate legal entity.